RIVALS
FOR POWER
OTTAWA AND
THE PROVINCES

RIVALS FOR POWER

OTTAWA AND THE PROVINCES

The contentious history of the Canadian federation

ED WHITCOMB

James Lorimer and Company Ltd., Publishers

Toronto

James Lorimer & Company Ltd., Publishers acknowledges the support of the Ontario Arts Council (OAC), an agency of the Government of Ontario, which in 2015–16 funded 1,676 individual artists and 1,125 organizations in 209 communities across Ontario for a total of $50.5 million. We acknowledge the support of the Canada Council for the Arts, which last year invested $153 million to bring the arts to Canadians throughout the country. This project has been made possible in part by the Government of Canada and with the support of the Ontario Media Development Corporation.

Cover design: Shabnam Safari
Cover images: Shutterstock (top) and *The Fathers of Confederation*, Rex Woods © House of Commons Collection, Ottawa (bottom)

Library and Archives Canada Cataloguing in Publication

Whitcomb, Edward A., author
        Rivals for power : Ottawa and the provinces : the contentious history of the Canadian federation / Edward Whitcomb.

Includes bibliographical references and index.
Issued in print and electronic formats.
ISBN 978-1-4594-1238-5 (softcover).--ISBN 978-1-4594-1239-2 (EPUB)

        1. Federal government--Canada--History. I. Title.

JL27.W55 2017   321.02'30971   C2017-900789-0
                                              C2017-900790-4

James Lorimer & Company Ltd., Publishers
117 Peter Street, Suite 304
Toronto, ON, Canada
M5V 0M3
www.lorimer.ca

Printed and bound in Canada.

CONTENTS

This book is dedicated to the Fathers of Confederation
who built far better than they knew,
and to the thousands of politicians
who have made Canada a superbly governed country for 150 years.

Preface

On July 1, 2017, Canadians will celebrate the 150th anniversary of Confederation. My contribution to that celebration is this history of Canadian federalism since 1867. It covers the background, the *British North America Act*, the union of the colonies, and how federalism has evolved over fifteen decades. It is a work of passion, because I cannot remember a time when I was not interested in the elements that went into making Canada a federal state.

In the 1950s, I travelled across western Canada with my parents and noted that the provinces did things differently. In Grade 8, I wrote an essay arguing that Louis Riel should be regarded as a Father of Confederation. In high school, I was well aware that Manitoba was responsible for our education and that Ottawa was responsible for the nearby Indian reserve, and I vaguely grasped that neither were working particularly well. At university, a number of courses in political science, history, and economics informed me about federalism, politics, government, administration, and the relations between central governments and regions in a variety of countries and empires.

As a European historian, I spent four years in England and France and travelled all over western Europe, noting things like the independence movements in Scotland and Brittany and the way the Swiss seemed to make a multinational country run as smooth as, well, a Swiss clock. I studied and lectured on the functioning of government, the creation and disintegration of countries, on civil wars, on the rise of nationalism, and on the differences between a unitary state such as France and the loose German federation with its many independent states. That academic career also led me to jobs in Nova Scotia and Quebec, which provided intellectual and other challenges for a lad from the prairies.

It is often said that federalism is the most talked-about issue in Canadian politics. One small example of this is that during my first week in the Foreign Service in 1975, a number of new officers were discussing Confederation; I clearly remember attempting to correct the one who said that Quebec had been forced to join the Dominion. The Department of Foreign Affairs had an office dealing with the provinces, and I considered an assignment there or a secondment to one of the provincial departments of intergovernmental affairs. Neither ambition came to fruition, but they certainly indicated a strong interest in federalism. The Foreign Service took me to four federal states—Yugoslavia, Indonesia, India, and of course Canada (Ottawa), all of which had significant problems between the centre and the provinces and among the provinces, all of which handled centre-regional relations differently. Foreign affairs involves many domestic issues, and I was desk officer for international energy when the Canadian government brought in the National Energy Program, an issue covered in detail in this book.

In that diplomatic career, I spent two decades reporting on insurrections, terrorism, and the efforts of dominant groups to impose their will on minorities and the resistance of the latter to those attempts. Issues such as those were major elements of my third career as the federal government's senior intelligence analyst for South and Southeast Asia. Afghanistan, Pakistan, India, and Sri Lanka all suffered from serious regional, religious, and ethnic divisions that cried out for decentralized government, but, in all four, over-centralization produced insurrection and civil war. Overall, I lived in four Canadian provinces and six foreign countries, and travelled extensively through most of Canada and fifty countries on five continents. While I did not make my career teaching federalism at a Canadian university, I did study it for five decades and from a hundred different perspectives around the world.

Studying the history of Canada's provinces became a hobby when I changed careers in 1975, and in 1982 I published *A Short History of*

Manitoba. That book must have interested others, because over nine thousand copies have been sold and it has been used in schools and universities. As retirement approached, I resumed work on the plan to publish histories of all the provinces, starting with *Alberta* and *Saskatchewan* in 2005 and finishing with *Quebec* in 2012. Each province entered Confederation by a different path, and each has had a different relationship with Ottawa. The knowledge of centre-state relations gained in a variety of countries helped me understand the evolution of centre-provincial relations in Canada, and the research for the provincial histories revealed both the broad thrust of Canada's federalism and the specific issues in each province's relations with Ottawa.

When the series was complete, the logical next step was a history of one of the most important themes in all those provincial histories, namely their relationship with the central government. The timing was perfect as retirement allowed Canadian history to become my fourth career. And the 150th anniversary of Confederation, when many Canadians might want to see a history of federalism written from a perspective that included studies of all of Canada's provinces and five centuries of centre-regional relations all over the globe, was just five years in the future.

Retirement allowed me to take a fairly exhaustive look at the literature, academic and otherwise, of some rather complicated aspects of Canadian federalism, such as the important court cases, constitutional issues such as the "spending power," the complexities of health and welfare programs, fiscal federalism, and Quebec separatism. Fortunately, Canada has been gifted with wonderful academics who have spent their careers delving into these mysteries and presenting them in ways people can understand. I had the time to peruse this literature, but whether I grasped their analysis is up to the reader to determine.

The result of all this is *Rivals for Power: Ottawa and the Provinces: The contentious history of the Canadian federation.* It also reflects conversations and communications with dozens of friends, colleagues, academics, and journalists over a very long period. Many of them helped in a variety of ways, commenting in detail on one or more chapters, providing general comments about the project or parts of it, offering advice on all manner of issues, and giving the encouragement that is essential for a project like this.

They include Dr. Jim Bickerton, Marc Bourie, Dr. R. Matthew Bray, Dr. Jorg Broschek, Clark Brownlee, Don Buckingham, Poppy Cummings, Dr. Adrian de Hoog, Dr. Janet Epp, Dr. Gerald Friesen, Dr. James Hiller, Dr. Harvey Lazar, Dr. Dan Livermore, David Malone, Dr. James McKillip, Dr. Peter Meekinson, Dr. Jim Mitchel, Rodney Mykle, Gar Pardy, Bob Plamandon, Margaret Poetschke, Robert Poetschke, Colin Robertson, Dr. Donald Savoie, Paul Turcot, Dr. Bill Waiser, Dr. Nelson Wiseman, and Dr. Donna Wood. Not specifically identified are about four dozen people who helped with the ten provincial histories and whose contribution is acknowledged in those books. James Lorimer and Laura Cook at Lorimer Publishers were particularly helpful. Of special importance was the helpfulness, professionalism, and friendliness of the staff of the Ottawa Public Library. My wife Kai and daughters Denise and Diana exhibited great patience and provided much support as this project unfolded.

It is normal practice to say that the author alone is responsible for whatever errors remain in the book, and that is absolutely true of this work. It must also be said that some of the people identified above did not agree with this interpretation of Canadian federalism. In spite of that, they thought the project worthwhile and did much to save me from errors of fact, even if they failed to correct alleged errors of judgment.

—Ed Whitcomb, May 2017

Introduction

At an international school, the students were asked to write an essay on the elephant. The American wrote on their economic importance, the German on their uses in wartime, the Frenchman on their sex lives. And the Canadian student's title was: "The elephant: A federal or provincial responsibility?"

In 2017, Canadians will celebrate the 150th year of Confederation, and the joke about the elephant illustrates just how important federalism has been in Canadian history and society. We will have much to celebrate because Canada is one of the oldest and most successful federations in the world. Many Canadians will want to understand the broad contours of what they are celebrating. Some will want to know a great deal about why Canada adopted a federal system of government, what it meant, how it works, how well it works, how it affects their lives, how it has changed, and how it might change in the future. This book gives some glimpses into these issues.

The Confederation we will be celebrating consisted of two separate but related developments. One was the adoption of a federal system of government; the other was the union of three British colonies into one big colony. On the matter of federalism, there were few models to copy, and the Fathers of Confederation spent years wrestling with the various ideas, issues, problems, and possible solutions. Eventually, they concluded that the only system that would work was federalism. In that system the responsibilities of government are divided between two orders of government, a central one and the provincial ones, both autonomous in the administration of their responsibilities. That is a very difficult system of government to make work.

Unfortunately, the exact demarcation of responsibilities between the two orders of government can never be written out clearly; opinions will differ over whether some issues fall under federal or provincial power or under both, and there will be overlap. Some responsibilities will not be identified, and new ones will arise. There is also a natural competitive instinct as both orders of government try to protect and enhance their power, serve their constituents, and win re-election. The Fathers of Confederation could not possibly have dealt with all aspects of federalism in a manner that would foresee future developments. Most of them disagreed with some of the different decisions and compromises that emerged, but they did agree that what they produced was the best document possible. They got most things right and a few wrong—overall they did better than anyone had the right to expect.

The other aspect of Confederation, the union of Britain's provinces, proved to be far more difficult to achieve at the time. The Province of Canada, which became Ontario and Quebec, was quite in favour of the proposals that emerged from the 1864 conferences in Charlottetown and Quebec City. It then took over two years for the pro-Confederation politicians in Canada, Great Britain, New Brunswick, and Nova Scotia to engineer the union of just three colonies, and PEI and Newfoundland said no to the scheme. But by July 1, 1867, the Dominion of Canada had a central government plus four provincial ones, and Canada was launched on the uncharted waters of its federalism.

These developments are explored in the first chapter, which takes the story up to the adoption of federalism at the Quebec Conference in 1866, and in the second chapter on the struggle to merge three colonies into one. Chapter 3 is a detailed analysis of the *British North America Act*, the *BNA Act*, of all the sections that affect federalism, and of the background to many of the debates over it. These include such issues as the "intentions" of the Fathers of Confederation, the type of federalism they created, the lists of responsibilities given to the two orders of government, the balance between them, questions such as which government was more important or sovereign, the fiscal arrangements, and debates over topics such as the Compact Theory. We also look at the myths that have since arisen, such as the idea that Canada became a country and Canadians became a nation at midnight, July 1, 1867. Myths are important, and we will celebrate them heartily in 2017, but it is valuable to know what is myth and what is reality.

After 1867, the new Dominion faced two very difficult challenges: making the new system work and incorporating the other colonies. BC and PEI were scheduled to join but, due to a number of blunders by the new central government, a small corner of the prairies became the next province: Manitoba. That development was premature by decades and created enormous problems for Ottawa and Winnipeg. Then BC was successfully courted with the promise of a railway, but since the promise could not be fulfilled, it asked to secede. It changed its mind with the completion of the Canadian Pacific Railway (CPR), one of the new Dominion's greatest achievements. PEI then spent itself into bankruptcy and had no choice but to join, and by 1873 the Dominion counted seven provinces. The incorporation of these three new provinces is covered in Chapter 4.

Three decades later, the settlement of the prairies led to the creation of Alberta and Saskatchewan, both treated differently from all the others with consequences that lasted for decades. Then, in 1949, Ottawa and London arranged for Newfoundland to become the tenth province, once more by a different process than any other province. Eighty-two years after Confederation, the original idea of a single political entity stretching from sea to sea was finally complete. Provincial status for Alberta and Saskatchewan is covered in Chapter 6, and that of Newfoundland in Chapter 9.

Making federalism work was arguably more difficult, and federalism itself has gone through so many phases and permutations that political scientists invented a whole lexicon of expressions to define it. Various texts use at least fifteen adjectives, including asymmetrical, authentic, classical, collaborative, competitive, confederal, confrontational, constitutional, co-operative, flexible, genuine, mixed, open, quasi-, subordinate, symmetrical, and unilateral. Of these, Canada has never been confederal or symmetrical, and it was only unilateral during the First and Second World Wars. How accurate the other adjectives are may be a matter of opinion, and several of them could apply at the same time even if they conflict. The following pages will describe some of these various forms of federalism and the conflicts and contradictions between them as they emerged in the debates or the flow of history.

The main issue leading to Confederation was that, in 1763, Britain found itself in control of a colony of sixty thousand French Catholics. The British wanted to turn them into good little Englishmen, but the *Canadiens* had no intention of being assimilated. The failure of assimilation was the main factor driving the politicians of the Province of Canada to accept federalism, the system that left Quebec's French Catholics in control of their lives while Ontario's English-speaking Protestants were in control of theirs. Provincial governments then controlled education, health, welfare, civil law, property, municipal government, local matters, language, and culture. The new central government was in charge of everything else, of "general" as opposed to "local" matters, of the overall economy and of expanding the colony to the Pacific and Arctic Oceans. In 1867, Nova Scotia and New Brunswick joined the Province of Canada in the new Dominion.

Chapters 4 and 5 outline the way federalism was implemented, and Chapter 6 covers the Golden Age of Federalism under Sir Wilfrid Laurier, a period when Ottawa concentrated on its responsibilities and the provinces on theirs. Chapter 7 documents how the election of Robert Borden and the Conservatives in 1911 renewed Ottawa's offensive in terms of encroaching on provincial jurisdiction, before the First World War turned the Dominion into a virtual unitary state. The war changed federalism, one of the most important changes being that in 1917 Ottawa entered the field of direct taxes. That had been a monopoly of the provinces, and Ottawa's taxes squeezed provincial revenue, as did the steady decline in the importance of federal subsidies. The problem of the "fiscal imbalance" has been a dominant theme in Ottawa's relations with the provinces ever since.

For six decades, the relationship between Ottawa and Quebec was generally harmonious but that came to an end when Ottawa launched a pension plan in 1927, welfare being a clear and accepted matter of provincial responsibility. The Depression (Chapter 8) was a disaster for federal-provincial relations, as the provinces could not finance their responsibilities and Ottawa spent the decade attempting to avoid action and responsibility for welfare. In perhaps the clearest examples ever of federalism's failures, the central government tried to do things within provincial power, and the province of Alberta tried to do things within federal power, with the result that policies that would have done much good were not implemented at all.

The Second World War (Chapter 9) turned Canada into a unitary state once more. Part-way through the war, the bureaucrats and politicians who ran the country so successfully as a wartime economy decided to continue running it as a peacetime economy. That required the creation of the welfare state by the federal government. The poorer provinces were willing to turn their constitutional responsibilities over to Ottawa; the richer ones were not, especially Quebec, which knew that federal policies reflected English-Protestant values, not French-Catholic ones. The co-operation and conflict between Ottawa and the provinces over the management of health, welfare, and higher education dominated federal-provincial relations and indeed Canadian politics from the Second World War into the twenty-first century. The issues and battles are explored throughout the rest of the book. They include unemployment insurance, the family allowance, aid to the universities, old age pensions, shared-cost programs, the fiscal imbalance, the Trans-Canada Highway, the CPP and QPP, Medicare, support for regional economic development, assistance to municipalities, and the evolving way all these issues have been handled. A further layer of confrontation emerged in the 1970s over control of natural resources (Chapters 12 and 13).

These issues affected the provinces in different ways, but the dominant clash was between Ottawa and Quebec. That eventually led to two referenda on whether Quebec would separate from the rest of Canada (Chapters 13 and 15). In a sense, the issue was the same as the one that produced Confederation in the first place, namely, the attempt by English-speaking Canadians to assimilate the Québécois and the determination of the latter to remain *maîtres chez nous*, "masters in our own house," to ensure *la survivance* of their distinct culture.

Underlying these tensions was the evolving nature of national identities. Before 1867, the term French Canadian applied to the inhabitants of the St. Lawrence Valley; by 1900, it meant anyone of French descent anywhere in Canada, except the Acadians. After 1960, the term once more came to mean French people in Quebec, the Québécois. Before 1867, there were three distinct English-speaking nations: the Irish, English, and Scottish. Over many decades, they evolved into a single English-speaking Canadian nation that gradually assimilated people of non-British origin. These national identities had a major effect on federal-provincial relations, and their evolution is documented in a variety of chapters. Until the 1980s, the First Nations

15

and Inuit were marginalized politically, having virtually no influence on federalism, a situation that has changed considerably since then.

Another theme that runs through the text is the fact that Canadian federalism is asymmetrical, that is, that different provinces are treated differently in the constitution and in practice. That is especially true of Quebec. Numerous examples of that are given in the *BNA Act* itself and in how Ottawa treated each province subsequently. For example, representation in the House of Commons was based on the principle of representation by population, but that principle was violated for each new province and then for the whole of Atlantic Canada. After the Second World War, the increasingly strong force of English-Canadian nationalism was reflected in the demands that federalism should be made symmetrical and all provinces should be the same and be treated the same. The battles that followed were in part over whether Quebec was a distinct society, whether it had special status, and whether special status should be specifically recognized in the constitution.

In the power struggles between the two orders of government, few matters have been as important or controversial as the federal "spending power." The *BNA Act* did not give Ottawa any such power, but in the mid-twentieth century the theory emerged that since Ottawa had access to any type of taxation, it should be able to spend revenue any way it chose, including in the launching of programs within "exclusive" provincial jurisdiction. It began doing so before the First World War, launched its first major program in provincial jurisdiction in 1927, and used its surplus revenue after the Second World War to turn most exclusive provincial responsibilities into shared ones. The use or misuse of this power is almost certainly the main cause of the rise of separatism in Quebec, and the "spending power" is explored in depth in half the chapters in this book.

The evolution of federalism documents the changing roles and situations of the provinces within the Dominion. On the east coast, Newfoundland simply remained aloof for the first eighty years. The Maritimes joined reluctantly because they knew the financial arrangements were inadequate, and much of their history has involved fighting for adequate financing and dealing with the consequences of that original mistake. For the first sixty years, Quebec was the most contented province but it gradually became the most discontented, and that change receives a lot of attention and detailed explanation. Ontario's relations with Ottawa were the opposite, as it spent the first century as the main champion of provincial rights and then became Ottawa's best provincial ally. The West's place in Confederation is very different, from being Ottawa's colony to partial autonomy, to exploited hinterland, to near-separatism, and back to full partnership. All these separate currents intermingle with each other in fascinating and sometimes unpredictable ways.

There are three arbitrators when Ottawa and the provinces clash over jurisdiction and power, namely, the politicians, the people, and the courts. The actions of politicians, the public, and the courts thus form themes that run through the entire text. Confederation was launched with the manipulation of elections by the pro-confederates. Ottawa was dominated for most of the first three decades by the Conservative party, but to balance that power the people began electing Liberal governments at the provincial level. When the Liberals became dominant at the federal level, the people began voting Conservative provincially. In both orders of government, politicians have found that public opinion provides one of the most important guides to the way federalism is managed. The interplay of politics and constitutionalism runs through the entire history of Canada.

The other arbitrator is the courts, and this text discusses numerous legal cases that helped define federalism. Originally, the ultimate arbitrator was the Judicial Committee of the Privy Council, the JCPC, in London, so that "vestige of colonialism" was attacked by those who disagreed with its decisions. Their criticisms in the 1930s launched the movement that led to patriation of the constitution in 1982, but that could not be done until Ottawa and the provinces agreed on an amending formula, a process that took over half a century to resolve, assuming it has been resolved. Eventually Canada's Supreme Court became truly supreme, and it has played a very important role in the relations between Ottawa and the provinces, with opinion divided as to whether that role is positive or not.

Many conclusions emerge from this study, one of the most important being that Canadian federalism has proved to be enormously flexible and resilient. We still live under that old, dusty 1867 British Act of Parliament. It has been formally amended very few times but has been changed repeatedly by convention, that is, by the decisions and actions of governments. In that sense, Canada has two constitutions: the written document, plus all the conventions and agreements that define the mechanics of how Ottawa and the provinces co-operate to manage the country. What governments actually do or do not do is perhaps as important as what the constitution says they can or cannot do. But the *BNA Act* and the way it has been implemented and interpreted has seen us through the creation of a federal union, the absorption of six more provinces, a variety of crises involving minorities, two world wars and a decade-long depression, the near-disintegration of the country, and massive change to the way the responsibilities of the two orders of government are actually managed. In spite of the conflicts, there has been an enormous degree of co-operation between Ottawa and the provinces on almost every matter that affects the lives of Canadians. And all this was achieved by discussion, debate, and compromise, which, to some, makes Canadian history less interesting than that of countries that addressed similar problems with violence, conquest, insurrection, and civil war. Notwithstanding that view, Canadian federalism is, indeed, one of our greatest achievements. Happy Sesquicentennial!

PART I
Adopting Federalism

CHAPTER 1
British North America to 1864

One hundred and fifty years ago, on July 1, 1867, the British government united three of its North American colonies into a single one, a development that is called Confederation. The three colonies were New Brunswick, Nova Scotia, and the Province of Canada. The new colony took the name of the largest, but modified it to the Dominion of Canada. The new Dominion was given a federal system of government with one central government and four provincial ones, as the Province of Canada was divided into Ontario and Quebec. Confederation thus refers to these two separate developments—the adoption of federalism and the union of Britain's North American colonies. The plan called for the inclusion of British Columbia, so the Dominion adopted the motto "from sea to sea," and, four years later, BC did become a province. The Dominion acquired Rupert's Land, a territory that included almost all of the continent of North America that drained into the Arctic Ocean. Covering half of North America, by geography, the new Dominion was the second largest political entity in the world. It still is.

At the time, the idea of governing states through a federal system was not new, but it was very rare. Debate about the possibility of adopting a federal system began in the Province of Canada in the 1850s because four previous British constitutions had failed, and the colony had become ungovernable. By 1864, there was broad agreement that federalism was the only system that would work, but it was far from clear what that system should entail, and the Fathers of Confederation did not have many models to guide them.

Over three years of intensive debate, they worked out the best scheme they could for the new political experiment. They did far better than anyone had the right to expect, and the fifth constitution—the *British North America Act* of 1867—was successful. It is still in effect, although it has been formally amended a number of times and informally amended many times more through changing usage of its terms. That constitution succeeded because federalism is the best form of government for countries containing different economic regions and multiple ethnic and cultural groups.

Federalism is, however, a very difficult form of government to manage. The interests of the central government and of one or more provinces often diverge, with each government legitimately representing the interests of its citizens. Government is about power, making decisions, and applying policies, so there is often competition and conflict between the two orders of government. The division of responsibilities between central and provincial governments is never fully defined and changes over time. So does the balance of power between them. The evolving relations between the centre and the provinces thus becomes one of the most important elements in the political, economic, and cultural life of a colony or country with a federal system of government. This book is the story of those relations through the first 150 years of Canadian federalism.

The achievement of Confederation through political negotiations and democratic votes must be seen in context. At the time, other nations were being united, for example, Germany and Italy through a series of very bloody international and civil wars. The unity of the United States was maintained by a civil war that took six hundred thousand lives. The United States had only recently conquered Texas and the Southwest from Mexico, and one by one the Native Americans south of the border were conquered or starved into submission. By contrast, the Fathers of Confederation achieved their goals through debate, compromise, politics, and diplomacy, a tradition that continued as their successors dealt peacefully with the acquisition of the prairies, negotiations with the First Nations, the entrance of other colonies to Confederation, the threat of secession, the divisions created by two world wars, the rise of Quebec separatism, and the alienation of the West. None of these issues was handled perfectly and some lives were lost, but none was settled by violence and force. Many of those issues demonstrate the way Canadians have handled federal-provincial relations and are described in detail in the following chapters.

New France, the Loyalists, and the Atlantic Colonies

The underlying reasons why Canada needed a federal system of government date from before the British Conquest of New France in 1763. New France, the French colony along the St. Lawrence, had a population of sixty thousand that was extremely homogeneous, being entirely French and Catholic. These *Canadiens* had developed a sense of identity different from that of the European French or the French Acadian colonists in the Maritimes. They were a nation in the cultural or social sense of the word, a people who saw themselves as distinct from other groups because of their shared history, religion, language, customs, traditions, attitudes, and values. Following 1763, isolated from France and dominated by English Protestants, they were determined to maintain their identity and way of life. That determination to survive as a nation, to preserve their culture, and to resist British attempts to assimilate them became one of the major defining characteristics of their nationalism. It is known as *la survivance*, and their history is of how they survived as a nation. The slogan on Quebec licence plates, *Je me souviens*, means "I remember," an acknowledgement of the *Canadiens'* history of struggle.

The first British constitution for Quebec, the *Proclamation Act of 1763*, created a government similar to that of the other British colonies along the Atlantic seaboard of what is now the United States. In those colonies, English Protestants constituted an overwhelming majority, and Catholics could not vote or hold public office. In Quebec there were only a handful of English Protestants, and the *Proclamation Act* proved to be quite impractical for a colony overwhelmingly French and Catholic. After a decade of confusion, the second British constitution for the colony, the *Quebec Act of 1774*, granted the *Canadiens* the thing most important to them: the right to live their lives as they wanted in terms of religion, language, culture, civil law, education, health, welfare, and land ownership. The *Quebec Act* became the bedrock of *Canadien* political culture, and they saw their survival as a distinct cultural group as dependent on the maintenance of the rights obtained in 1774. That has never changed, and one of the great achievements of Confederation is the preservation of Quebec's distinct culture.

Ten years after the Conquest, the American War of Independence produced a wave of English-speaking refugees known as the Loyalists. Most of them settled in the Maritimes or west of Montreal, leaving the *Canadien* community essentially intact. To accommodate this new group, the *Quebec Act* was replaced by the *Constitutional Act of 1791*. This *Act*, the third constitution for the colony, was the first to officially use the name Canada. It divided Quebec into two colonies: Lower Canada, where the *Canadiens* were the majority, and Upper Canada, where English-speaking American Protestants were the majority. Both colonies would have elected assemblies, and elections were called to select politicians who were known as Members of the Legislative Assembly, or MLAs. Power, however, continued to rest with the governors appointed by Britain. The *Canadiens* soon became expert at playing the game of electoral politics and for them the main objective was *la survivance*, the protection of their right to live their lives as they wanted. In contrast, the main interest of English-speaking MLAs was usually economic development.

The Loyalist immigration in the Maritimes led to the separation of New Brunswick from Nova Scotia in 1784. Both colonies were dominated by English-speaking Protestants. Prince Edward Island had already been separated from Nova Scotia in 1769, so there were six British North American colonies by 1800: the oldest, Newfoundland; the three Maritime ones; and Lower and Upper Canada. Britain had little difficulty governing Newfoundland and the three Maritime colonies. The Canadas were a different matter, and their government eventually became dysfunctional. It was the political problems in the Province of Canada that led to the adoption of federalism for all the colonies. First Nations in all these colonies had no role in government whatsoever. They were not involved in any of the discussions, were not able to vote until 1960, and did not achieve a role in First Ministers' conferences for another twenty years after that.

In the early 1800s, there were few clashes between French- and English-speaking Canadians. There were almost no *Canadiens* in Upper Canada, and the English-speaking minorities in Lower Canada were privileged as it was a British colony. In fact, French- and English-speaking people had few contacts with each other. Both colonies were beset with political problems caused mainly by the exploitation and abuse of privilege and power by small cliques of influential citizens. Rebellions broke out in 1837, prompting Britain to appoint a new governor, Lord Durham, to make recommendations for better governance of the Canadas. He proposed that the *Canadiens* be assimilated into British culture and recommended that the two colonies be combined into one, to be called the Province of Canada. Because there had to be separate governance for matters such as education and civil law, the new colony was divided administratively into two halves called Canada East and Canada West, but people continued to use the terms Upper and Lower Canada and sometimes still do.

Since *Canadiens* constituted more than half the population of the united Province of Canada, the British had to devise a means to prevent them from dominating the Assembly. Though the population of Lower Canada substantially exceeded that of Upper Canada, Durham recommended that the two halves of the united province each elect forty MLAs (later increased to sixty-two) and that the English-speaking minorities in Lower Canada be overrepresented. Those two undemocratic features ensured that about two-thirds of the MLAs were English speakers. Unfortunately for Durham, the main goal of English-speaking MLAs remained economic development, on which their opinions differed, while the main goal of the *Canadiens* was to prevent assimilation, on which they were united. The assimilation policy included barring the use of French in the new assembly, but defiant *Canadien* MLAs spoke in their own language on the very first day of debate. A wise governor and the English-speaking MLAs ignored the protest, and French continued to be used in the assembly. The new policy of assimilation had suffered its first serious setback. In 1848, the *Canadiens* obtained the right to use French in the Assembly and the courts, and it was never again challenged.

Political Paralysis and Federalism

The new government in the Province of Canada continued to function as before, but after 1848, Britain gave both Nova Scotia and Canada democratic government in the form of control of local matters. Power over those matters was transferred from the British governor to an executive based on a majority of the MLAs in each assembly. In the Canadian Assembly the English-speaking MLAs were divided into loose factions, with a large group calling itself the Reformers, a smaller faction consisting of Conservatives, and many MLAs not affiliated with either. *Canadien* politicians were similarly divided on many issues other than assimilation, with a large conservative faction known as the Bleus and a smaller, radical faction known as the Rouges. These unstable and undisciplined factions had great difficulty combining to form governments, and elections failed to produce stable majorities. Governments could only be formed if they included *Canadien* MLAs and, because they were more united than the English-speaking MLAs, they came to wield great influence within these governments. That was the reverse of what Durham and his supporters had hoped to achieve.

In the 1850s, the weak coalitions faced a number of issues on which British Protestants and *Canadien* Catholics had very different views, particularly matters concerning education and religion. Governments could not deal with problems such as defence against the possibility of American aggression, the withdrawal of British military support, the pending cancellation of a free-trade agreement with the United States, or building transportation links to the Maritime colonies. French- and English-speaking Canadians also had different views about the future of their colony. The *Canadiens* were relatively content with their families, communities, and homeland along the St. Lawrence, while many English-speaking Canadians were interested in economic development and expansion into the western prairies. During this period, Britain's interest in its North American colonies was changing. It had not previously favoured a union of all its colonies, but now it definitely wanted to reduce the cost of administration and defence, and the pending victory of the North in the American Civil War carried the threat of invasion. British investors also wanted a single, stable government to deal with in the colonies, and Britain gradually came to favour the union of the colonies.

Newfoundland, Nova Scotia, New Brunswick, and Prince Edward Island experienced very different historical development from each other and especially from that of the Province of Canada. Their main common denominators were the facts that they were all British colonies and that they all bordered the Atlantic. By the 1850s, all of them were jealous of their identities and powers and were very loyal to Great Britain. All but Newfoundland had government responsible to the people in local matters, but municipal government had not developed and local MLAs had enormous influence over roads, forests, property, and contracts. When the inhabitants of these four colonies peered beyond their local horizons, they looked first and foremost to Great Britain, second to New England, and then perhaps to each other or the West Indies. The Province of Canada was of little interest or importance to any of them, and they saw it as a confused society, incapable of dealing with its political problems, less than reliable in economic negotiations, and more self-satisfied than its circumstances warranted.

By the late 1850s, many of the politicians in the Province of Canada were dissatisfied with their situation. They included the leaders of three of the main factions in the Assembly—George Brown of the large Reformer faction, John A. Macdonald of the smaller Conservative faction from Upper Canada, and George-Étienne Cartier of the large Bleu, or Conservative, faction from Lower Canada. In 1858, a Conservative-Bleu government fell and the new Reform-Rouge government lasted only two days. Cartier and Macdonald formed a new coalition and asked Alexander T. Galt to join to give it more support in the Assembly. Galt believed that federalism was the only solution to the political problems of the Province of Canada, and he wanted to include the four Atlantic colonies in the scheme. He made acceptance of that position a condition for joining the government. Cartier and Macdonald did not want a federal system of government, but they agreed to his demand because they believed it was harmless. Few politicians were interested in Galt's proposal, but it remained a plank in the Conservative-Bleu platform.

In the 1850s, George Brown's Reformers were increasingly frustrated with political instability and with many of the decisions governments did manage to make. They liked the existing unitary government, but they wanted it to be based on the principle of representation by population, or "rep by pop." Since the population of Upper Canada now substantially exceeded that of Lower Canada and the gap was increasing, that change would give English-speaking Protestants a large and growing majority in the Assembly. They could then pursue a major objective that had been shelved for twenty years, namely assimilating the *Canadiens*. But federalism also had appeal for the Reformers because it would provide a separate government for Upper Canada, which English-speaking Protestants would dominate, free of the influence wielded by *Canadiens* in the current government. Reformers were therefore increasingly of the view that if they could not base the current unitary system on rep by pop, then the next best option was a federal system in which the central government and the two provincial governments would be based on rep by pop. Brown abandoned the dream of a unitary government and accepted the necessity of federalism. In 1859, his Reform Party endorsed federalism and Brown introduced the proposal into the Assembly, where it was soundly defeated. Like the Conservatives, the Reform platform retained federalism as a plank, but, unlike the Conservatives, many Reformers were genuinely committed to it and never abandoned that goal.

Cartier liked the status quo because he and his followers were in a powerful position in the Assembly and a dominant position in most governments. By the early 1860s, however, he realized that the adoption of rep by pop was inevitable because London could not allow a Catholic minority to override the interests of a Protestant majority indefinitely. Cartier needed a new means to protect *Canadien* culture, and federalism would provide a separate government completely under the control of *Canadiens* for Lower Canada. Such a government would have to be given full control of matters affecting the daily life of *Canadiens*, thus ensuring *la survivance*. The fundamental compromise that underlay federalism was emerging: Brown had to accept it in order to obtain rep by pop in the central government, and Cartier had to accept it in order to obtain French-Canadian control of their own lives in an autonomous province. In the mid-1850s, John A. Macdonald was as unenthusiastic about federalism as Brown and Cartier. He wanted a strong, unified state, unhindered by provincial governments, and he never changed his mind.

By the winter of 1863–64, political manoeuvring and stalemate had reached a level that exasperated both Brown's Reformers and Macdonald's Conservatives. On March 14, Brown proposed that a committee be established to identify a replacement for the dysfunctional constitution, a proposal that was accepted. He then formed a committee of twenty MLAs, including the leaders of the four major factions—himself, Cartier, Macdonald, and A.A. Dorion of the Rouges—plus powerful ministers such as Galt.

These politicians were well aware of the various solutions that had been discussed. One was to reform the existing unitary system to eliminate its weaknesses. Another option was a confederal system in which Upper and Lower Canada would become separate colonies once again, but would have some joint administrative bodies to manage things such as canals on the St. Lawrence River. Federalism was another option, one for which the United States offered an obvious, but flawed model. Another example was the British Empire itself, where the government in London controlled trade, defence, foreign affairs, and public land, while colonial governments controlled local matters. This option implied that the existing government would be replaced by three new ones: a central government with responsibility for common or general issues, plus two provincial governments, one for each of Upper and Lower Canada, with responsibility for local issues. Oddly enough, the existing constitution provided another model, in that there were separate systems of law and education for the two halves of the colony. All of these options had been discussed for years in political circles, in the newspapers, and among members of the public.

The challenge for Brown's committee was to identify which of the options would be the best and how it might be refined to suit the circumstances of Canada. The chaos of the previous decade indicated that pragmatism was not their strong suit, but by 1864 their frustrations had driven them to the point of seeking compromise. In spite of themselves, they were evolving from petty politicians into pragmatists. A majority of the English-speaking committee members wanted to reform and retain the existing system. The main reform they wanted was rep by pop, which would give Upper Canada twenty additional seats and form the basis for a strong and stable government. The *Canadiens* were, of course, united in their opposition to this model. Since no solution was possible without their support, that option was effectively dead. There was little support for a confederal union of two separate colonies with some joint institution to manage common interests. By process of elimination, the MLAs were left with only one option: the Province of Canada must have a federal system with a central government plus two provincial ones.

The committee met eight times over two months, with twelve of its members agreeing to the federalist option; three were opposed, including

Macdonald. On June 14, Brown tabled the recommendation for federalism, which was adopted by a vote of 59–48. Later that day, as if to demonstrate the urgency of dealing with that proposal, the Conservative government of Étienne Pascal Taché and Macdonald fell by a vote of 60–58. It was the fourth government to fall in three years. The political system established by the 1840 *Act of Union* had come to the end of the road.

Since another election would not likely produce a better outcome, the Governor General Sir Charles Stanley, Viscount Monck, urged Macdonald and Brown to negotiate with each other. Monck was strongly in favour of a union of all the colonies, and he played a major role in solving the crisis and adopting federalism. Brown appears to have been the first to respond to Monck's pressure. He realized that the only way his committee's recommendation could be implemented was if his Reformers joined with the Bleus and Conservatives in a coalition government, with the overriding goal of adopting a federal system of government. Since he and Cartier now agreed on the federal option, the question was whether Macdonald would join the coalition that was emerging. Macdonald temporarily abandoned his position favouring a unitary system, but he never stopped trying to impose it or, at least, to make the central government so strong that the system would be in effect unitary. On June 22, 1864, the Grand Coalition took office with four Conservatives (Taché, Cartier, Macdonald, and Galt), and two Reformers (Brown and Oliver Mowat).

The agreement establishing the Grand Coalition reflected some of the most important political compromises ever made in North America. The Coalition's stated purpose was to negotiate a union of British North American colonies based on the federal principle. Cartier had accepted that the central government would be based on rep by pop. Brown and Macdonald accepted that Lower Canada would be restored with responsibility for the issues that would put *Canadiens* in complete control of their own lives. And Brown had ceded to Macdonald's insistence that they try to entice the Maritimes to join from the beginning, rather than establishing federalism in Canada first. The Coalition issued a statement saying that, according to the principles of federal government, local matters would be handled by local bodies and general matters by a general legislature. They invited the four Atlantic colonies to join, but made it clear that if they remained aloof, the Province of Canada would adopt a federal system for itself.

The Coalition had to figure out how to make federalism work and how to divide responsibilities between the central and the provincial governments. Another problem was how to combine the British form of government, with its unwritten constitution, and the American form of federalism, with its written constitution. Work proceeded quickly, and by the end of August, they had drafted a detailed plan for a federal system of government. The next step was selling that plan to the Atlantic colonies.

Uniting the Colonies: The Charlottetown Conference

Fortunately, events in the Maritimes were creating the conditions that would lead to the second goal of Confederation, the union of most of the colonies. The Maritimes had too much government for too few people. Britain wanted to combine the three colonies into one, but all of them had different priorities and needs, as well as strong senses of local identity. Since 1862, Lieutenant Governor Arthur Hamilton Gordon of New Brunswick had been discussing Maritime union with the premiers of all three colonies, and it was debated in the Nova Scotia Assembly in March 1864. On March 28, Premier Charles Tupper of Nova Scotia wrote the other two premiers, proposing a meeting to discuss the union of the Maritime provinces. Under British pressure, the three Assemblies agreed to appoint delegates to discuss union. The politicians then did what politicians often do when responding to unwanted pressure—nothing.

The Canadians were aware of the proposed meeting and were much more interested in union than the Maritimers themselves. Canadian economic development depended upon massive borrowing in London, and British bankers would be far more confident dealing with a single, stable government than with four or five small ones. As the United States had indicated that it would not renew the Reciprocity Treaty of 1854, which had spurred significant growth of Canadian exports, uniting all the British colonies in a single economic market would help offset the pending loss of access to the American one. A single colony might be better able to defend itself in case of confrontation with the United States. And the idea of one colony stretching from sea to sea held attraction for those who dreamed great dreams. On June 30, Governor General Monck wrote his Maritime colleagues asking if the Canadians could attend their upcoming meeting. They agreed, and a meeting was scheduled in Charlottetown on September 1, with Canadian politicians attending as observers.

Besides being observers rather than delegates, the Canadians were set off from the Maritimers by several other factors. With seven members, the Canadian contingent was the largest. Having debated the issues for a decade in general and for five months in detail, the Canadians had a vast amount of knowledge about federalism and political union. All members of the Canadian delegation were government ministers subject to the discipline of cabinet solidarity, while both government and opposition parties were represented in the three Maritime delegations. The Canadian delegation was united in its objectives; the other delegations represented a variety of opinions in their colonies and attended the Conference as individuals rather than party representatives. In short, the Canadians did not have to "divide and conquer" the Maritime delegates as they were already quite divided and very ripe for conquest.

While the Maritime delegations had little interest in uniting their three colonies, hosting the Canadians had some value to them. They had followed closely the Canadian debate over federalism, and they knew a federation of colonies would preserve their governments, offer possible solutions to some of their problems, and create opportunities for those who found the local scene too confining for their ambitions. They also desperately wanted a railway connecting their region to Lower Canada and that required Canadian co-operation. Negotiations for that and for economic co-operation had occurred spasmodically over the years, producing much frustration but at least some of the participants at the Charlottetown Conference knew each other. They all became even more familiar when Canada dispatched a hundred-man delegation to tour the Maritimes, sixty-five of them being members of the Assembly or the Legislative Council. It was led by D'Arcy McGee, a brilliant choice as he was among the most personable and popular of Canadian politicians, an Irish Catholic from Quebec, a man of vision who could capture imaginations with his wonderful, Irish-accented oratory.

The Conference began on September 1, and the idea of Maritime union was quickly shelved as none of the three governments was really interested in it. The status of the Canadians was upgraded from observers to delegates, and the twenty-five politicians got down to the real business of the

Conference, namely listening to the Canadian delegates outline the details of their federal scheme. The Canadian delegation had arrived with carefully prepared presentations of the various aspects of the plan and a well-developed strategy for selling it. Macdonald led off with an overview of how the union of all the colonies would solve many problems and create the basis for a prosperous and peaceful future. Cartier supported him, which eased Maritime fears of domination by Upper Canada. Brown explained how the system would work, that is, how to meld American federalism with British cabinet government. The Canadians had already decided that the new federal assembly, or lower house, would be based on rep by pop so that was not a matter for negotiation.

Brown proposed that the upper house contain twenty senators from each of three regions, which the Canadians defined as Upper Canada, Lower Canada, and the Maritimes. Accordingly, provinces would not have equal representation in the Senate, as was the case in the United States, and central Canada would outnumber the other three colonies two to one. That meant that both the lower and upper houses would be based essentially on rep by pop, and the upper house would not bring regional or provincial balance to the lower one. A key question for the Maritimes was whether they would accept that both lower and upper houses would be dominated by central Canada.

Brown explained the proposed division of responsibilities between the two orders of government. Drafting the two lists had not presented many problems for the Grand Coalition, and they presented few problems for the Maritimers. The principle was simple: the central government would be responsible for general matters, the provinces for local ones. The new central government would thus handle trade and commerce, money and banking, navigation, the post office, criminal law, weights and measures, Aboriginal affairs, defence, and overall economic development. The provinces would handle property, natural resources, civil law, education, health, welfare, and municipal government. Finally, Galt explained Canada's proposals for the financial details of taxation and expenditure under the new system.

Although the Canadian Coalition had endorsed the federalist option rather than a unitary government, the debate on the relative merits of the two systems re-emerged at Charlottetown. Macdonald and many other English-speaking delegates still preferred a unitary government. The four *Canadien* delegates were completely opposed, as were many Maritime delegates who were determined to maintain local legislatures with autonomy and meaningful roles. The advocates of unitary government were probably a majority, but no solution was possible without the support of the *Canadiens* and those Maritime delegates who agreed with them. No minutes were kept of the presentations or discussions, which maintained maximum flexibility, avoided giving ammunition to potential opponents, and limited debate outside the conference hall.

It was clear that the Canadians were going to implement a federal system in their colony if the broader talks with the Maritimes failed. The choice facing the Maritime delegations was therefore between remaining separate colonies or joining in the wider federal union the Canadians had just outlined. While the Nova Scotia and New Brunswick delegates generally endorsed federalism, the Island delegates were much less pleased with what they were hearing. The Canadians were willing to help with a railway connection, which would benefit Nova Scotia and New Brunswick, but they showed little interest in helping Prince Edward Island deal with its economic problems. And with only a couple of MPs and senators, PEI would have virtually no influence in the new central government.

What mattered for the Canadians, however, was support from Nova Scotia and New Brunswick, and the Conference was thus an overwhelming success. The reports of the balls, dinners, parties, and speeches suggest that delegates were almost giddy with the level of agreement they had reached so quickly and easily, and with the prospects of creating something far greater than a mere union of colonies. Britain had repeatedly separated and united colonies, but a union of all would be new, as would the federal system of government. Also new was the fact that this dispensation would be initiated by the colonies themselves, and it might lead to the development of a new nation and a new country, about which a few delegates, politicians, and newspaper editors were already waxing eloquent.

Filling in the Details: The Quebec Conference

The delegates agreed to meet at Quebec City just one month later to work out the details of the scheme. In the meantime, after the work and fun of the Charlottetown Conference, they went on a tour of Nova Scotia and New

Brunswick. One purpose was to become more familiar with the various regions of the proposed super-colony. Another was to build support for the new creation, which was furthered by lavish entertainment by local dignitaries. These activities had a positive effect on the delegates themselves, on civic leaders, on the press, and presumably on the public. Missing from the action plan, however, was any attempt to promote the actual deal or provide information on the scheme. Those gaps would be filled in only after the Quebec Conference had worked out the details.

The delegates did not seem to realize that two problems were developing with this approach. One was that the more the delegates partied with each other, fed off each other's rhetoric, and enjoyed the attention, the oysters, the champagne, and their increasingly overly optimistic predictions for the future, the more they grew out of step with other MLAs, with their own constituents, and with the realities of the different colonies, not to mention the substantial number of *Canadiens* who voted Rouges and were not involved at all in the discussions. The second was that those who cheered them on at celebrations, dinners, and train and steamship stops along the route knew that something very important was developing, but did not know exactly what it was. Many of them were in for a major shock when they did see the details. Later, on September 26, a summary of the delegates' conclusions was published in the *Montreal Gazette*, but it was too vague to give readers a real sense of what was being created.

On October 9, thirty-three delegates from five colonies met in Quebec City. This time, Newfoundland decided to see whether joining such a union would solve any of its manifold problems. Canada sent twelve delegates, nine Conservatives and three Reformers. Of them, four were *Canadiens*, and once more there was no representation at all for the Rouges. The delegations from the Atlantic colonies—seven each from New Brunswick and PEI, five from Nova Scotia, and two from Newfoundland—all contained representatives from both government and opposition. By now John A. Macdonald was the dominant player and the chief drafter of the various clauses, a role that reflected his two decades in government.

In Quebec City the debate over federal versus unitary systems surfaced once more. The supporters of unitary government could not prevail because French Canadians and many Maritime delegates would never accept it. As the *Canadiens* insisted, the provinces were given exclusive control of all the spheres of responsibility deemed essential for *la survivance* of the *Canadien* nation. The federal government was allocated everything else. A difficult issue was which order of government would be allocated residual power, that is, power over things not assigned to either order of government or matters that might arise in the future. Some wanted residual power to rest with the provinces; others advocated for it to rest with the new central government. The result was a compromise, as the *BNA Act* gave the provinces residual power over all local matters and the central government residual power over everything else.

Macdonald's continuing struggle for a unitary government was reflected in his rather odd proposal that the central government alone would be based on the principle of democratic government. That would give the power the provinces had won in 1848 back to the lieutenant governors. And since it had been decided that the central government would appoint lieutenant governors, Macdonald's proposal meant that the provinces would become, in effect, colonies of the central government. New Brunswick's Charles Fisher introduced a crucial motion stating that both orders of government would be democratic. It passed without opposition, and another of Macdonald's attempts to create a unitary government failed.

The main debate in Quebec was over the allocation of seats in the Senate. That was not because other issues were less important but rather that they were easier to resolve. The allocation of Senate seats was, in contrast, very controversial and has never been resolved to everyone's satisfaction. The Canadian proposal at Charlottetown was endorsed with Upper Canada, Lower Canada, and the Maritimes identified as regions entitled to twenty-four senators each and with the Maritime seats distributed between its three provinces. Newfoundland would have additional seats should it join. If Rupert's Land was acquired and BC joined, the West would be treated as a single region, eventually also acquiring twenty-four senators. Unlike American senators, Canadian ones would be appointed rather than elected, and the appointment would be made by the federal government rather than the provincial ones. These provisions ensured that the Senate would provide an echo of the House of Commons, rather than a powerful voice for the provinces and regions.

The financial provisions were left much as Galt had outlined them at the Charlottetown Conference. It was not practical for each province to continue collecting customs, so that responsibility was transferred to the central government. Then, as customs had provided the overwhelming majority of revenue for the individual colonies, the central government had to return a large part of its customs revenue to the provinces to finance their continuing responsibilities. Given that the central government would have the more expensive responsibilities, it could collect taxes by any means, and the provinces were limited to the federal transfers, direct taxes, and the royalties from natural resources. These provisions were deemed adequate by most delegates.

The delegates at Quebec dealt quickly with dozens of clauses drafted by John A. Macdonald on issues such as the roles of the governor general, the lieutenant governors, and the courts. Issues crucial to the functioning of government such as political parties or the roles of the cabinet, prime minister, and premiers were not mentioned because these institutions were adopted from Britain, where the constitution was a matter of accepted precedent. It was agreed that the new super-colony would buy Rupert's Land from the Hudson's Bay Company. Britain would provide financial support for that purchase and the construction of the Intercolonial Railway connecting Lower Canada and the Maritimes. Building a railway to Red River and perhaps the Pacific was part of the general understanding, but was not mentioned in the *BNA Act*, although both railways were absolutely essential to Confederation. Finally, the new entity would take the name of the largest colony, Canada.

The delegates finalized their work on November 4 in a document called the *Quebec Resolutions*, seventy-two clauses that set out how they thought the new federation would be organized. It was a tremendous achievement, but the delegates overestimated what they had accomplished. Those from Nova Scotia and New Brunswick were seriously out of touch with their fellow MLAs and constituents, those from PEI and Newfoundland had major reservations about the new constitution, and the opinions of the *Canadien* Rouges had not even been solicited. Nevertheless, the delegates set off on a tour of the Province of Canada, where they were well received and the *Quebec Resolutions* were published on November 8.

Throughout the process, no one questioned that Great Britain was sovereign in the colonies and would remain so if they were to unite. It was Britain's intention that the colonial governments sort out what they wanted to do, then submit their wishes to London for modification, approval, and drafting into British law. To confirm that the *Quebec Resolutions* reflected the views of the colonies, it was understood that they would be submitted to the five assemblies for approval. There was no intention to submit the resolutions to the people in general elections, as such elections involved many issues and no delegation had obtained all it wanted for its colony. The plan to obtain the approval of the five assemblies ran into immediate difficulty, touching off two and a half years of further debate, elections, crises, and massive British intervention to obtain the necessary level of support.

Nonetheless, by December 1864, the march to Confederation was well underway, and British North America had undergone a remarkable political evolution. Only ten months previous, the Canadian Assembly was in chaos, stable governments could not be formed, decisions could not be taken, and elections had become pointless, while the Atlantic provinces were adrift with growing problems and uncertain futures, and both Canada and the Maritime colonies faced the real possibility of absorption into the United States. It was little wonder that the delegates who produced this remarkable turn-around were sometimes intoxicated with their achievements, with plans for future greatness, and with their own speeches.

CHAPTER 2
Towards Confederation, 1864-1867

The Quebec Conference drafted a federal constitution for all of Britain's North American colonies. The next stage was having the assemblies of the five colonies adopt it and requesting the British Parliament pass it into law. The process failed almost immediately, and it took two and a half years of very difficult work to cobble together a union of just three of the five colonies. Only two colonies followed the prescribed process: the Province of Canada, which approved the resolutions, and PEI, which rejected them. The New Brunswick elections of 1865 and 1866 were fought on the issue, the first one rejecting it and the second one endorsing it. But the campaigns involved many other issues, and elections had been ruled out as a means of approving the deal. The Nova Scotia government did not submit the Resolutions to the Assembly or even make Confederation an issue in an election, and Britain forced the colony to join. The resolutions were never submitted to the Newfoundland Assembly, but Confederation was rejected in the 1869 election. This chapter will examine the convoluted process by which three of the five BNA colonies were united into one, forming the basis of modern Canada.

The resolutions were published on November 8, 1864, and immediately copied in newspapers throughout the colonies. That was the first time politicians who had not been part of the delegations knew exactly what had been agreed. There followed an immediate outburst of debate, newspaper articles, speeches, meetings, and conversations. On November 23,

Alexander T. Galt, one of the chief architects of the scheme, defended it in a major speech that was widely distributed. He said that the deal was really quite simple: the old colonies were being rolled into one, and a new order of government was being created alongside the existing ones, which would retain control of local issues. All that was needed to implement the change, he suggested, was for the colonies to ask London to do so, and there was no need for conventions, elections, or ratification. That optimistic, overly simplistic, and somewhat false view was immediately challenged.

Upper and Lower Canada Approve Confederation

In the Province of Canada, the motion to approve the resolutions was introduced to the Assembly on February 3, 1865. Macdonald said it was a treaty and that, as such, it could be accepted or rejected, but not amended. That was a good debating position, but the resolutions were not a treaty and they were changed. Since the plan called for the division of the colony into two provinces, there were really two debates, one by the MLAs from Upper Canada and another by those from Lower Canada. Upper Canada was most enthusiastic about the new dispensation as it was the homeland of George Brown's Reformers, who had obtained almost everything they wanted. The new province was given control of matters of local importance, where laws would reflect the values of English-speaking Protestants. Macdonald's smaller Conservative faction could boast of a powerful central government. For Upper Canada, the *Quebec Resolutions* were a "win-win" proposition, and on March 11, their MLAs approved them by an overwhelming vote of 54–8.

In Lower Canada, French Canadians were much less favourably disposed to the deal. The restoration of a separate provincial government dominated by French Canadians was certainly welcome, but the main debate was over whether the new province would have the power and autonomy to protect French-Canadian culture from a central government overwhelmingly dominated by British-Canadian Protestants. The Rouges did not believe *la survivance* was sufficiently protected or that British Canadians would not use their preponderance in Ottawa to interfere with French-Canadian rights. Rouge leader A.A. Dorion said that the seventy-two resolutions really created a unitary government and represented the latest attempt to assimilate French Canadians.

This position was given credence by the fact that some English-speaking Canadians were saying that Confederation would create a new nationality, which implied that their "old" nationality would disappear. British Canadians also were saying that the central government would be very powerful, which implied that the provinces would be relatively weak. Some *Canadiens* criticized the adoption of rep by pop since it would put them in a permanent and growing minority position. They said that provincial control of education was an illusion since the central government could veto provincial legislation, and they flagged the potential abuse of the federal power of disallowance.

The Bleu press defended the deal. On July 11, 1864, *Le Courrier du Canada* said that a new general government would not have the right to interfere in a provincial legislature. Cartier's paper, *La Minèrve de Montréal*, said that the local government would have all the powers necessary to handle economic, civil, and religious affairs. The Bleu papers argued that French-Canadian MPs would be able to prevent the central government from interfering in the provinces, echoing the views of the three French-Canadian cabinet ministers, Cartier, Taché, and Hector-Louis Langevin. To deal with criticisms of the scheme in the Maritimes, pro-confederates there said that the resolutions could be changed. That undermined Cartier, who was trying to convince French Canadians that the rights guaranteed them could not be changed.

Overall, the Bleu response to the Rouge criticisms was that Confederation would not create a strong and dominant central government, that Lower Canada would be liberated from the Union of 1840, and that the colony would be a distinct and autonomous province in a loose and decentralized federation. Rep by pop would not make Upper Canada dominant as two-thirds of the senators would come from Lower Canada and the Maritimes. Since the House of Commons would only be concerned with general issues, it did not matter that it was based on rep by pop. Cartier argued that federalism was the only viable solution because the current system could not continue, restoring a separate colony of Lower Canada was not realistic, and the only alternative to Confederation was annexation by the United States. Langevin and Cartier said that the central government would not deal with matters of race, nationality, religion, or local issues, and French Canadians "would have their own province with their own parliament and their own government." There would be "a state within a state," with the "full exercise of [French] rights" and recognition of "national independence."

In spite of misgivings, the arrangements were satisfactory to a majority of French-Canadian politicians, to the Catholic Church, to the English-speaking business class in Montreal, and to the British minorities whose culture and distinctiveness were well protected. On March 11, the MLAs from Lower Canada approved the resolutions 37–25, with French-Canadian MLAs voting 27–21 in favour. The Rouges claimed that a majority of French Canadians opposed Confederation, but the facts suggest otherwise as pro-confederates won all the by-elections between 1864 and 1867. Of the twenty-one French-Canadian MLAs who voted against the resolutions, seven were defeated in the 1867 election, three switched sides and won re-election as pro-confederates, and the seats of three others who did not run were won by the pro-Confederation side. Only five of the twenty-one anti-confederates were re-elected, indicating that French Canadians definitely endorsed Confederation.

Overall, the vote in the Assembly of the Province of Canada was 91–33. The MLAs had voted their province out of existence, transferring half its responsibilities to the new central government and half to the new provinces of Quebec and Ontario. On July 1, 1867, thirty years of political and constitutional confusion came to an end, along with a century of failed attempts at assimilation. Lower Canada became Quebec once more, this time as one of four provinces in the new Dominion of Canada. Champlain's settlement at Quebec City was once more the capital of a province stretching from Gaspé to the Ottawa River, and Toronto was once more the capital of Upper Canada under its new name of Ontario.

The Flawed Approval Process in New Brunswick

The *Quebec Resolutions* had a very different reception in the Maritimes. Opposition began to mount as details and rumours circulated during the Quebec Conference. The main concerns were a likely increase in tariffs and taxes, the effects on trade, the idea of the Maritimes paying part of the cost of a railway to the Pacific, and the inadequate representation the provinces would have in the super-colony. One of the main demands, the building of the Intercolonial Railway, had not been fully addressed, and it was not clear that Britain was committed to providing the necessary financing. The debate over defence suggested that the Maritimes would help defend central Canada, not the other way around, and the idea that union would protect the Atlantic provinces from the United States was ridiculed.

When the New Brunswick delegates returned from Quebec, they discovered that they had mishandled the negotiations and misread public opinion. People immediately grasped that New Brunswick would be virtually powerless in the new federation, with almost no representation in Ottawa. A storm of protest erupted, and Premier Samuel Leonard Tilley decided not to submit the *Quebec Resolutions* to the Assembly as required by the agreed process. The second most powerful minister, Albert Smith, declared his opposition to the scheme. He argued that it would decrease the province's influence and increase taxes. He said the subsidy of eighty cents per capita was inadequate, and pointed out a major flaw in the trade-off of customs for the subsidy, namely that customs revenue for Ottawa would grow over time, but Ottawa's subsidy to the province would not. His position was supported by the mercantile classes, because the province traded mainly with the United States.

In response to such criticisms, Tilley and other delegates suggested that taxes and tariffs would not be increased, that the Maritimes would have enough political strength in Ottawa to prevent it from spending money in central Canada and on acquiring Rupert's Land, and that the Intercolonial Railway might terminate in Saint John rather than Halifax. They had no proof for any of these assertions because none of them were true. The pro-confederates said that New Brunswick's industries would gain access to the larger central Canadian market, but the Saint John merchants were skeptical. Tilley said that Britain favoured Confederation, but he could not provide any evidence since Britain's actions had been discreet and behind the scenes.

Instead of asking for a vote in the Assembly, Tilley called an election for February–March 1865. The main newspapers came out against the agreement. Irish Catholics opposed it because they saw Upper Canada as dominated by Protestant Orangemen, and Acadians had no interest in being an even smaller linguistic minority in a much larger, English-dominated federation. There was skepticism about the worth of Canadian promises, since Canada had reneged on previous agreements. The pro-Confederation side used the threat of potential invasion by the United States, but the American government made clear that no such threat existed, and British governors had always had full authority to move troops between colonies.

Smith and the anti-confederates won the election. Every delegate to the Quebec Conference was defeated. The popular vote was fairly close, however, because most objections related to the detailed provisions rather than the concept of Confederation itself. The best alternative to Confederation was closer relations with the United States. The United States, however, was not interested in building railways from Maine to the Gulf of St. Lawrence, and in the spring of 1865, it announced the termination of the free-trade agreement that had sustained New Brunswick's prosperity for a decade. Increased trade with Canada and Nova Scotia was a poor alternative, but it was the only one. Smith's coalition began to weaken, and a by-election in Saint John in November became a crucial barometer of opinion. Tilley told Macdonald that it would take considerable money to tip the scales, and Macdonald duly sent $5,000, which helped the pro-Confederation candidate win by a substantial margin.

The outcome was still very much in doubt, so Britain intervened openly. A dispatch of June 24, 1865, ordered all the lieutenant governors in the Maritimes to use their influence to impose the Confederation scheme. In June, Premier Smith visited London, where he met Colonial Secretary Edward Cardwell. The latter made it clear that Britain was fully in support of Confederation. The actions and attitudes of the British government became a significant, if not crucial factor. London had not previously made its pro-Confederation views public because it had hoped that the colonial assemblies would decide to unite on their own initiative. Now Lieutenant Governor Gordon was ordered to intervene, and he published correspondence with London that proved the British government was solidly behind Confederation. It now seemed unpatriotic to oppose the mother country's wishes, especially for the Loyalist province. Britain also suggested that its support for the Intercolonial Railway depended on Confederation being adopted, a rather heavy-handed hint for the province.

Smith still commanded a majority in the Assembly, so Lieutenant Governor Gordon precipitated a crisis. On April 6, he arranged for the Legislative Council to send an address to Queen Victoria, urging Britain to unite the colonies. There was no precedent for an appointed council to address the monarch on a political issue. Smith resigned because Gordon's actions indicated a lack of confidence in his government and a blatant interference in politics. A resolution stating that Gordon had engaged in unconstitutional conduct was signed by a majority of MLAs, but Gordon called for a new election for June to resolve the alleged constitutional crisis that he had precipitated.

At that point New Brunswick found itself threatened by invasion by an Irish political faction known as the Fenians. They were Irish-Catholic veterans of the American Civil War who entertained the notion that they could advance the cause of Irish independence by attacking British colonies such as New Brunswick. They posed no military threat, but they did cross the border and burn a customs house. A few troops sent from Halifax put a quick end to the alleged threat, but the incident diverted attention from Gordon's questionable call for an election. The incident was used to reinforce the dubious argument that Confederation would make all the colonies more secure. Fenian appeals to Irish Catholics in New Brunswick backfired as the Catholics felt that they had to demonstrate their loyalty to Britain, which meant endorsing Confederation.

Gordon's actions touched off a nasty electoral campaign. Smith attacked Gordon for misusing his authority. Gordon published accounts of his meetings with Smith showing that they had been discussing the implementation of Confederation. Tilley used his significant influence with the Prohibitionist movement to lock up the Protestant vote on the side of Confederation. Though Smith's alternatives to Confederation lay in ruins, Tilley was still not certain of victory. He telegraphed Macdonald asking for $40,000 to $50,000 to help persuade the undecided. This was a very substantial sum per voter, but Macdonald willingly complied. Tilley also promised that he would fix the other problems that had been raised in the final negotiations scheduled for that winter in London. Confederation was but one issue in the election that reversed the 1865 vote, with Tilley winning thirty-three seats and the anti-confederates reduced to eight.

The new Assembly met in June 1866, but Tilley was still afraid to submit the *Quebec Resolutions*, and they were approved instead by the appointed Legislative Council. In August, Tilley and his delegation sailed for London for the final round of negotiations. A few minor changes were made, but Tilley failed to fix the problems as he had promised. He was, however, allegedly instrumental in selecting a name for the new political creation. He remembered a verse in the Bible that stated that God had "dominion also from sea to sea." No one knew what a dominion actually was, but it sounded quite fine and so the new federation was named the Dominion of Canada. It was a wise decision as it differentiated the new entity from the colony of Canada, which had been established in 1791. On July 1, 1867, New Brunswick became one of the four provinces in the new Dominion of Canada.

Nova Scotia Fails to Approve Confederation

Nova Scotia followed a completely different course in its evolution into a Canadian province. There, the 1863 election was arguably the most important in the history of the province and one of the most important in Canada. Charles Tupper's Conservatives won a majority on a platform that included the idea of uniting the three Maritime colonies. His main goal was a union of the five colonies, and he never deviated from that vision, never questioned its wisdom, never weighed the advantages against the disadvantages. Over the next four years, he did everything he could to make it happen, and he succeeded. He and the other Nova Scotian delegates agreed with the outline for the new federation and did not fight particularly hard to strengthen the Senate, to obtain equal representation, or to obtain a larger per-capita grant.

When Nova Scotians learned of the terms on November 8, the main Halifax papers supported them, but opposition immediately developed among ordinary people. Indeed, there was not actually much of a debate because few people had anything good to say about the proposal. One of the Liberal politicians, William Annand, pointed out the most serious flaw, namely that the eighty-cent subsidy represented only 25 per cent of the customs revenue Nova Scotia had previously collected and could not possibly cover the responsibilities left to the province. He argued that Canada would spend the customs revenue collected in Nova Scotia buying Rupert's Land and building transportation elsewhere. Nova Scotia's contingent of nineteen MPs would not be able to influence federal policy, and Nova Scotians would have to emigrate to find jobs. A major concern was that Nova Scotia's tariff rate was 10 per cent and that would almost certainly increase with Confederation. Having fought for and won democratic government, it would now lose control over many matters to a parliament dominated by central Canadians.

This opposition developed into a well-financed and organized political movement. Since January 1865, the prominent politician Joseph Howe had been criticizing the arrangements in a series of letters published anonymously in the *Novascotian*, letters that brilliantly summed up all the criticisms being made, and he became the leader of the Antis. Tupper knew that the Assembly would not approve the resolutions so, like Tilley in New Brunswick, he did not submit them for approval. Confederation was not even mentioned in the 1866 Speech from the Throne. Like Tilley, Tupper said he would fix any problems in the next round of negotiations in London. Neither Tupper nor other supporters made an adequate effort to explain the deal, and some of the arguments they made were specious.

The key factor in Nova Scotia's road to Confederation was Britain's determination to force the colonies to unite. Lieutenant Governor Richard MacDonnell was ordered to support Confederation. He refused to do so because that meant siding with one party in a domestic political debate, a violation of democratic government. He was removed and his successor, Sir Fenwick Williams, had no such qualms. He interfered with the anti-Confederation campaign and supported Tupper by providing lavish entertainment and strong hints of appointments for MLAs who might be persuaded to favour the scheme. A number of MLAs were seen visiting Government House, and it was noted that they changed sides on the issue and later received rewards such as Senate appointments.

Though there was no debate on the *Quebec Resolutions*, some reference to it could hardly be avoided. William Miller, who had opposed Confederation, introduced a motion calling for the appointment of a delegation to attend the final round of negotiations in London, where it could seek better terms. Appointing such a delegation could possibly be interpreted as approval of the proposed union. The crucial vote carried 31–19, with seven MLAs who had previously opposed Confederation switching sides. Without their change of heart, the motion would have been defeated 26–24. It was not clear why Miller and the others changed sides, but strong suspicion was that they were bought off. That was as close as Nova Scotia ever came to approving Confederation.

The London Conference

The centre of action then moved to London, where the British government had the task of turning the *Quebec Resolutions* into legislation. In July 1866, cabinet approved a draft act that identified the cost of Britain's contribution to the deal. Accordingly, London would provide guarantees for Canada to borrow £5 million to help build the Intercolonial Railway and purchase Rupert's Land. These guarantees finally solved problems that had lingered for a decade. The officials then awaited the final revisions the colonial delegates might make once they arrived in London. In the meantime, Britain united the colonies of Vancouver Island and British Columbia in preparation for the expansion of the new super-colony to the Pacific.

The third and final meeting, the London Conference, lasted officially from December 4 to 21, though colonial delegates were debating the issues with British officials and politicians from the time they arrived in London until the legislation was approved by Parliament in March 1867. There was more debate over the major issues, but no substantive changes were made, and Maritime delegates had no significant success obtaining the changes they had promised. Neither, apparently, did Macdonald, who remained determined to make the federal government even more powerful. His Conservative colleague Langevin said he had to watch Macdonald like a hawk to ensure that he did not slip in language strengthening the central government.

The delegates' final draft was then sent to the Colonial Office. There, experts turned it into legislation, a process that went through a number of stages. One major change was that fisheries were made a federal responsibility, rather than a shared one like agriculture. The debate over responsibility for residual power was renewed, but the final draft confirmed the decision of the Quebec Conference so that power remained divided between the two orders of government. The legislation was introduced into the House of Lords in early February 1867, passed by the House of Commons on March 8, given royal assent on March 29, and implemented on July 1. During this period, Britain appointed Macdonald as the Dominion's first prime minister, and he got on with the job of selecting the first cabinet, identifying future senators and judges, and finalizing the arrangements to create the new central government and the provinces of Ontario and Quebec.

The three colonies that formed the Dominion of Canada thus entered Confederation by very different routes. The process that called for the *Quebec Resolutions* to be approved by each Assembly was only followed in the Province of Canada and PEI. The government of New Brunswick knew it could not obtain the approval of the Assembly, so it called an election but was overwhelmingly defeated. That new government was undermined by its own failures and the actions of Britain, the Province of Canada, and the pro-confederates. It was manipulated into a new election, which it lost and New Brunswick was then arguably on board. Nova Scotia never approved the *Quebec Resolutions*, but Britain forced it to join Confederation anyway. The Assembly of Prince Edward Island debated the *Quebec Resolutions* on March 29, 1865, and rejected the deal by a vote of 23–5. Newfoundland rejected the deal in the election of 1869 and did not change its mind for another eight decades. But with approval of the Province of Canada, the manipulation of the vote in New Brunswick, and the overriding of opinion in Nova Scotia by the British, the Dominion of Canada was born on July 1, 1867. The various processes followed indicate just how difficult a task it was and how great an achievement the politicians had accomplished. And though there was misrepresentation, manipulation, and bribery, Confederation was achieved without violence, warfare, or conquest, a sharp contrast to the way nations were being united or preserved in Europe and the United States.

CHAPTER 3
The Constitution of 1867

The implementation of the *British North America Act* on July 1, 1867, marked the culmination of a process that had first been broached in the late 1850s. The specific proposal for federalism and for the union of the colonies had developed through seven fairly distinct stages. They included George Brown's committee, which met from March to June of 1864; the work of the Grand Coalition in July and August; the Charlottetown Conference; the Quebec Conference; the negotiations and deal-making over the next two years; the talks and negotiations in London after October 1866, including the London Conference; and the final drafting of the *Act* from January to March of 1867.

This chapter will provide a detailed description of the sections of the *BNA Act* that apply to federalism and the union of the three colonies. It will examine the exact wording of the *Act*, the issues involved in the constitution, and some of the myths that have since arisen about Confederation. It will analyze important issues such as residual power, the federal power to veto provincial legislation, the importance of the responsibilities of the two orders of government, the question of sovereignty, and the relative power of the two orders of government. The story of the evolution of Canadian federalism will resume in Part II, with this analysis providing the foundation for understanding the ebb and flow of the various issues over the last 150 years.

The *British North America Act*

About half of the *BNA Act*'s 147 sections refer to federalism. The first paragraph explains why the British government passed an act uniting three colonies into one. Accordingly, "the Provinces of Canada, Nova Scotia, and New Brunswick have expressed their desire to be federally united into one Dominion . . ." The truth, of course, is that it was Britain that wanted the union, and the Assemblies of Nova Scotia and New Brunswick never expressed any such a desire. Other reasons for passing the *Act* included promoting the welfare of the provinces and the empire, providing a constitution, and providing for the admission of other colonies.

Section 5 states that "Canada shall be divided into four provinces, named Ontario, Quebec, Nova Scotia, and New Brunswick." The next one explains that the existing Province of Canada was being divided into the new provinces of Ontario and Quebec. Sections 21 to 36 explain the Senate and the allocation of its seats on the basis of equality of regions: twenty-four each for Ontario, Quebec, and the Maritimes, with the latter divided equally between Nova Scotia and New Brunswick. Senate appointments are made by the governor general, upon recommendation by the prime minister. The House of Commons is covered in Sections 37 to 52 and, as George Brown insisted, it is based on the principle of rep by pop. Its 181 members were allocated to Ontario (eighty-two, a gain of twenty), Quebec (sixty-five, a gain of three), Nova Scotia (nineteen), and New Brunswick (fifteen). Quebec's representation was fixed at sixty-five, and that of other provinces was to be adjusted every ten years to reflect any changes in the ratio of their populations to that of Quebec.

Numerous sections explain the changes necessary to convert the three colonies into four provinces. Sections 64 and 88 declare that the status and powers of Nova Scotia and New Brunswick "shall, subject to the provisions of this *Act*, continue to exist as at the Union . . ." Ontario and Quebec also maintained the status they had enjoyed as the Province of Canada. These articles confirm that the politicians who wanted to reduce the status of the provinces to that of municipalities had lost the debate. When Britain granted its colonies democratic government, it had retained the power to "disallow" colonial legislation, and its governors had the power to "reserve" a bill if they thought Britain might want to disallow it. Britain retained those powers over Dominion legislation (Sections 56 and 57), and its power to disallow and reserve provincial legislation was transferred to the federal government and the lieutenant governors (Section 90). No change was made to these powers.

The heart of the constitution is Sections 91 and 92, which identify the division of responsibilities between the two orders of government, the most important element in any federal constitution. Section 91 begins by saying that the Queen, represented by the federal government, can "make laws for the peace, order, and good government of Canada, in relation to all matters not . . . assigned exclusively to the . . . Provinces . . .". Then, "for greater certainty" regarding the meaning of peace, order, and good government, a list of subjects that are within "the exclusive [power] of Parliament" is provided. The federal responsibilities include the regulation of trade and commerce, the raising of money by any mode, the postal service, defence, navigation and shipping, the seacoast and fisheries, interprovincial or international ferries, currency and banking, patents and copyrights, Aboriginal affairs, naturalization, marriage and divorce, criminal law and penitentiaries, and various safety matters such as lighthouses or quarantines. Finally, the federal government has residual power over matters not assigned to the provinces.

Provincial powers are listed in Section 92, which begins: "In each Province the Legislature may exclusively make laws in relation to matters . . . hereinafter enumerated," and then lists fifteen such items. They include amending provincial constitutions, direct taxation, public lands (natural resources), hospitals and asylums (health and welfare), municipal institutions (local government), local works, property and civil rights, and provincial laws and prisons. The allocation of local works to the provinces is qualified to exclude interprovincial or international transportation, and communications and public works declared by the federal government to be to the overall advantage of Canada or of two or more provinces. The last sub-clause, 16, defines the residual power of provinces: "Generally all matters of a merely local or private nature in the Province." Although Section 91 gives Ottawa the power to make laws for the "peace, order, and good government of Canada," the provinces have always made laws for peace, order, and good government within their borders, so that is definitely not an "exclusive" federal power.

Education was one of the issues that had led to deadlock in the Assembly of the Province of Canada, and it was delicately handled in Section 93, which says that the provinces "may exclusively make laws in relation to education . . ." A number of clauses then spell out minority education rights, but the wording is fairly clear: education is a provincial responsibility, but the existing legal rights of Protestant and Catholic minorities in the four provinces have to be respected. If they are not, the federal government has the right to intervene to protect them.

Two responsibilities, agriculture and immigration, could not easily be assigned to either order of government, so they are listed as shared (Section 95). Since conflict is inevitable in federal systems, one order of government had to be given paramountcy, in this case the central one. Other responsibilities were necessarily assigned to both orders of government, such as the right to borrow money, but these are not shared. A number of other provisions divide up the duties for courts and jails. The federal government was assigned responsibility to implement treaties that Great Britain signed with other countries (Section 132). That was necessary as Britain had to ensure that its treaty obligations would be honoured by its colonies even if they adopted federal constitutions, but foreign affairs remained solely the prerogative of the British government. One of the most significant sections covered the transfer of customs revenue to Ottawa and the subsequent requirement for Ottawa to return part of it so the provinces could execute their responsibilities (Section 118). Each province received a grant of eighty cents per capita based on the 1861 census, plus annual grants to assist with administration. The last two Sections, 146 and 147, provided for the admission of Newfoundland, PEI, and British Columbia if requested by their legislatures.

The Intentions of the Fathers of Confederation

The debates on the *Quebec Resolutions* had revealed wide differences of interpretation over what the proposed provisions meant. Some of those debates have been resolved over the years, some have never been resolved, and new ones have been added to the constitutional saga. Such differences of opinion are a fundamental and inevitable characteristic of federalism, and they often go to the heart of politics because the outcomes affect the power, wealth, and lives of the people in every province. It also reflects the balance of power between the central and provincial governments, both of whom represent the same citizenry. The history of Canadian federalism is largely the story of co-operation and conflicts between the two orders of government, and the ultimate conflict is over power, over which order of government makes the decisions that affect Canadians. This section will summarize a number of the issues that have arisen over the past 150 years and relate them to the debates of the 1860s and the *BNA Act*.

Many of the debates have been couched in terms of what the Fathers of Confederation may or may not have "intended" when they drafted the various clauses. There is no agreement, however, on who the Fathers were, and there were certainly more than the group that met at Charlottetown. The Fathers could include the twenty members of George Brown's constitutional committee, the members of the Grand Coalition, and the delegates to the Charlottetown, Quebec, and London Conferences. The governor general, the lieutenant governors, and British colonial secretaries and their officials played large and perhaps crucial roles. These architects had a lot of different intentions, views, and interests, and many of the them made compromises and changed their positions during the debates. The discussions at the three conferences were held in secret, no notes were taken, and even when the politicians wrote editorials or letters, or made speeches, one cannot always know whether they meant what they said. Since 1867 these ambiguities have allowed people to pick and choose various pieces of evidence for what they think the Fathers "intended," usually to support their views on what they wish the constitution actually said or meant.

Genuine or Quasi-Federalism?

One of the major debates in Canadian political history is over the question of whether the *Act* established a genuine form of federalism, often referred to as classic federalism, or if the central government was so strong vis-á-vis the provinces that the system was only "quasi-federal." Whatever the "intentions" of the Fathers, the *Act* does not say that the two orders are equally sovereign (genuinely federal) or that the central government is dominant (quasi-federal). The first sentence in the *Act* says that the provinces are to be "federally united," a very clear statement of intent to create a federal system. Section 92 identifies the "Exclusive Powers" of the provinces, and "exclusive" means that the central government cannot intervene. Sections 91 gives Parliament power only for "matters not . . . assigned exclusively to the . . . Provinces." Those phrases suggest that both orders of government are autonomous in their spheres and that the system is therefore genuinely federal.

On the other hand, a number of clauses suggest that the central government is dominant, which implies that the system is quasi-federal. The central government was given the power to veto provincial legislation, but by convention that power was only to be used if such legislation harmed the wider interests of the Dominion or was outside provincial jurisdiction. Ottawa was given the authority to declare any provincial work a federal matter, but that was intended to apply to infrastructure that affected other provinces, such as transportation links. Ottawa was given authority to collect revenue by any means while the provinces were restricted to direct taxes, which were not important at the time. It therefore is not clear whether the *Act* established a genuine or a quasi-federal system, and that lack of clarity has persisted ever since.

Another debate centres on whether the *Act* assigned the more "important" matters to the central government, which might suggest that the system was designed to be quasi-federal. For English-speaking Canadians, the important matters of trade, commerce, taxes, and banking were assigned to the central government. For French Catholics and many Maritimers, the important matters of education, health, welfare, civil law, and property were assigned to the provincial governments, as was the very important economic subject of natural resources. Thus both lists of responsibilities contained "important" matters, and that was the win-win agreement that made federalism such an obvious option for both French and British Canadians and all of the colonies. Defence and foreign affairs are often identified as important tasks assigned to Ottawa, but defence was not important after 1867 and foreign affairs remained a British prerogative until 1931.

Ottawa and the Provinces: Equally Sovereign? Equally Powerful?

Another important debate about federalism concerns the question of whether both orders of government are equally sovereign or autonomous in their areas of responsibility. It is a rather odd debate, since the *BNA Act* makes clear that they are, in fact, equally autonomous. The first sentence of Section 92 states that the provincial legislatures "may exclusively make laws" in their areas of responsibility, that is, they are autonomous in those areas. Section 91 states that the central government can make laws "in relation to all matters" not assigned to the provinces, that is, it is autonomous in all those areas. So both orders of government have full power to make laws in their areas of responsibility, and neither has power to make laws in the other's area of responsibility.

A variation on the debate about relative importance and autonomy concerns the question of which order of government is more powerful. The federal government had the right to declare any local work as being in the Dominion's interest. This was a common-sense provision that would, for example, allow it to build the Welland Canal, which is entirely within Ontario's borders but forms part of an international waterway. Ottawa needed that power to obtain land for general purposes such as building a railway, post office, or a military base. The power is limited by the phrase "for the general advantage of Canada or . . . two or more provinces." The provision has worked well, and Ottawa has not used this power to dominate the provinces.

Ottawa was given the ability to raise taxes by any means, which certainly suggests "power." But Ottawa was given costlier responsibilities at the time, it had to return part of the customs revenue to the provinces, and many provincial responsibilities were paid for through municipal taxes and church tithes. It is not clear at all that citizens paid more in taxes to Ottawa than they did to both the provincial and municipal governments, plus tithes to the churches that administered education, health, and welfare. And larger budgets are only one of many factors defining the relative power of competing governments.

The fact that the provinces were restricted to mere "local" issues might imply that the Fathers "intended" the provinces to be weaker. But constitutionally the word *local* meant within provincial borders, and many local issues were seen as being very important by their constituents. Municipalities fell under provincial jurisdiction, so Montreal, Toronto, and Halifax were "local." The CPR was of great significance, but so were the extensive railway networks within each province, and the latter probably carried more freight and passengers than the CPR. The road from Cornwall to Windsor was local but hardly unimportant. In fact, almost all of an ordinary citizen's dealings with governments or institutions came under provincial control, and they were almost certainly the most important matters for those individuals.

A related issue is the relative balance of power between the federal and provincial governments and changes in that balance. The balance reflects the relative importance of the two sets of responsibilities at any given time. Historically, the most important example is federal responsibility for defence, which turned Canada into a virtual unitary state during the two world wars. Both wars were then followed by trends towards a weakening of the federal government and increasing power for the provinces. For many other responsibilities, it does not matter which ones are becoming more or less important at any time, and such shifts do not affect any alleged balance between the two orders of government.

After the Second World War, a number of factors combined to increase greatly the importance of three provincial responsibilities: health, welfare, and education. Provincial and municipal spending mushroomed at the same time as federal spending on defence was declining. That is often cited as evidence of a swing in the balance of power, but it is not clear how having a hundred thousand fewer soldiers and a hundred thousand more teachers and nurses weakened Ottawa's capacity to fulfill its duties, and it certainly did not lead to the provinces dictating to Ottawa in areas of federal responsibility. The following chapters document fluctuations in the relative importance of federal and provincial responsibilities, in the capacity of the two orders of government to meet their obligations, and in the effects of those factors on their relations.

During the Quiet Revolution of the 1960s, the phrase *maîtres chez nous*, "masters in our own house," became popular in Quebec. It expressed the goal of Quebec nationalists and was endorsed by all the province's political parties. It meant that French Canadians in Quebec, not Ottawa or the local English-speaking business class, were to be in charge of their own lives. In fact, Sections 92 and 93 of the *BNA Act* had clearly made French Canadians *maîtres chez nous* because these clauses gave Quebec control of almost every aspect of a citizen's private life: home, business, farm, and property; schools, hospitals, and institutions; the laws that affected a citizen, unless they committed criminal acts; and culture. These issues were all handled in the citizen's language and according to the individual's values and interests. What the Québécois meant when they used the phrase after 1960 was that they wanted Ottawa and English-speaking Canadians to recognize that the Québécois still intended to be governed by laws made in Quebec City and not Ottawa. That issue eventually led to the

57

near breakup of the country. Of course, Section 92 also made Upper Canadian Protestants and Maritimers "masters in their own houses," but the phrase is only used in reference to French Canadians in Quebec as they continued their centuries-old quest to avoid assimilation.

Under the *BNA Act*, the federal government had to return part of its revenue to the provinces to allow them to execute their responsibilities. The amount of eighty cents per capita was grossly unfair, because the different colonies had very different types and levels of revenue and expenditure. Customs duties had accounted for 75 per cent of New Brunswick's revenue, 72 per cent of Nova Scotia's, and only 56 per cent of Canada's. The new subsidy would provide 80 to 90 per cent of the revenue for Nova Scotia and New Brunswick, about 65 per cent for Quebec, and about 50 per cent for Ontario, and consume around 20 per cent of the federal budget. That was far more than adequate for Ontario, a little less than adequate for Quebec, and woefully inadequate for the Maritime provinces. The formula often left Ottawa with more money than was needed to finance its responsibilities and the provinces with less than they needed to finance theirs. This came to be called the "fiscal imbalance," although there are other definitions of this term, and it has been a major element in the relations between Ottawa and the provinces ever since 1867.

The Provinces: Equal or Distinct?

One of the important aspects of any federal constitution is whether the provincial governments are all treated the same, which is known as symmetrical federalism, or whether they are treated differently, which is known as asymmetrical federalism. Canadian federalism has always been asymmetrical: the provinces have never been equal, and Ottawa has never treated them equally. There are at least a dozen specific examples of asymmetrical provisions in the *BNA Act*, a clear indication that the Fathers had no intention of treating all provinces the same. The American Senate is based on a symmetrical system with two seats per state regardless of population, but in Canada different provinces at different times have had twenty-four, twelve, ten, six, four, three, or two senators. Senate seats in Quebec were allocated differently than those in other provinces. Civil law in Quebec is different than in other provinces. Minorities had different degrees of protection in different provinces, and federal subsidies were different. The Intercolonial Railway benefited the provinces east of Ontario;

the CPR benefited those west of Quebec. All provinces entered Confederation with different debts, subsidies, promises, rights, and numbers of senators per capita. And ever since, Ottawa has treated the provinces differently, with special treatment often reflecting political imperatives.

A Pact between Provinces or Peoples?

One of the major controversies of Confederation is the question of whether it was a pact (or compact), and, if so, whether it was between provinces or between peoples. The fundamental problem that led to Confederation was that French Catholics and British-Canadian Protestants in the Province of Canada had different values and therefore wanted different laws and government priorities. The basis of Confederation was, in fact, the informal agreement between Brown and Cartier that Canada had to have a federal system of government so that English-speaking Protestants could not interfere in the lives of French Canadians and vice versa.

Those two leaders represented the largest French- and English-speaking groups, which gives credence to the idea of Confederation as a pact between peoples. But the large Rouge faction of French Catholics opposed the deal; the Acadians were not part of the process; and the English-speaking colonists were not united on the merits of Confederation and belonged to three national groups, Irish, Scottish, and English. In fact, not one of the members of the Grand Coalition that drafted the scheme was of English background. Confederation was based on an unwritten understanding between two linguistic groups, not a pact or compact between two peoples, nations, or races. Confederation would have been a pact between provinces if the process agreed at the Quebec Conference had been followed, namely to have the agreement approved by the assemblies of the five colonies. But it was approved by the Assembly of the Province of Canada and not by Upper Canada (Ontario) or Lower Canada (Quebec), or the assemblies of Nova Scotia and New Brunswick.

An amendment process is an essential part of any constitution. The *BNA Act* was a British law, so the British Parliament could amend it simply by passing a law, and the *Act* states that the provinces can amend their own constitutions (Section 92.1). Most changes to the constitution were made by convention, however, meaning that Ottawa or one or more provinces took action that was not covered by the *Act* or that violated its provisions, but was either upheld or not challenged in the courts. Almost immediately after Confederation, Ottawa began making changes without seeking formal amendments simply by announcing a new policy or negotiating some arrangement with one or more provinces. Although the *Act* assigned trade to Ottawa, the provinces continued to promote trade abroad and no formal amendment was ever made to legitimize this very important convention. Similarly, sections of the *BNA Act* could become ineffective simply by failure to use them over a sufficiently long period. Federal powers such as disallowance and reserve fell into disuse, although they technically still exist. Most federal programs in health, welfare, education, and local economic government have represented changes to the constitution based on convention rather than amendment.

Myths about Confederation

Over the years, many myths have developed about Confederation and what it did or did not achieve. One is that "Canada" was created in 1867. In fact, Canada became a political entity with the *Constitutional* or *Canada Act* of 1791, and that name was simply passed on to the larger Dominion. It is often suggested that Confederation made Canada a country, but it remained a British colony until 1931. There are numerous references to Canadians becoming a nation on July 1, 1867. In fact, nations take centuries to evolve, and in 1867 the new Dominion was populated by First Nations, French Canadians, Acadians, English, Irish, Scots, and Americans, many of whom felt their prime "national" loyalty was to Britain, their province, or ethnic group, and certainly not to "Canada." A favourite myth is that Sir John A. Macdonald was the most important Father of Confederation, but that title must be shared with George Brown and George-Étienne Cartier, as it was their view of federalism that prevailed, not Macdonald's. Other myths are explored in detail in this book, including the idea that Ottawa was given all the "important" responsibilities, or that swings in the relative balance of power seriously affected the ability of Ottawa to handle its responsibilities. None of the myths diminish the near-incredible accomplishment of the Fathers of Confederation, but they have proven very valuable for nation-building over the past 150 years.

PART II
The First Seventy Years

CHAPTER 4
Implementing Federalism, 1867-1878

On July 1, 1867, the denizens of the new Dominion of Canada launched themselves on the uncharted waters of federalism. Implementing this new system involved numerous challenges, in addition to the old ones that had brought the union into being. It was not entirely clear that federalism was a panacea for these problems, but it did offer a new way forward. The next thirty years would see the Dominion address most of these challenges, but not without undergoing a series of crises that threatened and then defined the new super-colony.

Confederation was implemented in very different ways in central Canada and the Maritimes. All the governments of Nova Scotia and New Brunswick had to do was ignore the responsibilities that the *BNA Act* assigned to the new central government and continue exercising those left to them. Both governments reduced the number of MLAs, ministers, and civil servants. The people were now citizens of the new Dominion, but for many years their prime loyalties would remain with their own provinces and the British Empire. In central Canada, the old government was completely abolished and its responsibilities divided between a new central government in Ottawa and the two new provincial governments of Ontario and Quebec. The central government inherited the magnificent Parliament buildings that had just been built, plus the vast majority of politicians and civil servants of the old province.

New Governments for the Dominion, Ontario, and Quebec

One of the first orders of business was electing assemblies for the new provinces of Ontario and Quebec, for the new Dominion, and for the old Maritime provinces. Britain wanted to make sure that the new system would be successful so, in effect, it rigged the first elections in Ontario, Quebec, and the Dominion. Two months before Confederation, Governor General Monck dissolved the Grand Coalition and called on John A. Macdonald to form a government. Technically, that was still the government of the old Province of Canada, but the plan was to ensure its re-election so it would become the government of the new Dominion. To reinforce his prestige and indicate its blessings, Britain made Macdonald "Sir John," a reward that annoyed his colleagues. The appointment gave him and the pro-federalists control of the government, the election machinery, and patronage, the latter being the ability to offer jobs immediately and make credible promises of jobs in the future. The "new" government was the old Bleu-Conservative coalition, plus a few Reformers, now calling itself the Liberal Conservative party. Most of the Reformers returned to their role as opposition and gradually merged with the Rouges and anti-confederates in the Maritimes to form the federal Liberal party. Macdonald's party allied itself with pro-confederates in Nova Scotia and New Brunswick such as Tupper and Tilley, and the Conservatives coasted to victory largely on the strength of Cartier's Bleus in Quebec. The cabinet was expanded to include three Maritimers and got on with the task of implementing Confederation.

Confederation required the creation of an entirely new government for Ontario. John A. Macdonald, his supporters, Britain, and Governor General Monck wanted to ensure that federalists dominated this government so, in effect, they also rigged the first Ontario election. Before the province was created, Macdonald appointed its first lieutenant governor and asked him to appoint John Sandfield Macdonald as interim premier. The provincial election was held at the same time as the federal one with the two Macdonalds dispensing patronage and promises, co-operating in the selection of candidates, and campaigning together. Sandfield won fifty out of the eighty-two provincial seats, while John A. won forty-nine of the eighty-two federal ones. The two Macdonalds then set out to govern Canada and Ontario as they thought they should be governed—with a strong central government and a weaker provincial one. Sandfield Macdonald adopted a subordinate position, even sending John A. drafts of Ontario legislation for his approval, comment, or amendment.

In spite of Ottawa's involvement, Ontario's provincial status worked as George Brown and the Reformers hoped it would. French-Catholic MPs and ministers in Ottawa no longer had influence on policies in the new Ontario, and the problems of administrative paralysis and instability disappeared. Sandfield Macdonald's regime forged ahead with a series of reforms in education, put the taxation of timber-cutting rights on a sound basis, and encouraged immigration from Britain. Government spending jumped 50 per cent in four years, but could not consume the huge federal subsidies Ontario received from the Confederation agreements.

Sandfield Macdonald's alliance with Ottawa was not successful. John A. Macdonald's majority rested heavily on Quebec, and he had to make a number of decisions that seemed to favour French Catholics especially in the case of rights granted to them in the new province of Manitoba, which infuriated English-Protestant extremists in Ontario. Sandfield had to support John A. and was seen as his lackey. Sandfield almost lost his majority in the 1871 election. Old, sick, and dispirited, he met the Assembly, lost several votes, and resigned. The Liberals took power, and their relations with Ottawa would be very different.

The defeat of Sandfield Macdonald's government in 1873 terminated one of the tactics John A. had devised in his plan to dominate the provinces. Under the new arrangements, it was possible for a politician to be elected to both the House of Commons and the Ontario or Quebec assemblies and nineteen politicians were elected to two assemblies in 1867. John A. Macdonald intended to use them to help dominate the two provincial governments. The Reform/Liberal Party of Ontario believed that the provincial and federal assemblies had to be completely separate. The new premier, Edward Blake, abolished the duel mandate system, saying that the Ontario government had to "be absolutely independent of the other in the management of its own affairs" and that all "interference in Ontario's business would be protested . . ."

In July 1867, French Canadians elected their first government ever. George-Étienne Cartier's Conservatives, or Bleus, easily won fifty of the sixty-five seats in the new provincial assembly and forty-five of the sixty-five federal ones. Cartier selected the first Quebec premier, Pierre Chauveau, who deliberately included English-speaking politicians in his cabinet. Since Quebeckers were generally satisfied with the deal, the Liberal/Rouge opposition grudgingly accepted it and the constitution ceased to be an important political issue. The new government began creating departments, a bureaucracy, and offices in Quebec City. A new assembly building emerged just west of the crumbling walls of the old city. The government had the support of most Catholic clergy, the Protestant minority, businessmen, and its powerful political partner, the federal government. The new provincial government's responsibilities were limited, and of those, the churches would continue to administer some of the most important. Relations with Ottawa were relatively smooth for the next half-century.

One of this government's first priorities was implementing the clauses in the *BNA Act* that gave Quebec responsibility for education while protecting the rights of Protestants. The government replaced the Council of Public Instruction with two separate organizations, one run by the Catholic Church, the other by representatives of the Anglican, Presbyterian, and Methodist Churches. The Protestant minority had full control of its education, which was confirmed in 1875 when Quebec abolished the Department of Education so that schools would be free from political interference. Health and welfare also continued to be administered by churches, so Protestants were in control of almost everything that touched their personal lives. *Canadiens* were now *maîtres chez nous* in Canada, and the English-speaking Quebeckers were essentially *maîtres chez nous* in Quebec, the best of both worlds for both groups.

Nova Scotia, the Reluctant Province

The first post-Confederation election in Nova Scotia was very different from those in central Canada. Confederation was generally met with anger or indifference. Charles Tupper and other pro-Confederation politicians were burnt in effigy, editorials bemoaned the death of their separate colony, and gloomy predictions were made for the future. For decades, Nova Scotia refused to make July 1 a holiday. Tupper's government implemented the administrative changes required by the *BNA Act* and reduced the size of the Assembly from fifty-five to thirty-eight members, and the size of the cabinet from five to four. On July 4, Tupper was replaced by a new premier, Hiram Blanchard, but Tupper ensured that the federal and provincial elections in Nova Scotia were postponed until the federal election had been held in Ontario, Quebec, and New Brunswick. The pro-confederates won in those three provinces so when Nova Scotians went to the polls on September 18, Confederation was a *fait accompli* constitutionally, legally, and politically.

The Antis who opposed Confederation contested all thirty-eight provincial and nineteen federal seats. Their leaders were Joseph Howe at the federal level and William Annand in the provincial wing. Their main goal was to convince Britain to allow the province to withdraw from the arrangement. The pro-Confederation side—Conservatives or Unionists—entered the 1867 election saddled with the blame for the terms of the agreement and for the way they had been forced on the province. They were accused of bribing their opponents, lying to London, abusing the lieutenant governor's powers, and mismanaging finances. The results took even the Antis by surprise. Tupper was the only pro-confederate to win a federal seat, and the Antis won thirty-six of the thirty-eight provincial seats. It was stunning proof that Nova Scotians were overwhelmingly opposed to Confederation and that Tupper had been wise not to seek any form of approval for the plan.

The new anti-Confederation MPs decided to take their seats in Parliament so they could argue the province's case, a move that implied recognizing the Confederation deal, and in Halifax the anti-Confederation MLAs formed a government with William Annand as premier. The Antis sent a delegation to London under Howe and Annand to convince the British government that Nova Scotia had been forced into Confederation against its will. In London, the colonial secretary refused to meet them: he was, after all, the one who had forced the colony into Confederation. Howe and Annand discovered that the British politicians and elites had no intention of seeing Confederation unravel.

It was soon evident that the criticisms of the Confederation scheme were correct. Nova Scotia's most serious grievance concerned the financial situation. After cutting the roads budget from $240,000 to $100,000, the province still had a deficit of $100,000. Its tariffs had been 10 per cent, compared to the former Canadian one of 15 per cent. Ottawa applied the old Canadian rate, imposed it on more items, and added taxes that were new to Nova Scotia, effectively raising the tax rate by over 50 per cent, with all the money flowing to Ottawa. Ottawa took over the branch rail lines that would be amalgamated into the Intercolonial Railway and then raised the fares. The harsher criminal code of the old Province of Canada was implemented. The few civil servants who retired from the old Canadian bureaucracy received pensions; those who retired from the Nova Scotian administration did not. Despite being home to one-tenth of the Dominion's population, Nova Scotians obtained only two of the five hundred jobs in the new federal administration.

Tupper was rewarded with a cabinet position in Ottawa, plus the job of convincing Howe that the most he could hope for were some improvements, changes which came to be known as "better terms." Ottawa offered to provide an additional $83,000 per year for ten years, the same amount New Brunswick had obtained in 1866. Macdonald negotiated the deal with Howe and refused to deal with any provincial minister to make the point that MPs, rather than provincial governments, represented the provinces in Ottawa. In December 1868, Howe accepted the offer. He does not seem to have pursued the other grievances, and the financial offer did not eliminate the deficit and would only last a decade. Since it was clear that Howe would enter the federal cabinet, "better terms" were in effect agreed between the prime minister and his new minister-in-waiting. Annand's government had no choice but to swallow its pride and accept the deal. One by one, the anti-Confederation MPs abandoned the cause or were bought off with positions or influence.

Macdonald's deal with Nova Scotia raised a serious issue regarding federalism. The BNA Act had been negotiated by delegates from the five colonies. In giving better terms to Nova Scotia, Ottawa was unilaterally changing Section 118, which identified the subsidies for all the provinces. Edward Blake, Leader of the Opposition in the House of Commons, argued that the terms of the BNA Act could not be changed without the approval of the provinces. That challenge was ignored, but it was the opening shot in the battle over how to amend the constitution, a battle that lasted for more than a century. It also demonstrated how easy it was for the federal government to change the terms of the constitution without formally amending the wording. Significantly, the British government said nothing about this change to its own legislation, and an important precedent was set by Ottawa and London. Most changes to the *BNA Act* from then on were made by unilateral action or bilateral agreements, not by formal amendments to the wording of the *Act*.

The "better terms" of $83,000 annually came to an end on July 1, 1877. When Premier Phillip Hill asked for an extension, Ottawa refused. In 1876, Ottawa finally had completed the Intercolonial Railway, fulfilling the promise that had been written into the *BNA Act*. It then refused to provide any more support for railways, its efforts now being concentrated on a railway to the Pacific, which would be paid for in part by Nova Scotians. Hill's successors carried on the battle with Ottawa throughout the rest of the century. They even threatened to separate, but their pleas went unheard. It was clear that the province's delegates to the various Confederation conferences should never have accepted the eighty-cent per-capita subsidy because it was, indeed, seriously inadequate for the responsibilities left to the provinces. The result was that demands for federal funds have been a staple of Nova Scotian politics throughout the 150 years of Confederation.

New Brunswick: Resigned to Confederation

In New Brunswick, people greeted Canada's first Dominion Day with resignation. Tilley and most of the politicians who had supported Confederation went off to their rewards in the new federal government. A number of minor politicians replaced them, A.R. Wetmore becoming the first premier of the Canadian province of New Brunswick. The Confederation debate had grouped most politicians into two loose coalitions, the Antis and the pro-confederates. The latter won the 1866 election, and remnants of that group remained in power after Confederation, tending to support the federal Conservatives. The losers from the Confederation debates were mostly Reformers or Liberals, and tended to support the federal Liberal party. Many of the MLAs had switched sides during the debates, and three of the first four premiers had in fact opposed Confederation. One of them, Premier Wetmore, commented that at least he had been right half the time.

As Wetmore and his new cabinet got on with the job of administering the diminished role left to the province, they discovered that the critics had been right about the inadequacy of the federal subsidy. A delegation sent to Ottawa to request a recalculation ran into the stark realities of Confederation about which the Antis had warned. Central Canadians had effective control of the levers of power, New Brunswick had few MPs and only one cabinet minister, and those politicians seemed to have more loyalty to the new federation than to their home province. The delegation returned to Fredericton empty handed. Five years later, Premier George King negotiated an increase in New Brunswick's subsidies plus a grant in lieu of the loss of export tariffs on American timber shipped down the St. John River. These arrangements temporarily eased the financial problem, but in 1877, the increase in subsidies came to an end and the province continued to suffer from serious financial constraints. Overall, New Brunswick went into relative decline after 1867 and Confederation was blamed for it, an accusation that had some merit.

Manitoba, an Unlikely Province

While the federal system was taking hold in the original four provinces, other colonies were edging closer to joining. Indeed, rounding out the Dominion would be one of Macdonald's greatest achievements. BC and PEI should have been next, since the blueprint definitely called for their inclusion. Instead, a number of developments and miscalculations propelled a tiny piece of the prairies to provincial status, and Manitoba became Canada's fifth province. Its conception was an accident, its birth premature by at least a decade, and the strange circumstances of its arrival on the scene created federal-provincial problems that endured for over half a century.

The Confederation scheme called for the purchase of Rupert's Land from the Hudson's Bay Company. Ottawa planned to administer it, develop it, and exploit it into the indefinite future or until its population was so large that parts of it could become provinces. This plan might have succeeded had it been properly implemented. Instead, numerous mistakes by the federal government led to a rebellion, which in turn led to the grant of provincial status. The first mistake was the failure to inform the roughly ten thousand inhabitants of the Red River Valley of Ottawa's plans. It was clear at Red River that the status of the prairies was about to change dramatically; it was not clear at all what those changes would be and how they would affect the local inhabitants.

A majority of the population was Catholic, mainly Métis, the offspring of French fur traders and First Nations women. But settlers were arriving from Ontario, British Protestants who acted as though they were going to dominate the new federal territory. Given the history of religious and racial animosity in Ontario, the Métis saw this as a clear threat, and events soon proved them correct. Unease was magnified when Canada sent expeditions to evaluate resources and conditions on the prairies. The new settlers questioned the validity of the land titles that had been issued by Lord Selkirk and by the Hudson's Bay Company, HBC, and the Métis had no legal titles to the homes and farms they had occupied for years. Ottawa then sent a survey team to mark out the land and to do so in square miles. That violated the existing pattern of land occupation with lots running back from rivers so that every farmer had access to water transportation. A young Métis by the name of Louis Riel stopped the survey team. That was not an act of rebellion against Ottawa since the HBC still owned the territory, but it was an unmistakable challenge.

The challenge should not have come as a surprise. In the summer of 1869, William McTavish, the HBC governor at Red River, visited Ottawa to warn the government of the growing tension. So did the main religious leader, Bishop Taché of St. Boniface, who wanted to obtain guarantees of rights for the French language and Catholic religion. Anglican Bishop Robert Machray sent warnings, and Joseph Howe, now a federal minister, visited Red River that October. The head of the survey party also conveyed his concerns to Ottawa. The federal government ignored all these warnings.

Instead, Ottawa exacerbated the situation by sending a lieutenant governor-elect to take control of the region. The appointment was not auspicious, as William McDougall was impulsive and inflexible, and, as Minister of Public Works, was the one who had sent the survey team and ignored warnings about the effects that would have. The timing was not auspicious either, as Canada had not yet assumed title to the territory. The authority of the HBC had virtually ceased to exist, and the inhabitants had created a provisional government to fill the vacuum. One of its first acts was to stop McDougall at the American border on November 2. He issued proclamations declaring, incorrectly, that title had been transferred and calling for the raising of troops. The latter was repudiated by Ottawa, and

McDougall was ordered to say no more. The threat of troops and the confusion over the title only served to increase anxiety in the colony.

In the absence of governance by the HBC, London, or Ottawa, with no experience in governing, and in very confused and tense circumstances, the provisional government carried on quite well. An assembly of French- and English-speaking members was elected and draft terms were prepared for negotiations with Ottawa. The inhabitants wanted title to lands already occupied, provincial status, control of public lands, better communications with central Canada, and money for public works. Riel was elected president, the HBC governor recognized the new government, and three delegates were nominated to negotiate with Ottawa. The fact that Ottawa agreed to negotiate with them implied that it too recognized the provisional government.

Before the delegates arrived in Ottawa, the situation in Red River changed dramatically. A group of Canadians who had never accepted rule by the Métis majority launched a revolt against the provisional government. It failed and sixty-five men were imprisoned. In February 1870, another attempt to overthrow the provisional government failed. One of the more extreme leaders, Thomas Scott, continued to promote jail breaks, to urge rebellion, and to insult the guards. He was tried and executed in March. That ended the turmoil in Red River, but it inflamed Orange Protestant opinion in Ontario where people demanded revenge and the suppression of Red River by force. French Catholics in Quebec had never paid much attention to the West, but now they became sympathetic to the plight of the Métis. This was the beginning of a very important trend. Prior to Confederation, French Canadians in Lower Canada had not regarded French Catholics in other colonies as being part of their nation; by 1900, they viewed French Canadians everywhere in Canada as part of the same nation. With the Dominion becoming seriously divided on religious and racial lines, the federal government's weak ability to deal with the situation grew weaker.

On arrival in Ottawa, two of the delegates were arrested for the murder of Scott. They were soon released, and agreement was quickly reached on the terms by which Manitoba would become a province. It was granted provincial status, with a government and dualistic educational system like Quebec's, and recognition of existing claims to land. It was allotted two senators and four MPs, which was vastly more than its population warranted. George Brown's great achievement of a central government based on the democratic principle of rep by pop had survived a brief three years, and Manitoba's overrepresentation was an important example of Ottawa making federalism asymmetrical for political reasons. While Ottawa conceded the necessity of provincial status, it had no intention of creating a province like the original four. Manitoba's area was limited to a small square around Winnipeg, about 150 kilometres on each side, roughly 4 per cent of the present province, a fraction of 1 per cent of the North-West Territories. These restricted boundaries were soon to become a major problem in federal-provincial relations, an irritant not solved until 1912.

More seriously, Ottawa retained control of natural resources in contrast to the situation of the original four provinces and that of BC and PEI, both of which joined Confederation after Manitoba. This made Manitoba a second-class province and the Dominion more asymmetrically federal. It meant that, when BC and PEI joined, the resources of six provinces could be exploited primarily for the benefit of their citizens, but the resources of Manitoba belonged to all Canadians. That was an act of discrimination that was not resolved until 1930, and it created an attitude of distrust towards Ottawa that has never died.

The federal government argued that it had to control natural resources in Manitoba in order to populate the prairies and to build a transcontinental railway. Neither argument was credible. The "postage-stamp" province was rapidly being occupied by settlers from Ontario, people with capital, experience in farming and government, and no need of government assistance. No province needed railways more than land-locked Manitoba, and Ottawa had built the CPR and the Intercolonial through provinces that controlled their own land. Besides, Ottawa had the rest of the prairies with which to subsidize the railway. In short, Ottawa bought Rupert's Land in order to have a colony, and while forced to cede provincial status, it had no intention of giving up ownership and control of land and resources. The *Manitoba Act* was approved on May 12, 1870, and Manitoba became Canada's fifth province on July 15.

Passing legislation was one thing, creating a viable province quite another. For years, the lieutenant governor wielded considerable power while political parties and leaders were gaining experience. The province immediately faced the question of an amnesty for the Métis leaders, an amnesty Bishop Taché of St. Boniface believed he had been promised. Instead, several leaders were arrested and found guilty of murder. Fortunately, a wise governor general commuted their sentences, and Riel fled to the United States. Though peace reigned at Red River, Ottawa did not recall the military force that had been raised in Ontario to deal with the insurrection. This expedition, numbering a tenth the size of the entire population at Red River, was bent on revenge for the execution of Scott. It did more damage in nine days than had occurred in nine months of Riel's provisional government. Thus did Manitoba become a province.

BC and Dominion from Sea to Sea

On the west coast, the British colony of Vancouver Island had existed since 1849, a lonely outpost of empire with a few hundred colonists engaged in agriculture and supplying the British navy. The gold rush of 1858 produced a flood of immigration to the mainland so on August 2, 1858, Britain created the separate colony of British Columbia, a name designed to make clear that the northern half of the Columbia River basin was British and not American. Worried that the gold seekers might venture into the Peace River country, Britain included that region in BC. The eastern border of the colony was fixed along the Rockies from the US border to the 120th meridian and then north to the 60th degree of latitude. Thus the colony of BC obtained a corner of both the prairies and of the Arctic tundra to add to its geographic variety, and it was larger than either Quebec or Ontario.

Britain could not afford two administrations on the west coast, and on November 19, 1866, it united the two under the name British Columbia. A number of immigrants from Canada and the Maritimes began to suggest that BC should join the super-colony that was being created on the east coast. Their motives were personal, financial, and even social. They had been shut out of government jobs and high society by the dominant English and HBC elite. They assumed they would replace that elite if BC became a Canadian province. They were also businessmen who hoped that Confederation would bring access to markets and an end to economic stagnation. Leaders soon emerged, such as Bill Smith, who had changed his name to Amor de Cosmos, "Lover of the Universe." The majority of white British Columbians were opposed to Confederation, and the vast majority of inhabitants, the First Nations, had no voice at all. Canada was many thousands of kilometres away, and it was extremely difficult to travel over land to Ontario. The English and HBC elites were fearful that Confederation would do what the Canadian faction wanted, namely, transfer power to them.

Prime Minister Macdonald arranged for Britain to appoint a pro-Confederation governor, Anthony Musgrave. He was thoroughly familiar with Confederation and his mandate was to bring about BC's entry into the union. Musgrave advanced the cause by helping to draft a very favourable set of conditions that Ottawa might accept in order to entice the reluctant colony to join. It was a negotiating position, so it asked as much as the politicians dared, much more than they expected. Accordingly, the federal government was to assume the colony's huge debt, give it an annual per-capita subsidy based on a population estimate larger than its ten thousand inhabitants, build public works including a wagon trail and telegraph connecting the colony to Lake Superior, and start building a railway within three years. Musgrave selected the delegates who met in Ottawa with George-Étienne Cartier, Macdonald being incapacitated, probably due to excessive drinking.

To the amazement of the delegates, Cartier accepted almost all of BC's demands and offered even more. Ottawa promised a huge annual subsidy and agreed to pay the annual interest on the cost of building a dry dock at Esquimalt. The population was said to be 120,000, more than ten times the actual figure, which would yield far greater per-capita grants than other provinces received, plus six MPs and three senators. Once more, rep by pop, the great achievement of George Brown, was being compromised. To their further amazement, Cartier promised a railway that was to be started in two years and completed in ten. To facilitate the building of the railway, BC was to give the federal government a strip of land twenty miles wide on both sides of the proposed railway in return for an annual grant of $100,000 in perpetuity.

The delegates returned to Victoria with terms that far exceeded their wildest dreams. Musgrave took advantage of the euphoria to call an election for the nine elected members of the Council. Not surprisingly, pro-Confederation candidates easily won every seat and, also not surprisingly, the Council unanimously agreed to the terms. But while BC celebrated, cooler heads in Ottawa wondered why Cartier had promised to build a railway that Canada could not afford. Conservative MPs sensed that the offer was financially impossible and perhaps political suicide. Fortunately, one of the BC delegates, Joseph Trutch, happened to be back in Ottawa. Without any authority from the BC government or Council, he assured the Conservative MPs that BC did not expect Canada to bankrupt itself honouring the terms it had just offered. Cartier promised the House of Commons that taxes would not be raised to pay for the railway, a promise that could not likely be honoured. Parliament approved BC's admission, and it became Canada's sixth province on July 20, 1871.

Macdonald found a good candidate for the province's first lieutenant governor, namely Joseph Trutch, the delegate who had said that Ottawa could violate its promises. He called elections for twenty-five MLAs and selected one of them, John Foster McCreight, to be the province's first premier. His government immediately went to work setting up Canada's newest province. Its tariffs and excise taxes were adjusted to the Canadian rates; the British civil service was replaced by British Columbians; a regular judiciary was established; municipalities were mapped out; and a free, universal, non-sectarian education system was created. In many ways, BC borrowed the best of the political and administrative systems from eastern Canada, a tradition that has been followed ever since.

Ottawa had bought BC, but it had not yet paid for it. The main form of payment was a transcontinental railway, to be started in 1873 and completed by 1881. When no surveyors appeared, those who were skeptical about Ottawa's overly generous terms began to think that the new province had been duped. Newspapers argued that if Ottawa did not honour its terms, then the province did not have to honour its part of the agreement, and it could and should secede. The demand that Ottawa honour its promises dominated provincial politics for a decade and became enmeshed in a series of related issues connecting federal and provincial politics, economics, finances, business, geography, and even surveying.

Before surveying could begin for the railway, a decision had to be made on what route to follow. People on Vancouver Island demanded that the railway start in Victoria, cross Georgia Strait on a series of bridges, traverse the Chilcotin Plateau, and continue on to the Rockies. People on the main-land demanded that it start at Burrard Inlet and follow the Fraser River to the Rockies. Macdonald's government made little effort to begin the survey and, in 1873, the Liberals, who had strongly opposed the railway, came to power in Ottawa. The main issue in the election was a financial scandal resulting from gifts to the Conservative Party from the consortium that was planning to build the Canadian Pacific Railway. Macdonald was thus the first prime minister to be defeated over the mishandling of matters relating to relations with the provinces.

The arrival of the Liberals coincided with the beginning of an economic depression, which doubly reinforced their intention to delay the railway. The new prime minister, Alexander Mackenzie, asked BC to renegotiate the contract and accept a carriageway and a telegraph line in the immediate future, plus a railway sometime later. This time it was Ottawa that was ask-ing a province for "better terms" and doing so just months after giving PEI "still better terms" than ones previously offered. Federalism was becoming quite confused, with every province obtaining different financial and other terms and different per capita representation in the Senate and Commons.

An infuriated Premier George Walkem took BC's grievances to London, because the new offer clearly violated the terms of union that Britain had helped negotiate. In January 1874, the Assembly unanimously passed a motion threatening to secede. The worried British colonial secretary, Lord Carnarvon, offered to mediate, which angered Ottawa as it believed that relations between the federal and provincial governments were now an internal Canadian matter. Ignoring Ottawa's view, Carnarvon proposed a new set of terms, and Ottawa made a counter-proposal. BC rejected these terms and threatened again to secede. In Ottawa, Governor General Lord Dufferin attempted to intervene, but Mackenzie rejected his advice.

Ottawa then offered $750,000 dollars annually in lieu of the broken promise. It was a disingenuous offer as it was not clear if it was compen-sation for past, present, or future delays or for all three. Lord Dufferin disagreed sharply with Mackenzie over it. Mackenzie also made promises that were contradictory, saying that he would build the railway, but not if it meant going into debt. Since building it would definitely mean going into debt, he was both promising to build it and saying he would not. Dufferin felt that the federal government had lost its credibility on the issue and asked London to mediate.

In the meantime, progress was made on selecting a route. It was decided that the terminus would be on Burrard Inlet, which meant that Victoria was doomed to become BC's second city. The next question was where it would go over the Rockies. The Crowsnest route east of Trail was unacceptable because the grades were too steep. The best route was the Yellowhead, going up the Thompson River from Kamloops, over the Rockies to Jasper, and on to Edmonton. It was surveyed and proven, and the section from Edmonton to Winnipeg would run through the best agricultural land on the prairies. That route was approved by the Mackenzie government shortly before its term expired. Then, the 1878 federal election returned Sir John A. Macdonald's Conservatives to power with building the transcontinental railway as their top priority. For reasons that are not clear, the route was changed to the Kicking Horse Pass west of Calgary, a mistake that retarded the economic development of the West and added greatly to the cost of the railway.

Ottawa then built the railway as quickly as possible, completing it in 1885. With the railway problem resolved, the federal and provincial governments quickly settled most other outstanding issues. BC gave the federal government 3,500,000 acres in the Peace River country in compensation for land along the CPR mainline that was not suitable for settlement. Ottawa promised again to begin constructing the Esquimalt dry dock. With the province's capital now definitely sited in Victoria, the main grievances of Vancouver Island had been addressed as much as they could be. For a few years, the relationship with Ottawa would be relatively tranquil.

PEI Spends Itself into Confederation

On the other coast, Prince Edward Island's absence from Confederation was unacceptable to both Ottawa and London. However, many Islanders saw a trade arrangement with the United States as a better option than Confederation, and talks were held on the possibility of exchanging access to the local fishery for access to the American market. This alarmed Ottawa, and in August 1869 it sent a delegation to Charlottetown to begin discussions for "better terms." The new premier, Robert Haythorne, informed

Ottawa that no proposal would be acceptable without a complete settlement of the problem of absentee ownership of land. Decades earlier, Britain had given most of the province's Crown lands to speculators, who left their lots undeveloped in hopes of selling them later for large profits. Leaving the land as wilderness seriously retarded PEI's development, and land was the most important issue the Island wanted dealt with if it joined Confederation. In January 1870, the Canadian government offered "better terms," including some small improvements over those covered in the *Quebec Resolutions* of 1866, plus an offer to help obtain a solution to the land question.

To Ottawa's surprise, "better terms" were rejected and indeed ridiculed by both pro- and anti-Confederation factions in the Assembly. Emotions ran high after decades of frustration with London over the absentee land ownership problem and five years of fruitless negotiations over Confederation. Arguing that under the proposed terms the province would be giving up £200,000 in customs revenue for £25,000 in subsidies, Edward Palmer asked "if there were three people in the Island who can read and write who are such absolute asses as to make such a sacrifice." There probably were more than three, but an overwhelming proportion of the population was clearly unimpressed with "better terms."

With Confederation shelved, the Island's attention turned to other issues, including building a railway. That was one of the worst decisions ever made by an Island government. No farm was far from a sea port and the volume of traffic would be insufficient to cover costs. These facts were clearly outlined in the Assembly, where the opposition argued that the railway would bankrupt the province and force it to join Confederation. Indeed, some saw it as a conspiracy to achieve just that. The government ignored the criticisms, and the railway bill was approved. Construction proceeded, costs ran over estimates, new branch lines were approved, and new governments added to the problems rather than addressing them. Soon the government had no choice but to ask Canada for financial support. Everyone knew what the price would be.

In December 1872, Haythorne's anti-Confederation Liberal government asked Ottawa for the "better terms" that the Island had rejected in 1870, plus much more, or "still better terms." In late February 1873, his delegation arrived in Ottawa, where it found the federal government in a generous mood. Ottawa offered to take possession of the railway, and PEI received an annual per-capita allowance of $45,000, plus another $45,000 annually in light of the fact that London had given away all the Crown lands. Canada would provide a loan of $800,000 to buy out the absentee land owners. Representation in the House of Commons was increased to six MPs, the third violation of rep by pop since it was adopted in 1867. As with BC, Ottawa promised something it could not deliver, namely "continuous communications" with the mainland, which were impossible in the winter. The promise was not even necessary, and failure to deliver on it poisoned relations with Ottawa. It is arguable that the promise was not fulfilled until the Confederation Bridge opened in 1997. Nonetheless, the terms were far better than what Nova Scotia and New Brunswick had received, more examples of asymmetrical federalism.

Haythorne returned to Charlottetown with "still better terms" and called an election to seek approval. The pro-Confederation Conservatives of ex-premier James Pope were miffed that the Liberals had negotiated a very favourable deal, so they campaigned on the promise that they could re-open the talks and get even more. Pope won eighteen of thirty seats, and in Ottawa his fellow Conservatives made some insignificant concessions so he could claim that he had won even more than "still better terms." Confederation was approved in May 1873, by an Assembly vote of 27–2 and the unanimous vote of the Legislative Council. There were no big cele-brations when PEI became Canada's seventh province on July 1, 1873—Dominion Day—nine years after the Charlottetown Conference.

Though PEI had now obtained far better terms than those of the *Quebec Resolutions*, the critics of those proposals, especially of the federal subsidy, were proven right. As it carried on with the tasks left to provinces, PEI soon found that the subsidy was quite insufficient for its responsibilities. In 1877, the L.H. Davis government introduced poll and property taxes to reduce the deficit and was defeated as a result. The incoming Conservative adminis-tration of W.W. Sullivan introduced new taxes, re-imposed four days of compulsory work on the roads for able-bodied men, and looked for ways to cut costs, including abolishing the secret ballot because it cost too much to administer. It used money from the land sales for general expenses instead of paying back the federal loan and tried to reduce the size of government and abolish the Legislative Council. Like the other Maritime provinces, the government of PEI began a long campaign to correct the errors made in the initial calculations of subsidies from Ottawa. While it has won significant financial concessions, the fundamental problem of the imbalance between its responsibilities and its revenue base has never been solved.

Another piece of the federal puzzle was fitted in when the Canadian Supreme Court was established in 1875. It was not in fact "supreme," because court decisions could be appealed to the Judicial Committee of the Privy Council, the JCPC, in London. The Supreme Court could in theory settle disputes between the two orders of government on matters of jurisdiction, but justices were selected by the federal government, that is, by one of the parties to such disputes. That was seen by the provinces as a conflict of interest, and the Court's early decisions reinforced that view as most of them favoured Ottawa. In the first three decades of Confederation, the JCPC often overturned decisions of the Supreme Court, which remained a weak institution until appeals to the JCPC ended in 1949.

Thus, within ten short years many of the goals of Confederation had been achieved or were well on their way to completion. The list is extremely impressive, and Canadians ever since have owed a massive debt of thanks to the Fathers of Confederation and the other politicians who put Confederation into practice. The main problem that led to Confederation, political instability in central Canada, was solved. The creation of Quebec and Ontario, with provincial control of education, health, welfare, civil law, and property, ended the problem of English-speaking Protestants dominating French Catholics and vice versa for at least sixty years. The new federation bought a quarter of a continent from the HBC, accepted provincial status for Manitoba, and enticed BC and PEI into joining.

Within a decade, Canadians had established the basis for a transcontinental economy and a genuine Canadian identity. The danger of absorption by the United States disappeared, and Britain withdrew its troops. By 1877, the new federal government and the new provinces of Ontario and Quebec were well established, the Maritime provinces were adjusting to their lesser roles, BC had democratic government, and Manitoba was developing into a properly functioning province. Of enormous significance is the fact that all this was accomplished without wars of conquest, wars against the First Nations, wars against foreign powers, civil war, or even the use of force within the colonies, the small exception being a few deaths and some property damage during the Red River Rebellion. The exact nature of federalism had not been worked out, though, and the next twenty years would witness many struggles to determine whether the new, huge, united colony would be a quasi-federal regime, in which Ottawa dominated the provinces, or a genuine federation, in which both orders of government would be autonomous in their areas of responsibility.

CHAPTER 5
Macdonald's Centralism, 1878-1896

In the first decade of Confederation, Canada's political leaders made enormous progress on implementing the new system of government and tackling the problems it was designed to solve. They had not, however, resolved the question of what kind of federalism was being created. The marriage of British constitutional practice with American-style federalism had produced a hybrid, and it was not yet clear exactly how the parts would work together. Some still argued that the central government alone was autonomous; others contended that both orders of government were autonomous in their areas of responsibility. Some argued that the central government was stronger and superior or should be; others believed that the two orders of government were equal.

Oddly enough, the answers emerged from a number of political battles and court cases that seemed relatively trivial on their own merits. They included issues surrounding appointing Queen's Counsels, inheriting property, fire insurance, granting liquor licences, playing billiards after a pub's closing time, settling the debts of a bankrupt bank, using a timber slide on a little river, dismissing a provincial government, financing Catholic schools, distributing the estates of the Jesuit Order, building railways in Manitoba, employing Chinese labour in BC, and determining Ontario's western border. Many of these issues dragged on for years, often overlapping with each other.

Defining the Powers of Ottawa and the Provinces

One issue that touched on many others was the position, power, and prerogatives of the lieutenant governors in the provincial capitals. In Macdonald's view, they were officers of the federal government, instruments of federal supervision, and had no direct link to the Crown in Britain. In the view of the provinces, they were part of their governments, occupied an equivalent position and exercised the same powers as governors general did in Ottawa, and represented the Crown in the provinces. The issue was crucial to the definition of Canadian federalism, because under Macdonald's interpretation the provinces would be subordinate to Ottawa and Canada would have a quasi-federal system. As time passed, it became clear that Macdonald wanted to use lieutenant governors the way Britain had used governors before initiating democratic government in 1848, that is, for the lieutenant governors to be in charge rather than the provincial cabinets.

One of the issues that helped answer the question was the appointment of lawyers as Queen's Counsels. These appointments were the prerogative of the Crown, and the question was whether that meant the lieutenant governors, the governors general, or both. The issue first arose in Nova Scotia in 1879, and the Canadian Supreme Court sided with Ottawa. It arose again in Ontario in 1885, when Premier Oliver Mowat argued that the prerogatives of governors general and lieutenants general had been divided between the two orders of government and were therefore equal. The JCPC in London supported him. The wording of the decision was unambiguous: ". . . the Lieutenant Governor of a province is as much a representative of [the Crown] for all purposes of provincial government as the Governor General is . . . for all purposes of the Dominion Government."

A complex dispute in Quebec helped clarify the roles of governors general and lieutenant governors. In 1876, the federal Liberals appointed a new lieutenant governor, the highly partisan Liberal Luc Letellier de St. Just. Ignoring three decades of democratic government, Letellier acted as though the cabinet reported to him. In March 1878, he dismissed the Conservative government of Bouchard de Boucherville, appointed as premier the Liberal leader, and the new government narrowly won the following election. All Letellier's actions arguably exceeded the powers of a lieutenant governor.

Then a federal election put Sir John A. Macdonald back in power and his Quebec MPs demanded that he dismiss Letellier. Letellier, Governor General the Marquess of Lorne, and Premier Joly all said that doing so would constitute interference in Quebec's affairs. Macdonald asked Britain for advice, and it replied that Macdonald had the authority to dismiss the lieutenant governor and that Governor General Lorne had to accept Macdonald's decisions. Macdonald then dismissed Letellier and replaced him with a Conservative. The issue taught both governors general and lieutenant governors that their powers were much more restricted than they had supposed and that they had to accept that it was the elected politicians who made the decisions.

Another seemingly trivial matter raised again the question of whether lieutenant governors were equal to governors general. Before Confederation, the estate of a citizen of Upper Canada (escheats) who died without heirs passed to the government, that is, the Crown as represented by the governor general. The death of an Ontarian raised the question of whether the Crown was now represented by the governor general in Ottawa or the lieutenant governor in Toronto. While the actual amount involved was small, the implications were enormous. According to Macdonald, only the governor general represented the Crown so the federal government should receive the inheritance. Premier Mowat argued that before Confederation, the government of the Province of Canada represented the Crown, and it had not surrendered that power in 1867, so its lieutenant governor still represented the Crown and Ontario should receive the inheritance. He also argued that both federal and provincial governments were fully autonomous so they both represented the Crown. Ottawa disallowed the Ontario legislation in April 1875. An Ontario court upheld Mowat's law, but the Supreme Court reversed that decision. Quebec supported Ontario by passing a law similar to Ontario's, and the Quebec courts upheld it. The matter was appealed to the JCPC in London, which supported Mowat's position, confirming that the provinces had legal equality with the central government, and lieutenants general and governors general were equal in status.

Another important legal case concerned a fire insurance claim in the small Ontario town of Orangeville (*Citizen's Insurance v. Parsons, 1881*). Mr. Parsons owned a hardware store, on which he had insurance policies with companies chartered by both Ottawa and Ontario. After his store burned, two of the companies refused to pay. When ordered to do so by the courts on the basis of a provincial law, they argued that insurance was a trade, that trade was a federal responsibility, and that the provincial law was therefore beyond the powers of the Ontario government. The Ontario court, the Supreme Court, and the JCPC all upheld the Ontario law. The JCPC ruled that the federal power over trade and commerce applied to the economy as a whole or to interprovincial or international trade, not to the regulation of a specific "trade" such as insurance within a province. Fire insurance policies were private contracts that were a matter of property and civil rights, which made them provincial. The decision was of considerable importance, because if the JCPC had ruled that regulating a business within a province was a matter of federal power over trade and commerce, then the province's control of property and civil rights could have been severely restricted.

Mowat had allies in the other provinces, including Premier A.G. Blair of New Brunswick. In 1887, the Maritime Bank there went bankrupt while holding deposits from the provincial government. The latter claimed that, as representative of the Crown, it had royal prerogative that gave it priority over other claimants for the bank's assets. The *Maritime Bank* case went to the courts, with Ottawa arguing that only the federal government represented the Crown because Confederation had cut the provinces' ties with the British Crown. Premier Blair argued that the New Brunswick lieutenant governor also represented the Crown. The provincial court agreed, the Supreme Court upheld that decision, and so did the JCPC.

This issue had now come before the JCPC so many times that Lord Watson, who penned the decision, decided to add the Council's specific view of Confederation. "The *BNA Act* . . . has not severed the connection between the Crown and the provinces; the relation between them is the same as that which subsists between the Crown and the Dominion . . . The object of the *Act* was neither to weld the provinces into one, nor to subordinate provincial governments to a central authority, but to create a federal government in which they should all be represented, entrusted with the exclusive administration of affairs in which they had a common interest, each province retaining its independence and autonomy . . . [and] the legislatures of each province continued to be free from the control of the Dominion and as supreme as it was before [1867]." By the time of Macdonald's death in 1892, his attempt to use lieutenant governors the way Britain had used governors prior to the 1848 grant of democratic government had failed. Lieutenant governors in the provinces had the same power as the governor general in Ottawa, and both positions were in fact largely ceremonial.

The Liquor Trade: Federal or Provincial?

Another area of conflict that helped define federalism involved a series of court cases over the control of the liquor trade. Nineteenth-century Canada was a male-dominated, hard-working, hard-drinking society with over four thousand pubs in Ontario alone. Liquor sales provided an important source of government revenue, and appointing inspectors and granting licences were important elements in the patronage system that greased the political parties. The question was whether the federal Conservatives in Ottawa or the provincial Liberals in Toronto could regulate the business, and since the *BNA Act* was silent on the matter, it soon wound up in the courts. In 1872, Ontario passed a law regulating the trade and Ottawa challenged it. The following year, Ontario passed another law transferring the power to issue licences from the municipalities to Queen's Park. That law came before the courts in the case of *Severn v. the Queen* and was found to be beyond provincial power. Ottawa then passed the *Scott Act* to regulate the trade across Canada. It was based on federal responsibility for trade and commerce and the belief that Canada should have a uniform law governing Prohibition. Oddly, that principle was contradicted by the fact that, under the *Scott Act*, each municipality could decide whether or not to impose Prohibition.

When the city of Fredericton introduced Prohibition under the federal law, a tavern owner, Charles Russell, argued that the law was beyond the power of the federal government (*Russell v. the Queen*, 1882). A New Brunswick court and the JCPC both upheld the federal legislation on the grounds that Prohibition fell under federal power over peace, order, and good government because alcohol consumption was a matter of public safety, like poisonous drugs or explosives, and an evil assumed to exist throughout the Dominion.

That was a major victory for Macdonald's belief in the superiority of the federal government, but it was his last. He was back in power following the 1878 election, fully aware of the political advantages of controlling liquor licensing. He passed the *McCarthy Act* in 1883, requiring taverns to have federal licences and establishing a network of federal inspectors who would, of course, be Conservatives. Macdonald hoped that would end the capacity of the provinces to license taverns and that it would undermine the patronage system of provincial Liberal regimes. The following year, Quebec Conservatives proposed the repeal of the federal law as an infringement of provincial powers, and they were supported in the House of Commons by Liberal leader Wilfrid Laurier, who declared that the law was as an infringement on Quebec's powers.

Ontario's Mowat thus had allies, but he was the one to take the lead in challenging the federal law. In 1884, Ontario passed a law regulating taverns; the federal government disallowed it. The issue went to court when tavern owner Archibald Hodge was fined $25 for allowing customers to play billiards past the legal closing hour of 7 PM. His lawyers argued in *Hodge v. the Queen* that Ontario could not pass laws regulating behaviour, that the matter was criminal and hence federal, and that Ontario could not delegate its authority to local municipalities. The Ontario court agreed with him, a higher court disagreed with that judgment, and the case went to the JCPC in London.

In a decision of great significance, the JCPC sided with Ontario on all the issues. It said that the Ontario law did apply, because a matter could be both federal and provincial in different aspects; that is, it did not have to be either federal or provincial in its entirety. Thus, Ottawa's right to legislate for public safety, as upheld by *Russell v. the Queen*, did not prevent a province legislating on the same issue on matters under its jurisdiction. Liquor was a local matter and was therefore provincial under Section 92. It also stated that Ontario had the right to delegate power to municipalities. Most importantly, the JCPC said that provinces were sovereign in the matters listed in Section 92, just as the federal government was sovereign in its spheres, and the provinces were not subordinate to the federal government's powers under peace, order, and good government. The wording was unambiguous: "the local legislature is supreme, and has the same authority as . . . the Parliament of the Dominion . . ."

Mowat then passed a law imposing heavy taxes on the pubs that had federal licences, a law that Ottawa quickly disallowed. That turned out to be a major mistake, because the case drew Ottawa's liquor law into question and the Supreme Court declared it beyond federal power, a decision upheld by the JCPC. In 1896, Ottawa referred another Ontario liquor law to the JCPC, arguing once more that Prohibition was a matter of peace, order, and good government. Lord Watson wrote the Council's decision, saying that the general federal powers identified in Section 91 did not allow Ottawa to overrule the provincial powers identified in Section 92. Watson may have been tired of these cases, because he went on to make a definitive statement on the issue. He said that apart from the matters listed in Section 91,

> *Parliament has no authority to encroach upon any class of*
> *subjects which is exclusively assigned to provincial legislatures*
> *. . . To attach any other construction to the general power . . .*
> *would . . . not only be contrary to the intendment of the act, but*
> *would practically destroy the autonomy of the provinces. If it were*
> *conceded that . . . Parliament . . . has authority to make laws [on]*
> *matters which . . . are . . . of local or private interest, upon the*
> *assumption that these matters also concern peace, order, and good*
> *government of the Dominion, there is hardly a subject . . . which*
> *it might not legislate, to the exclusion of the provincial legislatures.*

He added that the federal government's general power "ought to be strictly confined to such matters as are unquestionably of Canadian interest and importance and ought not to trench upon [provincial powers]."

Minority Rights and French-Canadian Nationalism

Another crucial matter that had to be determined was the role the federal government would play in the protection of minority rights. The *BNA Act* specifically protected the rights of Protestants in Quebec, but did not give Catholics in other provinces the same degree of protection. The New Brunswick government decided to establish a single, non-denominational, government-run system of schools, which would be free for all citizens. Until then, education had been provided mainly by Protestant and Catholic churches with financial support from the government. The new system would inevitably reflect the views of the Protestant majority and was therefore rejected by the Catholic minorities. The new law did not abolish Catholic schools, but it meant that Catholics would have to pay for them in addition to paying taxes for public ones.

Catholic appeals to the provincial Assembly fell on deaf ears. Some Catholics refused to pay school taxes, and the government began prosecuting them. The Church took the issue to court and lost. It then appealed to the federal government to protect minority religious rights by overturning the legislation. Riots broke out in the Acadian region of New Brunswick and lives were lost. French-Canadian MPs in Ottawa were sympathetic to New Brunswick's Catholics, but they faced a very difficult dilemma: If Ottawa could veto legislation regarding education in one province, then it could do so in others, including Quebec. And one of the main reasons French Canadians had endorsed federalism was precisely because it gave the provinces control of education. While French-Canadian MPs were conflicted by the crisis, Macdonald found an easy way to deal with it. The *BNA Act* had guaranteed the rights of Catholics that were based on law, but New Brunswick's support to Catholic schools was merely an arrangement. The federal government was not then under any constitutional obligation to protect the separate schools, and Macdonald refused to disallow the legislation. Then the New Brunswick government worked out compromises that preserved the common system of education, but allowed Catholics to function within that system. In this case, federalism was working exactly as planned.

Other developments outside the borders of Quebec added to the English Protestant/French Catholic hostility that Confederation was designed to avoid. In 1885, Louis Riel led a second uprising in western Canada. He was found guilty of treason and sentenced to hang. The federal Conservative government, including three Quebec ministers, allowed the hanging to proceed although it was argued that Riel was insane. French Canadians were outraged, and Honoré Mercier renamed the provincial Liberals the "Parti National" to make it easier for Conservatives to support him. His main objective was putting the interests of French Canadians first, as opposed to the provincial Conservative practice of supporting federal policies. Mercier led the Parti National to victory on June 29, 1887, on an anti-Ottawa, anti-Conservative platform. His government endorsed a new interpretation of French-Canadian nationalism, of Confederation, and of the role of the Quebec state. According to this interpretation, it was the duty of the Quebec government to protect French-Canadian rights across the country since Quebec was the homeland of the French-Canadian nation.

These developments reflected the emerging Compact Theory of Confederation, which argued that it was an agreement between the provinces. John A. Macdonald's continuous attempts to weaken provincial governments were now seen as a threat in Quebec, as they had been viewed in Ontario since at least 1873. The federal government had repeatedly used its power to disallow provincial legislation, far more than Britain had ever done. Ottawa was using its power to assert dominance over the provinces, not just to prevent provinces from passing laws that seriously harmed the Dominion's general interests or those of other provinces. Mercier's Parti National and Mowat's Liberals began to co-operate, and the Ontario-Quebec axis was founded. To give weight to their demands, Premier Mercier called for the first interprovincial conference in Canadian history, to be held in Quebec City in October 1887, with Mowat as chairman. Quebec's main grievance was that federal subsidies were quite inadequate for Quebec's needs. Mercier argued that, in 1867, the provinces had given up customs revenue of $12 million in return for subsidies of $2.75 million. Since then, federal customs revenue had increased to $24 million, while the subsidies had only increased to $3.34 million.

Macdonald declined to attend the conference, so it became a premiers' conference. Premier Mowat did not want federal subsidies increased, as Ontarians would pay most of the bill, but he wanted even more to have allies for his battles with Ottawa. The Liberal premiers of Nova Scotia and New Brunswick came, as did Conservative Premier John Norquay of Manitoba, a province engaged in bitter struggle with Ottawa. Only the two least populous provinces, BC and PEI, declined to attend—Ottawa had given them per capita financial support far in excess of that received by other provinces and that might have influenced their decisions.

Mowat drafted most of the twenty-two resolutions that were adopted. They called for an increase in federal subsidies to $4.3 million, for half the senators to be appointed by the provinces, for an end to the federal power of disallowance, for having the courts rather than the federal government make decisions on the constitutionality of provincial laws, for provinces alone to establish voting lists, for MLAs to have the same privileges as MPs, for provincial agreement before Ottawa could declare local infrastructure as federal, and for recognition of Ontario's claim to its western border.

All of these demands were designed to reduce federal influence over provincial affairs, and they represented a clear and strong political challenge to Macdonald's centralist view of Confederation. Macdonald ignored the conference, but he responded to the pressure that it created. Just one year later, he stopped disallowing Manitoba's railway legislation and he recognized Ontario's border in 1889. Over time, most of the other resolutions were adopted, confirming the victory of provincial rights over federal centralization.

Mercier had far more success addressing an issue that had long bedevilled his predecessors. His solution produced another needless federal-provincial dispute, one that spoke volumes about the attitudes of English-speaking Protestants. The issue was purely internal to Quebec, namely the disposition of revenues from the Jesuit's estates. When the Jesuit Order was banned in 1774, the government confiscated its estates and used the revenue for education. After the Order was allowed to return in 1814, it wanted to regain control of that revenue. Other Catholics disagreed, and the problem dragged on for decades.

In 1887, the Mercier government decided that the issue had to be resolved and asked the Vatican for guidance. The resulting compromise called for $400,000 to be divided between various Catholic bodies and for $60,000 to be given to the Protestant churches, a fairly accurate per-capita distribution from property that had originally been public lands. Quebeckers were generally satisfied, but Ontario's militant Protestants objected strongly to the Vatican having influence over any political affairs in Canada. They exerted strong pressure on Macdonald to veto the legislation. Macdonald refused, arguing that the issue fell exclusively under provincial jurisdiction. Federalism was working as its architects intended, and the issue demonstrated again that Macdonald would not use federal power to intervene in religious or cultural matters.

These developments reflected another stage in the evolution of French-Canadian nationalism, this time led by an MP, Henri Bourassa, whose views were based on the writings of Lionel-Adolphe Groulx. Bourassa argued that Confederation was a pact between two founding nations, French and English, and not just between provinces. Ottawa, he alleged, was violating that agreement by failing to protect French rights because it was dominated by English-speaking MPs. This new nationalism reflected French-Canadian fear of being "swamped" in the new Dominion. Quebec's population grew from 1.2 million in 1871 to 2 million four years later, but half a million people left the province. The rest of Canada grew faster, and Quebec's share of federal MPs dropped from 65 of 181 at Confederation to 65 of 213 in 1896. Quebec was thus increasingly unhappy with its position within Confederation and with the workings of the *BNA Act*, and increasingly nationalistic as a result.

Railways and Rivers: Ottawa vs. Manitoba, BC, and Ontario

Meanwhile, on the prairies a major intergovernmental clash had developed over the building of railways in Manitoba. For Ottawa, the key issue was financing the CPR, so Macdonald gave it a monopoly on rail transit on the prairies. Every farmer and businessman had to travel to the lone CPR line to deliver or obtain goods, no matter what the distance, time, cost, or inconvenience, and the CPR was able to set freight rates at three times those in central Canada. The main priority of the Manitoba government was the construction of other railways to provide competition for the CPR, to lower freight rates, and to provide branch lines. The Conservative government of John Norquay therefore chartered railway companies to meet the needs of the province's population, and Macdonald disallowed them to meet the needs of the Dominion. Norquay passed more railway bills; Macdonald vetoed them. Norquay's failure to protect the interests of his province undermined his party, and more and more Manitobans voted Liberal. Macdonald began to realize that while he had the constitutional authority to disallow Manitoban legislation, the political cost was too high, and in 1880 he stopped vetoing Manitoban railway charters. At the same time, Norquay pressed Ottawa for control of natural resources. The province submitted long reports on the unfairness of its treatment and its need for revenue from those lands. Ottawa refused, but offered increased subsidies.

Manitoba was not the only province to fight major battles with Ottawa over the building of the CPR, but BC's problems were over the ethnicity of the workforce. White labour was employed to build the railway over thousands of miles from eastern Ontario to Revelstoke, BC, but the CPR claimed that it needed Chinese labour to complete the short section to the Pacific. That would be very advantageous to the CPR, as Chinese workers were willing to work and live in terrible conditions and could be paid far lower wages than white workers. Opposition to the Chinese presence mounted rapidly, reflecting racism, concerns about health, and negative effects on the wages of white workers.

BC passed a law requiring companies to obtain licences to use Chinese labour; Ottawa disallowed it. BC imposed a poll tax to raise the cost of bringing in Chinese men; the Supreme Court overturned it. Ottawa disallowed a $10 licence on workers imposed by the province in 1878. BC passed more laws to bar Chinese workers; Ottawa used various methods to disallow or veto them. But thanks to Chinese labour, the CPR was finally completed on November 7, 1885. Ottawa then began responding to BC's demands by imposing an increasingly high head tax on Chinese immigrants. Immigration declined, and relations between Ottawa and the province improved.

At the same time, there was no relief in Macdonald's problems with Mowat's Ontario. In 1881, a dispute broke out over the control of rivers inside the province. A lumberman, Peter McLaren, built a timber slide on a small tributary of the Ottawa River called the Mississippi and charged fees for other lumbermen to use it. One of them, Boyd Caldwell, refused to pay, and McLaren got a court order to stop Caldwell from using the slide. Caldwell appealed to the provincial government for support. Mowat passed a law, the *Rivers and Streams Act*, confirming that anyone could use timber slides, but they would have to pay a fair fee. In response to a request from McLaren, Macdonald disallowed the law.

An Ontario court upheld the provincial legislation, and Mowat passed the law again in 1883. Macdonald disallowed it again. Mowat passed it a third time in 1884, and Macdonald disallowed it again. McLaren took the case to the Supreme Court and lost, and then to the JCPC, where he lost again. Mowat then passed the legislation a fourth time, and Macdonald let it stand. It is not clear why Macdonald vetoed this legislation, since it involved property rights, a small local river, and natural resources—all provincial matters—and was of no general interest to the Dominion. The matter was vital to Ontario, however, because if Ottawa could veto legislation affecting a timber slide on a little river, it could intervene in almost any economic matter in the province. The best explanations for Macdonald's actions may well be his personal animosity towards Mowat, annoyance over the fact that Mowat was winning all the battles, and the fact that McLaren was a Conservative.

The *Rivers and Streams* case was a milestone in the development of federal-provincial relations. At the 1864 Quebec Conference, no one questioned the concept that the federal government should take over Britain's right to veto provincial legislation that went beyond provincial powers or threatened the broader interests of the Dominion or of other provinces. In 1868, Macdonald had stated that the power of disallowance should be used carefully and rarely, and he followed that policy during his first term, as did Mackenzie's Liberal government. But in the *Rivers and Streams* case, the central government disallowed provincial legislation that did not threaten any general Dominion interest. Those vetoes violated the convention upon which Britain's power of disallowance was based; they violated the spirit upon which that power was passed to Ottawa in the *BNA Act*; and they violated Macdonald's own 1868 guidelines. Macdonald's actions were seen as an abuse of a power that had previously been regarded as legitimate, and they seriously undermined public support for the power of disallowance. The constitution was not amended to remove the power of disallowance, but it was used less and less frequently from then on, and only for legitimate reasons.

Ottawa and the Ontario-Manitoba Border

During the 1880s, a dispute over Ontario's western border came to have a major influence on federal-provincial relations. At Confederation, Ontario's territory included the watershed of the north shore of Lake Superior. The northern and western borders beyond that had not been demarcated, but Upper Canada had long disputed ownership of that territory with the

HBC. The 1783 border with the United States ran from Fort William (now Thunder Bay) to Lake of the Woods, and Ontario accordingly claimed Lake of the Woods as its western border with the line then running straight north to Hudson Bay. When the federal government purchased Rupert's Land in 1870, it inherited the HBC's claim. The area in dispute was an enormous 370,000 square kilometres.

Jurisdiction had to be determined because lumber companies, prospectors, and settlers were moving into the area. Ottawa proposed that Manitoba's border be extended to a point just east of Fort William, run north to the watershed of Hudson Bay, and eastwards along that watershed to Quebec, a proposal that would have given Manitoba half of modern-day Ontario and rendered Ontario the fourth largest province. Ontario was outraged, partly because it had long administered part of the territory. Control of natural resources was a major factor. Ontario controlled its own, but Ottawa controlled those in Manitoba. In proposing to extend Manitoba's borders, Ottawa was trying to keep control of a vast stretch of valuable timber and potential mineral wealth. Manitoba would have the administrative burden; Ottawa would have control and the revenue, and Mowat regarded Ottawa's proposal as a blatant money grab.

After the 1878 election, Macdonald passed a law fixing Manitoba's border at Fort William. Premier Mowat threatened to secede from Canada. He got Manitoba to agree to submit the case to the JCPC, with him drafting the questions that would be submitted. Macdonald had been seriously outmanoeuvred, because now the main protagonists were Ontario, which was determined to win, and Manitoba, which had little interest in the case. The JCPC sided with Ontario. Macdonald then asserted that Ottawa controlled land that First Nations had surrendered to the Crown. Mowat won that battle before an Ontario court in 1885 and before the Supreme Court two years later and then before the JCPC.

Ontario's victories had contradictory effects on the state of federal-provincial relations. On the one hand, they helped create a more viable balance of power by making the provinces somewhat more powerful and Ottawa somewhat weaker, a lot weaker than Macdonald wanted. They did not, however, threaten Ottawa's control of its responsibilities as listed in Section 91 or its ability to raise money by any means, which made it the main tax-collector in the Dominion. On the other hand, Mowat's victories widened the imbalance between Ontario and the other provinces, and between central Canada and the other regions. One province, Ontario, contained over 40 per cent of Canada's population, wealth, and seats in the House of Commons, and central Canada almost always dominated the federal government. This made Canada and its federalism very different from other federal states such as Germany, Switzerland, the United States, or India, where no province or state had a dominant influence on the federal government. Dealing with the imbalance between Ontario/central Canada and the other provinces has been a major and somewhat unique theme in Canadian federalism, an important feature of federal-provincial relations, and of Canadian politics ever since 1867.

By the 1890s, Canadian courts, provinces, political parties, and the public had answered the question left dangling at Confederation, namely whether the system represented genuine federalism or quasi-federalism. And the answer was genuine federalism. That had been confirmed by a number of decisions made by the JCPC, which reflected political, geographic, economic, and cultural realities in Canada and often upheld the decisions of Canadian courts. Macdonald had failed in his attempts to use various devices and clauses in the *BNA Act* to make the provinces subordinate.

Politics had played a large role in defining the limitations to federal power. Political calculations were certainly important when Ottawa chose not to intervene with provinces that limited the rights of minorities. Ottawa also discovered that the use of the power of disallowance was resented by citizens whose provincial governments were acting on their behalf. The workings of a two-party political system had also come into play. Macdonald's goal of using provincial Conservative regimes to support federal Conservative policies undermined those parties in Ontario, Quebec, and Manitoba, and reinforced provincial Liberal parties in Nova Scotia, New Brunswick, and Ontario. Those provincial Liberal governments then became a natural opposition to the federal government, a check on its ambitions, a balance to its power. Since the federal Conservatives were centralizers, the opposition Liberals took the opposite position and defended provincial interests, a further check on Ottawa's power.

In a sense, the degree of centralization written into the *BNA Act* reflected three circumstances that did not endure. One was the unusual influence of the American Civil War and the alleged threat that conflict posed to the British colonies. Another was the plan to purchase Rupert's Land and build a railway to the Pacific, two huge yet short-term expenditures. The third was the lingering power of Britain to veto Canadian legislation and Ottawa's power to veto provincial legislation. The British veto was well on the way to oblivion before Confederation, and Britain used it only once after 1867. Ottawa inherited the veto, but, like Britain, found that it was not a power that could be used effectively when provincial governments and the public were determined to have provincial laws and interests prevail.

Other factors played a role. Identification with the provinces remained very strong; identification with Canada took many years to develop. Though federal projects like the acquisition of the prairies and the building of the CPR were hugely important to the Dominion, they were not particularly important to many Canadians. On the other hand, things that were small were often hugely important to individuals, such as the local schoolhouse and the road to the nearest town. The Fathers may have underestimated the geographical, economic, historic, and cultural diversity of the federation they were creating—a centralized system simply did not reflect the underlying facts.

CHAPTER 6
Laurier and the Golden Age of Federalism, 1896-1911

The election of the federal Liberals under Wilfrid Laurier in 1896 marked one of the most significant changes in Canadian political history and in federal-provincial relations. Macdonald and his supporters had never really accepted that federalism meant that both orders of government were autonomous in their respective areas of jurisdiction. The Laurier Liberals did. As leader of the Opposition, Laurier had declared publicly that he believed in genuine federalism, and he had long supported provincial rights.

Laurier came to power with the help of the provincial Liberal regimes in Nova Scotia, New Brunswick, Ontario, and Manitoba, all of whom believed strongly in provincial autonomy in their own areas of responsibility. He then forged one of the strongest and best federal governments in Canadian history, including four former provincial premiers: Oliver Mowat from Ontario, William Fielding from Nova Scotia, Andrew Blair from New Brunswick, and Henri-Gastav July de Lotbinière from Quebec. The West was represented by the powerful former Manitoba Attorney General Clifford Sifton. The Laurier cabinet unquestionably had a deep appreciation for the rights, responsibilities, and problems of provincial governments.

Canada entered almost two decades of relative peace on the federal-provincial side of politics. Peace between Ottawa and the provinces was actually relatively easy to attain. The main thing Ottawa had to do was simply stop trying to dominate the provinces, and that was the policy

Laurier pursued. The period after 1896 was the Golden Age of Federalism and of federal-provincial relations. Both orders of government knew and followed the rules, both had a great deal to do in their respective spheres, and both had growing revenue from a boom in the world economy to spend on their respective tasks. The two orders of government worked as partners in supporting the growing population and prosperity of a colony that was moving towards nationalism internally and towards independence internationally. Involvement in the Boer War and the build-up to the First Word War became important issues for Ottawa, but had little direct effect on its relations with the provinces until after the First World War began.

The Manitoba Schools Question

Before Laurier could get on with his own challenges, however, he had to settle a major conflict from the Conservative era. That was the Manitoba Schools Question, one of the most difficult, complex, and important issues ever to dominate the federal-provincial agenda. When Manitoba entered Confederation in 1870, French-speaking Catholics outnumbered English-speaking Protestants, but both were given equal rights in education and in the official use of language. Massive immigration produced a large English-speaking Protestant majority, plus a dozen ethnic groups with various religious and linguistic cultures. The situation in the 1890s was completely different from that of 1870 and from that of central Canada, and in 1890, the Liberal government of Thomas Greenway cancelled government support for religious schools.

That measure violated the federal *Manitoba Act of 1870* and provoked an immediate protest by Catholics throughout Canada. Macdonald's government was in an almost impossible position because any federal action was bound to upset Protestants, Catholics, or both. He procrastinated for a year, which meant that the option of disallowing the legislation lapsed. His plan was to keep the issue in the courts and hope that they produced a solution. The Manitoban courts declared the legislation within provincial power and the JCPC in London agreed. The next question was whether Manitoba's Catholics could appeal to Ottawa to overturn the provincial law. That issue also went to court and eventually to the JCPC, which ruled that Ottawa did have the power to overturn the provincial legislation.

In March 1895, the federal government issued an order demanding that the government of Manitoba restore the rights of the religious minorities. Ottawa did not, however, have the power to enforce the order, and the federal Liberals opposed it. Laurier argued that if Ottawa protected the French minority in Manitoba, other minorities would demand similar protection and that would lead to conflict rather than harmony. He argued that the provinces were autonomous in education, and the solution was to negotiate an acceptable agreement. In the election of 1896, the Church in Quebec issued instructions for Catholics to vote Conservative. But Quebeckers were well aware that if Ottawa could intervene in Manitoba to overthrow provincial legislation, then it could intervene in Quebec. That was a precedent few of them were willing to see established, even if it meant abandoning Manitoba's French-Catholic minority. They defied the Church and voted for provincial rights, the federal Liberals, and their native son Laurier.

The Manitoba Attorney General Clifford Sifton had been elected to Parliament, so Laurier put him in charge of negotiating a settlement with his former colleagues, that is, to yield to Manitoba as gracefully as possible. Premier Greenway had won the war and was willing to make some concessions: religious instruction could be provided in public schools for half-an-hour at the end of the school day, and schools with a significant number of Catholic students had to have some Catholic teachers. French was not restored as an official language, but bilingual instruction could be provided if ten pupils in any school spoke French. That right was extended to every linguistic minority in recognition of the fact that French was only one of many languages now spoken in the province. Manitoba's French Catholics had no choice but to accept the outcome. Laurier's "Sunny Ways" had triumphed, and politics had trumped the courts as the proper forum for dealing with such issues. It was a huge victory for provincial rights; it was not so for the constitution. Manitoba's actions were unconstitutional, but Ottawa did not have the political power to enforce its remedial legislation school-by-school throughout the province of Manitoba.

Co-operation and Confrontation over Logging and Hydro-Electric Power

With that crisis out of the way, Laurier and his new government could turn to other matters. In 1898, the United States passed a tariff law designed to prevent the importation of lumber from Canada. The goal was to import logs and have all the processing work done in the United States. Canadian companies demanded that Ottawa impose an export tax on logs sufficiently high to offset the American tariff and keep the processing jobs in Canada. That request clearly fell under federal responsibility for trade and commerce, but Laurier was interested in a broad economic deal with the United States and did not want his plans complicated by a dispute over lumber.

The companies then went to Ontario's Liberal government, now headed by Arthur Hardy. The provinces controlled resources, and Hardy passed a law saying timber could only be cut if it was then processed in Ontario. Under pressure from American companies, the United States asked Laurier to disallow the legislation. Laurier refused, and the courts upheld the Ontario law. Subsequent Ontario legislation seemed to touch on federal jurisdiction, and Ontario changed it when Ottawa identified problems and threatened to disallow it. Ontario's law led to processing within the province, and it was then applied to other resources. Excellent co-operation between the two governments was an important factor in the development of the Canadian lumber and mining industries.

Other issues were not so easy to resolve, such as the control of hydro-electric development, which produced some conflict between Laurier and Ontario's James Whitney, who led the provincial Conservatives to power in 1905. His victory was another example of how federalism was evolving. Throughout the Conservative ascendency in Ottawa from 1878 to 1896, one of the main pillars of opposition to Ottawa was the Ontario Liberal government. Laurier's victory in 1896 put Liberals in power in both Toronto and Ottawa, but the election of Whitney restored the old Conservative-Liberal rivalry. Now, however, the positions were reversed, with the federal Liberals inheriting Macdonald's responsibility to manage the overall interests of the Dominion and the provincial Conservatives inheriting Mowat's imperative to stand up for Ontario.

Ontario was determined to use its vast hydro-electric resources to build the economy, and Ottawa was certainly interested in economic development anywhere in the Dominion. Both had constitutional grounds for becoming involved, with the provinces responsible for the rivers and Ottawa responsible for navigation on them. Whitney set up what became

Ontario Hydro to create a province-wide monopoly. Hydro-electric firms petitioned Ottawa to disallow the relevant provincial legislation, but Laurier backed off. He wrote: "the power of disallowance should not be exercised, except in cases of extreme emergency . . . where the interests of the Dominion . . . are likely to suffer." He added that he could detect no great support for disallowing the legislation, and if there was, it was up to the Ontario electorate to demand that their provincial government make the change.

Alberta and Saskatchewan Become Provinces

Central Canada was not the only area where rapid economic development was leading to changes in federal-provincial relations. With the prairie population and economy surging, the time was rapidly approaching for new provinces to be carved out of the North-West Territories. The region had a Legislative Assembly in Regina and its executive controlled some local matters. In May 1900, the Territorial Legislature asked Ottawa to begin discussing the conditions for granting provincial status. The pressure increased when the territorial government of Frederick Haultain won a resounding victory on the issue in 1902. That same year, the federal Conservative Party announced its support for provincial status, so Haultain supported them in the next federal election. Bowing to the inevitable, Laurier's Liberal government promised provincial status if it won the election of 1905, which it did.

A decision had to be made as to whether there would be one, two, or three provinces on the prairies, that is, whether Manitoba would be extended westward to BC or whether the area between them would become one or two provinces. There was little support for extending Manitoba westwards, and Premier Haultain and many others wanted the remaining area to be a single province so it would have a strong government to deal with Ottawa. For that reason, many central Canadian politicians wanted the prairies to be divided into several provinces and it was they who controlled the federal government that would make the decisions.

Two provinces were created: Alberta, named after a daughter of Queen Victoria, and Saskatchewan, named after the largest river on the prairies. They were divided roughly into equal parts at 110 degrees longitude, with their northern borders fixed at 60 degrees north latitude. That was the same as BC's northern border, but well north of Manitoba's, and Manitoba was bitterly disappointed with its inferior size. The rationale for dividing the prairies into three provinces proved correct, as three different societies developed with three provincial regimes that were seldom able to present a united front to Ottawa, unlike the regions of Ontario and Quebec with their single governments.

Control of Crown Lands and natural resources was another issue of contention. At Confederation, the original provinces retained control of natural resources, as did PEI and BC when they joined. In the United States, new states controlled natural resources and were equal to the older states. But when Manitoba was carved out of the Territories, it was not given control of resources, and Alberta and Saskatchewan were treated in the same manner. The main arguments were that the federal government had to control land in order to build railways and attract immigrants. The arguments were specious. There were no political problems building the CPR and the Intercolonial Railway in provinces that controlled their own natural resources, and immigrants were attracted to all parts of Canada regardless of which government controlled the land. The West needed railways more desperately than the other provinces, and the area was being given provincial status because the prairies had already been largely settled.

Other facts suggest that Ottawa simply wanted to maintain control of the Prairie economy. In the 1870 land survey, seven sections per township were set aside to support education. Though education was a provincial matter, Ottawa refused to surrender that land in 1905. Saskatchewan's Premier Walter Scott requested that all land in northern Saskatchewan be turned over to the province. That land could not be used to promote immigration, but Ottawa refused. Ottawa's argument that it needed land sales to finance railways was also contradicted by the fact that it gave generous compensation to the provinces in return for retaining control of resources. As with so many federal-provincial disputes, the real issue was power.

The most important controversy concerned education. Since education was a provincial responsibility, it should not have been an issue at all. The system in the North-West Territories included both non-denominational and religious schools with a single body to administer all of them. Education was not an issue in the negotiations and discussions leading up to provincial status. Laurier then decided to restore French-Catholic education rights as they had been in 1875, when the French were a significant part of the Prairie population. It was a blatant attempt to dictate a key element of education policy for the two new provinces after they gained control of education. It is not clear why Laurier took this tack as it clearly violated his views on provincial rights, as well as the solution he had devised for the Manitoba Schools Question. It also revived the animosity between French Catholics and English-speaking Protestants, the very problem Confederation had been so successful in solving.

Laurier's chief western minister, Clifford Sifton, resigned in protest. The Opposition Conservatives took up the defence of provincial rights, trading places with Laurier, who had always defended them when he was in opposition. An acrimonious and divisive debate took place in the House of Commons. Laurier had miscalculated, and he was forced to back down. The outcome was that the school system would be public, religious minorities could establish their own schools with government support, and the language of instruction throughout was English.

Another question was whether provincial politics would continue to be non-partisan, as the Territorial government had been, or whether the eastern Canadian two-party system would be imposed. Municipal governments had always been based on the non-partisan principle, as was the Territorial government and most Westerners wanted to retain that system in their new provinces. For political reasons, Laurier decided to impose the federal party system, that is, the federal Liberal party system. On September 1, 1905, he appointed a Liberal, George Bulyea, as Alberta's first lieutenant governor four days before Alberta became a province of the Dominion. Instead of calling an election and asking the leader with the most seats to form a government, Bulyea appointed another Liberal, Alexander Rutherford, as Alberta's first premier. That put Liberals in charge of the new administration well before the first election. This, of course, is what Macdonald had done for Conservatives in Ontario and Quebec before their first elections, and Laurier had learned well from the master.

With pro-farm and pro-immigration policies, support from Ottawa, and loads of patronage, the Liberals won the first Alberta election with twenty-three of twenty-five seats, and they went on to win another four successive elections. Safely ensconced in office, the Liberals rewarded the northern part of the province for its support. Edmonton was made the capital and also the seat of the provincial university. Half the civil service from the old Territorial government in Regina was transferred to Edmonton, and construction began on a new Legislative building overlooking the North Saskatchewan River. Given the way it was established, the close links between the federal and provincial Liberal parties and governments, and the fact that the dominant Liberal in the old Territorial government, Frank Oliver, became Laurier's new Minister of the Interior and chief lieutenant on the Prairies, relations between Ottawa and Alberta were excellent. Albertans got on with the challenges of building a new province and did so with great success.

Laurier selected another Liberal, A.W. Forget, as Saskatchewan's first lieutenant governor, and four days later, Saskatchewan became a province. Many people expected that Haultain would remain premier, but he had supported the Conservatives in the 1904 election. He had also fought with Laurier on the controversial issues surrounding the creation of the two provinces. So Laurier had Forget appoint another Liberal, Walter Scott, as premier and Haultain was not even asked to speak at the celebrations when Saskatchewan became a province. Scott quickly organized a provincial government including good Liberals, none of whom had served in the Territorial government. Their main job was to get the new provincial Liberal party elected, and they had ten weeks in control of the government to arrange the desired result.

The Liberals created more constituencies in the north where they were popular and fewer in the south where Haultain and the Conservatives had support—so much for George Brown's principle that democracy should be based on rep by pop. With pro-farm and pro-immigration policies, support from Ottawa, and loads of patronage, the Liberals easily won sixteen of twenty-five seats, and the provincial Liberal party became a bastion of federal Liberal strength for decades. Regina remained the capital, but unlike in Alberta and Manitoba, there was a sense that government institutions should be fairly distributed around the province. The university was therefore situated in Saskatoon, the provincial jail in Prince Albert, and the mental hospitals in Battleford and Weyburn. With Liberal regimes established in

Saskatchewan and re-elected in Ottawa, the relations between the two governments were set for decades of co-operation.

The Imbalance between Revenue and Responsibilities

Halfway through his second term, Laurier decided to tackle the problem of subsidies that had marred the workings of federalism since 1867. Perhaps the biggest miscalculations the Fathers of Confederation had made were in underestimating the proportion of customs revenue that Ottawa had to return to the provinces in order for them to fulfill their remaining responsibilities. Almost every year after Confederation, one or more provinces complained to Ottawa that they could not pay their way. Provincial legislatures passed motions outlining the case for more funds, and premiers beat a steady path to Ottawa to present their cases. Ottawa often replied that the provinces should raise taxes, cut spending, and live within their means. The cases were so compelling, however, that Ottawa repeatedly increased its transfers to the provinces by various means, usually calling each such deal a "final" one. Politics played a huge role, as friendly provincial administrations received favourable treatment. These ad hoc adjustments were bandages, not solutions, and each one created a different relationship between the federal government and whichever province received the latest deal. Between 1867 and 1927, there were twenty-six increases to the subsidies, twenty-one to provinces governed by the same party as Ottawa, all coming shortly before or after federal elections.

The statistics paint a clear picture. In 1868, the subsidies provided half the revenue of all the provinces; by 1906, they provided a quarter. In 1868, the subsidies consumed 20 to 25 per cent of the federal budget; by 1906, that had fallen to under 10 per cent. At first, Laurier handled the problem the way his Conservative predecessors had, with one-off deals arranged province-by-province, and hints that more might come to friendly provincial governments. The subsidies provided to the new provinces of Alberta and Saskatchewan were very generous and were certainly noted by the other provinces, especially in the Maritimes. But with the economy booming and Ottawa's revenues rapidly growing, the highly politicized ad hoc approach was increasingly unacceptable. To address the issue, Laurier called the first-ever heads of government meeting, set for January 1906, which was followed by a second conference in October. The federal subsidy was raised from $6.7 million to $9.3 million, a long jump from the $2.2 million of 1867. There was a special addition for BC because of the needs created by its small, scattered population and mountainous geography.

Unlike the case of all ad hoc adjustments of the past, the *BNA Act* was amended to reflect the changes. The Maritimes still complained that they had been disadvantaged, and in 1912, the new federal Conservative government of Robert Borden provided them a cash settlement of $2 million. Laurier's "final" settlement was no more final than the previous ones because it did not solve the original problem of an inadequate formula. Within five years, the grants were again insufficient and declining as a percentage of provincial revenue, prompting another predictable chorus of provincial complaints. By the time the Depression hit in 1930, this imbalance between federal surpluses and provincial deficits was one of the most serious problems facing Ottawa and the provinces.

Immigration and Borders: Ottawa vs. BC and Manitoba

When Laurier came to power, the problems over Asian immigration had not been solved. Many of the Chinese workers brought to BC to complete the CPR had remained, and more had joined them. Their presence was bitterly resented by the white population for a combination of reasons including racism, fears that they drove down wages, and health concerns as Chinese immigrants were crowded into slums. In response to public pressure, the BC Legislature continued to pass bills restricting the flow of Chinese immigration, and the federal government kept disallowing those bills in response to pressure from the companies that employed Chinese labour. In 1907, Premier Richard McBride's government passed yet another bill restricting Asian immigration. There were anti-Chinese riots in Vancouver, and Laurier allowed some reductions in the rate of immigration from Asia. Of the thirty provincial acts disallowed by the Laurier government, twenty of them affected BC, almost all concerning immigration policy. The positions of the two governments were simply irreconcilable, and the only option for Ottawa was to disallow the bills that the BC Legislature kept passing to reflect the interests and wishes of its white population.

Another issue that had bedevilled federal-provincial relations since 1870 was that of the borders of Manitoba. Few issues irked Manitobans as much. Manitoba's Conservative Premier Rodmond Roblin argued that Manitoba had become a third-class province, not controlling natural resources like the original four, and now greatly inferior in size to its sister Prairie provinces. But Roblin was Conservative, and Laurier refused to deal with him. The main issue in the 1911 federal election was free trade with the United States, with the Liberals in favour and the Conservatives opposed. Free trade was very much in the interests of the Prairies, and Alberta and Saskatchewan voted overwhelmingly for Laurier. Roblin threw his powerful political machine behind the victorious federal Conservatives, and Laurier lost the election partly because he had played politics for too long and treated a province too unfairly. Ottawa's relations with Manitoba thus played an important role in two of the most important federal elections in Canadian history, the one of 1896, which brought Laurier to power, and that of 1911 which sent him back to the Opposition benches for the rest of his long and illustrious career.

CHAPTER 7
The First World War and the Twenties, 1911-1929

The election of a federal Conservative government in 1911 began a new chapter in federal-provincial relations. Indeed, it witnessed the beginning of a new form of federalism that gradually replaced the genuine or classical version of the previous several decades. Robert Borden's new Conservative administration had a very different view of federalism than Laurier's Liberal government, and Canada was about to experience a sea change in the relations between Ottawa and the provinces.

By 1911 the task of building the Dominion from sea to sea had been largely achieved. Ottawa's remaining responsibilities were less important and less costly, but the surge of global prosperity was still running strong and Ottawa had spare cash to spend. Federalism is characterized by competition between the centre and the provinces as each regime strives to maintain or increase its power, ensure its re-election, and satisfy the needs and demands of its constituents. So Borden's Conservatives were soon looking for new things to do and new ways to spend money.

They did not have far to look, because the cost of provincial responsibilities was rapidly increasing, especially for roads, education, and welfare. Borden therefore decided to help the provinces with their affairs. And since governments and politicians like to control the money they spend, Ottawa began attaching conditions to its grants. The twentieth-century federal invasion of provincial jurisdiction had begun. It has continued ever since, in fits and starts, leading to a form of mixed federalism in which Ottawa is involved in almost every matter of "exclusive" provincial responsibility. The movement was almost entirely one-sided as there are almost no examples of provinces invading federal jurisdiction, and certainly none that provoked the political crises that often resulted from federal encroachment on provincial affairs. Classical or genuine federalism has never been restored and never could be.

Borders and Natural Resources

Before getting involved with the provinces, however, Borden had debts to pay. The Conservative regimes in Manitoba and Ontario had helped him win, and they both wanted their borders extended northwards. On April 1, 1912, Manitoba's border was moved from 53 to 60 degrees latitude and along the Hudson Bay shoreline to include the rivers draining the prairies. Ontario and Quebec were both expanded north to include all of the Hudson Bay Lowlands, with their new mutual border fixed at 79 degrees longitude. Manitoba grew by 350 per cent, and Ontario and Quebec more than doubled. Manitoba eventually gained access to the sea with a railway to Churchill on Hudson Bay; Ontario, with a railway to Moosonee on James Bay. The three provinces were satisfied, but others thought that they too should receive something from Ottawa. Saskatchewan objected on the grounds that it should have access to the sea, and the Maritime provinces demanded money as they had contributed to the purchase of the territory back in 1870. Borden ignored their complaints; they were just part of the game of federalism.

Another issue fared less well. Ottawa still controlled natural resources in the Prairie provinces, but by 1911 the argument that it needed them to promote settlement was irrelevant. The three Prairie provinces expected that resources would be turned over to them. Borden had promised to do so in the 1908 election, but now he did not like the idea of helping Liberal administrations in Alberta and Saskatchewan. Pressure on Ottawa produced no movement. A conference between the three premiers and Borden led to a standard delaying tactic, as Borden asked them for a written report. Nothing came of that, and Borden said that the issue had to be discussed with the other provinces. That guaranteed failure, because other provinces would demand some compensation. The outbreak of the First World War in 1914 provided further excuse for delay and the issue remained unresolved.

Ottawa's Invasion of Provincial Jurisdiction

Borden's new government proceeded with plans to help all the provinces address their needs. There was no political advantage in increasing the subsidies that had been declining for years, but specific programs would be quite visible and hence politically attractive. The first such program provided support for the construction of local roads and highways, although anything purely "local" was a matter of "exclusive" provincial responsibility. Without an amendment to the *BNA Act*, such a program would be a technical violation of the constitution. The grants also carried conditions that would lead to federal involvement in the administration of the money, and that meant both duplication and interference. Liberal opposition parties in Ottawa and the provinces opposed the program on the grounds that it was unconstitutional.

Provincial governments, whether Conservative or Liberal, did not object to this violation of rights because they stood to receive funds to help meet the burgeoning need for more and better highways. Federal conditions might not be much different than their own and meeting them was seen as a small price to pay for the larger roads budgets. Liberal premiers, however, believed that a Conservative federal government would ensure that more money went to Conservative provincial regimes, which was a very valid concern. The bill passed the House of Commons in November 1912, but was vetoed by the Liberal-dominated Senate as a violation of the constitution. Interestingly, Ottawa made no attempt to build an interprovincial highway, which would have been fully within its jurisdiction.

The First World War and Federalism

Developments in Europe soon put Ottawa's new approach to federalism on hold. On August 4, 1914, Great Britain declared war on Germany. As a colony, Canada was automatically at war, but the degree of Canada's contribution was a matter for Canadians to decide. Fortunately for the relations between Ottawa and the provinces, most Canadians were enthusiastic in their support for the war effort. One of the first manifestations of this spirit involved a rare example of a province invading federal jurisdiction over defence. Three days before Britain's declaration of war, British Columbia's Premier Richard McBride bought two submarines that had just been built in the Seattle dockyards, an action that was constitutionally, legally, and financially questionable, if not illegal. A few days later, a grateful federal government bought them from McBride, Canada's first war hero.

Throughout the war the provinces strongly supported Ottawa, and powerful provincial politicians joined the federal cabinet. Everyone understood that peace and unity were necessary on the home front in order to fight the war in Europe. Federal, provincial, and municipal politicians of all parties took leadership roles in supporting recruitment, selling bonds, and promoting the war. The constitution gave Ottawa all the powers it needed to fight a war. On August 14, Parliament passed the *War Measures Act*, transferring its constitutional powers to Borden's cabinet, allowing it to govern through the simple issuance of government orders rather than the cumbersome process of legislation. That *Act* effectively suspended the entire constitution, including any provincial powers Ottawa chose to override. Ottawa took control of many matters that were under provincial authority, such as prices and wages or civil and property rights. In effect, Canada became a unitary state for the duration of the war plus one year. There were numerous and serious problems in Canada during the war, but they did not become federal-provincial issues because of the high level of co-operation among all the governments and the willingness of provincial governments to place the war effort above their local needs and rights.

One issue later led to serious and continuous problems between Ottawa and the provinces, and that was Ottawa's method of financing the war. Ottawa could collect any type of revenue, but the provinces were limited to direct taxes. After 1867, Ottawa made no attempt to collect direct taxes, so by 1914 it was an established convention that the provinces alone collected them. That situation changed as a result of Canada's enormous losses fighting in Europe. By 1917, the size of the Canadian contingent could not be maintained by voluntary recruitment, and Ottawa decided to introduce conscription. Many Canadians objected. The war had created an economic boom with enormous profits for some companies and their shareholders, that is, for the rich. People demanded that if Ottawa was going to conscript the sons of the poor, it must also conscript the money of the rich. Therefore, to soften opposition to military conscription, the government decided to collect direct taxes from corporations and individuals as a wartime measure that was clearly linked to military conscription.

Those earning over $2,000 paid a minimum tax of 1 per cent, and thirty thousand Canadians and many corporations were paying income tax by 1918. The tax accounted for less than 1 per cent of government revenue, but the administration to collect it was established and the rich survived the experience of paying it. After the war, Ottawa decided to continue collecting direct taxes. There was good justification as the war created huge federal expenses, including a massive debt to pay off, annual interest on that debt, heavy costs for health and pensions for veterans and their families, and the cost of various post-war adjustments. In addition, in 1917, two transcontinental railways had to be nationalized and amalgamated into the Canadian National Railway, with Ottawa assuming its huge debt. Ottawa's income tax then created a new and serious problem for the provinces. Citizens were more willing to pay taxes to the distant federal government than to their provincial ones, so Ottawa's tax limited the degree to which taxpayers would tolerate higher provincial taxes. This magnified the existing fiscal imbalance, the fact that Ottawa was able to collect more revenue for its responsibilities than the provinces could collect for theirs.

The Great War changed forever the way Canadians acted and thought, and federal-provincial relations was just one of many areas that were affected. It is in the nature of governments to wield as much power as they can, and Ottawa was reluctant to give up the enormous power the war had bestowed on it. Soon after the war, it became clear that the pre-war balance between the provinces and Ottawa would not be restored, as there were strong arguments for extending or even making permanent parts of the transfer of provincial power that had taken place. One factor was that Ottawa now had a strong and successful bureaucracy with fewer federal responsibilities to keep it occupied, while provincial administrations had stagnated for four years with their more limited roles and small budgets.

The war created major problems related to the health and pensions of veterans. Health and welfare were provincial responsibilities, but soldiers and veterans were federal, and that blurred the lines between Ottawa and the provinces regarding the health and welfare of hundreds of thousands men and women and their families. Federal programs to deal with their post-war care included pensions, health facilities, a program to deal with venereal disease, and the establishment of a number of employment offices to help veterans reintegrate into the peacetime economy. The provinces welcomed these federal initiatives and willingly participated in such programs because they were needed, they were caused by the war, they were usually small and of limited duration, and they did not pose fundamental challenges to provincial rights. These excellent examples of federal-provincial co-operation were largely phased out in the 1920s. In 1919, the federal government also established a Department of Health primarily to deal with the Spanish flu, an epidemic directly related to the war that killed as many Canadians as the war itself.

Other federal programs definitely upset the provinces. As he had done in 1911, Borden began launching programs in areas of provincial jurisdiction in matters not related to the war, programs for which the provinces were to pay half the cost, but that also carried conditions the provinces had to meet. The program providing assistance for technical education was criticized by Ernest Lapointe, the leading Quebec Liberal MP, on the grounds that it was a violation of provincial jurisdiction. Another program supported local highway construction, paying 40 per cent of the cost, but subject to federal standards. This was the first program in which Ottawa insisted that the provinces make matching grants. The provinces entered these schemes as they could not afford the rapid expansion of highways that the new age of cars and trucks required.

Ottawa also announced a program to build houses that would help address a lack of construction during the war, as well as provide jobs for veterans. Few things could be as "local" as a private house on a little piece of property—housing was clearly within provincial jurisdiction. Federal bureaucrats wanted to dictate standards for size, cost, construction materials, and water supply. Ontario pointed out that an additional set of housing standards would produce endless and needless complications. A compromise was reached in which provinces submitted plans and if Ottawa accepted them, it could not then interfere in their implementation. Thousands of houses were built before the program lapsed in 1921.

Growing Resistance to Ottawa's Invasion of Provincial Responsibilities

These programs were significant in other ways. Ottawa argued that it had to continue collecting direct taxes in order to pay for the war, but part of that revenue was now going towards programs in provincial jurisdiction that the provinces could not adequately fund because their revenue sources were being squeezed out by Ottawa's continued collection of direct taxes. This was a vicious circle financially, administratively, and politically. Other patterns were emerging: in different provinces, Ottawa was paying varying portions of the costs of different programs and setting different levels of conditions, creating a patchwork of programs, and making federalism more asymmetrical. Each program forced provinces to shift their spending towards priorities set by Ottawa, although each province's priorities differed from those of Ottawa and from those of other provinces. Ottawa was starting to influence, if not dictate, provincial spending decisions and impose uniform policies in spite of the very different needs of the provinces.

Quebec had not objected to the concentration of power in Ottawa during the war, but now Premier Louis-Alexandre Taschereau's Liberal government was determined to modernize and develop the province with a network of roads, hydro-electricity, and more social welfare programs. The federal government was involving itself in all these matters, and in November 1920, Taschereau gave a major speech criticizing federal intervention in provincial matters. Until that time, relations between Ottawa and Quebec had been quite cordial because Ottawa had restricted its actions to federal responsibilities as outlined in the *BNA Act*. Now Ottawa was deliberately and systematically encroaching on provincial turf, and Quebec was becoming a critic of the federal government. Taschereau's 1920 speech was the first indication that Quebec would resist federal encroachment, a battle that has gone on ever since. The English-speaking provinces did not object as strongly, establishing another pattern in which Quebec and the other provinces reacted differently to Ottawa's incursions. Eventually, these issues and patterns almost led to the breakup of the country.

Taschereau's opposition came at a favourable time. The wartime concentration of power in Ottawa's hands was a temporary phenomenon, even though Ottawa had been somewhat successful in clinging to it after the war. The wartime shift in the balance of power had interrupted, but not reversed the trend towards greater provincial activity. The importance of the functions assigned to the Dominion's central government in 1867 was still declining, while the importance of responsibilities assigned to the provinces was mushrooming with the need for roads, social welfare, urban infrastructure, education, and support for local industry. The 1920s would see a further relative weakening of federal power as Ottawa entered a period of minority governments and weak majority ones.

The phase-out of the post-war programs was facilitated by the 1921 election of the federal Liberals under William Lyon Mackenzie King. He did not believe Ottawa should be involved in provincial matters. That belief was reinforced politically by the fact that his largest contingent of MPs came from Quebec, whose government, elites, and people did not believe that any government should be heavily involved in social issues, especially the federal one dominated by English-speaking Canadians. King's view was reinforced economically by the fact that Ottawa had huge debts to pay for the war and the nationalization of the railways. King had matured under Laurier's vision of Canada, and intervention in provincial affairs was identified with Conservatives, with Macdonald and Borden, with the *War Measures Act*, and with conscription. All of these were poisonous politically in Quebec. Across Canada, the predominant political-economic philosophy still suggested that matters such as economic decisions, health, and social welfare were best left to companies, individuals, families, churches, and charities.

The Courts Define Federal and Provincial Roles

During the war and post-war period, the courts were also active in further defining the respective roles and powers of the federal and provincial governments. An important example was the *Alberta Insurance Reference* case of 1916. It dealt with a 1910 federal law that required all insurance companies to have federal licences. The Supreme Court decided that the law exceeded federal power, and the JCPC in London agreed; both decisions restricted Ottawa's power under its responsibility for trade and commerce. In the *Board of Commerce* case of 1922, the Supreme Court again reinforced a more narrow interpretation of Ottawa's responsibility for trade and commerce.

The 1914 *War Measures Act* overrode provincial responsibilities, but its legitimacy came into question in 1918 when Ottawa issued an order stating that provinces required federal approval to issue bonds. Quebec challenged it, and Ottawa backed down. Another important case involved Ottawa's 1919 *Combines and Fair Prices Act*, which attempted to control prices. Three years later, the courts rejected it on the grounds that there was no current national emergency that would justify such intervention in the economy. Other cases, such as *Reciprocal Insurance*, determined that Ottawa could not declare an action to be criminal and then claim responsibility for that matter because Ottawa had responsibility for criminal law.

The *Snider* case of 1925 marked another serious restriction of federal power. In 1907, Ottawa passed the *Industrial Disputes Investigation Act*, allowing the federal Ministry of Labour to appoint a board to deal with industrial strikes and lockouts. In 1925, the Toronto Electric Commission asked for a board to be appointed to deal with its labour problems, an action that was challenged on the grounds that the matter was in provincial jurisdiction. Several courts upheld the law, but the JCPC in London overturned it on the grounds that labour relations were matters of property and civil rights, and there was "no emergency putting the national life of Canada in . . . peril."

The effect of this series of court cases, dating back to the 1880s, was to ensure that Ottawa's residual power under peace, order, and good government could only be used by the federal government to intervene in provincial affairs if there was a genuine national emergency affecting more than one province, that is, if the peace and order of Canada were actually threatened. Local disputes such as a strike in Toronto clearly did not meet that test. Ottawa was persistent though, and in 1928, it licensed a fish cannery on the grounds that since the fishery was federal, processing fish must also be federal. The Supreme Court regarded that as an exaggeration, and the JCPC agreed. Though these decisions restricted the federal government's potential power, Ottawa continued to manage its own responsibilities quite well, and Canada survived in spite of the fact that Ottawa did not regulate things like fish-processing plants, liquor licences, insurance companies, and local labour disputes.

New technologies often raised questions as to which government should regulate them. Travel by airplane had become practical with some flights being within provincial borders while others crossed provincial or national borders. In 1919, Ottawa passed a law regulating air travel, which Quebec challenged in 1927. The courts declared that air travel was a matter of national importance, so Ottawa won that battle. Radios were another important new technology that required regulation, with some radio stations having purely local audiences while other broadcasts reached audiences in other provinces or the United States. Ottawa sought to regulate them, and Quebec's challenge to the federal *Radiotelegraph Act of 1927* failed.

The fact that Ottawa had won two battles after a long series of defeats did not represent any new transfer of power to Ottawa or any real reversal of trends in the balance of power between the two orders of government. The cases were entirely different, and the decisions made sense, even if some disagreed with them. Basically when Ottawa tried to exceed its powers, the courts usually supported the provinces; when new technologies came along that were national rather than local in scope, the courts made them federal responsibilities. That conformed to the *BNA Act*'s definition of the difference between general and local responsibilities and between federal and provincial jurisdiction.

Old Age Pensions

Federal-provincial relations entered a new phase in the late 1920s. The issue was old-age pensions, and the result was the specific, deliberate, successful, and permanent entry of Ottawa into an "exclusive" area of provincial jurisdiction. Attitudes towards social welfare reflected values, which differed between French Catholics and English-speaking Protestants. Welfare was therefore made a provincial responsibility in 1867. Later in the century another significant difference emerged, in that Quebec's French Catholics trusted their Church rather than their government on such matters, while other Canadians increasingly wanted governments, rather than churches, to administer social welfare programs.

The *BNA Act* accommodated such differences extremely well, and by 1920, there were nine provinces in five geographic or economic regions and the differences between provinces were greater than in 1867. Under the constitution, each province could, if its citizens demanded, develop a pension program according to its own circumstances, politics, views, needs, and capabilities. For several decades, the provinces had in fact been introducing social welfare programs for needy groups such as the blind and single mothers. The provinces had discovered that the costs of new programs usually exceeded estimates, and they were therefore carefully approaching other forms of welfare acutely aware of the many demands on their limited budgets, and the fact that budgeting is often a zero-sum game: the more they spent on welfare, the less there would be for everything else.

The possibility of a federal plan was debated in the early 1920s, and in 1925, a House of Commons committee recommended one. This was a problem for Mackenzie King because welfare was provincial, and it was thought that a purely federal plan would require a constitutional amendment, a course of action he did not want to pursue. There was an argument, however, that a shared-cost program with the provinces might not require an amendment because any province joining the federal plan would, in effect, be giving its consent to the change. The Conservative opposition argued that if Ottawa could pay 50 per cent without an amendment, then it must also be able to pay 100 per cent, and welfare either was or was not in provincial jurisdiction. Quebec was strongly opposed to any federal program, BC favoured a federal-provincial scheme, and the other provinces waited to see what a federal plan would entail.

When the draft legislation was debated, Mackenzie King took the position that the constitution prevented Ottawa from introducing a purely federal plan. He managed to dodge the issue throughout 1925, but in 1926, his minority government was facing a scandal that threatened to topple his regime. His survival depended on the votes of just a few western Labour MPs. Two of them—James S. Woodsworth and Abraham A. Heaps— decided to take advantage of the situation to achieve their goal of a federal pension program. They offered to support either a Conservative or a Liberal government if it brought in a pension plan. The Conservatives rejected the offer out of hand; Mackenzie King agreed to a shared-cost plan against the wishes of some of his ministers. Woodsworth and Heaps held their noses to avoid the smell of the scandal, King survived the crisis, and Canada received its first major federal welfare program. The plan was approved on March 26 by a vote of 123–120, but was then defeated in the Senate by a vote of

45–21 as a violation of the constitution. King had the Commons pass it again in 1927 and persuaded Liberal Senators to let it stand.

That year, Ottawa entered the provincial field of social welfare in violation of the constitution. Three leading Quebec lawyers, including future prime minister Louis St. Laurent, provided Quebec Premier Taschereau with the legal opinion that the program was beyond the power of the federal government. Taschereau did not challenge it in the courts, probably because Quebec was the only province opposing it on constitutional grounds, and he did not want to stand in the way of the other provinces. Instead he proposed a federal-provincial conference to find a solution satisfactory to all parties. That never occurred, and the constitutionality of the program was never challenged in the courts.

BC joined the program, followed in 1929 by the three Prairie provinces and Ontario. The Maritime provinces could not afford their 50 per cent, and Premier Taschereau refused to participate on constitutional grounds, so none of the needy seniors in the four eastern provinces received pensions. Canada then had two types of provinces, those with a pension scheme and those without, another example of asymmetrical federalism. Ottawa's share of the burden was paid from taxes collected in every province so the program transferred money from the four eastern provinces to the five western ones. Paradoxically, the Maritime provinces were poorer than the ones where their money was spent. In 1931, Ottawa increased its share to 75 per cent, disproving Mackenzie King's arguments that federal involvement was legal providing it paid only 50 per cent of "provincial" plans. With that increase in federal funding, Nova Scotia and PEI signed on in 1933, followed by New Brunswick in 1935. Quebec knuckled under in 1936 for the same reason that King knuckled under in 1926—its minority provincial government needed support from other MLAs to avoid political defeat. An argument was advanced that the program was "voluntary," because, in theory, the provinces did not have to join. History clearly demonstrated the opposite: the provinces could not avoid joining, because their taxpayers would not tolerate paying for a scheme from which they received no benefit.

The 1927 pension plan marked the emergence of a new theory concerning federalism, a theory known as the "spending power." According to it, since the Fathers of Confederation had given Ottawa the power to raise revenue by any means, the federal government therefore had the power to spend it on anything it wanted, be it individuals, provinces, or organizations. And if provinces "voluntarily" accepted federal funds, then they had accepted that the federal plan was within Ottawa's constitutional power. There was no discussion of such an idea during the Confederation debates, and in contrast, the *BNA Act* stated several times that the provincial responsibilities were "exclusive," and they could hardly be exclusive if Ottawa could spend money in those areas. The theory of the "spending power" also ignored the fact that federalism was adopted specifically to ensure that Ottawa could not interfere in welfare, education, health, and culture in Quebec. It is difficult, if not impossible, to believe that any French-Canadian politician would have accepted a statement in the constitution that allowed Ottawa to spend money on these matters, and the Fathers of Confederation could not have reconciled such a clause with the term "exclusive" that defined provincial matters.

The 1927 federal Old Age Pension Plan was questionable on other grounds. The money Ottawa paid for its share of pensions in the nine provinces was collected in those nine provinces. Had their citizens wanted their taxes spent on welfare, they had every opportunity to pressure their provincial governments to launch such programs. Indeed, that is exactly what the citizens were demanding and what their provincial governments were doing as fast as their finances allowed. Priorities varied from province to province, as did resources and needs, so the "one-size-fits-all" federal program on pensions distorted public spending on everything else. Ottawa also introduced the program on the principle of "take it or leave it," with Ottawa dictating the conditions but actually paying less than half as the provinces had to pay their half plus administrative costs. Need also varied widely between provinces due to demographics, family patterns, and standards of living. The program was thus most valuable to the Maritimes and least attractive to Quebec. The cost of living varied everywhere, so the value of the pension also varied between provinces, between regions within provinces, and between urban and rural areas. On paper it was "one-size-fits-all," but Canadians came in a wide variety of sizes!

Battles over Natural Resources

In the late 1920s, several other battles were unfolding between Ottawa and the provinces over a perennial problem—control of natural resources. One battle was in central Canada, where Ottawa was still fighting Ontario and Quebec for control of the development of hydro-electricity. Ontario wanted to exploit the vast potential of the St. Lawrence and Ottawa Rivers, the latter in co-operation with Quebec. Rivers were natural resources, a provincial matter. Mackenzie King wanted to build or improve locks on both rivers, and navigation was a federal matter. He also wanted to use the revenue from electricity sales to pay for the locks. The politicians and civil servants in Ottawa concluded that federal control over navigation gave it control of the water that produced the electricity. That suggested the rather strange fiction that boats could sail through a hydro generating plant.

Ontario's Conservative Premier Howard Ferguson regarded Ottawa's position as completely unacceptable. If Ottawa could use its authority over locks to control the electricity generated beside them, it could control the hydro-electric power on any river within the province that was navigable anywhere. Interpreting that broadly, as Ottawa was prone to do, could give the federal government control over a considerable portion of Ontario's economy, since it was increasingly based on cheap hydro-electric power. This was a new and perplexing development, as Ottawa had not previously questioned Ontario's complete control of power plants at Niagara, where Ontario co-operated directly with a foreign government, namely the state of New York.

Ferguson argued that Ottawa's responsibility for navigation on some river could not give it control of power generation, and such an interpretation would transform Canada from a federal union into a unitary state. Quebec's Premier Taschereau, who was even more concerned with Ottawa's penchant for interfering in provincial jurisdiction, supported Ferguson. To cement his alliance with Taschereau, Ferguson repealed a law known as Regulation 17, which had restricted the use of French in Ontario's schools to the great annoyance of Quebec. Taschereau then publicly backed Ferguson in a speech at the centenary of the founding of the University of Toronto. With Ferguson on the platform, Taschereau gave a very clear account of his view of Confederation:

> *Every Canadian must understand that 60 years ago we formed not a homogeneous country but a confederation of different provinces for certain purposes, with a distinct understanding that each of these provinces should retain certain things . . . traditions, creed, laws, national aspirations, language, and a heritage were abandoned by none of the contracting parties. To live and endure the spirit as well as the letter of Confederation must be respected.*

These disputes had a serious long-term effect on Canada. Since Confederation, Ontario had viewed appeals to the JCPC in London as essential for protecting provincial jurisdiction from federal encroachment. In the 1920s, Ottawa wanted to patriate the constitution and make it a Canadian, rather than British, Act of Parliament. Ontario was opposed because the federally appointed Supreme Court would then replace the JCPC as the final arbiter of federal-provincial disputes. Since the two governments were competing in various legal disputes, that was the equivalent of one of the teams in a hockey game appointing the referees, a blatant conflict of interest. Quebec agreed. Provincial opposition would postpone the patriation of the constitution for half a century and ultimately make amendment extremely difficult. In 1931, Ontario obtained British agreement that sections of the *BNA Act* that affected provinces could not be amended without provincial agreement. It was the logical conclusion of the federal-provincial disputes the JCPC had heard over the previous half-century, and it was one of the greatest victories ever for provincial rights.

Another dispute over resources broke out when the Prairie provinces once more put the question of control of natural resources on the federal-provincial agenda. By then, Ottawa's excuses for retaining control were hardly credible, but the issue had become more complicated. At first, the Prairie provinces had been satisfied with the compensation Ottawa provided for the loss of revenue from those resources, but by 1920, they calculated that Ottawa had earned more than it had returned to them and they wanted that money. At the same time, BC demanded the return of the unsettled land in the Peace River valley that it had transferred to Ottawa to help pay for building the CPR some forty years earlier.

Mackenzie King applied his most successful tactics—he procrastinated while creating difficulties in the way of a solution. In negotiations with Alberta in 1926, Ottawa insisted that when it handed over the lands that had been set aside to finance schools, Alberta had to administer those lands according to the terms of the 1905 *Alberta Act*. That meant that Ottawa would still be dictating how the lands were used after passing ownership of them to Alberta. These conditions threatened to re-open the 1905 debate over separate schools, which was always a potentially explosive issue. John Brownlee's United Farmers government resented the attempt to impose federal views on education, and the negotiations stalled. King had important allies in the West, however, and one of them, Saskatchewan's Liberal Premier Stuart Gardiner, convinced King that the situation was simply too unjust to remain unresolved.

A federal-provincial conference in 1927 produced agreement. This time, the Maritimes did not object as Ottawa was meeting many of their demands with a separate agreement, and Ontario and Quebec were more concerned about their own fight with Ottawa over control of hydro-electricity. With agreement in principle, all that remained was the details. With those, King resorted to the politics of divide and conquer, hoping to negotiate a deal with the province that would accept the least and then force the others to accept the same terms. By 1929, he had negotiated deals with the three Prairie provinces, and agreement with BC followed in February 1930. The deals came into effect in 1930 through an amendment to the *BNA Act*, sixty years after Manitoba entered Confederation as a second-class province, forty-five years after the completion of the CPR, twenty-five years after the creation of Alberta and Saskatchewan as second-class provinces, and twenty years after almost all good agricultural land had been settled. The timing could not have been worse; within months, the Great Depression made any remaining agricultural land almost worthless, and the decline in the price of minerals and lumber made further exploitation of the non-agricultural land less profitable.

Maritime Grievances Boil Over

While King was fending off the western provinces, he was also facing growing demand in the Maritimes for a fundamental correction to the original Confederation bargain. After the First World War, a combination of circumstances wrecked the Maritime economies. Young, educated people fled the region in search of jobs, leaving fewer workers to support an aging population. As the region's proportion of Canada's population declined, its representation in the House of Commons fell from forty-three MPs in 1883 to thirty-one in 1921—fewer voices crying out for more attention. At the same time, Maritimers watched in frustration as the Prairies obtained provincial status, special financial treatment, overrepresentation in Parliament, extension of borders for Manitoba, and special freight rates, while Ontario and Quebec received huge extensions of territory. In the late 1920s, ancient grievances and current frustrations exploded in the Maritime Rights Movement. The governments, business and professional groups, and the general populace of all three provinces demanded a fair share of the advantages of participation in the Canadian common market. Their specific demands were for transportation policies that recognized their needs, tariffs that protected their coal and steel industries, and support for the development and use of Maritime ports.

After winning the 1926 election, Mackenzie King responded to the pressure partly because the Conservatives were gaining votes in the Maritimes. King's short-term response was typical—he appointed a commission to investigate the complaints. The Duncan Commission duly documented the serious deterioration in the Maritime economies and provided numerous recommendations to address the problems. Mackenzie King then made another typical response by providing the minimal concessions that he calculated would meet enough of the concerns to defuse the protest movement. Ottawa increased its grants to Nova Scotia by $875,000, to New Brunswick by $600,000, and to PEI by $125,000. It reduced freight rates by 25 per cent and promised assistance to improve harbour facilities. These concessions made things better and allowed provincial politicians to claim some victories in their relations with Ottawa. The Depression then struck the fragile Maritime economies and the hardships of the 1920s started to appear like good times.

CHAPTER 8
The Depression, 1929-1939

In the autumn of 1929, Canada descended into the worst economic depression in its history. It was a national and global catastrophe. The cycle of "boom and bust" had gone on for centuries, with periods of high economic activity followed by periods of stagnation, falling income, unemployment, and poverty. The recession that began in 1929 quickly became far worse than previous ones. To protect their assets, banks called in loans and the amount of money in circulation declined. As people spent less, factories laid off more and more employees, the unemployment rate in Canada jumped to over 20 per cent, and farmers and others received less for their products.

Canadians who ran out of money went to their municipal offices to obtain relief so they could pay the rent and purchase food and fuel. There was nothing new in this—in the recession that followed the First World War, municipalities had provided relief to needy individuals and families, and those programs had been maintained in the 1920s. What was new in 1929 was the overwhelming demand. Municipal governments could not deal with the crisis; provincial governments had to come to their assistance, and it was soon clear that the municipalities and provinces did not have the financial resources to handle the demand. By then, the federal subsidy had fallen from 60 per cent of provincial revenue in 1867 to 10 per cent, while the cost of provincial responsibilities had risen significantly. The provinces had all been borrowing heavily to meet their needs, while the federal government balanced its budgets, paid down its debts, and began launching major and permanent programs in provincial areas of responsibility. The Depression brought the problem of this "fiscal imbalance" to the fore of the federal-provincial agenda.

When this crisis was debated in the House of Commons on April 3, 1930, the Opposition accused Prime Minister Mackenzie King of being heartless. King lost his temper and said that he would not give "a five-cent piece" to a Conservative provincial government. R.B. Bennett, Leader of the Official Opposition, said what Canadians wanted to hear—if elected, his government would provide action. He was elected, and on July 28, a special session of Parliament approved $20 million in immediate assistance for the provinces. There was no precedent for such a sum; it amounted to almost 5 per cent of the federal budget, ten times the amount Ottawa had spent on relief since the First World War. The grants were unconditional, but the municipalities were to pay for the first 50 per cent of relief, the provinces for the next 25 per cent, and Ottawa for the remaining 25 per cent. This was sound accounting practice, but it produced a very serious distortion. The poorest municipalities could not pay their share so they could not receive the provincial share, and the poorest provinces could not qualify for the federal payment. In the perverse way that welfare sometimes works, taxes collected in the poorest municipalities and provinces were actually being transferred to the richest, the reverse of what was needed.

Ottawa soon abandoned the 50–25–25 formula in favour of one under which each government would pay one third. That was more wishful thinking, since many municipalities could not pay their third and neither could the Prairie provinces. Nevertheless, this formula remained on the agenda throughout the Depression, although Ottawa paid different percentages of relief costs in different provinces, and the provinces paid different percentages of the costs of their municipalities. The federal share eventually worked out to around 40 per cent, not some mathematical and bureaucratic division of one-third each across the country. This and other welfare issues created a set of federal-provincial squabbles that lasted throughout the decade.

The situation was complicated by the facts that unemployed people migrated from rural areas to cities, from city to city, and from province to province, so that those who applied for relief might not be resident in the municipalities and provinces where they made the application. This became one of the most cogent arguments for federal schemes covering all the needy, wherever they might be. While providing this assistance, Ottawa made two things very clear. One was that the federal government had no permanent responsibility for relief, and it was just providing some financial assistance to help the provinces in hard times. The second was that the assistance was short-term, because it was assumed that the economic slow-down was a temporary phenomenon. The economy would presumably right itself in a short time, and everyone hoped things would get better "next year."

Independence and Amending the Constitution

In the meantime, another federal-provincial issue was developing. Canada remained a colony after 1867, but step by step, it moved towards independence. In 1926, Britain acknowledged the independence of its self-governing Dominions and work progressed on implementing that decision. One problem was that Britain could not simply declare that Canada was independent, as only Britain could amend the Canadian constitution. No solution emerged at the federal-provincial conference of 1926, and the question arose again in 1930. Premier Howard Ferguson of Ontario was concerned that independence might leave the federal government in sole control of amending the constitution. He argued that the BNA Act resulted from an agreement among the provinces and that it could only be amended with the consent of all nine provinces. Other premiers, particularly Quebec's Louis-Alexandre Taschereau, supported him, and Prime Minister Bennett promised that there would be no amendments without consultation with the provinces.

No agreement was achieved so the 1931 *British Statute of Westminster*, which recognized Canadian independence, included a statement that the *Statute* did not overrule the *BNA Act*. Britain would continue to make amendments anytime it received a request from the Parliament of Canada, but a request that affected matters of provincial responsibility would require the support of the provinces. Bennett made this very clear when he addressed the House of Commons on June 30, 1931. He referred to "the apprehension of some provinces that . . . a Dominion government might encroach upon the jurisdiction of a provincial legislature. . . . Lest it be concluded . . . that the rights of the provinces as defined by the BNA Act had been by reason of this Statute curtailed, lessened, modified, or repealed, a section of the Statute . . . declared, with the unanimous consent of the provinces, that such was not the case."

Failure to Deal with the Depression

While these constitutional problems were unfolding, the earlier optimistic hopes for an end to the "recession" of 1929–30 were proving unfounded. Bennett's massive infusion of $20 million into provincial relief programs, his plans to reverse the recession with huge increases in tariffs, and his other efforts to deal with the crisis were unsuccessful. Unemployment in 1930–31 remained at very high levels, and the Prairie provinces continued to face bankruptcy. Bennett called for a federal-provincial conference for 1931 to discuss the overall situation and the possible solutions. It resulted in a continuation of the federal grants, but the acrimonious debates harmed relations between Bennett and the premiers.

Further federal-provincial conferences in the early 1930s failed to deal with the Depression. Bennett kept demanding that the provinces tighten the administration of relief, but the provinces lacked the funds to help all those who needed assistance. In July 1931, he introduced the *Unemployment and Farm Relief Act* to provide grants to the provinces for make-work projects. Such projects created new infrastructure, but cost far more than direct relief because material had to be bought. After a year of experimenting with make-work projects, Bennett informed the 1932 federal-provincial conference that Ottawa was terminating them. Three issues were now entangled: the financial weakness of the provinces, the issue of unemployment insurance that the federal government was advocating as a panacea to the economic problems, and the fact that the constitution would have to be amended because unemployment fell within provincial jurisdiction.

Unemployment insurance, UI, was quite different from relief. The idea behind it was simple in theory: namely, to establish a system whereby employers and employees paid an insurance premium into a fund, and when a person became unemployed, the fund would pay a minimal amount until the person found another job. Such a program had to be compulsory, apply to all provinces, and be managed by government. The scheme would not cover short-term workers or the more than one million people on relief. In the short term, the introduction of a UI scheme would have made the situation worse, because employees and employers would have less to spend after paying their premiums. The amount of money in circulation would have declined, exactly the reverse of what was needed when deflation was a principle cause of unemployment. One major winner from an unemployment insurance scheme would be whichever government implemented it. It would have collected premiums for months before having to make any payments, and the employers and employees would have paid for the first forty weeks of relief for a worker who lost his or her job. UI was, in effect, a method of increasing taxes on companies and employees. That explains in considerable measure why Ottawa and the provinces spent much of the Depression fighting over control of any new program. As a result, not one Canadian benefited from any UI scheme during the 1930s.

As the Depression ground on, Bennett continued to transfer large amounts of money to the provinces, usually without conditions. By 1932, that money was spent and the situation remained the same, if not worse. Many people thought that the provinces were not administering the funds properly, that the "easy money" was encouraging laziness, and that unqualified people were taking advantage of the programs. Bennett began cutting back on the grants and attempting to introduce some form of accountability for the funds. That was a problem for every province, and to them, it represented a violation of the constitution and unwarranted federal interference in provincial jurisdiction.

At a federal-provincial conference in 1932, Bennett proposed an amendment to allow Ottawa to introduce a UI scheme in which the provinces would have to provide some of the initial funding. Premier Taschereau asked what it would cost, but Ottawa had not worked out any of the details. The premiers were not enamoured with a request for a blank cheque without any idea of how effective or costly such a program might be. This conference, like all the others, was not helped by the fact that Bennett was a terrible chairman with a strong penchant for bullying and little talent for compromise. The conference was a failure, and unemployment remained at 30 per cent with 1.5 million people on relief.

By January 1933, the western provinces were again facing bankruptcy, but Ottawa remained inflexible. The gulf between them was widening, with the provincial governments focused on dealing with those who needed relief while Ottawa seemed more interested in a UI scheme and the constitutional amendment that program would require. In March, Bennett told the four western premiers that they would have to place their spending under federal control in order to receive further aid. They were outraged because their situation was so desperate and obvious. Manitoba, for example, was spending 55 per cent of its budget on interest payments, and the idea that it required federal supervision of the portion left over for everything else, including relief, seemed ridiculous. Other provinces such as Ontario were still demanding that Ottawa stop collecting direct taxes so they could pay for relief. Ottawa refused. Another federal-provincial conference failed to produce agreement, and Ottawa had to continue paying part of all provincial relief costs and making loans to the western provinces.

In 1933, the electorate of BC began writing a new chapter in the history of the Depression when it elected a Liberal government under the leadership of the flamboyant, energetic, and open-minded Duff Pattullo. He was possibly the first Canadian politician to move beyond aiding the victims of the Depression to addressing the root causes of it. His plan was for a massive government investment in infrastructure called "work and wages," so massive it would wipe out unemployment. At a time when Ottawa was grudgingly granting around $40 million annually to the provinces out of a budget of around $500 million, he proposed an $800-million federal program, with Ottawa to spend $200 million on its own public works and loan $600 million to the provinces for theirs. He also urged Ottawa to establish a central bank, which could increase the money supply, an idea championed a few years later by Alberta's Social Credit government. Bennett refused to help with Pattullo's plan or listen to his advice on creating credit.

By this time, BC was having serious problems borrowing money on the market and was dependent on grants from Ottawa, which insisted on limitations on BC's budget deficit. Pattullo decided to launch his program, even though it would produce a deficit of $2 million. Ottawa refused to extend more loans, and BC headed towards bankruptcy. Pattullo accused Ottawa of trying to run the province, and demanded that Ottawa provide more assistance and stop collecting direct taxes. Bennett was forced to back down because a declaration of bankruptcy by a province like BC would harm Canada's credit rating.

Pattullo was a Keynesian economist years before John Maynard Keynes published his famous study in 1936, and he made a very prophetic comment about the Depression and the Second World War: "If [there was] another war, they would use the last dollar . . . They'd use the national credit . . . That's what we propose to do. We will use the national credit for a war on poverty." Unfortunately, provinces did not control the "national credit," but in 1939 Ottawa spent its way out of the Depression by fighting a war on Germany, as he had predicted. Pattullo was the first premier to argue that deficit spending and increasing the amount of money in circulation could solve the economic crisis—other premiers would join him, but Ottawa rejected his theory.

In December 1933, the four western premiers asked Ottawa to take over relief for transients and the homeless, to establish a federal UI scheme, to refinance provincial debts, and to introduce more programs for relief work. Bennett was not interested. On January 17, 1934, he told the provinces that Ottawa was going to stop providing assistance by the end of July because, in his view, the provinces were wasting money. This was the background to the failed federal-provincial conference of January 1934. At the next conference, Bennett argued again that the municipalities were wasting money and that the provinces were trying to shift the burden of responsibility to Ottawa, but refusing to transfer power. Accordingly, Ottawa would no longer provide for one-third of provincial relief.

Bennett's new plan called for the provinces to prove their level of need, after which they would receive federal funds. In the meantime, each province was told how much money it would receive over the next six months. There was no consistency to the calculations, so they appeared to be as much political as financial. The premiers were furious. There had been no consultation and the new proposals represented a 22 per cent decline in funding. The provinces cancelled public works projects and unemployment increased, but the federal deficit fell to $20 million, the lowest it had been since 1929. Ottawa then launched its own public works program with a budget of $40 million.

By then, politics had become a serious complicating factor. When the Depression began, six of the nine provinces had Conservative governments. By 1935, four of them had fallen to the Liberals: BC and Nova Scotia in 1933, Ontario and Saskatchewan in 1934, with New Brunswick and PEI set to go Liberal in 1935. Bennett was as aware as Mackenzie King that provincial parties supported their federal cousins, and that the more he gave Liberal provincial governments, the better it was for the Liberal Opposition. The Liberal premiers were equally aware of the politics of it all, and federal-provincial conferences became more strained as more of the seats around the table were occupied by new Liberal premiers such as Pattullo and Ontario's Mitch Hepburn. It was also increasingly clear that the Conservatives were heading for defeat when their mandate expired in the summer of 1935.

By the autumn of 1934, several things had become clear. The early predictions that the Depression was a short-term phenomenon seemed like ancient history. The routine of saying that every year's federal grants to the provinces were a one-off adjustment had become meaningless. The federal government's position that it had no responsibility for relief had become a myth. The Depression was leading to the rise of extremist governments in Europe and to increasingly radical ideas in Canada and the emergence of strong socialist parties. Finally, it was clear that the provinces were not going to approve any amendment that transferred their responsibilities to Ottawa unless Ottawa made some equal gesture to strengthen provincial taxation powers.

Bennett's New Deal

In the late fall of 1934, an increasingly desperate Bennett made some fateful decisions. He concluded that he had done everything possible under the existing system, so the system itself had to be changed. Since the provinces would not agree to transfer responsibilities, he would simply seize those powers through legislation. He concluded that free enterprise was no longer working and that massive government interference in the free market was required—federal interference, of course. Typically, he kept his thinking largely to himself. On January 3, 1935, a surprised nation, including his own cabinet, heard Bennett announce the most sweeping changes to government, the economy, and federal-provincial relations that had ever been put forward. And this was to be implemented in spite of the views of provincial governments or the *BNA Act*.

Bennett's New Deal program contained eight important pieces of legislation. Three of them, known as *Hours of Work*, *Weekly Rest*, and *Minimum Wages*, were designed to create more jobs by reducing the amount of work done by those who had jobs. The *Insurance Act* would establish a federal UI scheme. The *Dominion Trade and Industry Commission Act* and the *National Products Marketing Act* were meant to control companies, and the *Farmers Creditors Arrangement Act* would assist agriculture. Finally, an amendment to the *Criminal Code* called the *Price Spreads Legislation* would prevent companies from gouging customers. All of these measures would allow Ottawa to regulate the economic activity of individuals and companies, effectively putting an end to free enterprise or laissez-faire economics, as well as provincial responsibility for these matters. None called for increasing spending or the money supply, the two policies that would have addressed the underlying causes of the Depression.

In the upcoming election, Bennett's challenge was to convince the public that he had discovered the right solutions and was best suited to implement them. That was a very difficult proposition, because he had argued for four and a half years that the Depression was a temporary emergency and that free enterprise worked in the long term. There were obvious constitutional issues, and the provincial governments of all political stripes were opposed to Bennett's deal. To many, Bennett's New Deal looked like an insincere act of desperation, and he could not shake the public's perception that he had failed. It was not for lack of effort, though. In 1930, Bennett had recognized the seriousness of the problem, had promised dramatic action, and had taken it. For four years, he had experimented with different types of relief and different arrangements with the provinces. None had worked, and in 1935, he proposed the most radical solutions ever seen in Canada.

Mackenzie King's Approach

Mackenzie King had not changed his views since 1929, namely that governments should balance their budgets through increased taxes and reduced spending. Keynesian economists would later say that these were the worst possible policies to follow. He had consistently criticized federal assistance to the provinces, and he was, in fact, far more conservative than Bennett. He made no promises to deal with the Depression because he did not have to. He said that the constitutionality of the New Deal legislation would have to be verified, but not what he would do if it was found to be within Ottawa's power. That was not a serious matter for the public, however, and constitutional experts had mixed views about the package of reforms. In the 1935 election, the Liberals actually lost popular support, but their 45 per cent of the vote was concentrated in the right constituencies and their representation in the Commons jumped to 173 of 245 seats, a solid majority that they hoped would outlast the Depression.

After the election, King vowed that there would be no more handouts to the western provinces. His first federal-provincial conference focused on the usual three issues: aid to the provinces, UI, and amending the constitution. The provinces wanted Ottawa to guarantee their loans so they could borrow at a much lower rate of interest. That would cost Ottawa nothing, but King demanded control over their spending and repeated Bennett's demand for the establishment of a loan council. That meant surrendering sovereignty to Ottawa, and the provinces refused. The provinces again asked Ottawa to withdraw from the field of direct taxes; it refused. The provinces demanded that Ottawa stop taxing mining companies since natural resources were provincial; it refused.

Politics intervened to temper King's tough approach. The Liberals owed their election in considerable measure to the support of Canada's six provincial Liberal governments, and King's cabinet colleagues said that those provinces had to be rewarded with larger federal grants. King was forced to increase funding to the provinces by 75 per cent. In return, all the provinces except BC, Alberta, and Ontario, agreed to co-operate with the proposed National Employment Commission, whose main purpose was to examine provincial expenditure. Once the political debt had apparently been paid, King went back to the pursuit of his policies by cutting the grants by 25 per cent. Now King had his Commission, and the provinces saw their grants shrink—they had been betrayed. Needless to say, Liberal Ottawa's honeymoon with the Liberal provinces was very short-lived, and the relationship was soon as strained if not more so than Bennett's had been.

King referred Bennett's New Deal legislation to the Canadian Supreme Court. The federal side was headed by the brilliant lawyer and future prime minister Louis St. Laurent, while the provinces sent their attorneys general and deputy ministers. The Court divided 3–3 on the three labour acts, *Minimum Wages*, *Hours of Work*, and *Weekly Rest*. The *Dominion Trade and Industrial Commerce Act* was declared unconstitutional by a 6–0 vote on the grounds that it affected property. St. Laurent argued that there was an emergency, and the *Insurance Act* was therefore federal under the peace, order, and good government clause. In a 4–2 decision, the Court said that if there was an emergency, then the legislation had to be limited to the emergency and not be a permanent transfer of power.

The Supreme Court rejected the federal argument that since it could collect money by any means, it could spend it on anything it chose, the so-called spending power. The Court said that Ottawa could not use the power of spending money to "indirectly accomplish" its goals. Otherwise it "would be permitted to invade almost any field exclusively reserved . . . to the legislatures in each province . . ." It rejected the argument that since the insurance premiums would be compulsory, they were a form of taxation for which Ottawa had unlimited power, and it upheld previous decisions that insurance was a form of property. The *National Products Marketing Act* was rejected on the grounds that trade and commerce did not trump provincial responsibilities and that commercial transactions were provincial. Finally, the court upheld two acts, the *Price Spreads Legislation Act* and the *Farm Credit Act*, as matters of banking, which was federal. The decisions were appealed to the JCPC in London, which upheld five of the Canadian court's decisions. While the Canadian Supreme Court had divided 3–3 on the three labour acts, the JCPC declared all three beyond federal power.

The JCPC's reasoning applied to a number of the underlying issues. Regarding federal spending power, it said that while Ottawa could collect funds by any method, "it by no means follows that any legislation which disposes of it is necessarily within Dominion competence." It supported the Supreme Court's argument that the peace, order, and good government clause did not give Ottawa the right to legislate on labour matters. Ottawa had also argued that it had the right to sign international treaties and then, under Section 132, apply them to the provinces. The JCPC rejected that argument, ruling that Section 132 applied to laws signed by the British government, not by Canada. That meant that Ottawa could only enter international agreements on matters within provincial jurisdiction if the provinces agreed. Lord Aikens summed up the decisions in a phrase that would become a famous definition of federalism. He said that while there had been evolution, the federal ". . . ship of state . . . still retains watertight compartments which are an essential part of her original structure . . ."

The New Deal legislation included some of the most important federal-provincial cases ever to go before the courts. The courts did not say that the constitution prevented Canadian governments from implementing the elements in the New Deal. They only said that six of the acts were in provincial jurisdiction and so the federal government could not implement them. There was nothing preventing provincial governments from passing such legislation if that was what they and their electorates wanted. It was not, therefore, the courts or the constitution that prevented politicians from taking action to end the Depression. The simple fact was that the provinces lacked the financial means to deal with the problem, and the federal government was unwilling to spend the money required. That was a political decision, not the effect of any constitutional restraint on its ability to deal with the problems. Ottawa had the main responsibility for agriculture, but it was Alberta's Premier William Aberhart and Quebec's Premier Maurice Duplessis who took the lead in protecting farmers from foreclosures on their mortgages. Ottawa could have built a trans-continental highway, just as it had built the CPR fifty years earlier. Finances were not a serious restraint either—a few years after the Depression, Ottawa increased its spending by 600 per cent.

Continued Stalemate

Instead of increasing spending on matters that were within its constitutional rights, Mackenzie King began cutting back on federal grants. Alberta did not have sufficient revenue to pay the interest on its bonds, but King refused to make another loan unless Alberta accepted supervision of its finances. Alberta then unilaterally reduced the interest rate on some bonds, in effect, defaulting on them. Saskatchewan was nearing a deadline on its bonds and could not pay the interest on them. If a second province defaulted, Canada's credit rating would be even more seriously harmed. Mackenzie King's strategy of toughing it out with the provinces had failed just as Bennett's had failed—King had no choice but to loan more money to the near-bankrupt provinces to protect Canada's credit rating.

Since 1930, the federal government had believed that some provinces and municipalities were wasting money, a belief held mainly by the rich and those with jobs. Mackenzie King shared that belief, and he established the National Employment Commission, or NEC, in 1936 to identify abuse and recommend better ways for dealing with unemployment. That Commission failed to find much evidence of abuse, but it did acquire real knowledge about the level of distress. As a result, its sympathies began to shift from a belief in the policies and attitudes of the federal government towards an understanding of the hopeless situation so many people were facing. Another of King's responses has received far more attention from academics, and that was the establishment of a Royal Commission to investigate the relationship between the finances and responsibilities of the two orders of government and to recommend changes to the constitution to address the imbalance. It was known after its chairmen as the Rowell-Sirois Commission. Although its mandate was to deal with the Depression, there was good reason to believe that King's real goal was to create an excuse to avoid action until the global economy rebounded. Evidence supporting that interpretation included the fact that a commission was first suggested in 1935, was only established in 1937, and did not report until 1940.

The mandate was also not quite as balanced as it appeared. Its real purpose was to study the imbalance within provincial finances and responsibilities. That imbalance had been known since 1864 and had gradually worsened, in part because of federal policies. The solutions were well known too. Either provincial responsibilities had to be transferred to Ottawa or some of Ottawa's taxing power had to be transferred to the provinces. Since this was a federally appointed commission, there was little doubt that it was expected to recommend the transfer of provincial responsibilities to Ottawa. The Commission received strong support from the poorest provinces and from Canada's left-wing and nationalist English-speaking elites, all of whom wanted a stronger federal government and more federal spending. The only source for any such transfers was the richer provinces of Ontario, Quebec, and BC, whose governments naturally saw the Commission as a threat. Playing rich and poor provinces against each other was the politics of divide and conquer, a good divisionary tactic for Ottawa, which could put the blame for inaction on the inevitable inability of the provinces to reach agreement. It offered no help dealing with the Depression.

Ontario's new Liberal Premier Mitch Hepburn became one of the Commission's most bitter enemies. BC's Premier Pattullo had no interest in participating in an academic exercise that might challenge his province's autonomy. Alberta's new Social Credit Premier William Aberhart was already at war with Ottawa over a number of issues, and he refused to meet the Commission. Premier Duplessis of Quebec argued that the federal government had no right to appoint a commission to study provincial finances. In Quebec City, Duplessis hosted the commissioners at a dinner at the Chateau Frontenac. He got quite drunk and began throwing wine glasses at the chandelier; one frightened federal civil servant considered himself lucky to have escaped down a staircase.

Hepburn made his position clear at his first meeting with the Commission in May. He said that federalism should be discussed by politicians, not a commission, and complained that prior to its appointment, Ottawa had consulted the western provinces, but not Ontario. Ontario would have to pay 50 per cent of any increased federal assistance, and any change would be towards increasing federal powers, which Ontario would never accept. He asserted that Canada was heading towards dictatorship. Instead of centralizing power, Ottawa should withdraw from the field of direct taxes, which it had entered as an emergency measure and then continued to exercise, contrary to the spirit of Confederation.

The detailed Ontario brief said that the problem was financial, not constitutional, and the federal subsidy to Ontario had fallen from 60 per cent of Ontario's revenue in 1867 to 3 per cent in 1937. Ottawa had also started taxing the mining and forestry industries that the constitution assigned to the province. The very idea of a federal role was questioned, as Hepburn pointed out that there were wide differences of opinion in Canada regarding state involvement in the economy and that the issue should therefore be left to each province. The Rowell-Sirois Commission thus had no hope of producing recommendations that would be acceptable to the four largest provinces, and the constitution could not be changed without their agreement.

Alberta's Social Credit Legislation

In the meantime, one provincial government had decided that there were solutions to the Great Depression, and that it would implement them unilaterally. That was the Albertan Social Credit government of William Aberhart. Social Credit was one of the most curious political phenomena in Canadian history and Aberhart one of the most interesting personalities. He was a very successful high school principal in Calgary and an even more successful radio evangelist. One evening in 1932, he read an account of the social credit theories of William Douglas and decided that they contained the answer to the Depression.

Neither Douglas nor Aberhart were ever able to explain very clearly what Social Credit was, but the basic idea was neither profound nor new. It was, quite simply, that depressions or recessions occurred when the amount of money in circulation was not sufficient to enable people to purchase the amount of goods that had recently been produced. As a result of the gap, goods went unsold, stores cut back their orders, factories laid off workers, the unemployed had less to spend, stores cut back their orders even more, factories laid off even more workers, and the vicious circle continued. That was actually quite an accurate analysis of what had happened in Canada since 1929 as the private banks had restricted the money supply, which reduced demand for goods and services, which then led to more unemployment.

The solution to this situation, according to the theory, was for governments to put money into the hands of consumers so they could purchase the goods that were sitting in the stores. The stores would send new orders and re-hire the unemployed workers to produce more. These workers would spend their new paycheques, stores would send more orders to refill their shelves, and the vicious circle would be broken. All this activity could be taxed to pay back the government's initial infusion of credit, and it would not therefore lead to inflation. This was a variation of theories of "soft money" that had circulated in the United States and western Canada for decades. So the main tenet of Social Credit was to increase the money supply, something either banks or governments could do if they wished. The theory had history on its side, as increases in the money supply in the past had ended depressions, the most famous example being the discovery of gold in South Africa in 1896, which ushered in the prosperous years before the First World War. There were no similar discoveries of gold or silver on the horizon, but banknotes were the other form of currency and nothing prevented governments or banks from issuing them.

With a new offer of hope, Aberhart led his new Social Credit party to a resounding victory in 1935. His government took a number of positive steps, but it had no idea how to implement its economic policy, partly because issuing currency was a federal responsibility. Time passed, and in 1937 a backbench revolt forced the government to act. It then passed a number of bills to regulate banking and currency. These were clearly federal matters, and Ottawa used its power of disallowance to overturn some of the legislation while the Supreme Court declared the rest to be beyond provincial power. The rejection of both the provincial Social Credit legislation and the federal New Deal represent one of the great paradoxes of Canadian history and perhaps the great tragedy of the Depression. The courts did not say that Canada could not have these laws, only that the federal government could not implement the New Deal legislation because those issues were provincial, and Alberta could not implement the Social Credit legislation because those issues were federal. The problem was not in the laws, but in the fact that it was the wrong government that was trying to pass them.

Interestingly, while Ottawa was vetoing the Albertan legislation, officials in the Bank of Canada and the Department of Finance were looking at ways to increase the money supply. Mackenzie King was far too conservative to accept such advice, but the outbreak of the Second World War changed his view. In the autumn of 1939, Ottawa issued hundreds of millions of dollars' worth of contracts for war material, recruitment, and other wartime needs. A small portion of the money came from credits created for the Department of Finance by the Bank of Canada. Since then, Ottawa has "created" credit when it felt that the economy required stimulus. There was, in fact, no financial or constitutional constraint preventing Ottawa from increasing the money supply during the Depression; the problem was conservative political attitudes.

Creating credit was one way of dealing with the causes of the Depression; massive spending on public works was the other. By the late 1930s, a serious gulf had opened up between three provinces and Ottawa on the issue of borrowing money specifically to create jobs. As early as 1933, BC's Premier Pattullo had advocated a massive program of public works to stimulate the economy. After his election in 1934, Ontario's Premier Hepburn began to urge the same policy. In 1936, Quebec's new Premier Duplessis began massive borrowing to spend on infrastructure, rural electrification, and loans to farmers so they could avoid defaulting on their mortgages. Years later, economists would be almost unanimous in saying that these were the correct solutions to the Depression, namely deficit spending to stimulate economic activity and increasing the money supply by having the Bank of Canada create credit.

Although the crisis dragged on into its seventh and eighth years, Mackenzie King's thinking had still not evolved since 1929, and he continued to believe that the solution lay in governments balancing their budgets. He was, however, increasingly under pressure from three different groups within Ottawa. One was his own cabinet, where more and more ministers came to agree with Minister of Labour Norman Rogers, who believed the government should be spending far more money. In the civil service, the governor of the Bank of Canada, Graham Towers, and Deputy Minister of Finance William Clark were coming to the same conclusion. A third source of pressure came as a surprise to King, indeed, as a shock. In May 1936, the government had set up the NEC with the mandate of searching out waste in provincial welfare programs and making recommendations to lower unemployment. It had failed in its first task because there was not much waste, but it did recommend a way to deal with unemployment, namely, a sharp increase in federal spending. On December 20, Arthur Purvis, the Chair of the Commission, recommended that Ottawa assume total financial and administrative responsibility for aid to the unemployed.

King was enraged when he heard the proposal. He was even more horrified when he discovered that Labour Minister Rogers had known for two months that these recommendations were coming. The prime minister regarded as treasonous the fact that his minister had not kept him informed of the Commission's thinking. King also found out that

143

Deputy Finance Minister Clark had agreed with the recommendation and was drafting a budget to increase spending on relief. After a stormy cabinet debate, the Commission was ordered to change its recommendation to suit King's views. It made modifications but would not change the basic thrust. King then did what he was best at, namely procrastinating, this time with the excuse that the Rowell-Sirois Commission had not yet reported. The political crisis passed; the crisis for those on welfare remained unchanged.

At the beginning of 1938, King was still determined to balance the budget, which would require cutting spending by $70 million. That was difficult politically, as the number of persons on relief increased from eight hundred thousand in October to one million in March. Finance Minister Dunning planned to introduce a balanced budget, but Rogers argued that $75 million should be borrowed and spent on public works. King and Dunning were appalled and the finance minister threatened to resign. Then Rogers threatened to resign. King, ever the superb politician and compromiser, cut the difference roughly in half and had Cabinet agree to spending $40 million on housing, roads, tourism, and manpower training. This looked like Canada's first Keynesian budget, but Dunning rejected Keynes when he introduced the budget. Ottawa had not adopted Keynesian economics, and the small budget deficit did not end the Depression. The Depression ended as a result of the outbreak of the Second World War in September 1939. Ottawa saw that challenge as justification for a massive increase in spending on the military—just as BC's Premier Pattullo had predicted seven years earlier.

PART III
Post-War Federalism

CHAPTER 9
The Second World War and After, 1939-1948

The Second World War had a more profound and long-lasting effect on Canadian federalism than the Great War. With the exception of Premier Duplessis in Quebec, the provinces enthusiastically supported the war effort and, as in the First World War, provincial politicians came to Ottawa to help. Parliament passed a *War Measures Act*, effectively suspending the constitution and giving the federal government all the power it needed to manage the economy, produce the needed war material, and control the population. The provinces were left with whatever Ottawa chose to let them administer, and Canada became a de facto unitary state for the duration of the war plus one year. Under that *Act*, over six thousand Orders-in-Council were issued, decrees that had the force of law. They were issued by a civil service that ballooned from forty thousand to more than 120,000 employees. Unity proved short-term, however, and Mackenzie King soon faced crises with Quebec, which believed the government would abuse its enormous power, and with Ontario, which believed Ottawa would not do enough with that power.

Before those political battles opened, Finance Minister James Ilsley brought down an emergency budget to launch the war effort. Federal spending would jump over 300 per cent, from around $600 million in 1938–39 to over $2 billion in 1939–40. It was financed by huge tax increases, massive borrowing, and the creation of money by the Bank of Canada. Ilsley explained the new policy of creating credit: "We can create additional supplies of money and use it to purchase what we need . . . Instead of taking money in the form of taxes or loans, we can put our new money into competition with . . . old money . . ." That was what Alberta's Social Credit regime had tried to do, the laws that Ottawa and the Supreme Court had vetoed. Ilsley financed the war mainly by taxation, but the credit that was created was twenty-five times as much as Ottawa loaned or gave to the provinces during the Depression and was spent in half the time.

Quebec and Ontario Challenge Ottawa's Wartime Policy

Quebec's Premier Duplessis soon found reason to be concerned with a wartime government in Ottawa. Quebec had been borrowing heavily on the New York market, but under the *War Measures Act* Ottawa vetoed Quebec's next bond issue, a clear indication that Ottawa now controlled the economy. Duplessis had fought a number of battles with Ottawa, and he believed that Ottawa would try to use the war to make a permanent shift in the balance of power in its own favour. To protect Quebec's interests as he understood them, he called an election for October 25, 1939. A new mandate would clearly threaten the war effort, and Ottawa could not allow the election of a provincial party on an anti-Ottawa and anti-war platform. Federal Minister of Justice Ernest Lapointe and three other ministers threatened that, if Quebec re-elected the Union National government, they would resign, leaving the province with no representation in the federal cabinet. And they promised that if Quebec elected a provincial Liberal government, the federal Liberals would not introduce conscription. With that intervention, plus ample federal funds, Adélard Godbout was elected and Ottawa's Quebec flank was secure.

By 1942, it appeared that conscription might be necessary to maintain the military effort. King was saddled, however, with the promise to Quebec not to introduce it and with the promise of his Quebec ministers to resign if he did. His solution was typical of the political genius that made him Canada's longest-serving prime minister. He decided to hold a national referendum on the question of releasing his government from its promise, though the promise had been made to Quebec, not to Canada. Predictably the referendum was approved by 64 per cent of Canadians, while in Quebec it was rejected by 72 per cent. One of the Quebec ministers, P.J.A. Cardin, resigned as promised; the others accepted King's reinterpretation of their promises and did not. Duplessis had argued that Quebec could not trust Ottawa, and the referendum proved him right. That helped him gain re-election in 1944, but during the war all was quiet on the Ottawa-Quebec front.

Ontario threw itself solidly into the wartime effort but in the opinion of Premier Hepburn and many others, Ottawa did not demonstrate a similar degree of enthusiasm. On December 18, Hepburn introduced a motion criticizing Ottawa's commitment to the war. A federal election was due in 1940, and King used Hepburn's challenge to call it immediately, with the main issue being his government's competence to fight the war. The federal Liberals were returned with a strong majority, and Canada was politically, financially, and constitutionally ready for the major war effort that would follow.

On July 10, 1940, one of Ottawa's favourite goals from the Depression years was realized. Alberta, New Brunswick, and Quebec dropped their opposition to federal control of unemployment insurance, and King obtained unanimous agreement for an amendment to the *BNA Act*, making UI a federal responsibility. This made no difference to unemployment as wartime demand was now resulting in labour shortages, but it would be useful in any future recessions. Significantly, this was the first amendment that affected the most important part of the constitution, the division of federal and provincial responsibilities.

Agreement on Financing the War, Disagreement on Changing Federalism

Everyone understood that Ottawa needed more money to fight the war. At a conference in the summer of 1941, Ottawa offered the provinces tax agreements by which Ottawa would collect all personal and corporate income taxes until one year after the end of the war. In return, Ottawa would provide payments to compensate the provinces for their losses. These agreements worked extremely well, and federal revenue rose steadily from around $600 million to $2.2 billion. By comparison, between 1939 and 1945, provincial revenue and expenses remained almost static at around $150 million annually. All the provinces accepted that the war was the top priority, and there was relative calm in federal-provincial relations from 1941 to 1945.

In January 1940, King received the report that the Rowell-Sirois Commission had been labouring over for four long years. It recommended that the federal government collect all taxes and return a fixed amount to the provinces without conditions so that they could maintain a national minimum of standards in social welfare. It also recommended equalization payments so that the poorest six provinces could provide services similar to those of the richest provinces. Co-chair Joseph Sirois disagreed with the recommendations but was persuaded to sign the report. Ottawa did not accept the idea of unconditional grants to the provinces, and adopting the report would require amending the constitution, a course King did not want to pursue. The report was clearly no longer urgent, but King called a conference for January 14, 1941, to consider it.

Manitoba, Saskatchewan, Nova Scotia, and PEI were in favour of the recommendations. Alberta and BC were opposed, and Ontario's Hepburn was predictably furious since he had strongly disagreed with the very idea of a federal study of provincial matters. He saw the report and the conference as an attempt by Ottawa to use wartime nationalism and patriotic fervour as levers to effect a permanent transfer of provincial power to Ottawa. Mackenzie King said they needed to settle the issues raised in the report in order to fight the war; Hepburn pointed out that the report addressed the Depression, which was over. King said that the changes did not endanger provincial autonomy; Hepburn said that they did. Hepburn also pointed out that the *War Measures Act* gave Ottawa all the power it needed to prosecute the war. Finance Minister Ilsley repeated King's argument that the changes would not affect provincial autonomy, an argument Hepburn called "ridiculous." The conference was a failure but did little lasting damage to political relationships.

The Welfare State: Federal or Provincial Responsibility?

Shortly after the war began, some rather optimistic and far-sighted civil servants and ministers began planning for the adjustments that would be required after the war. They did not want a repeat of the chaos, unemployment, strikes, riots, and recession that had followed the First World War. A core of highly trained and ambitious bureaucrats was assembled, centered on graduates from Queen's University who had studied the theories of John Maynard Keynes. Those theories, called Keynesian economics, postulated that during boom times, government should collect more money than it spent in order to take some of the pressure off inflation. Then, when the economy slowed, government would spend more than it collected to stimulate spending, production, and employment. The civil servants concluded that after the war, Ottawa should launch a comprehensive program of spending on health and welfare to maintain a minimal level of economic activity and avoid a recession. There was nothing new in the concept of the welfare state, and European governments had begun crafting them in the 1880s. What was new in the thinking in Ottawa was the idea that the federal government should implement welfare, rather than the provinces who had constitutional responsibility for it. The civil servants did not seem to appreciate that the Fathers of Confederation had given "exclusive" control of health, welfare, and education to the provinces for good reasons, and those reasons had not changed.

In fact, the differences between English and French Canadians had widened since Confederation. In 1864, neither group wanted welfare managed by any government. By the 1940s, however, many English-speaking Canadians wanted their governments to be heavily involved in providing welfare services, especially the federal government. In Quebec, on the other hand, the vast majority still wanted welfare to be provided by the Church they trusted, rather than their provincial government or especially by the English-dominated government in Ottawa. French-Catholic views of the objectivity of the federal government were also affected by the fact that they did not hold one of the important economic portfolios or one of the top twenty positions in the civil service, and the priorities Ottawa identified were not those of most French Canadians.

Since the provinces were all developing their welfare systems to suit their own circumstances, there was in fact no need for federal involvement. The argument of the civil servants was that federal action was required in order to establish minimum levels of welfare, to establish "national standards" of service, and to implement Keynesian economics. All three arguments were flawed. There was always a minimum level for any program, namely that of the poorest one. The argument that standards had to be the same across Canada ignored the fact that circumstances were different in every province, and Canada had a federal constitution because of those differences. In a country overwhelmingly English-speaking, "national standards" also meant English-Protestant standards. And Keynesian anti-cyclical economics could not be implemented by fixed welfare payments, because such payments could not be adjusted to reflect periods of boom or bust.

In late 1942, the left-leaning economist Leonard Marsh was directed to draft a study on a federal welfare state. His report hit the cabinet with a thud on March 15, 1943. He argued that the federal government should have a major role in ensuring that people were healthy, educated, and employed. The proposed programs included health insurance, enhanced UI, workman's compensation, family allowances, and public works. The estimated cost was $900 million, almost twice the annual federal budgets of the 1930s. King sensed the political dangers of proceeding with the proposals as did some of his most powerful ministers, including Ilsley, T.A. Crerar, and C.D. Howe. However, the new left-wing party that had emerged during the depression, the Co-operative Commonwealth Federation, or CCF, had strongly endorsed the concept of a federal welfare state, and its popularity was surging. In 1942, the federal Conservatives adopted the welfare state and added the adjective "Progressive" to their name. That same year, the Ontario Conservatives adopted a similar program, which was key to their victory over Hepburn's Liberals in 1943.

Mackenzie King was not one to ignore such omens, and he was infinitely flexible in terms of principles and policies. His cabinet reversed itself and promised the welfare state in the January 1944 Speech from the Throne. It would deliver a national minimum of social security, full employment, broadened unemployment insurance, contributory old age pensions, insurance against accidents and sickness, and assistance for families and housing. Canada was now officially heading for a federally dominated welfare state and its political sequel—fierce and continuous battles between Ottawa and the provinces.

Although most of the programs of the new welfare state would be within provincial jurisdiction, Ottawa did not wait for discussions with the provinces to launch them. One of the first building blocks for the system was the family allowance, popularly known as the baby bonus. The payments would be $8 per month per child under sixteen for the first four children and $5 for additional children, a very large amount for a poor family. The estimated cost was $250 million annually, 50 per cent of Ottawa's entire pre-war budgets. King's Quebec lieutenant, Louis St. Laurent, argued that it did not violate the constitution because Ottawa could give money to any individual. This was the "spending power" argument that the courts had struck down with their rejection of the Bennett New Deal. It also reversed the position Mackenzie King had taken on the *1927 Pension Act*, when he stated that a welfare program financed entirely by Ottawa required a constitutional amendment, the policy he had followed with UI in 1940. Duplessis had been right to argue that Ottawa would take advantage of the war to permanently increase its power at the expense of the provinces.

St. Laurent also said that Ottawa was responsible for general economic activity and had a moral duty to do more for people. The *BNA Act* assigned no such responsibility to Ottawa, and by St. Laurent's interpretation, Ottawa could launch programs in almost any provincial field of jurisdiction. That statement and the defence of the spending power were, in fact, denials of federalism as a form of government. In Parliament, the Conservative Opposition challenged the constitutionality of the program and pointed out that it was seemingly aimed at voters in Quebec and the upcoming election. But the baby bonus was literally a motherhood issue, and the bill passed by a vote of 139–0.

Ontario's Premier George Drew was outraged. Ottawa's action was clearly an invasion of provincial jurisdiction, and Ontario was still the main defender of provincial rights. In 1942, his party had adopted a comprehensive and coherent program covering the entire span of welfare issues and had begun to implement it after winning the 1943 election. Ad hoc federal programs like this one threatened to weaken Ontario's capacity to set priorities and manage the overall issue of welfare. The main factor slowing the implementation of Ontario's programs was financial constraints that reflected the 1942 wartime tax agreements, which Ontario had accepted so Canada could fight the war properly. Now, with the war still raging and Ontario's revenue frozen, Ottawa was diverting a substantial portion of its revenue into provincial matters. The Ontario Conservatives were fully aware of how political King's action was. A majority of his MPs came from Quebec and their re-election was crucial to King's. Quebec had a higher birth rate than Ontario, and the new program would transfer money from Protestant Ontario to Catholic Quebec.

A year later, the government was still elaborating its overall plan to establish the welfare state. In February 1945, the plan went before cabinet, where it received a mixed reception. Some ministers such as Crerar were still strongly opposed and said it would lead to serious problems with the provinces. St. Laurent somewhat disingenuously and incorrectly replied that any proposal for federal action would meet the objections of Duplessis, who had just been re-elected with a large majority. A divided cabinet decided to proceed, no one being quite sure where Mackenzie King stood, possibly including himself. The federal government finally had a clear and unified set of policies covering taxation, spending, economic growth, the government's role, politics, and the means to avoid constitutional restraints. It would make some reductions to taxes and the debt, but it would maintain tax rates far above what was necessary to cover its own responsibilities.

Ottawa certainly did not plan to reduce its level of taxation sufficiently to allow provinces to raise theirs. Maintaining the tax rates would perpetuate the inability of the provinces to provide sufficient welfare and justify the continued federal role. It would also perpetuate the degree to which power had shifted in Ottawa's favour during the war. One crucial element in this integrated plan was the retention of the wartime tax agreements, with complete federal control over the collection of personal and corporate income taxes and succession duties. By 1945, Ottawa was collecting 85 per cent of total federal and provincial tax revenue. Whether clothed in the rhetoric of welfare, the good of the people, or the need for national standards, the real issue was power.

On April 12, 1945, C.D. Howe presented the House of Commons with a white paper on welfare. Accordingly, Ottawa would take responsibility for maintaining a "high level" of employment and a good standard of living, to be achieved by increased support for health and welfare, transportation, natural resources, housing, public works, rural credit, increased coverage for UI, and maintaining minimum prices for agricultural products and fish. Four days later, Mackenzie King called an election for June 11. The

Progressive Conservatives and the CCF had endorsed programs as comprehensive as that of the Liberals, so the public's choice was which party they trusted to introduce the federal welfare state. The Liberals entered the fray having demonstrated that they could control the economy, keep the country united, produce an enormous military arsenal, avoid inflation, and manage problems with the provinces. In spite of this record, the baby bonus, the platform, and all the advantages of incumbency, Mackenzie King's Liberals received only 40 per cent of the vote. It was, however, concentrated in the constituencies that mattered and translated into a slim majority of 125 out of 245 seats in the House of Commons.

The 1945 Conference on Taxes and Welfare

With his renewed mandate, Mackenzie King's government proceeded with what was essentially the bureaucracy's vision of a modern welfare state as endorsed by its Liberal masters in their desperation to win the election of 1945. No one seriously questioned that the issues were under provincial jurisdiction, and a federal-provincial conference was called for August 6, 1945. It was the first heads of government conference since the disastrous one of 1941. The nine premiers were presented with Ottawa's plans for the welfare state and with the request that the temporary wartime tax agreements be made permanent. A number of the programs would be shared-cost ones, in which the provinces paid a portion while Ottawa determined all the conditions. Overall, these programs would represent a massive transfer of power from the provinces to Ottawa. Regarding the constitutional issue, the senior civil service and cabinet seemed to have concluded that amending the constitution was too difficult and indeed unnecessary. Ottawa had unilaterally changed it with pensions in 1927 and the baby bonus in 1944, and the thinking in 1945 was that the new federal welfare schemes could be implemented unilaterally or through federal-provincial agreements. If so, that was a terrible, indeed inexplicable, reading of the Canadian political scene, because Ontario, Quebec, Alberta, and Nova Scotia were strongly opposed to federal programs for welfare.

For the taxation agreements, Ottawa offered a grant of $12 per capita, which would produce a minimum of $138 million annually for the next three years. All the premiers said that was inadequate. The federal offer would have made it difficult, if not impossible, for the provinces to have adequate programs in almost any field, and the shared-cost programs would have given Ottawa a large degree of control over provincial spending priorities. Drew, Duplessis, and Alberta's new premier, Ernest Manning, rejected the welfare proposals out of hand. Duplessis did not believe that a province could be autonomous if the federal government was collecting taxes on its behalf. He believed Ottawa would use such a system as leverage on his government, and he was determined not to renew Quebec's tax agreement. BC was not opposed to Ottawa's welfare plan, but rejected the financial arrangements.

One of Mackenzie King's strongest critics was a fellow Liberal, Nova Scotia Premier Angus L. Macdonald. He had joined the wartime cabinet and returned to Halifax with a deep hatred for Mackenzie King, a strong mistrust for his actions and words, and a good understanding of his tactics. He told the meeting that the proposals would destroy provincial autonomy and independence. Macdonald joined Duplessis, Drew, Manning, and BC Premier John Hart, which meant Ottawa now faced opposition from the powerful premiers of all five of Canada's regions. On the last day of the conference, St. Laurent pleaded with Ontario and Quebec and made the dubious argument that Ottawa needed more taxes because of the war. Drew and Duplessis walked out of the meeting.

The most enthusiastic provincial support came from Premier Tommy Douglas and the new CCF government of Saskatchewan. After the conference failed, Saskatchewan developed a welfare state that was as good as the one Ottawa had designed. Ontario proceeded with the one the Conservatives had outlined in 1942. Other English-speaking provinces followed suit, providing all the provinces with tailor-made welfare systems to suit their circumstances. Until 1960, French Canadians would continue to trust their Church more than their government, and their welfare system remained fundamentally different from those in the rest of Canada.

The conference was thus a failure, if not a fiasco. That may well have been King's objective, because it then appeared that Ottawa wanted to respond to popular demand but the provinces had prevented it from doing so. The only positive thing to emerge from the conference was agreement that officials would meet to discuss the issues over coming months, and the first ministers would continue the meeting the following year. Interestingly, the failure of the conference had no apparent effect on Canada's adjustment to post-war realities. The recession Ottawa feared never materialized, a major miscalculation for a group who had managed the war so superbly.

As the April 1946 meeting approached, Finance Minister Ilsley seemed desperate to have the provinces sign new taxation agreements so he increased the federal offer from $12 per capita to $15, a jump of 25 per cent. All the provinces except Ontario and Quebec signed agreements covering the period 1947–1952. The federal grants were greater than what those taxes would have yielded if collected by the provinces themselves, which meant that Ottawa was losing money. That called into question the argument that the agreements were necessary to help Ottawa finance the welfare state. Ontario and Quebec were also losing money, but they were in stronger financial positions than other provinces. Ottawa announced that it was leaving "tax room" for the provinces that did not join. Accordingly, federal taxpayers in Ontario and Quebec could be given a credit of 5 per cent of their personal or corporate taxes if the two provinces decided to collect that amount themselves, a process that would not affect the amount taxpayers paid. Neither province took advantage of the opportunity.

Ottawa made little attempt to actually follow Keynesian economics after the war while some provinces such as Quebec did, and both Ottawa and the provinces continued to develop the welfare state. Ottawa's two main arguments for maintaining control of direct taxation—to implement the welfare state and manage the economy—proved to be highly questionable. The remaining argument was that Ottawa wanted power and control. That, of course, was precisely why Duplessis refused to countenance the scheme. Ottawa's plans for the welfare state were also based on the assumption that there would be no more wars. In 1949, Canada was at war again, defence spending mounted quickly, and Prime Minister St. Laurent admitted that Canada could not have afforded both the welfare state and the Korean war.

On November 15, 1948, St. Laurent replaced Mackenzie King as prime minister. In his address to the nation that day, he promised a "national standard of social security and equality of opportunity . . ." Ontario Premier Drew had become leader of the federal Opposition, and he said that his main priority was federal-provincial relations and attacked the government for amassing power. By then, however, Ottawa had succeeded in setting a new course for federal-provincial relations. The era of shared-cost programs had definitely arrived. Federal involvement in provincial areas of jurisdiction would grow exponentially, increasingly blurring the "watertight" compartments of responsibility outlined in the *BNA Act* and confirmed by the courts in 1937. The 1950s would see the adoption of dozens of such programs with substantial federal involvement in welfare, then health, then education, and then local government and local economies. That, in turn, would lead to blow-back from the provinces, led this time by Quebec.

Newfoundland Becomes a Province

One of the greatest achievements of this period was the admission of Newfoundland into Confederation, the completion of the process begun in 1864. In the early 1930s, Newfoundland had gone bankrupt, and its government was replaced by a British-appointed Commission that was to govern until the colony was self-supporting again. The war produced prosperity, and the conditions were met for restoring democratic government. That became complicated because the Second World War convinced both Ottawa and London that Newfoundland should become a Canadian province. The war highlighted Newfoundland's strategic importance, and Canada's large investment in military facilities gave it a stake in the colony's future. There was also concern that the colony might remain heavily under Washington's influence, a sort of east-coast Alaska. In 1943, the British government began examining options other than the restoration of democratic government, even though it was advised that any other course would be illegal and unconstitutional.

In July 1943, Ottawa let London know that it was interested in having Newfoundland as the tenth province. Secret negotiations began between Ottawa and London, which meant that the people of Newfoundland were not aware of the most important developments affecting their future. There were almost no indications that Newfoundlanders wanted to join Canada. If democratic government was restored, the new assembly might decide that Newfoundland should remain a self-governing colony or it might demand tough terms for joining Confederation. It was better, therefore, for London and Ottawa to steer the colony into Confederation before democratic government was restored.

Instead of announcing elections for a new assembly, Britain said that Newfoundlanders would elect a National Convention to recommend options for governance, options which would be put to the people in a referendum. It was unclear why a Convention was needed since there were only two options in terms of governance, continue with Commission government or restore democratic government. There were, however, three options in terms of future status, namely to remain a colony, become a province of Canada, or become an independent country. On June 21, forty-five delegates began the National Convention. Many of them said that there were only two options for governance. Some of them were open to the idea of Confederation, but only if democracy was restored first so that a new elected government could negotiate a deal and a new assembly could ratify or reject it.

The Convention met from September 1946 to January 1948. The governing Commission would not allow its records to be examined, so the option of its continued governance could not be properly debated. The Confederation option concerning status was debated at length, and the debates were broadcast on the radio. The minority who favoured Confederation dominated the debate, as Joey Smallwood talked endlessly of the riches that would flow from Ottawa should Newfoundland become a Canadian province. He proposed that a delegation be sent to Ottawa to examine the possibility of Confederation, but the motion was defeated 25–17. A motion was then passed to send delegations to both London and Ottawa. In London, they were made to wait, received coldly, and offered no encouragement—a sad reception given Newfoundland's outstanding contribution to Britain's recent war effort. In Ottawa, the delegation was warmly greeted at an official dinner with Prime Minister Mackenzie King and several cabinet ministers and senior officials.

On October 19, Ottawa sent the governor its proposed terms for joining Canada, and they were debated in the Convention from November 6, 1947, to January 15, 1948. On January 23, Smallwood introduced a motion to include the Confederation option on the referendum ballot. It was defeated by a vote of 29–16, so the referendum ballot would offer only the two options for governance: the continuation of Commission government or the restoration of democratic government. That was not the outcome London wanted, so it simply added the one that it did, the one the Convention had just decisively rejected: Confederation. Britain thus overruled the decision of the democratically elected delegates who had spent a year and a half fulfilling their mandate. The wording on the ballot was slanted to help obtain the desired outcome. Option One was a continuation of "Commission of Government for a further period of five years," a choice with an uncertain future. Option Two was "Government as it existed in 1933," but the reference to 1933 was negative as that was the year the old government had collapsed. The third option was "Confederation with Canada." London and Ottawa were probably pleased if voters found it confusing that two of the options were about governance and one was about status.

The advocates of restoring democracy were furious. Newfoundland had now been betrayed twice, first when London established the Convention instead of restoring democracy and now when the options identified by the Convention were altered to include Confederation. The pro-Confederation champions had most of the advantages in the referendum campaign— better leadership, unity, and organization. They promised pensions, family allowances, UI, social benefits, and transfer payments, all to be paid for by Canadian taxpayers. Their opponents could promise little or nothing, certainly not support from London. The anti-confederates were divided between those wanting democracy and continued colonial status and those open to Confederation after the restoration of democracy. Smallwood portrayed the anti-confederates as lackeys of the rich merchants, but it was the Smallwood campaign that was well financed. Much of that money came, apparently, from Canadian companies with ties to the federal Liberal Party. Smallwood accused the Antis of being unpatriotic towards Britain, an odd accusation as it was his faction that wanted to abandon London for Ottawa.

In spite of all the pro-confederates' advantages, they obtained only 41.4 per cent of the vote in the referendum of June 3, 1948. Restoring democracy had the support of 44.6 per cent and 14.3 per cent of voters supported a continuation of the Commission. Had there been only the two options recommended by the Convention, the restoration of democracy would have won easily. For the next referendum, the choices were restoring democracy, a matter of governance, or joining Canada, a matter of status.

Two of the British-appointed Commissioners intervened on the side of the pro-Confederation group, a violation of their neutral positions. Smallwood criticized the Catholic Church to rally the Protestant vote, a successful exercise in divide-and-conquer politics. The rich merchants were accused of wanting to restore the corrupt practices of the past and protect their positions as exploiters. In this referendum, restoring democracy gained three points to 47.6 per cent, but Confederation gained 11 per cent for a majority of 52.3 per cent. Ottawa declared that the vote was honest and the majority clear, and London naturally accepted the outcome it had helped engineer.

Even though it had been decisively rejected in the first referendum, Britain left the Commission in control. The governor then appointed seven delegates to negotiate with Ottawa, ensuring that at least five were pro-Confederation. Since the war, the colony's financial situation had deteriorated and the delegation demanded a large increase in subsidies over that offered by Ottawa the previous December. Ottawa refused to budge, and negotiations dragged on through October and November. Ottawa finally made a small concession on December 11 and promised to appoint a Royal Commission within eight years to examine the province's financial situation and perhaps recommend changes.

The new grant was for $6.5 million for three years, declining to $2.25 million over the following five years. Ottawa took over most of the colony's debt and took ownership of the railway, the source of the greatest bleeding of provincial revenues. There was not much else to negotiate, because the *BNA Act* spelled out what responsibilities lay with provincial governments. The main change was that fisheries became federal and the new province lost control of its greatest natural resource. The Commission accepted Canada's terms on January 26, 1949, the most important decision it made during its fifteen-year reign and possibly the most important decision ever taken by a Newfoundland government.

The next stage was for Britain to make Newfoundland a province of Canada. This was a problem because Section 146 of the *BNA Act* provided for the admission of other colonies that requested it in the form of "Addresses from . . . (their) Legislatures." Since Newfoundland had no legislature, Canada asked Britain to amend the *BNA Act* to eliminate the requirement. In the British House of Commons, Sir Alan Herbert noted that this proposal violated the *BNA Act.* In Canada, the *Globe and Mail* pointed out that the process violated the *BNA Act,* the Agreement of 1933, and the sovereignty of the people of Newfoundland. It was all to no avail—Britain passed the legislation on March 31, 1949, and the subsequent court challenge failed. As with Nova Scotia and New Brunswick, the terms of union with Canada were never debated or approved by an elected legislature as required by the original agreement and in this case by the Canadian constitution itself.

On March 31, 1949, Newfoundland became Canada's tenth province. The next step was to establish a new provincial government to take over from the Commission. This was tricky as the referendum had just rejected the option of restoring democratic government, but in fact it was democratic government that had to be restored. The proper way to proceed was for the governor to call elections and ask the leader of the party with the most seats to form a government. Instead, on April 1, the Canadian government appointed Smallwood, a man with no legal political standing whatsoever, as premier. He then appointed a cabinet to govern the province prior to an election. He called a convention of proconfederates for April 28 and turned the participants into the provincial Liberal party. They then elected him as their leader and he then called a provincial election for May 27.

The federal government rushed to deliver pension and child allowance cheques. Smallwood claimed credit for them and threatened voters with their loss should they not vote Liberal. The Antis scrambled to turn themselves into a political party, took the name Progressive Conservatives, and attempted to mount a campaign. They had no chance—Smallwood's Liberals took 65 per cent of the popular vote and twenty-two of the twenty-eight seats. Democratic government had been restored, making a farce of the referendum that had just rejected it. Newfoundland now had both Confederation and democratic government, both of the two opposing options on the second ballot. The path to that curious outcome had been smoothed with political machinations, the overruling of the elected Convention, the misuse of government offices, the acceptance of outside financial support, the manipulation of delegations and of referenda questions, the violation of the constitution, and vote-buying on an unprecedented scale, even if Ottawa's cheques were technically legal. And this by a Convention that had been appointed in 1933 to replace an allegedly corrupt regime!

The federal Liberal government's manipulation of Newfoundland's politics produced excellent results in terms of federal-provincial relations. The federal and provincial Liberal parties in Newfoundland were essentially one, and they were both run by Smallwood. He selected the federal Liberal candidates and ensured that they won election—their job in Ottawa was to represent the interests of Newfoundland and of Smallwood. He selected a federal backroom politician, Jack Pickersgill, a Manitoban with excellent connections in Ottawa, to be Newfoundland's cabinet minister and ensured that he was elected in a constituency he may never have heard of before. Federal funds flowed into Newfoundland, the standard of living shot upwards, Liberals won repeatedly at both provincial and federal levels, and the referenda campaigns became the stuff of song and legend. Smallwood was a hero, the federal Liberals had a strong ally in St. John's, and Confederation was completed to the satisfaction of London, Ottawa, and eventually of most citizens of Newfoundland and Labrador. It would be a long time, however, before Newfoundlanders would regard themselves as Canadians, and they remain to this day a very distinct and much-loved group within the Canadian family.

CHAPTER 10
St. Laurent and Diefenbaker, 1948-1963

On November 15, 1948, Mackenzie King's long tenure as prime minister came to an end. He had changed his views on many aspects of government, always bending with the winds and making the necessary compromises required to stay in power. In contrast, the new prime minister, Louis St. Laurent, had very fixed views about government. He was a strong Canadian nationalist and believed that government should have a major role in the economy, that is, that the federal government should. While Ottawa's comprehensive plan for the welfare state had been rejected in 1945, St. Laurent believed that it should still be implemented on a piecemeal basis, with provincial co-operation if possible, without it if necessary.

Before St. Laurent could launch his series of welfare and economic initiatives, however, there were several constitutional issues he wanted to settle. By 1949, Britain had amended the *BNA Act* ten times regarding matters that did not affect the provinces. St. Laurent decided to obtain an amendment stating that Ottawa could make such changes itself. He informed the provinces of Ottawa's intention, but Opposition Leader George Drew knew that federal and provincial views might differ on what matters were exclusively federal and argued that the provinces had to be consulted and not just informed. Ottawa's view was that it alone would decide if a matter was exclusively federal and Britain passed the amendment. The premiers could do nothing about it, but it was not an auspicious way to begin relations with them.

St. Laurent's second constitutional initiative concerned the Supreme Court. When it was created in 1875, it was not, in fact, "supreme," because its decisions could be appealed to the JCPC in London. St. Laurent wanted to end such appeals to eliminate one more tie with Great Britain; the provinces opposed the change because the JCPC had often upheld their positions. St. Laurent ignored them again and eliminated appeals to the JCPC by an Act of Parliament in September 1949. Since then, scholars have not found conclusive proof that the Supreme Court has consistently or overwhelmingly sided with Ottawa, though that may reflect the fact that the provinces regarded it as part of the central government and were therefore reluctant to appeal to it. Ending appeals to London thus reduced the number of cases heard, and the courts played a less important role in federal-provincial relations than they had before the change.

The third constitutional issue that St. Laurent wanted solved was agreement on a formula for amending the constitution on issues that affected federal-provincial relations, and he wanted to terminate the convention by which such appeals required unanimous agreement. At a conference on January 10, 1950, the Prairie provinces supported a formula that would make change easier, but Ontario did not. Duplessis said that nothing in the constitution could be changed without unanimous provincial consent because "when Confederation was discussed and decided upon, it was based on the principle of complete provincial autonomy." After St. Laurent's unilateral moves on the other issues, the provinces were not in a good mood and no agreement emerged.

Education: Ottawa vs. Quebec

A serious battle broke out between Ottawa and Quebec when the federal government decided to become active in the promotion of culture and education, areas previously seen as the prerogative of individuals, groups, institutions, and provincial governments. English-speaking Canadians were increasingly alarmed at American cultural influence, and in 1949, St. Laurent appointed a Royal Commission under Vincent Massey to recommend a federal role. The main thrust was on culture, but it also looked at the state of higher education. Its assertion that the federal government had the right to be involved in "general" educational matters violated the letter and spirit of the *BNA Act*. Duplessis refused to co-operate with the Commission, and Massey ignored the objections of powerful Quebec organizations such as the Montreal Chamber of Commerce and the St. Jean Baptiste Society.

In 1951, the Massey Commission made a number of recommendations for a federal role in strengthening culture as well as providing grants to universities. The latter was clearly political as Ottawa intended to send cheques directly to the universities and colleges so they would know who their benefactor was. This federal program was unnecessary because the provinces could have increased university funding, if that was their priority, and if Ottawa reduced its level of taxation to allow the provinces to increase theirs. Ottawa refused to do that, creating the self-serving argument that federal money was necessary to fill the vacuum. The English-speaking provinces were willing to accept the federal largesse, but the proposal provoked one of Duplessis's most famous fights with Ottawa. He accepted the grants for a year, but when Ottawa refused to change the program, he ordered the universities and colleges to refuse the grants.

St. Laurent had, in effect, made education a "shared" responsibility instead of an "exclusively provincial" one. No formal amendment was proposed to legitimize this very significant change. The initiative also reflected one of the key characteristics of federal encroachments on provincial affairs, which came to be called "cherry-picking." In financial terms, higher education was no different from any other level of education and no level was as well funded as it should have been. Provinces had responsibility for all levels, so they had to allocate their education budgets from primary to university depending on numbers, needs, and finances. Not having any overall responsibility, Ottawa could identify any need such as universities, ignore the rest, and initiate a program that made Ottawa look like it cared, unlike the provinces, which were being stingy with all their programs. The matter was really about power and politics, not funding education.

The Development of Shared-Cost Programs

In 1948, Ottawa decided to expand the 1927 shared-cost program for old age pensions. It did not question that pensions were provincial matters, and a federal-provincial conference resulted in agreement on significant improvements to the regime. Ottawa assumed complete responsibility for pensions for every senior over the age of seventy, and needy seniors between the ages of sixty-five and seventy would receive pensions, with the provinces administering the program and Ottawa paying for half the costs with conditional grants. Paying pensions directly for those over seventy was regarded as beyond Ottawa's constitutional powers. Duplessis pointed out that social welfare was an exclusive provincial responsibility, but he could not let Quebeckers lose pensions for which they were being taxed by Ottawa. He acquiesced on the program, but insisted that the *BNA Act* be amended to state that the provinces remained paramount in the field of pensions.

In 1951, Ottawa and the provinces agreed to an amendment, Section 94A, making federal pensions legal but leaving the provinces paramount. There was now no clear pattern regarding the need for amendments to allow Ottawa to launch programs in areas of provincial responsibility. It had introduced old age pensions in 1927 without an amendment, introduced UI in 1940 with one, introduced the baby bonus in 1945 without amendment, and now changed the 1927 pension program with an amendment. That pattern, or non-pattern, would continue as Ottawa became more and more involved in provincial responsibilities, sometimes with amendments to legitimize the constitutional change, usually without amendments, and with the decisions on whether to make an amendment likely to reflect politics rather than constitutional logic or consistency.

The St. Laurent government proceeded with an impressive series of new programs. This reflected both a major increase in general governmental involvement in the economy and in the private lives of Canadians, as well as a transfer of power from the provinces to Ottawa. The method St. Laurent followed was shared-cost programs and the use of the federal "spending power." In St. Laurent's view, the constitution was not being violated and no constitutional amendment was required to legalize shared-cost programs, a rejection of the courts' 1937 decision that Ottawa could not use its unlimited power of taxation to encroach on provincial responsibilities. This was especially significant in that St. Laurent was the federal lawyer who lost the 1937 case, and he was now overruling the Supreme Court. St. Laurent's view was that if the provinces agreed to a federal proposal, then they had "voluntarily" accepted the change. It was also argued that Ottawa had every right to impose conditions on its gifts or grants, and if the recipients accepted those conditions, again, no violation of the constitution had occurred. This system allowed Ottawa to get around the constitutional division of responsibilities without seeking amendments. The English-speaking provinces approved of this constitutional theory; Quebec definitely did not.

Using this mechanism, Ottawa launched a number of programs to fill in the gaps in the welfare state. In 1948, health grants were provided to the provinces for hospital construction; treatment of cancer, diabetes, and tuberculosis; rehabilitation; surveys; and training. New programs included the *Blind Persons Act* in 1953, the *Disabled Persons Act* in 1954, an expanded role under the *Unemployment Assistance Act* in 1955, and hospital insurance in 1957, as well as programs for civil defence, vocational training, forestry, flood control, youth training, and building the Trans-Canada Highway. In 1953, conditional grants accounted for 18 per cent of federal payments to the provinces and 6 per cent of provincial revenue. Ten years later, they accounted for 77 per cent of federal transfers and 22 per cent of provincial revenue, a 400 per cent increase. Ottawa determined the conditions of these joint programs, but paid only half the cost or less.

Duplessis objected to these encroachments on provincial jurisdiction, arguing that the federal government should respect the constitution, that its actions should be based on the "rule of law." He did not want the constitution changed, just honoured. Nevertheless, he made his decisions on these proposed programs individually and pragmatically. If he believed a program threatened Quebec's autonomy, then he refused to participate. If he thought it was not a serious challenge or if the cost of rejecting it was too high, then he participated. Quebec thus refused to participate in grants to the universities, hospital insurance, civil defence, and the Trans-Canada Highway. But it did join the programs for hospital construction, health, tuberculosis, cancer, assistance to the old, and assistance to the unemployed whose insurance benefits had been exhausted.

Duplessis could not prevent Ottawa from launching these programs and using them to concentrate more and more power over provincial responsibilities in its own hands. The statistics told the tale. The percentage of provincial revenue earmarked for these programs in Quebec quadrupled between 1930 and 1960, at which time it amounted to 37 per cent of the budget. From 1933 to 1945, the percentage of Quebec's taxes collected by the federal government jumped from 47 per cent to 82 per cent, while that collected by the province fell from 10 per cent to 7.3 per cent, and the percentage collected by municipalities fell from 43 per cent to 7 per cent. Federal spending on the provinces went from 43 per cent of the federal budget in 1940 to 17 per cent by 1960. In the 1940s and 1950s, the federal budget increased twenty times, much of it now spent on programs in areas of provincial responsibility. Ottawa was launching this impressive series of programs as the 1947 tax agreements were coming up for renewal. Under these agreements, Ottawa collected income tax for seven provinces and returned a slightly larger amount as annual grants. Ontario and Quebec had refused to participate on the grounds that provinces could not be autonomous if they were dependent on receiving their revenue from Ottawa. In 1952, Ontario joined the other seven, and Quebec stood alone in refusing to allow Ottawa to collect its taxes.

Along with the development of the welfare state, the 1950s saw the completion of two of the most important infrastructure projects in Canadian history, the St. Lawrence Seaway and the Trans-Canada Highway. Both had been on the drawing board for decades, and both involved major issues of federal-provincial relations. The construction of the St. Lawrence Seaway was one of the best examples of co-operation between two orders of government. By 1951, the development of both a better system of locks and of the hydro-electric potential had become urgent, and Ottawa abandoned its attempts to control Ontario's electricity production. Under the new plan, Ottawa paid for the locks and Ontario paid for the power plant. The Seaway allowed ocean-going vessels to visit ports close to the centre of the continent and it gave Ontario an enormous amount of hydro-electric power.

Another of Ottawa's major shared-cost initiatives was the Trans-Canada Highway. Local roads were provincial matters, and each province had created a network of roads and connected them to those in neighbouring provinces and states. In 1948, Ottawa decided that a unified Trans-Canada Highway was needed, a decision that fit well into its nationalist strategy. There was no constitutional problem with Ottawa building the entire road—it had the right to declare any provincial work to be of national importance, and it could therefore knit provincial roads into a national network under its own control and improve them to whatever standard it wanted. It also had the financial capacity to build the entire project. Instead, Ottawa decided that the provinces should pay half the costs of a road that had to be built to Ottawa's plans, rules, and specifications. That decision turned a simple federal project into a serious political, administrative, and financial problem and added years to the period of construction.

Ottawa insisted on having a wide road allowance, but would not cover the costs of acquiring the larger right-of-way. The improved roads required access lanes and intersections—Ottawa said that was a provincial responsibility. Ottawa insisted on determining the route and setting minimum standards for the entire road. The route created problems for provinces like Ontario, where 90 per cent of the population lived in the south while the road would run through the north, and BC, where the cost of building through the mountains was excessive. Ottawa's demand that all provinces follow its contracting policies was unacceptable to Quebec, where the highways department was an important part of the ruling party's patronage system.

The project played havoc with provincial budgets and planning. The English-speaking provinces did not believe they could turn down the fifty-cent dollars for roads they needed anyway. To obtain those funds, however, they had to divert money from other departments and roads to the Trans-Canada. The Maritime provinces could not afford their 50 per cent, so Ottawa paid 90 per cent, making the project a form of equalization and another example of asymmetrical federalism. Quebec simply refused to join in the scheme, but did build its roads to an adequate standard and connected them to ones in Ontario and New Brunswick, thus demonstrating that federal involvement was not actually necessary. As a result of these problems, the project that began in 1948 was not completed until 1965, about the same length of time it took to plan, survey, and build the CPR.

The question that must be asked is why Ottawa did not simply build the entire road itself. For Canadian taxpayers, the cost would have been the same. The answer is probably very simple. By making it a shared-cost program, Ottawa forced the provinces to pay half the cost of what was, in fact, a federal project. The money saved was then available to launch more shared-cost programs, each of which imposed Ottawa's priorities on the provinces. Canada was moving towards the type of government John A. Macdonald had wanted: a dominant federal government with the provinces reduced to the role of glorified municipalities. English-speaking Canadians seemed in broad agreement with Ottawa's thrust; French Canadians definitely were not. The gulf between English and French Canadians was steadily widening, a contradiction of the image many people had of an emerging pan-Canadian nationalism.

Quebec's Growing Opposition to Federal Policies

The battles Quebec had been having with Ottawa since the 1920s were of concern to all French-speaking Quebeckers, and organizations like the Chamber of Commerce strongly urged Duplessis to appoint a commission to do an exhaustive study of the situation. He responded in February 1953, with a Royal Commission named after its chairman, Justice Thomas Tremblay. It identified three basic premises: that federalism was a compact between two peoples; that Quebec was the home of one of those peoples; and that its government was the principal defender of that people's interests. Quebec therefore had a special status, was sovereign in its areas of responsibility, and had to have the fiscal powers to execute those responsibilities. The only government that could protect the French-Canadian nation was that of Quebec, and it could never be dependent on Ottawa.

Not surprisingly, the Commission found numerous examples of Ottawa's meddling in Quebec's affairs. It found that the 1867 division of responsibilities was still a proper reflection of the fundamental differences between Quebec and the rest of Canada. It specifically rejected the spending power argument on the grounds that it made a farce of the division of responsibilities. It denied the assertion of the Massey Report that the federal government could involve itself in education, and its main recommendation was that Ottawa respect the constitution and stop using levers such as the spending power to encroach on provincial jurisdiction. The Commission reported just as Quebec was entering a profound period of change, and its recommendations for a return to the neat pre-war division of responsibilities was out-of-date and that discredited its findings.

The fact that part of the analysis was old-fashioned diverted attention from the main impact of the report. It was, in fact, a very clear and detailed statement of Quebec's unique situation and of the necessity for the province to be in charge of the lives of Quebeckers, to be *maîtres chez nous*. That part of its findings resonated strongly with French Quebeckers of every class and political persuasion. The main effect of the report may well have been its influence on the provincial Liberals, who were becoming about as nationalistic as Duplessis but determined to use the state instead of the Church to protect French culture and independence, and to use it actively rather than passively. English-speaking Canadians concentrated on the message of preserving Quebec as it was, which in their opinion was backwards, while French Quebeckers saw the report as documenting the very great danger Ottawa's centralization of power was posing to *la survivance*. The importance of the Tremblay Report lay in the latter, and it was a key ideological basis of the Quiet Revolution of the 1960s, which was quite forward-looking.

As Quebec was increasingly annoyed with Ottawa's policies, so too St. Laurent was annoyed with Quebec's resistance to those policies. A war of words erupted in the summer of 1954, with St. Laurent asserting that Quebec was "a province like the others." Duplessis replied that it was sad that a prime minister from Quebec would say that all provinces were similar, and he argued that surrender would mean Quebeckers were no longer masters in their own house. He accused St. Laurent of turning the other provinces against Quebec and attacked St. Laurent's claim that the tax agreements were temporary. The confrontation that had begun in 1945 was coming to a head.

Duplessis finally came to the conclusion that the war over taxation had to be won at any cost. Ottawa's taxation policy allowed an abatement of up to 5 per cent of personal income tax if provincial governments wanted to collect it, but Quebec had not taken advantage of the proposal. In 1954, Duplessis announced that Quebec was going to introduce a personal income tax and that it would be 15 per cent of the federal rate. If Ottawa did not raise its abatement to 15 per cent, a Quebecker's combined federal and provincial income tax would jump by 10 per cent, and the question was which government would be blamed for the increase created by this double taxation. Duplessis also promised that part of that revenue would be spent on the universities, which undermined Ottawa's argument that its program was necessary because the provinces were not adequately funding higher education.

Duplessis was well prepared for the battle. The Quebec government had defended its case at federal-provincial conferences, both in numerous detailed and well-argued submissions and in the press. Every annual provincial budget had stated that Ottawa was collecting taxes in violation of the constitution and the 1942 agreement, and that it was taking more from Quebec than it was returning. The fact those statements were partly incorrect was irrelevant—they were also partly correct and made excellent propaganda, which was what mattered in a political battle. Duplessis never missed an opportunity to press his case. When Canada provided assistance to war-torn Europe, he said that Ottawa spent taxpayers' money abroad, while he spent it in Quebec. His folksy assessment of federal policy was that Ottawa was like the thief who stole your watch and then returned the watch chain, calling it a gift. St. Laurent was also acutely aware that Duplessis had won the elections of 1944, 1948, and 1952 mainly on a nationalist platform of defending Quebec from Ottawa. That meant that over two-thirds of Quebec's French-Canadian vote was behind Duplessis, and his policies were uniting all the nationalists in the province.

After acrimonious exchanges, the two leaders met and St. Laurent agreed to increase Quebec's "tax room." Duplessis was victorious and he offered Ottawa the face-saving gesture of reducing the proposed provincial tax to 10 per cent. Quebec thus increased its revenue by 10 per cent of the amount that Ottawa had collected and Ottawa lost that amount. The fact that Quebec was now collecting the tax meant it had to develop the bureaucracy necessary to administer it, which reinforced its administration and enhanced its political and administrative autonomy. This arrangement was a major change to the 1952 tax agreements, which were just two years into their five-year term. The English-speaking provinces had not been consulted, and the deal meant that Ottawa had, in reality, agreed to special status for Quebec. Duplessis was hailed in Quebec and this was perhaps his greatest political victory, certainly his most important economic or financial one. Successor regimes in Quebec reaped the benefits, and the increased spending of the Quiet Revolution could not have been effected had Quebec not been in control of its own income tax collection.

Unemployment Insurance, Taxation, and Hospital Insurance

Unemployment insurance was another program that St. Laurent believed should be improved and expanded. UI helped the unemployed for a certain period, but the provinces were responsible for those who remained unemployed after the payments ran out, that is, for welfare. In 1955, Ottawa began paying 50 per cent of the cost of provincial programs for these "unemployables," the ones who could not find jobs. Ottawa also made a significant change to the criteria for eligibility, by including seasonal workers who had not worked long enough to qualify for payments under the existing scheme. Those additional amounts were, in effect, welfare payments rather than insurance payments, a further confusion of the line between federal and provincial responsibilities. The new system also transferred money from provinces with a high proportion of full-time workers to ones with a high proportion of seasonal workers and was therefore a form of equalization.

In preparation for the renewal of the 1952 tax agreements, Ottawa made a new proposal in January 1956. It called for the federal government to give an abatement of 10 per cent of its personal income tax collection, 9 per cent of its corporate income tax, and 50 per cent of its succession duties so that provinces could collect those amounts without taxpayers being "double-taxed" by the two orders of government. The new policy maintained the option of letting Ottawa collect the amounts for the provinces, and Ottawa encouraged them to do so by offering more than they would obtain collecting the taxes themselves. But now the English-speaking provinces were starting to follow Quebec's lead, and the provinces demanded a larger share of the revenue. Agreement was reached in March 1957, with eight provinces opting for Ottawa to collect their share, with Ontario choosing to collect its own corporate income tax and succession duties, and with Quebec continuing to collect all three of its own taxes.

The new formula represented a major change. From then on, provincial revenue would increase at the same rate as federal revenue, and the provinces would not be punished if they chose to collect the taxes themselves. In effect, Ottawa had abandoned one of the main policies it had tried to impose since 1942, namely domination of the economy through the collection of all personal and corporate income tax and succession duties. Now the provinces had regained control over their revenue even if they allowed Ottawa to continue collecting it. They were catching up to Quebec, and the allegedly "backwards" Duplessis must have been amused.

A separate part of the agreement provided for Ottawa to give unconditional "equalization" grants to the poorer provinces, known as "have-not" provinces, so that they could provide a level of service comparable to that of the richer or "have" provinces. This reflected a change in attitudes in central Canada and in the federal government, the recognition that federalism worked mainly to the advantage of Ontario and Quebec and that the federal government should tax the richer provinces and redistribute some of that wealth to the poorer ones, whose economies had not been blessed with the same degree of federal support as central Canada had always enjoyed. Equalization grants have been an important element in federalism ever since and were entrenched in the constitution in 1982.

The "fairness" principle of the equalization system had to be seen in context, however. Under the shared-cost programs, the more provinces spent, the more money Ottawa had to transfer to them by its 50–50 formula—Ottawa created the programs, but the provinces determined the amounts spent. Richer provinces spent more per capita than poorer ones, sometimes far more, and they therefore received more from Ottawa. To a certain extent, the equalization system just countered the unfairness of the shared-cost programs. A notable example was the Trans-Canada Highway. As with the CPR, the costs of construction were highest in BC and northern Ontario, so Ottawa spent much more per capita in these two "have" provinces than in the others. Another problem was that it was almost impossible to compare the amount each "have-not" province received from Ottawa's equalization program to the total amount each province received from Ottawa's 50 per cent of the shared-cost programs. The confusion allowed almost every province to argue that it was paying more into Confederation than it was getting back, and the confusion increased with every new program or change to existing ones. The politics of the game may well have been as important as the cash flows, with every politician trying to make his constituents believe that they were bringing more to their areas or provinces than was being taken away. That has never changed.

By the mid-1950s, the St. Laurent governments enthusiasm for both the managed economy and the welfare state was starting to fade. A major factor in its changing perspective was that the financial calculations behind the 1945 proposals had proven to be wrong. The bureaucrats who had drafted the plans for the federal welfare state assumed that there would be no more wars, an assumption that defied thousands of years of history. They estimated that defence spending would be $250 million annually in the post-war period. The development of the Cold War and the outbreak of the Korean War pushed the defence budget to $2 billion. By the mid-1950s, it was clear that Ottawa could not afford both its defence budget and the welfare state, and the cuts had to come from the ambitious welfare plan.

St. Laurent abandoned the public works program that was designed to create jobs. In explaining this reversal of policy, he said that although the government's proposals had been rejected at the 1945 federal-provincial conference, many of its elements had since been put into effect. Public works was being abandoned now because, he said, Ottawa did not want to be involved in detailed projects. The shared-cost program for those who had exhausted their unemployment payments was also coming to an end. In the House of Commons, the government was accused of abandoning the 1944 plan for the welfare state, and St. Laurent did not deny it. The crunch would come with the ongoing debate over hospital insurance.

Hospital insurance was one of the last issues tackled by the St. Laurent government. When Ottawa's overall plan for a welfare state was rejected by the provinces in 1945, Saskatchewan established its own program. That, of course, demonstrated that federal involvement was not essential for the creation of the welfare state. British Columbia soon followed, and naturally those two governments campaigned from then on for Ottawa to pay for part of their plans. Some other provinces were equally strongly opposed, especially Ontario, which believed that insurance was a private matter, and Quebec, which saw hospitals as a provincial responsibility. The genius of federalism was that in a situation like that, each province could do what suited it and none had to tailor its plans to suit Ottawa or other provinces. The assumption made by Saskatchewan, which proved to be correct, was that if there was a national plan, it would be a copy of Saskatchewan's. In the context of Canadian federalism, this amounted to the Saskatchewan tail wagging the Canadian dog, and it was not the last time it happened.

St. Laurent was opposed to health insurance and had no appetite for another battle with the provinces. He also knew that the Saskatchewan plan had cost far more than its government had estimated. This was a common problem with new programs—opposition parties usually accused governments of underestimating the cost of new programs, and the opposition parties were usually right. Nevertheless, St. Laurent was well aware of growing popular demand for government support and of the fact that both the CCF and the Progressive Conservatives could attract Liberal votes if the federal government did not act. The cabinet was seriously divided on the question, but powerful ministers such as Paul Martin Sr., backbenchers, and some provinces pressured the prime minister into introducing a plan.

In April 1957, the House of Commons unanimously passed the *Hospital and Diagnostic Services Act*, which covered a range of hospital services and suggested the government was still moving forward on social issues. St. Laurent was still a very clever politician, however, and the scheme was designed to be postponed for years. It would only come into operation when five provinces with half Canada's population signed on. Since Ontario and Quebec were opposed, the scheme was dead at birth. St. Laurent thus ended his tenure as prime minister heading a government in retreat on a number of federal-provincial issues while it pretended to be still marching forward with the implementation of the welfare state.

Diefenbaker and the Maritimes, the West, and Quebec

In 1957, twenty-two consecutive years of Liberal government in Ottawa came to an end with the election of a Progressive Conservative government. It was unique in many ways. For the first time, the country had a prime minister who was neither British nor French as John Diefenbaker was of German ancestry. He was more sympathetic to "ethnic" Canadians and First Nations than his predecessors, less so to the English-French problem. His cabinet was the first in history in which central Canadians were not a majority. For the first time ever, the interests of Atlantic Canada and the western provinces were high on a federal government's agenda, and not just in terms of doing enough to defuse outbreaks of regional discontent. Ottawa, Toronto, and Montreal were not pleased to lose what had been a monopoly on power since 1867. Federal-provincial relations were in for a change.

One of the first areas to benefit from the new configuration of the federal government was the Maritimes. In Ottawa, defending Confederation as a fair, national deal gave way to accepting that federal policies had indeed distorted economies across the land in favour of central Canada and that something had to be done to make Confederation fair for all provinces. For those provinces, genuine co-operation replaced coercion, confrontation, and inattentiveness as the dominant themes of federal-provincial relations, at least for a while. In Ottawa, the change began in the dying days of the Liberal regime and accelerated rapidly under Diefenbaker.

In New Brunswick, the new and dynamic Conservative government of Premier Hugh John Flemming wanted much more federal support than had been forthcoming under the Liberals. He called a meeting of the three Maritime premiers to develop a common approach to Ottawa. In 1957, for the first time ever, Maritime politicians succeeded in having a major federal party include their demands, the Atlantic Manifesto, in a national election platform. Flemming and the other Maritime premiers then helped elect Conservative MPs, and gains in the Maritimes were crucial to Diefenbaker's defeat of the federal Liberals. Flemming's reward was federal assistance for the building of a new hydro-electric dam at Beechwood, something Ottawa had refused at the same time as it was pouring millions into the St. Lawrence Seaway. There followed a rash of federal spending, support for other power plants, support for feasibility studies, loans for projects, and especially the formalization of unconditional equalization grants designed to allow Maritime provincial governments to narrow the gap between the services they provided their citizens and the national average.

PEI followed New Brunswick as its government willingly accepted the new programs of grants initiated by the Diefenbaker government, especially the unconditional Atlantic Adjustment Grants that allowed the province to improve the quality of administrative programs, grants that were soon absorbed into the equalization program. PEI eagerly joined the federal programs for Roads to Resources, the *Agricultural Rehabilitation and Development Act* (*ARDA*), the Fund for Regional Development (FRED), and the Atlantic

Development Board (ADB). Next door in Nova Scotia, the Conservative regime of Premier Robert Stanfield enjoyed the same federal attention and programs as New Brunswick and PEI.

Newfoundland did not fare nearly as well. While most provincial regimes had better relations with federal governments of the same political stripe, most were also wise enough to maintain a decent relationship with the federal Opposition party, hedging their bets in case their federal friends were defeated. Premier Joey Smallwood chose to regard federal Progressive Conservatives as a permanent enemy. That put Newfoundland in a rather poor position when the Conservatives won the 1957 election with the support of Conservative regimes in the Maritimes. Those three regimes and the federal Conservatives knew that Liberal Ottawa had pumped many millions of dollars into Liberal Newfoundland and little into the other Atlantic provinces.

The 1949 Terms of Union with Canada provided that within eight years, a commission would investigate Newfoundland's finances to determine if the amount of the federal grants was sufficient to provide a level of public services equivalent to that in the Maritime provinces. The Liberal government in Ottawa appointed John McNair who, as former Liberal premier of New Brunswick, was thoroughly familiar with the issues and presumably sympathetic to fellow Liberals in both Ottawa and Newfoundland. In May 1958, he recommended a federal grant of $8 million with no time limit, instead of the $15 million Smallwood expected. Smallwood was furious and attempted to make a major political issue of it. By then, however, Conservatives ruled in Ottawa, and they were not about to be bullied by a premier who had ensured they won no seats in Newfoundland. They accepted McNair's recommendation but limited it to four years, a major political and financial setback for the premier.

Labour relations became another problem in Newfoundland's relations with Ottawa. In order to attract foreign investment, Smallwood provided foreign companies with a docile and underpaid labour force. In 1959, the International Woodworkers of America (IWA) went on strike against the Anglo-Newfoundland Development Company, a producer of pulp and paper. On February 12, 1960, Smallwood broadcast a highly emotional speech saying there was a war underway between Newfoundland and a foreign union containing agitators, criminals, and Communists. He accused the IWA of breaking laws and asked the federal government to send the RCMP. Although Ottawa was obliged to respond automatically to such a request, Prime Minister John Diefenbaker was a libertarian who had chafed at government abuse of police power. He was appalled at Smallwood's handling of the strike and refused to send the police. Smallwood then sent the St. John's Constabulary and used the death of one of them to outlaw the union. The absence of the RCMP did not lead to the chaos Smallwood had predicted, and it appeared that Diefenbaker was right—the issue was strike-breaking, not law and order.

One positive element that came out of the strike was the final termination of the federal power of disallowance. When Newfoundland passed the bill decertifying the IWA, there was pressure on Ottawa to disallow it, and Diefenbaker must have been sorely tempted to strike another blow at his enemy. But Diefenbaker refused to disallow Smallwood's controversial legislation, arguing that the power of disallowance made the federal government judge and jury of the appropriateness of provincial legislation. Since 1867 Ottawa had disallowed 112 provincial laws, sixty-eight before Laurier, only sixteen between 1905 and 1921, and the last one in 1943. No federal government has since contemplated using that power, although it was never removed from the constitution. Allowing Smallwood's legislation to stand did not improve relations between the two governments, and decent relations were only restored in 1963 when Smallwood's Liberal friends returned to office in Ottawa.

On the prairies, people felt as neglected by the St. Laurent government as they did in the Maritimes, and one issue was the same as Ottawa ignored Regina's repeated requests for assistance building a dam on the South Saskatchewan River. One example of federal delay was the appointment of a Royal Commission to study the project. As far as Saskatchewan was concerned, enough studies had been done and all the facts were known. Another problem was Ottawa's insistence on a role in the allocation of the power and the exploitation of minerals under the flooded areas, both of which were provincial matters. In 1957, the South Saskatchewan Dam was high on the agenda of the new prime minister who was, of course, from Saskatchewan. The project was approved in July 1958, and the largest infrastructure project in the province's history was opened in July 1967. Like the Maritimes, the four western provinces were also pleased to co-operate with Ottawa on a large number of shared-cost programs and federal initiatives to develop their economies.

While federal-provincial co-operation worked well in a number of cases, that did not happen in BC. There, Premier W.A.C. Bennett saw the mighty rivers as the province's economic engine and the key to the re-election of himself and his Social Credit government. One project was a dam on the Columbia River. The Columbia is an international river, so any agreement on its development had to involve the Canadian and American governments. Bennett wanted to develop hydro-electric power on both the Columbia River and the Peace River at the same time, selling power from the Columbia project to the United States to pay for the construction of the dam on the Peace River. Ottawa wanted Canadian power projects to serve Canadian consumers, and it favoured short-term exports of power so the electricity would be available when demand grew in Canada. The dispute with Ottawa represented yet another attempt by the federal government to use its responsibility for trade to override a provincial responsibility for natural resources. Ottawa had forgotten that it had lost all the previous battles with Ontario and Quebec over control of hydro-electric power, and it seriously underestimated the premier of British Columbia.

The struggle between Victoria and Ottawa reached epic proportions. Bennett nationalized BC Electric and amalgamated it with the provincially owned BC Power Corporation to form the BC Hydro and Power Authority. As a Crown corporation, BC Hydro could not be taxed by Ottawa, but the provincial government could devise numerous means to obtain financial and political benefits from it. In 1962, Ottawa and Victoria were still at loggerheads over the deal, but a federal election was looming. For the first time, Bennett intervened in federal politics, urging people to vote Social Credit instead of Conservative. That helped reduce the federal Conservative government to minority status, and to obtain Social Credit support in the next election, the Conservatives accepted BC's position on sales to the US. Bennett went on to yet another electoral victory, while the federal Conservatives' mishandling of the issue contributed to their defeat in 1963.

Ottawa's relations with Quebec also underwent important changes after the 1957 election. By then, Duplessis was tired of the seemingly endless battles with the federal Liberals. He understood that the federal Conservatives had a much greater respect for the provinces, and in 1957 and 1958 his support was crucial to Diefenbaker's victories. Unlike St. Laurent, Diefenbaker had no major battles with Duplessis, who died on September 7, 1959, and co-operated very well with his successor, Paul Sauvé, who tragically died just four months later. Both governments wanted to resolve problems, and one of the most important was that of federal aid to universities. Premier Sauvé negotiated a face-saving arrangement by which Ottawa allowed Quebec to collect an additional 1 per cent corporate income tax, an amount roughly equal to what Ottawa would have provided the universities. The Quebec government was then to provide grants to the universities equal to that amount. The province's complete control over education was preserved and the universities got their money. The ease with which they reached a solution demonstrated the real problem—when Ottawa sought to exercise power and control, Quebec resisted; when Ottawa did not, co-operation was welcome.

More Federal Programs, More Problems

One area where the Diefenbaker government was in full agreement with St. Laurent was that of shared-cost programs. Both saw them as the basic formula for federal-provincial co-operation into the distant future, as the means to develop and manage the entire economy, and as a way of avoiding the difficulty of constitutional amendment. In the 1950s, Diefenbaker's criticism of shared-cost programs was that there were not enough of them and existing ones were underfunded. Doing more was a key element of the Conservative campaigns of 1957 and 1958, and the Conservatives received strong support across the country, including in Quebec.

The new federal government moved quickly to honour many of its promises. It turned the hospital insurance scheme into reality by dropping the condition that it could only begin when five provinces with 50 per cent of the population signed on. Five smaller provinces then joined the scheme, another four in 1959, plus Quebec in 1961. This program represented another major building block in the welfare state, making it possible for all Canadians to afford hospital treatment. It laid the foundation for Medicare because Saskatchewan used the money freed up by Ottawa's contributions to hospital insurance to launch the next program in its plan for the welfare state, namely Medicare.

The onset of a recession in 1958 was met with shared-cost programs, one of which supported public works constructed in winter when unemployment was always highest. A major program was called Roads to Resources, in which Ottawa paid part of the cost of roads running from south to north within provincial boundaries in order to tap forestry and mineral resources north of the agricultural zones. This was part of the government's "Northern Vision." Shared-cost programs were also used to enhance tourism, two famous examples being the reconstruction of the Fortress of Louisbourg and the building of the Cabot Trail, both on Cape Breton Island where the decline of coal mining was leading to severe economic problems.

St. Laurent had introduced equalization in the 1957 tax agreements, but Diefenbaker was the first prime minister to embrace the concept with genuine conviction. He began a very deliberate policy of transferring money from wealthy provinces to poorer ones, and from urban to rural areas within provinces. Both policies cost him votes in central Canada and the cities, but earned him votes elsewhere. The calculation of the equalization formula was made more fair, being based on a national average of income, including all sources of revenue. Two huge programs addressed the economic discrepancy between city and country within every province, namely *ARDA* and FRED. The local problems they addressed had previously been seen mainly as provincial responsibilities and were defined as provincial in the *BNA Act*.

Under the Conservatives, existing shared-cost programs received additional infusions of federal money and new programs were launched, five major ones and 15 smaller ones. No area of government activity seemed too small for a special program, such as assistance in building houses and vocational schools. In parallel, the abatement on personal income taxes was increased to 13 per cent so that provinces could raise more money for their programs, including their portion of the shared-cost ones. Statistics documented the burst in federal activity in shared-cost programs, from a budget of $144 million in 1958 to $606 million in 1962. This was built on the foundation of St. Laurent's programs, and in the decade from 1953 to 1964, federal spending on such programs increased twelve-fold, from

$75 million to $935 million. Those funds were matched by the provincial share, an indication of how much provincial spending was now being determined by federal initiatives.

Federalism and Quebec Nationalism

After the defeat of the Union National government in 1960, relations between Ottawa and the new Liberal government in Quebec deteriorated as a result of a complex set of developments. The rapid increase in the number of shared-cost programs was a major factor, as Quebec knew that it was being forced to accept more and more programs essentially devised for English Canada, programs that did not reflect Quebec's priorities or values, programs that were in provincial jurisdiction. French Canadians had never been well represented in the federal civil service that designed these programs, and they were even less well represented in cabinet and the Conservative caucus than under the Liberals. That produced a growing feeling that Ottawa and the rest of Canada did not understand or care about Quebec's views and concerns, a view that correctly reflected federal policies since at least the 1920s. The CCF had almost no representation in Quebec and was far more supportive of "national" policies than the other federal parties. In the early 1960s, Quebec was increasingly disenchanted with the rest of Canada, particularly the federal government, which happened to be Conservative.

The growing problems between Ottawa and Quebec also reflected a profound change in the way French Canadians in Quebec viewed themselves. By 1960, many of them had come to the conclusion that French Canadians outside the province were rapidly being assimilated into English-Canadian culture, a view solidly supported by statistics. French Quebeckers increasingly redefined themselves as Québécois, as separate from French Canadians in other provinces. This was a historic shift in their nationalism, from seeing themselves as part of a pan-Canadian nation to seeing themselves as a nation exclusively identified with the territory and political state of Quebec. The government of the Québécois was the one in Quebec City, not the one in Ottawa. There were exceptions, of course, the most famous being Pierre Elliott Trudeau, but the majority of Québécois endorsed the French nationalist view. English-speaking Canadians, on the other hand, were likely to regard Ottawa as their national government and the provinces as their local ones. The rise of Québécois nationalism had profound effects on politics within Quebec, between Quebec and Ottawa, and between Quebec and the rest of Canada. In terms of federal-provincial relations, the Québécois were dealing with a prime minister who believed very strongly in a single, pan-Canadian nationalism that included all ethnic groups. He rejected out of hand the idea that English Canadians and French Canadians had some sort of special place amongst Canadians, and the implication that all others—including himself—were second class-citizens.

In the late 1950s, Quebec experienced a dramatic and rapid change in society marked by an extremely swift decline in the influence of the Catholic Church. It was inevitable that the state would replace the Church as the provider of health, welfare, and education, and the Union National had been moving in that direction. Then, on June 22, 1960, the UN was replaced by the Liberals under Jean Lesage. As the Opposition, the Liberals had adopted policies to reflect the new realities, but they were also determined to resist all federal encroachments on provincial jurisdiction; to control their own programs in health, welfare, and other provincial spheres; and to maintain and increase the province's control of adequate revenue to achieve those goals. The Quiet Revolution was not an overall rejection of the past, as many English-Canadians thought, but the maintenance of the goals of successive Quebec governments since 1867, only with the state replacing the Church to deliver public services and champion nationalism.

Had the 1867 division of responsibilities still been in effect, the change in Quebec would have presented few difficulties to federal-provincial relations. By 1960, however, Ottawa had taken a major role in health, welfare, education, and local infrastructure. Given the sums involved, turning down federal shared-cost programs was no longer a viable option. The stage was set for a dramatic clash between the two governments, as Ottawa sought to maintain and expand its involvement in provincial affairs while Quebec sought to prevent any further incursions and to force Ottawa out of existing programs.

The first strong hint of serious confrontation came at a federal-provincial conference in October 1960. Newly elected Premier Jean Lesage announced that Quebec would now join all the shared-cost programs it

185

had been boycotting, but only on a temporary basis. He said that these programs were in provincial jurisdiction, and he expected Ottawa to pull out of them and turn over to the Quebec government the amount of money it had been spending on those programs. What Ottawa and the other provinces did about those programs in the rest of Canada was of no concern to Quebec, but federal programs within provincial jurisdiction would no longer be rejected as Duplessis had done in some cases, or tolerated, as he had done in others. The government of Quebec would now take control of all the programs for which it was constitutionally responsible, replacing both the Church as the administrator and the federal government as a prime source of funds. The initial enthusiasm English-Canadians had shown for the Quiet Revolution started to evaporate when they realized what it was really about.

At this conference, Lesage found support from a number of provinces, especially Ontario, Manitoba, Alberta, and PEI. Manitoba Premier Dufferin Roblin complained that the federal programs were seriously distorting provincial priorities, and PEI Premier Walter Shaw complained that provinces never knew when Ottawa was going to launch or change a program. Like Duplessis, they now saw the rapid growth of shared-cost programs as a threat to provincial autonomy. They said the programs were forcing them to accept federal priorities in their own areas of responsibility. The Atlantic premiers said their provinces could not afford to accept or reject federal offers.

In fact, by 1960, the post-war policy of shared-cost programs had become a major problem for all eleven governments. Many of the programs had been launched without overall planning, clear objectives, or rational standards. A number of programs were launched deliberately before federal elections, the baby bonus and hospital insurance being excellent examples. Some programs included equalization elements that overlapped the equalization program itself, especially in Atlantic Canada. The objectives of the ARDA and FRED programs were so vague that provinces had to submit proposals and wait for Ottawa to decide if they met the criteria.

Some programs addressed the problem of recessions but were then retained for political reasons after the recession was over, an example being additional aid to the unemployed, which was continued during the prosperous years of the mid-1950s. There was support for some roads, some educational facilities, and some medical programs, but not for others that were arguably as deserving. Ordinary hospitals received grants while mental hospitals did not, which caused provincial governments to spend on general hospitals and ignore mental health institutions. All shared-cost programs violated the most basic principle of democracy, namely that the governments that spent money—in this case the provinces—should be responsible for raising it, so that taxpayers could make informed decisions regarding their taxes, services, and governments. Another complaint was that federal requirements for auditing were excessive, complex, time-consuming, and duplicated provincial auditing.

Diefenbaker was not persuaded, and the October 10 meeting was a failure. However, Ottawa did respond in that the rapid growth in shared-cost programs that had characterized federal-provincial relations over the previous decade slowed down, and some programs were phased out. The other major issue in federal-provincial relations, the renewal of the 1957 tax agreements, led to the complete abandonment of the 1942 tax system. It was replaced in 1962 by tax collection agreements, in which each province set its own income tax rates as a percentage of the federal one and Ottawa collected the taxes for them. This time, eight provinces agreed to having Ottawa collect their taxes, Quebec continued administering all its taxes, and Ontario collected its own corporate income tax and succession duties.

Under the agreement, the provincial share of federal income tax rose to 16 per cent and would continue rising by 1 per cent a year until it reached 20 per cent in 1966. If the provinces wanted an even higher level of taxes, they had to pass laws to that effect. Several provinces did raise their tax rates, and Ottawa's post-war goal of imposing uniform provincial tax rates throughout the country came to an end. The fact that rates were then different in different provinces did not create any serious problems for the Canadian economy, calling into question Ottawa's rationale for imposing uniform rates after 1945.

Diefenbaker was defeated in 1963, twenty years after the federal civil servants dreamed up the welfare state and the centre-dominated federation. Part of that plan now lay in ruins or sat on the shelf. It had proven impossible for the federal government to maintain control of provincial income taxes and succession duties. Ottawa had been partially successful in implementing Keynesian economics—but only partially. There was no comprehensive federally administered welfare state, and in particular, Ottawa had failed to impose on Quebec the sort of control it came to exercise over the English-speaking provinces in the 1950s.

The 1945 welfare scheme had nevertheless been implemented in some major areas. Provincial governments in English-speaking Canada now accepted that Ottawa had a permanent role in welfare, education, health, and local infrastructure. All four of those areas had ceased to be under the "exclusive" control of the provinces as allocated in the 1867 *BNA Act*. They were now, in effect, shared jurisdiction, although the constitution continued to identify them as provincial. What had not been settled was how big or small the respective roles of the federal and provincial governments would be in those new shared areas and how Quebec would fit into the puzzle. This would have to be worked out in an environment in which both Ottawa and the provinces were on the offensive in terms of expanding the role of the state and their roles in these four areas. And that would produce the most serious clashes in the history of Canadian federalism.

CHAPTER 11
The Pearson Years, 1963-1968

Defeat in 1957 came as a great shock to the federal Liberals, who had come to believe that only they could govern Canada. They soon replaced the aging St. Laurent with Lester "Mike" Pearson, the Minister of Foreign Affairs. He was intelligent, friendly, and a great compromiser and deal-maker, but he had no particular views on where Canada should go or what the federal government should do, though he understood that relations between English and French Canadians were strained.

Co-operative or Confrontational Federalism?

The federal Liberals decided to outflank the Conservatives on the left by promising Medicare, a contributory pension plan, and a number of programs to provide more assistance for welfare, health, education, and local infrastructure. The proposed pension plan and Medicare scheme would be the biggest and costliest programs ever launched by Ottawa in provincial jurisdiction. Pearson also announced his intention to create better relations with the provinces, to practise "co-operative federalism," to respect provincial jurisdiction, and to have consultations and input into the drafting of new programs, plus better co-ordination in their implementation. One such statement came in a speech in December 1962, where he called for "the greatest possible constitutional decentralization," in light of the fact that "it is now clear . . . that French-speaking Canadians are determined to become directors of their economic and cultural destiny in their own . . . society."

The two sets of promises—more federal welfare and health programs and better relations with the provinces—were completely incompatible. The Liberal government of Quebec had demanded an end to new shared-cost programs, the right to opt out of existing ones with full compensation, and a better balance between federal and provincial revenue. These views were increasingly shared by other provinces, particularly Ontario. The platform the Liberals adopted for the 1962 and 1963 elections called for a sharp increase in the very types of policies that were poisoning federal-provincial relations.

In the next five years, Pearson was very successful in achieving the first set of goals, the expansion of the Canadian welfare state. But that was at the expense of better relations with the provinces, especially Quebec. When Pearson's Liberals won office in 1963, less than 5 per cent of Quebec's population supported separatism, and there were no separatist parties. By the late 1960s, support for separatism had more than doubled, over a quarter of Quebec's population or roughly one-third of the Québécois were becoming strongly nationalist, and there were three official separatist parties, plus one terrorist group.

Ottawa misjudged the Quebec government's attitude towards federalism and the strength of its commitment to protecting Quebec's autonomy and regaining control over provincial responsibilities. It also misjudged Quebec nationalism, a problem that seems endemic in Canadian history. In fact, Premier Lesage was as determined as Duplessis to resist federal incursions into Quebec's jurisdiction, and Ottawa would find him a tougher opponent than Duplessis had ever been. The scene was set for a showdown on federalism, or rather, for a number of showdowns.

On April 5, just three days before the 1963 federal election, Lesage laid down an ultimatum: whichever government was elected would have twelve months to meet Quebec's demands. If it failed, Quebec would unilaterally increase its rate of income tax. The 1963 Quebec budget debate highlighted the problems Ottawa's shared-cost programs were causing the province. A major example was the federal program to support technical and vocational training. Quebec's programs in this field were not nearly as extensive as those of other provinces, a clear reflection of cultural differences, values, and priorities. As a result, in 1962, Ontario had qualified for over $200 million of Ottawa's matching funds, while Quebec had only received $28 million. Lesage said that the system was unfair, unjust, and a violation of the spirit of Confederation. He demanded the same amount as Ontario had received and said the real solution was to abolish such programs, and let the provinces get on with the job of managing their responsibilities.

Lesage's statement in the budget debate was unequivocal: "This situation is totally unacceptable to Quebec." Opposition Leader Daniel Johnson went much further: "We now have to see whether this freedom of action [Pearson's promise of decentralization] can be had within a Canadian Confederation, or whether we must turn to the solution offered by the movements for independence." Johnson pointed out that in 1942 Ottawa seized 100 per cent of income taxes as a temporary wartime measure, but since then had forced the provinces to beg to get back a share of a tax that was rightfully theirs. Ottawa alone was deciding what share of income taxes could be collected by the provinces. "This situation is wholly incompatible with the political sovereignty . . . of Quebec." He supported Lesage's demand that Ottawa withdraw from social services and allow the province to collect more taxes. Those two measures, he said, would end the quarrelling.

After winning the 1963 election, Pearson called a federal-provincial conference for July. At that meeting, Lesage repeated all of Quebec's objections to Ottawa's policies and programs. He argued that all federal joint programs should be terminated with compensation, and that Quebec should receive 25 per cent of personal and corporate income taxes and 100 per cent of succession duties. Lesage stated that Quebec would oppose any new federal policies "because each [encroachment] is a threat to the autonomy of the province [and sets a precedent for the next one]." In effect, he rejected the two main federal Liberal promises—the contributory pension plan and Medicare. He added that Quebec should receive $15 million in compensation for the programs Duplessis had not joined. At that conference, Ontario Premier John Robarts also complained about shared-cost programs and proposed that provinces be given a list of them and allowed to choose which ones they wanted to join. Ottawa rejected that proposal.

The new Pearson government had no intention of abandoning its ambitious plans for completing the welfare state. That resolved the contradiction between pursuing those programs and having better relations with the provinces; the winner was the federal welfare state, the loser federal-provincial relations. From then on, "co-operative federalism" would consist largely of meetings and rhetoric, while Ottawa's actual policies would be in the direction of more interference in provincial jurisdiction.

English Canadians accepted the idea that "co-operative federalism" was in effect because many of them, including their nine provincial governments, approved the shared-cost programs. The Québécois and their government in Quebec City overwhelmingly rejected these new initiatives, and for them, Pearson's proposal, which was hardly new, represented "confrontational federalism." English-speaking Canadians, including academics, regarded new federal initiatives as quite acceptable and indeed desirable; the Québécois and their elites regarded them as a massive threat to the goal they had been pursuing since the Conquest, *la survivance* as a distinct culture, the avoidance of domination and assimilation by English-speaking Canadians.

One new policy was the Municipal Development and Loan Plan. Municipalities and local infrastructure were provincial responsibilities, but Finance Minister Walter Gordon said that measures that promoted employment were federal, a principle that could apply to any local project that required any amount of labour. The statement indicated ignorance of both the constitution and history, because the constitution did not assign employment to Ottawa and history showed that the provinces had always been involved in creating jobs. The federal plan was to be implemented directly by MPs in the municipalities within their constituencies, cutting out the provincial governments altogether. The provinces were not enthused; Quebec threatened to penalize any municipality that accepted such funds, and Ottawa was forced to abandon its plan. Instead, the $400-million budget was allocated to the provinces on a per-capita basis for them to administer however they wanted, if they chose to manage the funds themselves. Saskatchewan, Manitoba, Ontario, and Quebec opted to administer the funds; the other six provinces allowed Ottawa to administer the new program for them.

The Quebec and Canada Pension Plans

The first major confrontation was over the proposed federal pension plan. Judy LaMarsh, the new Minister of Health and Welfare, established a committee to examine the questions involved in a federal-provincial contributory pension plan. The resulting hastily and poorly drafted plan was introduced into the House of Commons on June 19, 1963, released as a white paper on July 18, and discussed at a conference on July 21–27. The plan was pay-as-you-go, with companies and their employees both contributing 1 per cent of salaries into a federal fund, of which 50 per cent could be loaned to the provinces. It would be portable between companies and between provinces, and Ottawa would administer it.

Inexplicably, the federal side did not expect problems. Quebec had been working on its own plan since 1962, and Lesage had warned Ottawa before the election against unilateral action on the issue. It was not, however, high on the list of Quebec's political, social, economic, or budgetary priorities. Ottawa's actions made it a top priority with the resulting annoyance that once more, and right after the election promise of fostering better relations, Quebec's priorities were being determined unilaterally by Ottawa's political agenda.

It was Ontario, however, that fought the first battles with Ottawa over the pension plan. Conservative Premier Robarts had set out to complete the welfare platform his party had adopted in 1942, and his plan ran head-on into the decision of the new federal Liberal government to do the same for the whole country. The Ontario government believed that most people could and should continue to handle pensions through voluntary private insurance schemes. The only role government should play was to help those who could not participate in private insurance. Private insurance had worked well in the past and worked well for other services such as dental costs, and it was how all governments had handled hospital insurance with government programs allowing poorer citizens to be included. In the spring of 1963, the Robarts government passed legislation requiring all companies to establish private, portable insurance schemes, and Ontario was working on a program to cover those unable to participate in the private ones. There was thus an unbridgeable gulf between Ottawa and Ontario, a classic political division of left-versus-right in terms of views, values, and politics; of federal-versus-provincial in terms of responsibility; and of Liberals-versus-Conservatives in terms of the political theatre.

Nothing was resolved at a federal-provincial conference on September 9–10, and the issue became a major focus of the September 25 Ontario election. LaMarsh's decision to enter the provincial campaign backfired when Robarts increased both his popular vote and the number of Conservative seats. A second draft of Ottawa's Canada Pension Plan, the

CPP, was discussed at a conference on November 26–29, with Ontario still the main opponent of the plan. At that conference, Lesage announced that, after the 1960 election, he had reversed the Duplessis policy of refusing to participate in the building of the Trans-Canada Highway, but now he regretted that decision as Ottawa had used the highway to enter a field of provincial responsibility. There were no responses to any of these points, and a third draft of the federal CPP plan was issued on March 17, 1964.

Lesage hosted the next conference, beginning on March 31, 1964. He and his government were tired of the battle over taxes and shared-cost programs, and they wanted a showdown. The stridency and determination of Lesage's opening statement took the guests by surprise. That itself was surprising, as Quebec had been complaining about these issues for decades. Lesage repeated his earlier threat that Quebec would raise taxes if Ottawa did not yield more tax points and would do so in its upcoming budget, which was due in just five days. Given that public opinion was on Lesage's side, Ottawa would have to concede or take political responsibility for the double taxation.

The main issue at the meeting, however, was pension plans. Quebec's had been completed just days before the conference, and Lesage decided to present it. The audience, which had just been briefed on the third draft of the CPP by Judy LaMarsh, was astonished. It was immediately obvious that the draft Quebec Pension Plan, the QPP, was far superior to the draft CPP. It was fully funded with contributions of 2 per cent from both employers and employees and with payments starting in twenty years rather than ten. Quebec would have complete control of a huge fund of forced private savings. The Quebec plan also included higher payments and good provisions for survivor, death, and disability benefits. The provincial delegates were overwhelmed, the federal ones embarrassed and humiliated. The federal plan could not be salvaged as it was impossible to have two radically different plans in Canada. The meeting was a shambles with Ottawa's pension plan in ruins, no agreement on taxes, no resolution of the opting out issue, and no clear indication of how Ottawa could proceed.

The mood of the federal delegation on the trip back to Ottawa was sombre and depressed, and some wondered whether Canada would even survive. That was another striking indication of how out of touch the federal government was. There was, in fact, no threat to the survival of Canada.

Ottawa had backed down before on taxes, would back down this time, and would back down again in the future. Ottawa could not win on the pension issue because it could not use the spending power to force provincial acceptance, since the pension plan would be based on contributions and not federal money. There was no pressing need for contributory pension plans, and the provinces had been slowly moving into the field. The only crisis was in the federal Liberal party when it realized that a Quebec government would succeed in defending provincial responsibility for pensions. Quebec's plan posed no problem to Canadian unity or to federalism; what it challenged was Ottawa's capacity to dictate social policy to Quebec.

The only solution to the problem was for Ottawa to copy the QPP and try to find some face-saving changes. Three people recognized that fact: Prime Minister Pearson; his principal secretary, Tom Kent; and Maurice Sauvé, a junior minister from Quebec. Without the knowledge of LaMarsh, Kent and Sauvé began secret negotiations with civil servants in Quebec City, which led to Pearson adopting a modified QPP and calling it the CPP. Quebec agreed to allow payments to begin in ten years instead of twenty. The contributions would be 1.8 per cent instead of Ottawa's proposed 1 per cent or Quebec's 2 per cent, another Quebec victory. The CPP could only be changed by agreement between Ottawa and two-thirds of the provinces containing two-thirds of Canada's population. Ottawa also agreed that neither plan could be changed without the agreement of Quebec, which gave Quebec a veto even though it did not contain one-third of the population. Those agreements made it almost impossible for political parties to play politics with either the CPP or the QPP, and within a year, contributory pensions ceased to be much of an issue in Canadian politics or in federal-provincial relations.

On April 16, Pearson informed the other provinces of the deal. The announcement meant that Ottawa and Quebec were making the big decisions by themselves and in secret. That was a matter of annoyance to other provinces, not to mention all the federal cabinet ministers who knew nothing of the secret negotiations. Ottawa achieved its goal of a "nation-wide" program, and the public announcement of both the CPP and the QPP on April 20 meant that the pension part of the crisis was over. Health and Welfare Minister LaMarsh knew nothing of the developments on the most important issue she and her department had been working on since the election. When told, she smashed the picture of Pearson that had sat proudly on her desk.

Robarts recognized that Ontario's plan for a mainly private pension system was dead. The question for him was whether Ontario should have a separate plan similar to Quebec's or join the CPP as the other English-speaking provinces were contemplating. This was one of the tougher decisions any Ontario government has ever had to make. Copying the QPP would give Ontario all the advantages that Quebec was deriving. But the exclusion of both Quebec and Ontario would severely weaken a national plan. Ultimately Premier Robarts was a Canadian nationalist, and he joined the CPP even though he never decided whether he had made the right decision.

The myth was created that Quebec had been "allowed" to "opt out" of the CPP and that Ottawa and the rest of Canada had made major "concessions" to the insatiable nationalistic demands of the Québécois. In fact, Quebec was setting up a plan for which it had every constitutional and legal authority and had not opted out of anything. In effect, the nine English-speaking provinces "opted in" to the CPP. The CPP/QPP was one of the most important programs in Canadian history and became a significant factor in old age security. Politically, the biggest loser was Ontario, although many English-Canadians in all provinces felt they had lost something because Quebec had not been forced to join the federal plan. Financially, the CPP/QPP was a huge success, with funds exceeding $500 million by 1966, the beginning of an enormous asset for the provinces to invest.

The fact that it was Quebec and not Ontario that forced Ottawa to back down reflected a major change that was underway in the country's political landscape. In the nineteenth century, Ontario had led and won the battles for provincial rights, preventing Macdonald from making Canada a quasi-federal state. It remained the main provincial obstacle to Ottawa's attempts to dominate the country in the first half of the twentieth century. But in the 1960s, the task of restraining Ottawa passed to Quebec, partly because Ontario failed in its traditional role. Robarts opposed Pearson's two main policies, contributory pensions and Medicare, but he lost both those battles. Control of taxation was a major factor. Ontario allowed Ottawa to collect taxes on its behalf, so its financial administration was not as competent and powerful as it had been before the Second World War. More important was Ottawa's relentless use of the spending power. As Canadian nationalism grew, Canadians outside

Quebec tended to accept Ottawa's arguments in favour of pan-Canadian standards and programs, and Ontarians were increasingly comfortable with policies that were made in Ottawa rather than in Toronto. That comfort level was facilitated by the fact that Ontarians accounted for over half of Canada's English-speaking population, and they dominated decision making in Ottawa.

Opting Out of Shared-Cost Programs

The Ottawa-Quebec City deal on pensions included the solution to Lesage's demands for tax abatements. Ottawa agreed to increase the abatement to 24 per cent of income tax and 75 per cent of succession duties, most of what Quebec had demanded. On the third issue, opting out, Lesage failed to achieve his goal, but won a small and confusing symbolic victory, one that has been seriously misunderstood ever since. Lesage's demand was that provinces be allowed to opt out of federal programs in provincial areas of jurisdiction and receive full compensation, that is, the amount of money Ottawa was spending on those programs. Quebec wanted to spend that money on any program and not necessarily on a similar program because, in its view, Ottawa had no right to launch programs in any area of provincial jurisdiction and set priorities for provincial spending. If other provinces wanted to spend their money on programs identified by Ottawa, that was their business, and Quebec had no interest in telling other provinces how to manage their affairs. But it had no intention of allowing Ottawa and the nine English-speaking provinces to tell it how to manage its own affairs. At the March 31 meeting, Pearson stated that Ottawa would continue to require national standards for shared-cost programs. "National standards" was the code word for Ottawa's view on any issue, and the statement meant that Quebec could not opt out of the federal programs. There was no change in Ottawa's policy of using the spending power to launch new programs in provincial areas of jurisdiction and to impose its priorities on the provinces. Pearson agreed, however, that Quebec could finance them differently. Under this arrangement, Ottawa increased its tax abatement to Quebec by twenty points, and Quebec collected that money itself and used it to pay its share of the same programs. The new system was made available to every province to avoid the impression that Quebec was being treated differently, but only Quebec took advantage of it. From then on, the term *opting out* referred to the way Quebec financed shared-cost programs, but many misinterpreted it to mean that Quebec was being allowed to opt out of the programs themselves.

Ottawa only applied the new arrangement for financing to programs that were deemed to be well established and unlikely to be cancelled. This was embodied in the *Established Programs Act*, the *EPA*, of April 1965. Accordingly, Quebec "opted out" of the federal tax system for twenty-nine well-established programs, but not for seventeen others, which were temporary or in areas of shared jurisdiction. The reason no other province followed Quebec's lead was that the change did not affect the programs themselves, and English Canadians did not care which order of government collected taxes for these programs. Quebeckers were not fooled—Ottawa was still determining how Quebec spent its own money, and Lesage had failed to change that situation.

The fact that Ottawa was still on the offensive in terms of encroaching on provincial responsibilities became evident at a meeting in March 1965. Ottawa announced new programs to provide loans to university students and extend the family allowance to sixteen- and seventeen-year-olds who were still in school or university. The family allowance had been an unconditional grant that had nothing to do with education, and the new proposal made it dependent on going to school, which discriminated against those who did not or could not, which was hardly the business of the federal government. Quebec threatened to go to court to block the new program. Quebec already had a similar program, which demonstrated that other provinces could also have them if they so desired. There was, in fact, no compelling reason for federal involvement other than political advantage, and the program was announced during an election. A compromise was reached by which Quebec received an additional tax abatement of 3 per cent and administered the program, while Ottawa administered it directly in the other provinces. Quebec could claim that it had defended its jurisdiction, Ottawa could claim that it had introduced yet another pan-Canadian plan, and another example of "special status" and conditional grants had been created.

The federal government and the English-speaking provinces had not come to terms with the fact that it was initiatives such as this that were making Quebec more and more distinct from the other provinces. In the first hundred years of Confederation, all the provinces handled these sorts of matters as they wished, and when they did things differently, none of them were "special" and none of those differences affected other provinces. Quebec had not changed, because it was still administering its responsibilities; it was the other nine provinces that were becoming different and "special" by allowing Ottawa to manage more and more provincial matters for them. Quebec was trying to maintain a genuine federal system; Ottawa and the other nine provinces were moving steadily and perhaps quickly towards a unitary form of government.

Perhaps more importantly, there was a growing feeling in English Canada that Quebec should, indeed, be a "province like the others." That meant that the one French-Catholic province should do things the same way as the English-Canadian provinces and not the other way around; it should have the same priorities and goals, implement the same programs to achieve them, and allocate the same proportion of resources to them. That was the twentieth-century version of assimilation, the goal of the *Proclamation Act of 1763* and of the *Act of Union of 1840*, the very thing Confederation was designed to avoid. Resisting assimilation had been the main objective of most French-Canadian politicians since 1791, of all Quebec governments since 1867, and especially of the Lesage government since 1960, namely to ensure *la survivance* of French culture in North America, to be *maîtres chez nous*, masters in their own house of Quebec. In as much as English Canadians understood the historical background to Quebec's determination to manage its own affairs, they increasingly disagreed that it should be permitted to do so. And in that, they were abandoning both the constitution and the rule of law.

The conflict between Quebec City and Ottawa continued to worsen throughout the 1960s. On April 5, 1965, Ottawa announced a "war on poverty" and a conference was called for December 7–10 to discuss it. The Quebec delegation headed by Premier Lesage and Ministers Eric Kierens and René Lévesque opposed it, because such a program would clash with a series of existing provincial programs that had the same goal. Another federal proposal for a health care program touched off such a bitter battle that federal and provincial civil servants ceased talking to each other.

Pressure mounted to deal with the complexity of all the programs Ottawa had launched over the years. Provincial criticism had been growing concerning the ad hoc approach that had been adopted to implementing new welfare programs and to the wide variety of conditions among those programs and between different provinces. Lévesque announced that Quebec was planning to integrate all of its social assistance, including family allowances, into a single whole. Quebec repeated the demand that Ottawa end its involvement, stop introducing shared-cost programs, stop abusing the spending power, and stop making payments directly to citizens on matters within provincial jurisdiction.

Ottawa rejected Quebec's position, arguing that its previous "concessions" only whetted Quebec's appetite for more, and said that Quebec had to accept that Ottawa had a responsibility to preserve national unity. Ottawa's arguments reflected the vicious circle that had come to characterize federal-provincial relations by the mid-1960s. It was Ottawa's continued interference in provincial jurisdiction that was fostering the rapid growth of nationalism and separatism, and driving Quebec towards increasingly intransigent stands on provincial rights. That in turn led Ottawa to insist that it needed more such programs to preserve national unity.

Some of these issues were resolved with the adoption of the Canada Assistance Plan, or CAP, in July 1966, with the approval of all the provinces. CAP united programs for old age assistance, blind persons allowances, and disabled persons allowances, plus the welfare aspects of unemployment insurance, into a single comprehensive program. It was subject to fewer conditions than the individual programs and marked the beginning of a trend away from detailed federal supervision. By uniting, simplifying, and rationalizing some of these programs, CAP proved to be one of the most successful federal-provincial initiatives of the Pearson years.

English- and French-Canadian Nationalism and the Rise of Separatism

The fundamental problem causing these tensions was that both English-speaking Canadians and the Québécois were becoming more nationalistic, and by then Canadians of English, Irish, Scottish, and other ethnic backgrounds had essentially merged into a single nation that could correctly be called "English Canadian." A fundamental characteristic of nationalism is the assumption that your national group is right and the others are wrong; that your group has solutions while the others cause problems; and that everything would be fine if others abandoned their misdirected and unjustified beliefs, values, and goals and adopted your correct ones. English-speaking Canadians increasingly believed that there was only one Canadian nation, that it included the French Canadians or Québécois, and that its members should enjoy common standards across Canada. The common standards, values, and rights they were advocating were, of course, their own, not the ones of the groups that had been assimilated or the ones of the Québécois, who had definitely and defiantly not been assimilated. English Canadians not only tolerated federal programs in provincial areas of responsibility, but they pressured the federal government to introduce more, and they believed that Ottawa had the right and indeed the duty to insist on common standards. That also meant that English Canadians were increasingly opposed to anything that smacked of "concessions" to Quebec, of "special status" for Quebec, or the recognition that Quebec was "distinct" or "a province not like the others."

English-Canadian misinterpretations of federalism, the *BNA Act*, the history of federalism after 1867, and the way it was evolving in the 1960s were reflected in the view that federalism was becoming "asymmetrical," and that this was a serious problem. In fact, the provinces had never been symmetrical and, with nine of them opting in to uniform federal policies, Canada was actually becoming more symmetrical. The problem was that federal politicians and civil servants and many English Canadians wanted policy to be completely symmetrical, the same in every province. They argued that policies should be uniform "from sea to sea," that the country needed "national standards," and that every citizen should be treated the same or was "entitled" to the same level of social services. Later, those arguments would be translated into rights, suggesting that anyone who disagreed was denying Canadian rights. All of these slogans denied the principle of federalism, and uniformity could only be achieved if the Québécois accepted the ideas, views, values, and priorities reflected in federal programs.

It was impossible for both Ottawa and Quebec City to be *maîtres chez nous* in terms of setting policies, objectives, standards, and priorities for health, welfare, and other matters in the province of Quebec, and of the two, it was Ottawa that was gaining in strength. It was gradually forcing Quebec's objectives into conformity with those of the rest of Canada. The failure to preserve its autonomy over provincial jurisdiction was increasingly clear to the Québécois. Duplessis had stood up to Ottawa by refusing to co-operate. Lesage had co-operated with Ottawa as a short-term expedient, pending Ottawa's withdrawal from the programs. Ottawa had refused, and the concessions he obtained were largely symbolic.

201

Lesage's failure to resist the tide of centralization was reflected in growing support for nationalism, for separatism, and for new ways to ensure *la survivance* against a seemingly all-powerful federal government. Key ministers such as René Lévesque and Paul Gérin-Lajoie were increasingly frustrated with Quebec's powerlessness, as were senior civil servants such as Claude Morin and Jacques Parizeau. By 1966, the Quebec Liberal regime was facing growing problems dealing with the rise of nationalism within its own ranks. A new party, the Rassemblement pour l'Indépendance Nationale (RIN), emerged to represent the nationalists. It was the first party to use the word "independence" in its name, another indication that Quebec and the rest of Canada were moving further apart. Another new party, the Ralliement National (RN), was also separatist but more conservative. At the same time, the most radical nationalists joined the Front de Libération du Québec, the FLQ, whose campaign of bombings and kidnappings gained sympathy, support, and strength throughout the 1960s.

Most importantly, the Union National reinvented itself under the leadership of Daniel Johnson. He had been in the Duplessis government and knew that the policy of refusing to participate in federal programs had failed. He had watched for six years as Lesage's attempt to gain the right to opt out of programs had also failed. Johnson was very aware of the strong nationalist winds blowing through the province and the dangers they posed for draining traditional UN support to the new, more extreme nationalist parties. He captured the spirit of the times in the title of his book, *Equality or Independence.* If Canada was based on two founding nations, if Quebec was the homeland of one of them, and if the federal government would not respect Quebec's jurisdiction, then what was needed was a redefinition of federalism to create a sort of bi-national country based on equality between Quebec and the rest of Canada. And if English Canada would not agree, then there were only two options left—the status quo, which few Québécois accepted, or independence, which more and more were endorsing.

Medicare

While the gulf between English Canadians and the Québécois was rapidly widening, Pearson moved to implement the second major promise of the 1963 election campaign, Medicare. That would touch off more battles with the provinces, the main opposition coming once more from Ontario, with Alberta as a close second. Saskatchewan had introduced a public Medicare system in 1959, the first such program in North America. The federal CCF naturally wanted a federal program, the Diefenbaker government appointed a Royal Commission to gather the facts, and the federal Liberals also endorsed Medicare.

Provinces other than Saskatchewan were also moving towards Medicare. When Medicare was announced in the 1963 federal budget, the provinces regarded it as inevitable because "free" Medicare would be politically irresistible. Diefenbaker's Royal Commission continued its investigation, and civil servants worked on a plan. In March 1965, Quebec set up a committee to study the issue. There were no federal consultations with the provinces, and at a conference on June 19, 1965, Pearson told a surprised group of premiers that Canada was to have a shared-cost Medicare program. Not all of the province's health programs were covered, and Ottawa's share would amount to around 40 per cent of provincial spending once Medicare was implemented.

Only Saskatchewan agreed. Alberta's Premier Ernest Manning said it was unnecessary, as well as being questionable constitutionally—he became the most articulate critic of the plan. Ontario's Premier Robarts was predictably angry and stated that it was "one of the greatest frauds that has ever been perpetuated on the people of this country." Quebec regarded it as yet another massive incursion into provincial jurisdiction: Minister of Health Eric Kierens was furious, as was another key minister, René Lévesque. The shared program would cost $1 billion annually, a quarter of it in Quebec, which meant that the Quebec government's spending on health would mount sharply. Its budget had already been prepared, citizens were resisting further tax increases, and once more Ottawa was attempting to dictate Quebec's priorities.

The provinces would be paying half the bill for the new health programs, and they had to meet four federal conditions: that the program be portable, comprehensive, universal, and government-run. Ontario had private plans, which did not meet these criteria, and by 1965, it had a government plan to cover those too poor to participate in the private ones. It did not believe that a national plan was needed and vehemently objected to the federal government's attempt to impose such a massive plan in an area of provincial jurisdiction. Alberta, by then the bastion of laissez-faire capitalism and "small government," did not believe in any government-run scheme. Manitoba agreed with Ontario and Alberta, but BC started to move towards Saskatchewan's position.

On July 27, 1965, Premier Robarts strongly condemned Ottawa for failure to consult the provinces and for using the spending power to force provinces to accept its dictates. He argued that the discussion of Medicare should be postponed until the completion of several major studies that were underway. He asked Ottawa to share the studies it had done, but Ottawa refused. Robarts did not believe Ontario could afford the plan and was upset that it would lead to the cancellation of private plans that had worked well for decades. That same month, Lesage once more demanded that Ottawa stop using its spending power to invade provincial jurisdiction.

Ottawa was also abandoning some other shared-cost programs that imposed federal standards. Pulling out of them would double the provinces' costs for those programs, since the public was accustomed to them and would demand that they be maintained. Ottawa was, in effect, jumping in and out of provincial areas of jurisdiction with its shared-cost programs, without any overall plan, imposing conditions and cherry-picking where and when it would become involved, change conditions, or withdraw, to the consternation of provinces that were trying to plan coherently for all of their responsibilities. Those were the complaints the provinces had levelled in 1960, and the problems had grown more severe. By 1966, seven of ten provinces still opposed the federal Medicare plan, and their opposition was growing because Ottawa had announced that it would make no more increases to the tax abatements. Ottawa's plan would therefore force the provinces to increase taxes, transfer resources from other programs to Medicare, or wait several years until they were in a position to participate.

Public opinion was strongly in favour of the single plan for the whole of Canada, and the *Medical Care Act* was passed by the Commons in December 1966, by a vote of 177–2. Pearson wanted the program to begin on July 1, 1967, the centennial of Confederation. Finance Minister Mitchell Sharp told him that Ottawa could not afford to launch the program that year, and it was postponed until July 1, 1968. Ottawa then cancelled other shared-cost medical programs, including cancer care and medical research, putting more pressure on the provinces to join. Saskatchewan and BC were the only provinces that joined Medicare at the beginning, but all provinces had joined by 1971. By 2000, Medicare was certainly one of the most successful and popular programs ever launched by any government in Canada.

The January 1966 Throne Speeches in Ottawa and Quebec showed that the differences between them were growing. The federal Speech said that Ottawa should expect "some assurance . . . that [Quebec] desired to preserve and strengthen Canadian unity . . . [and] if federal compromises merely increased the appetite for concessions, then the country was in for trouble . . ." One week later, the Quebec Throne Speech referred to two concepts of Canada, one favouring "a more and more unitary type of Canada with powers centralized in Ottawa . . .", the other "a healthy and constructive division of powers" that would enable French-speaking Canadians "to develop according to their aspirations . . ."

These issues formed an important backdrop to the 1966 Quebec election, which most people expected Lesage to win. The outcome was a shock. The Union National won and the two new separatist parties, the RIN and the RN, polled almost 10 per cent of the vote. A very substantial majority of the Québécois had voted nationalist, including many Liberals, and a significant part of that nationalist vote was either separatist or willing to consider separatism. The new premier, Daniel Johnson, said that Quebec would not participate in any more federal programs in provincial areas and that Ottawa should withdraw from all the programs it was involved in. That, of course, was what Lesage had said in 1960, and his failure to protect Quebec's autonomy was a major factor in his defeat.

At the same time, Ottawa was beginning to change its views on several aspects of its relations with the provinces. Since 1954, it had yielded to provincial pressure to allow the provinces a larger and larger share of the income taxes and succession duties that Ottawa alone had collected under the wartime agreements. By 1966, nine provinces were receiving 25 per cent of the personal and corporate income tax collected by Ottawa, and Quebec was receiving 45 per cent. Ottawa decided that it was time to put an end to its reluctant retreat from the wartime collection of 100 per cent of those taxes. Ottawa was also becoming concerned that provincial dependence on federal programs was destructive of good government. If left unchecked, that trend would suck Ottawa further and further into the detailed administration of programs and into increasing conflict with all provinces, especially Quebec.

Federal Finance Minister Mitchell Sharp therefore announced at a conference in September 1966 that Ottawa intended to make all the provinces opt out of the system whereby the federal government collected taxes for their portion of the shared-cost programs. The nine English-speaking provinces would thus be forced to collect the taxes themselves, as Quebec had been doing. They would receive a final tax abatement of seventeen points, which would eliminate the impression that Quebec was achieving "special status," but federal conditions would still apply to the programs. From then on, any increase in provincial tax would have to come from their taxpayers and not out of Ottawa's share.

The main debate at the October meeting, however, was over education. Since 1950, Ottawa had been giving grants to universities, but it decided to replace that program by paying half the operating costs of universities and to do so by giving the provinces a further abatement of four points of personal income tax and one point of corporate income tax. It also decided to cancel the shared-cost program for technical and vocational education and pay the full amount. It argued that manpower training prepared people for work and was thus an economic matter and hence federal. By that definition, almost any school course could be defined as federal, and Premier Johnson flatly rejected the argument: training was education and education was provincial.

The federal proposals were vague, hastily prepared, and poorly presented. There had been no warning that these changes were coming, and the provinces were given one day to reply, prompting many panicky phone calls back to provincial capitals. All the provinces were upset with the proposals and the way they were announced, as these programs had been very valuable to them. Johnson gave a detailed presentation of Quebec's position, demanding full control of social policy, a massive reallocation of resources, and recognition in the constitution that Canada was based on two nations. There was little support from the other provinces, and none from Ottawa.

After several days of rancorous debate, Ottawa refused to alter the thrust of its policies, but Pearson sweetened the pot by increasing the amount of the equalization grants. That was the politics of "divide and conquer" as the deal pitted the poorer provinces against the richer ones. Since debate was proving futile, some premiers started to leave, and Pearson quipped that he supposed the meeting was adjourned. One provincial representative said he had never been to a meeting where federal positions were so poorly prepared and presented. In March 1967, Parliament passed legislation implementing its new policies on manpower and training at the same time as Medicare was being put into effect. These changes all reflected the fact that the struggle was really over power, and Ottawa was still determined to use its fiscal power to dominate Quebec. The stage was set for even more bitter battles between the two governments and for the sequel of rapidly increasing support for Quebec separatism.

The Constitution and Foreign Affairs

In 1967, the centennial of Confederation, Premier Robarts took a leadership role in easing federal-provincial tensions by hosting a meeting of premiers to celebrate the work their predecessors had done a century before and discuss the current state of the nation. It was called the Confederation of Tomorrow Conference. The Union National had been demanding constitutional change, and while Robarts had no similar demands, he saw a need for a thorough discussion of the issues. Ottawa definitely did not want such a discussion, but other provinces wanted some changes. The main result of the Conference was that Ottawa was forced to accept that constitutional change was now on the national agenda, which led to the first of many constitutional conferences in February 1968.

Another issue of increasing importance in the 1960s was the desire to agree on a formal amending process for the *BNA Act*, so the *Act* could be patriated from London and become a purely Canadian document. Work had proceeded well under the chairmanship of Diefenbaker's Minister of Justice Davie Fulton, and was continued after the 1963 election by the new Liberal Minister of Justice Guy Favreau. By October 14, 1964, there was agreement with all the provinces on what was called the Fulton-Favreau formula.

Nationalist Québécois wanted the constitution to state that Canada was a compact between two races, to recognize that Quebec was the homeland of the French-Canadian nation, and to recognize "special status" and the fact that Quebec was "not a province like the others." They forced Lesage to withdraw his agreement to the formula he had just accepted. Tactics then became crucial, because if the Quebec nationalists won recognition of Quebec's status first, both sides could get much of what they wanted—recognition of Quebec's special status, constitutional reform, an amending formula, and patriation. But if English-speaking nationalists had their way, Canada would have an amending formula and patriation first, and then Quebec would not likely be able to obtain the constitutional reform it wanted because the English-speaking provinces would be able to veto it.

Later in the decade, the position of some other provinces hardened on the related issue of appointing Supreme Court justices. There was no clear pattern of pro-federal decisions by the Court, but the belief that it was pro-federal was considerably strengthened in 1967 when it had to determine whether the resources off the coast of BC belonged to the province or to the whole country. Ottawa's case was not particularly strong because natural resources on the mainland were provincial, and those under the Pacific would not have belonged to Canada if BC had not joined Confederation. BC was supported by Ontario and the Atlantic provinces, and Premier Lesage argued that the issue was political and should be settled by negotiation. The Supreme Court found for Ottawa, and the decision strengthened provincial demand for a role in the selection of Supreme Court justices.

In the last year of the Pearson era, the constitution replaced the welfare state as the main battleground in federal-provincial relations. On the Quebec side, the replacement of Lesage by Daniel Johnson marked a very significant shift. Neither Duplessis nor Lesage had questioned the *BNA Act*; what they demanded again and again was simply that Ottawa respect it and obey the rule of law. Johnson, however, wanted the *Act* fundamentally changed to recognize Quebec as the government of the Québécois, that is, to recognize the equality and duality of the two races. He argued that Quebec must regain full powers over social security, family allowances, education, culture, municipal affairs, and regional economic development, and have the right to sign agreements with foreign countries and a role in communications policy if the matter was provincial. He also argued that the Supreme Court should not be the final court of arbitration since it was appointed by Ottawa and was two-thirds English Canadian.

On the federal side, Pierre Elliott Trudeau had become Minister of Justice, and he was one of the most anti-nationalist of all Quebeckers. He rejected separatism, special status, and nationalism, and argued that the best protection for French culture and language was a partnership of French and English within a strong federal government. He rejected the argument that French Canadians outside Quebec had been assimilated and that the Québécois constituted a nation separate from the other French Canadians. He wanted a guarantee of rights for French Canadians everywhere, to be enshrined in a charter within the constitution, which was then to be patriated from London. His concern was with the rights of French Canadians as individuals, not as a group, and certainly not as Québécois. Trudeau wanted a stronger Ottawa and weaker provinces, especially a weaker Quebec. There was little room for compromise between his position and that of Johnson.

These differences came to a head at the federal-provincial conference in February 1968, shortly before Prime Minister Pearson retired. In several speeches, Trudeau had taken a very hard line with the UN and other nationalists. Pearson was not pleased with that approach, but Trudeau received a strong and positive response in English Canada and some support in Quebec. Pearson opened the conference with the warning that the survival of Canada was at stake, but the main confrontation was between Trudeau and Johnson. While Johnson argued that the constitution should be changed dramatically, Trudeau replied that there was nothing wrong with the BNA Act as long as Ottawa respected provincial jurisdiction.

The problem with that, of course, was that Ottawa had not respected provincial jurisdiction for decades, and any debate over the division of powers between Ottawa and the provinces was bound to demonstrate clearly that Ottawa was involved in a wide range of fields of "exclusive" provincial responsibility. Johnson failed to make a good case, and Trudeau won a clear victory. The fact that the debate was televised made him the main contender to replace Pearson—who better to stand up to the "insatiable demands" of Quebec nationalists for "concessions," "opting out," and "special status" than a tough, informed, perfectly bilingual, and highly articulate Québécois? The conference was, of course, a failure, a harbinger of another decade and a half of such failures.

In one particular area, Quebec was clearly on the offensive, and that was foreign affairs. The BNA Act left control of foreign affairs in the hands of Great Britain, where it had remained until Canada became independent in 1931. Many people assumed that Ottawa inherited control of foreign affairs from Britain and that only the federal government could conduct relations with other countries, but the constitution was never amended to state that. In fact, a number of provinces had maintained offices abroad for years, promoting their interests, including trade, which was constitutionally a federal monopoly.

As part of the Quiet Revolution, Quebec followed the English-speaking provinces into a more active role abroad, but it also upped the ante. In 1961, it opened the *Maison du Québec* in Paris, catching up to a number of English-speaking provinces that had offices in the UK and the US. Quebec also demanded the right to negotiate agreements with foreign countries and to send delegates to international conferences if the subjects were provincial under the *BNA Act*. Ottawa insisted that it alone had such authority. Both sides were half right and half wrong—relations with foreign countries had to be federal, but Ottawa had neither authority nor expertise to handle matters that were provincial.

After considerable tension, gamesmanship, clashes, rhetoric, and embarrassments, the two sides were driven to compromise by politics, mutual interest, and common sense. It was agreed that delegations to international conferences would be headed by federal officials but could be staffed with provincial ones, that provinces could negotiate agreements with foreign countries but Ottawa had to sign them, and that Ottawa could negotiate umbrella agreements covering culture and education under which provinces could work out formal agreements with those countries.

Agreements between Ottawa and France in 1964 and 1965 allowed Quebec to develop student exchanges and to train civil servants in France. In 1967, these programs were furthered when Ottawa and the new Johnson government signed a seventeen-point agreement on education, culture, and research. These agreements, however, were overshadowed by the crisis produced by Quebec's drive for international recognition during the 1967 centennial celebrations. Foreign heads of state were invited to visit Canada, including French President Charles de Gaulle. Premier Johnson had been cultivating Quebec's relationship with France, and de Gaulle had been all too happy to encourage him. After a royal reception, de Gaulle addressed a large rally from the balcony of Montreal City Hall, enthusiastically shouting, *"Vive le Québec libre!"* An infuriated federal government terminated the visit, and Canada's relations with France reached a new low.

De Gaulle's hasty departure did not put an end to the problems. In February 1968, the tiny African country of Gabon invited Quebec to a conference on education and treated the delegation as though it were from a sovereign state. Canada broke relations with Gabon and launched a full-scale diplomatic campaign to ensure that no country treated provincial delegations as though they represented Canada. By the end of Pearson's regime, however, this problem had been largely put to rest.

Pearson, the Maritimes, and the West

In the Pearson years, peace and harmony reigned between Ottawa and the Atlantic provinces. The Pearson government continued the basic thrust of the Diefenbaker regime, which had begun treating the region as a full-fledged but disadvantaged part of the country. The four provinces continued to lag far behind the rest of Canada, a gap that would have increased greatly were it not for equalization grants. These were unconditional, so the provinces spent them according to their priorities and felt a great deal of gratitude towards Ottawa. The shared-cost programs with their federal standards and qualifications also created few problems.

Unlike some other provinces, the Atlantic ones did not have any option but to accept the grants with whatever strings were attached, and the fact that these grants distorted their priorities was just a political and administrative price to pay for "fifty-cent dollars." Indeed, none of them had enough revenue to cover any of their responsibilities, so if a federal shared-cost program helped them with one area but not another, that at least meant progress on one front. They could also use the large, unconditional equalization grants to cover their portion of the shared-cost programs. The main problem with this situation was a long-term one—these four provinces were losing their independence to the politicians and civil servants in Ottawa. They were becoming, as Sir John A. Macdonald had wanted, glorified municipalities administering federal programs. At the time, that seemed a small price to pay or, rather, one that had to be paid no matter the long-term consequences.

During the Pearson years, the relations between Ottawa and the western provinces were largely peaceful. Saskatchewan, of course, was delighted when Ottawa applied its Medicare system to the whole of the country; Alberta protested but was powerless to stop it. The main complaint of the western provinces was that Ottawa seemed to be obsessed with the problems of Quebec at the expense of attention to Western issues.

The Pearson era had begun on an optimistic note, with a new and invigorated national government replacing one that had descended into confusion and chaos. Pearson set out to complete the welfare state, and six years later, Canadians enjoyed a superb pension program and a Medicare system. A plethora of other programs provided assistance to educational facilities and students, to areas of health and welfare that had fallen through the cracks of previous programs, and to local infrastructure and municipalities. Pearson did achieve his goal of completing the Canadian welfare state.

These initiatives, however, produced continuous conflict with the provinces and with the two largest, Ontario and Quebec, in particular. The Government of Ontario could be, and was, brushed aside. Quebec City could not be ignored, because the Québécois still insisted on being in charge of their own lives. But Premier Lesage lost almost every battle to stop Ottawa from encroaching on Quebec's constitutional responsibilities. The result was growing nationalism, the appearance of separatist parties, and a wave of terrorist bombings. Paradoxically, English Canadians were increasingly of the opinion that Pearson had made too many "concessions" to Quebec and were less and less willing to accept what had been reality since 1867, namely, that Quebec was not "a province like the others." Pearson was replaced by the man many English Canadians and some Québécois thought could rein in Quebec, a Quebecker of half-French and half-Scottish ancestry named Pierre Elliott Trudeau. He would have to deal with Pearson's legacy—a superb welfare state that could not be sustained financially and a deepening crisis in federal-provincial relations.

PART IV
The Modern Era

CHAPTER 12
The First Trudeau Regime, 1968-1979

No prime minister had such an effect on federalism as Pierre Elliott Trudeau. He held the office for fifteen years, interrupted only by the nine-month reign of Joe Clark's Progressive Conservatives in 1979–80. His two regimes are among the most controversial in Canadian history, with Canadians highly polarized along regional, ethnic, linguistic, economic, and political lines, some supporting him to the point of hero-worship, others regarding him as one of the worst prime ministers in history. He was unique amongst prime ministers in that federal-provincial relations and constitutional issues dominated his entire period in power, producing some of his greatest triumphs and greatest failures.

In part, the mixed record stems from the contradictions in his personality, his speeches, and his actions. In his earlier career, he was a strong believer in classic or genuine federalism, the idea that each order of government should stick to its responsibilities. Then, as prime minister, he launched several of the most centralizing policies in Canadian history. He was a sharp critic of nationalism, especially as found in Quebec, but was a very strong Canadian nationalist. He entered politics because he believed that the central government had yielded too much to Quebec, and he argued that all provinces should be treated the same even as he treated them differently, especially Quebec. His alleged opposition to special status for Quebec fit into the English-Canadian nationalism that was rapidly growing, and English-Canadian academics strongly endorsed Trudeau's view and supported him politically. English-speaking Canadians believed that he spoke for Quebec, but while many Québécois voted for Liberals in federal elections, they often voted differently in provincial elections and it was far from clear who spoke for Quebec.

One of the first issues Trudeau dealt with was the report of the Bilingual and Bicultural Commission. One of Pearson's first acts as prime minister had been the appointment of a Royal Commission to study the state of "bilingualism and biculturalism" in Canada. Canada had, in fact, been multilingual and multicultural for at least four hundred years, and many Canadians did not accept that English and French should enjoy privileged positions. The Commission's recommendations would almost certainly affect federal-provincial relations, because provinces with large ethnic and linguistic minorities were angered by the idea of being relegated to second-class status, and any recommendations the Commission might make for a federal role in advancing linguistic or cultural rights were bound to interfere with provincial jurisdiction over those matters. Paradoxically, that concern applied to Quebec, the home of most of the people who were the prospective beneficiaries of any new federal initiatives. No Quebec premier had ever raised concerns with "bilingualism and biculturalism" at federal-provincial meetings, and no premier wanted federal involvement in these issues at the provincial level.

The Commission did not report in time for Pearson to take any action, but Trudeau was very strongly in favour of the recommendations regarding bilingualism. To make French Canadians feel more at home everywhere in Canada, his government launched a massive program to ensure that they could deal with the federal government in their own language. He was determined to ensure that they occupy a fair proportion of the important positions in the federal cabinet and civil service. Trudeau was equally strong in his opposition to the second half of the Commission's mandate, the promotion of biculturalism. To Trudeau, biculturalism meant recognition of the French Canadians as an ethnic group, and he was well aware that Canada was hardly bicultural. Trudeau therefore replaced the idea of biculturalism with *multiculturalism*. That policy was especially popular among minorities and in western Canada, where bilingualism was highly unpopular. Multiculturalism was also a direct rejection of the Compact Theory of federalism and the views of Quebec's government, because it meant that the Québécois were not one of two dominant ethnic groups, but just one of dozens, all of which were sort of equal in everything but language.

For the majority of Québécois nationalists, federal bilingualism policies were of little value and multiculturalism was both an insult and a political threat. What they wanted was to strengthen French language rights inside Quebec, which was accomplished through a series of ever-tougher language laws. Those laws seriously upset Quebec's Anglophone population, the federal government, and the population of the English-speaking provinces. Throughout the 1970s, language policy became an increasingly important federal-provincial issue, mainly in terms of the way it hardened attitudes between Quebec, Ottawa, and the other nine provinces. The Québécois felt that Ottawa and English Canada were interfering in their provincial matters; Ottawa and English Canadians felt that Quebec was denying constitutional rights to its non-French minorities. These linguistic issues then formed an increasingly important backdrop to other federal-provincial relations and English-French relations, including the debate over the constitution.

More Incursions into Provincial Affairs

Battles over the control of social policy came just as quickly. One of the first clashes between Trudeau and Quebec was over family allowances. Since 1944, the federal government had been paying an allowance for young children. Quebec had not objected at the time, but in the 1960s nationalists in the Lesage government such as René Lévesque began arguing that family allowances should be an exclusive provincial matter. In 1967, Quebec created its own program, which differed from the federal one by having a progressive scale of payments depending on the size of the family. Then, in 1969, the Johnson government demanded that Ottawa transfer its program to Quebec. Ottawa refused, partly because the two governments were now competing for the loyalty of the province's citizens, and family allowance cheques from Ottawa or from Quebec City were important weapons in the battle for the hearts and minds of the Québécois. Trudeau accelerated the policy of his predecessors in becoming more and more involved in local economic development, which was constitutionally an encroachment on provincial jurisdiction. In 1969, Ottawa established the Department of Regional Economic Expansion (DREE) to give itself a large, rapidly growing, and highly visible role in local development, especially in Quebec. Quebec and other provinces criticized DREE, as its programs were developed by federal officials and presented on a "take it or leave it" basis. In 1970, Ottawa established the Department of Urban Affairs and Housing. The *BNA Act* gave the provinces exclusive responsibility for municipal affairs (Section 92.8), public land (Section 92.5), property (Section 92.13), local works (Section 92.10), and "all matters of a purely local . . . nature" (Section 92.16). Nevertheless, the new department launched more and more programs in municipal affairs, and it attempted to become involved in urban planning. The rationale advanced was that urban problems were "national" since they existed in all Canadian cities. But cities had always faced problems and that hardly made their problems "national" rather than local. Indeed, by Ottawa's logic, urban affairs were international. Nor did the theory explain why the Fathers had made these matters provincial, why Ottawa had left them alone for a century, or why Ottawa was determined to become more and more involved in them in the 1970s.

In addition to the traditional desire of federal politicians and bureaucrats to expand their power, the new initiatives were driven by Ottawa's desire to increase direct contacts with the public, to let them know that Ottawa was as important a government and benefactor as the provincial governments. In particular, it was increasingly driven by the desire to make Quebeckers look to Ottawa, to see themselves as Canadians first and Quebeckers second. Naturally Quebec governments of any stripe would object to these encroachments on constitutional grounds, and Ontario was concerned over administrative problems such as duplication and co-ordination. Other provinces welcomed federal spending in their cities, but these new initiatives became yet another element and often an irritant in federal-provincial negotiations.

The Department of Urban Affairs lacked the knowledge and administrative base of municipal governments and operated on the fringes of the other governments, launching initiatives here and there, starting and ending programs in ways not fully co-ordinated with the other governments, and often acting for political and short-term imperatives, adding nothing that could not have been provided by the same taxpayers through their municipal and provincial governments. The taxpayers were increasingly confused about which order of government should be credited or blamed for urban problems. Ultimately, Ottawa recognized that the political costs exceeded the benefits, and the department was abolished in 1979.

One of the worst examples of Ottawa's use of its constitutional powers to gain more control of local economic development was the construction of Mirabel airport northwest of Montreal. The selection of the site became one more unnecessary battle between Ottawa and Quebec City and a striking example of federal economic and political mismanagement. Quebec wanted a new airport east of Montreal to facilitate the economic development of the Montreal–Trois-Rivières–Quebec City axis. Airports were a federal responsibility, but Quebec believed that its responsibilities for local matters such as roads, urban areas, and the local economy, as well as the costs it would incur facilitating access to the airport, should give it a role in the selection of the site. It saw the issue as a shared responsibility and proposed a joint committee to select a site satisfactory to both governments.

While negotiations were proceeding, Prime Minister Trudeau dramatically arrived by helicopter at Ottawa's preferred site at Mirabel, northwest of Montreal, and announced that Ottawa's decision on the location was final. Ottawa expropriated an area far greater than needed for the airport itself so that industries would be located on land controlled by Ottawa rather than the municipalities. Farmers, municipalities, and the Quebec government were furious. The poor location and continued squabbling ensured the failure of the venture, and Mirabel became one of the great white elephants of federal transportation policy. In one of the ironies of Canadian history, the airport that Mirabel was designed to supersede, Dorval, was renamed Pierre Elliott Trudeau International Airport.

As the fiscal situation tightened, the provinces continued their criticisms of the shared-cost programs. By 1970 there were seventy-nine such programs, and the provinces complained that they had to join new ones because of public pressure to take advantage of the fifty-cent dollars, the public seemingly ignoring the fact that it was also paying Ottawa's 50 per cent. Spending fifty-cent dollars encouraged overspending, and the provinces, not Ottawa, decided how much would be spent. So while the provinces could not reject Ottawa's programs, Ottawa could not control the costs of the programs and the inevitable result was that costs, waste, and political squabbling continued to grow.

Ontario in particular argued that the system had to be changed. In 1968, Ontario's treasurer said that the shared-cost programs were heading for catastrophe unless Ottawa yielded more tax room, a demand now more than twenty years old. Ottawa refused and said that the provinces had to increase their tax rates if they wanted more revenue, telling them, in effect, to raise their taxes in order to participate in federal programs. In 1968–69, Ottawa was unwilling to negotiate new tax agreements; at the same time it was increasing its tax revenue, making it more difficult for the provinces to increase theirs, and it was beginning to cut back on transfers to the provinces, which called into question both its right and its ability to dictate conditions.

At the Constitutional Conference of June 1969, Ottawa distributed a working paper replying to provincial criticisms of its use of the spending power. The unexciting title was "Federal-Provincial Grants and the Spending Power of Parliament." In reply to the criticism that Ottawa launched programs without consultation, it said the provinces were free not to participate. History, however, had demonstrated that public pressure would, in fact, force the provinces to participate. In reply to the criticism that the programs affected provincial priorities, it said that national priorities were more important. That was a subjective argument no province would accept. In reply to the argument that some provinces were taxed for programs not implemented in those provinces, it said that MPs from all provinces participated in federal policy formation. That was untrue of provinces that had no MPs on the government benches and a substantial exaggeration of the influence of backbench MPs. The paper ignored two of the most serious criticisms: that the programs gave Ottawa a role in provincial areas of responsibility, and that they were often announced without prior consultation.

The paper gave four reasons why Ottawa should have a significant role in social issues. It had to be able to redistribute income between individuals and between provinces; it had to build a sense of community; it had to create uniform standards across the country; and it had to spend money on social issues in order to stabilize the economy. The idea that Ottawa "had" to do all these things was subjective and political, a view of federal politicians, bureaucrats, and their supporters that was not shared by provincial politicians, bureaucrats, and their supporters. The document indicated that Trudeau had no intention of reducing Ottawa's role in the welfare state or of abandoning the practice of attaching conditions to its programs. Somewhere along his personal journey, he had abandoned his earlier faith in genuine federalism.

By the time Trudeau became prime minister, three constitutional issues had become political priorities, at least for some people: a re-examination and perhaps rejigging of the division of responsibilities, the adoption of an amending formula, and patriation of the constitution from London. The first of the many constitutional conferences of the Trudeau era took place in February 1969, following negotiations, talks, and discussions that had continued since Pearson's failed 1968 conference. Two things were different in that Ottawa had a majority government under a tougher prime minister and new Quebec Premier Jean Jacques Bertrand was more flexible. The underlying problems were the same, however, and the respective positions were even more entrenched. Trudeau was determined to add to the *BNA Act* an amending formula and a charter of rights and freedoms that included language rights, and then to patriate the *Act*. The English-speaking provinces did not want enhanced language rights or a charter, but they now wanted some of their own issues added to the agenda. Trudeau's first federal-provincial conference failed to settle any of the issues, and so did the next five.

The Canadian political landscape changed dramatically when Quebec Premier Bertrand called an election for April 29, 1970. Under Robert Bourassa, the pro-federal Liberals elected seventy-two of the 108 MLAs. Support for the Union National fell dramatically as much of the nationalist vote went to the new Parti Québécois of René Lévesque. As with Lesage's victory a decade earlier, the meaning of Bourassa's victory was misread by many observers including, once more, the federal government. The Liberals were back in power, but the nationalist vote had increased dramatically and the Liberal victory depended in considerable measure on the fact that the nationalist vote was split between the UN and the PQ. But Bourassa's

Liberals were a federalist provincial party, and the election was wrongly seen as an endorsement of federalism.

Almost before the new Bourassa government could settle in, it faced a crisis provoked by the kidnapping of a British diplomat, James Cross. On October 10, a second group acting independently kidnapped cabinet minister Pierre Laporte. That threw some people into a panic, particularly Mayor Jean Drapeau of Montreal and several members of the Bourassa cabinet. Others such as René Lévesque; Claude Ryan, editor of the influential newspaper *Le Devoir*; and some business and labour leaders urged the Quebec government to negotiate over the release of the prisoners. The Bourassa government was divided on what course of action to take, which gave the impression of dithering. On Wednesday, October 14, the RCMP told the federal cabinet that the best course was to continue its investigation. Instead, at 3 AM on Friday, October 16, Ottawa invoked the *War Measures Act*. Parliament was told that the *Act* was required because an insurrection was underway to overthrow the government of Quebec. The House of Commons approved the *Act* by a vote of 190–16 without seeing any evidence of an apprehended insurrection, or for any of the other arguments that had been advanced.

At 4 AM on that Friday, 12,500 soldiers, plus the RCMP and the provincial and municipal police, began implementing the *Act*. More than 450 people were arrested, and ten thousand houses were searched. The sweep produced no proof that an insurrection was underway or even being planned; no missing arms or explosives; and no leads regarding the kidnappers. The FLQ cell holding Laporte panicked and murdered him on October 17. Two months later, normal police work led to the discovery of Cross's kidnappers and Laporte's murderers. The imposition of the *War Measures Act* infuriated the PQ, labour leaders, nationalists, civil rights advocates, and the general public, and anger mounted as it became clear that the federal government had no evidence to support its decision. In Quebec, the main political legacy was a strengthening of the independence movement, increasingly strained relations between Ottawa and Quebec City as well as between Trudeau and Bourassa, and a lasting distrust of the Trudeau Liberals by the PQ and many of the Quebec intelligentsia. It did, however, make Trudeau very popular in English Canada, where people mistakenly thought that he had "put Quebec in its place." Six years later, the Québécois who had supposedly been put in their place elected the province's first separatist government.

The Victoria Conference

Throughout this period, constitutional talks continued between federal and provincial leaders. The next formal round began with a First Ministers' meeting in September 1970, where the mood, at least, was positive. Unlike Premier Lesage and his predecessors, Bourassa was not demanding that Ottawa restore and respect the 1867 division of responsibilities. Unlike Premier Johnson, he was not demanding a new constitution that would recognize Canada as being based on two founding partners. Bourassa knew that the neat power division of 1867 no longer existed and could not be recreated. Whatever the constitution said, health, welfare, and education were no longer "exclusive" provincial responsibilities, and the division of responsibilities could now be discussed in terms of modern realities.

In January 1971, Trudeau sent his right-hand man Marc Lalonde and his Cabinet Secretary Gordon Robertson to Quebec City to identify Bourassa's minimum demands for a constitutional settlement. Those demands were not unreasonable, and Ottawa decided they could be accommodated by the federal government. Lalonde and Robertson visited the other nine provinces to identify their minimum demands and to convey Quebec's views and Ottawa's acceptance of them. Justice Minister John Turner later toured the provincial capitals to confirm their agreements. Between January and May, the concerns of Ottawa, Quebec, and the other provinces were met to a degree acceptable to all. An amending formula was agreed upon, giving vetoes to Ontario, Quebec, and any two provinces from Atlantic Canada or the West that had 50 per cent of their respective populations. The provinces would have a role in the selection of Supreme Court justices, and three of them had to come from Quebec. All this was drafted into the *Victoria Charter*, the result of four years' work, seven First Minsters' meetings, nine formal meetings of ministerial committees, fifteen formal meetings of subcommittees, and countless hours of bilateral talks, drafting, and re-drafting.

The first ministers agreed to meet in Victoria on June 14, 1971. It was expected that they would have a final look at the document, sign it, congratulate each other, and pop the champagne corks. The governments,

223

caucuses, or legislatures could pass it or reject it, but they could not change it. The *Charter* would then be sent to London, where the government would pass the necessary legislation, happy to be rid of the Canadian problem left over from the distant days of colonialism. Canada would have its constitution, Trudeau would have his *Charter of Rights*, the provinces would have the changes they had requested, and the eleven governments could get on with matters of more interest and importance to their citizens.

That optimism was shattered when it became clear that Bourassa had made one of the biggest political blunders of his career, one of the biggest and most damaging blunders in the entire history of federalism. The "bottom line" of demands that he had given to Lalonde and Robertson at the beginning of the process turned out not to be the bottom line for his cabinet. Minister of Social Affairs Claude Castonguay had been presiding over a study of the whole range of social issues. The conclusion of that study was that Quebec had to integrate all the social programs that affected its citizens. That was not possible when, for example, Ottawa controlled unemployment insurance while Quebec controlled the welfare of the unemployed. The only way all the programs could be fully integrated was if Quebec or Ottawa was the paramount power for all of them, and to Castonguay, that meant Quebec.

When the pensions acts were passed in 1951, the constitution was amended by Section 94A to give Ottawa the power to enter the field, but left the provinces paramount over pensions. Now, just before the Victoria meeting, Castonguay convinced Bourassa that a similar amendment had to cover the entire field of social policy and be part of the new package of constitutional reforms. In effect, Castonguay was demanding that Ottawa and the other nine provinces accept that the constitution state that while the provinces no longer had "exclusive" responsibility, they at least retained "paramountcy." Gordon Robertson was shocked when informed of Quebec's new condition and said that Bourassa had to inform Trudeau immediately of such an important change. A betrayed Trudeau was predictably furious. The other nine premiers were equally shocked. They had accepted Quebec's "bottom line" as part of the compromises, and they and Trudeau saw the new demand as a trick, as evidence of bargaining in bad faith, as proof Quebec's demands were insatiable and that new ones would be added as soon as old ones were accepted.

Instead of celebrating their agreement at Victoria, the first ministers engaged in intense and bitter discussions including a closed thirteen-hour meeting. Trudeau had no intention of recognizing provincial paramountcy over federal programs, and the other nine provinces would not yield to a new demand after agreeing to the former "bottom line." Bourassa failed to obtain approval for the change, but seemed to accept that Quebec had gained all it could. The Conference was a disaster, and, as a desperate attempt to keep the issues in play, the participants agreed on a ten-day delay while they consulted their cabinets. This was window dressing as it was only Bourassa who had to convince his cabinet that the deal was both final and the best possible.

In his *Memoirs*, Trudeau describes his objections to Quebec's demand. According to his interpretation, they had agreed that there would be shared jurisdiction, but the last-minute proposal meant that Quebec would control the programs. Ottawa would then be collecting the money, and Quebec would be spending it as it wished. Other provinces would follow Quebec's lead, and Ottawa would become the tax collector "for a confederation of shopping centres." This was an odd interpretation, because provincial paramountcy over social programs did not mean that the only federal role in such programs was to give money to the provinces. Paramountcy meant that Ottawa could not initiate shared-cost programs if they clashed with provincial ones in the same area. That was the case with the CPP/QPP deal, and it was functioning extremely well. The suggestion that Canada might become a "confederation of shopping centres" was indeed absurd—shopping centres are not governments, and Trudeau's suggestion implied that the provinces, including Quebec, would disintegrate into a bunch of politically independent collections of retail stores. Trudeau's extreme exaggeration masked the real issue, which was power: Ottawa had successfully made health, welfare, education, and local development "shared" responsibilities rather than "exclusive" provincial ones, and it would not accept that the provinces were at least still paramount in what used to be their exclusive powers.

Back in Quebec City, Bourassa was surprised by the reaction to the Victoria package. The three opposition parties—the UN, PQ, and New Democratic Party (NDP), which had replaced the old CCF—were outraged with the failure to obtain recognition of Quebec's paramountcy over social policy. So, naturally, were other hard nationalist groups such as the St. Jean Baptiste Society and the major unions. Soft nationalists within Bourassa's own cabinet such as Claude Castonguay were angry, and even federalists such as *Le Devoir* editor Claude Ryan regarded the *Victoria Charter* as a sell-out. The cabinet was in crisis, and an all-night session resulted in Bourassa reversing his recent endorsement of the *Charter*. Trudeau was outraged and became convinced that Bourassa could not be trusted and was too weak to be premier. Bourassa's announcement of the rejection of the *Victoria Charter* was, however, applauded by MNAs from all parties in the Quebec Assembly.

The Conference foundered on Bourassa's mishandling of the negotiations, but Ottawa and the nine English-speaking provinces would almost certainly have rejected Castonguay's demand if it had been included in Bourassa's initial "bottom line." Throughout the constitutional debate of the 1970s and 1980s, it was clear that Ottawa and the nine provinces would not accept that the government of Quebec should have or regain paramountcy over education, health, and welfare. The fundamental compromise of Confederation—that every province must control these matters—was dead, and the constitution was not going to be changed to recognize that the Québécois were *maîtres chez nous* on matters of social policy.

Quebec's rejection of the *Victoria Charter* downgraded constitutional issues for several years, but they certainly did not disappear. Trudeau's biggest dream upon entering politics lay in ruins, possibly forever. He never forgave Bourassa, and the relations between the two Quebec-based politicians and political parties were often hostile. In Quebec, Bourassa became the latest in a long series of premiers who had failed to guarantee *la survivance* of Québécois culture against the assimilating pressure of Ottawa and English-speaking Canadians. The failure of the *Victoria Charter* was a disaster for the participating governments, for Quebec, and arguably for all of Canada.

It was particularly a disaster for federalists in Quebec. The failure gave credence to the PQ argument that Quebec's aspirations could never be met within Canada. After the Conference, the top civil servant, Claude Morin, resigned from the government, joined the PQ, and wrote an article in *Le Devoir* on May 23 saying that, after ten years of negotiating with Ottawa, he had concluded that the federal government was "barely willing to let us operate a province under supervision." He said that "the inevitable tendency of the present federal system is to erode the power of Quebec . . . What is now at stake is the very existence of an effective Quebec capable of solving our problems, the very existence of the only political entity we can truly control and employ." Many Québécois agreed with him; few, if any, English-speaking Canadians did. Public opinion polls documented the trend, with support for independence at 8 per cent in 1966, 16 per cent in 1970, 21 per cent in 1973, and 24 per cent in 1976. Amongst the Québécois, the figures were 24 per cent in 1970, 30 per cent in 1973, and 41 per cent in 1976. Support for the new PQ jumped from 23 per cent before the Victoria Conference to 30 per cent in 1973.

Constitutional Battles in the Mid-1970s

Problems with the shared-cost programs continued into the 1970s. In May 1972, Ottawa unilaterally introduced major changes to the universal pension and the Guaranteed Income Supplement (GIS), changes that affected Quebec's programs and its overall plan to integrate and rationalize all its welfare programs. Castonguay almost resigned in frustration. The resentment over the way Medicare had been introduced and its cost led the other provinces to share Quebec's opposition to the programs. Once more, this movement was led by Ontario, which produced a paper in 1972 listing all the shared-cost programs and identifying a series of problems with them. The main criticisms were that they interfered in provincial jurisdiction, made it difficult for the provincial government to control its overall expenditure, and made it difficult for the premier and cabinet to control the departments that were involved directly with Ottawa in administering the shared-cost programs.

Trudeau narrowly held onto power in the 1972 election but his re-election with a majority in 1974 led him to renew the effort to address constitutional issues. At a dinner with the premiers on April 9, 1975, he proposed that they patriate the constitution using the amending formula accepted at Victoria and leave all other issues for future debate. There was agreement to take another look at the issues. Cabinet Secretary Gordon

Robertson was sent to discuss this proposal in more detail with the premiers. Trudeau repeated the proposal in a letter to the premiers dated March 31, 1976. That letter also raised the issue, or rather made the threat of asking Britain to patriate the constitution with or without the agreement of the provinces. This proposal was unprecedented—no federal government had ever hinted that it could act alone in matters that affected the provinces. This new approach was, indeed, an implicit denial of the principle of federalism.

Trudeau's letter was not well received by Alberta, Saskatchewan, and BC, all of whom now wanted the other issues resolved before the constitution was patriated. The main objection, however, came from Quebec City. Since it was Trudeau and English-speaking Canadians who wanted patriation, Bourassa correctly saw that withholding agreement was a good bargaining lever for Quebec's demands. That list had been steadily growing and now included the right to opt out of federal programs with full compensation, complete control of culture and education, a Quebec veto on future amendments, limitations on the federal declaratory and spending power, increased control over immigration, and constitutional guarantees for Quebec's responsibility for the French language and culture in Quebec. Direct meetings between Trudeau and Bourassa made things worse, and after one in March 1976, an angry Trudeau publicly referred to Bourassa as a "hot-dog eater," suggesting that he was uncultured and shallow.

The premiers held several meetings in 1975 and 1976, during which the four western provinces tabled a list of fifty-seven examples of federal intrusions into their jurisdiction. They rejected Trudeau's proposal regarding patriation, and their chairman for the meeting, Alberta Premier Peter Lougheed, conveyed that decision to Trudeau in a letter dated October 14, 1976. It said that the provinces wanted a number of issues solved before patriating the constitution: clarification and expansion of powers over culture, communications, and natural resources; a role in appointing senators and Supreme Court judges; limits on the federal spending and declaratory powers; and more aid to deal with regional disparities. In the summer of 1978, the premiers produced a longer list of federal powers that they wanted restricted or transferred.

Canadian Nationalism vs. Quebec Nationalism

Bourassa called an election after only three years, another major political miscalculation. The Quebec electorate did not favour separation, but the PQ had adopted a clever strategy: campaigning on a platform of good government rather than independence and the promise of a future referendum on the possibility of negotiating independence from Canada. The electorate could now get rid of Bourassa without voting for independence, and that was exactly what it did. On November 15, 1976, Quebec's first separatist government was elected with 41 per cent of the vote and seventy-one seats. Separatism was not dead, as Trudeau had been saying, and his leadership, policies, and practices were increasingly being questioned and even blamed for the rise of separatism. He had, after all, gone to Ottawa in 1965 to counter the growth of nationalism in Quebec, but the result had been the exact opposite. And he had personally contributed to Bourassa's defeat by undermining him with public criticisms and insults and reluctance to compromise, leaving little of federalism for Bourassa to defend.

The election of a separatist PQ government ended English Canada's complacency towards Quebec and ushered in two decades of serious and bitter political debate and constitutional manoeuvring. To deal with the ongoing crisis, all the governments reinforced the sections of their bureaucracies that dealt with other governments. Numerous studies were launched and reports released. Premiers' meetings established task forces that made more studies, and common positions were gradually adopted. One was the condemnation of Ottawa for intervening in court cases involving provincial ownership of resources, which was seen as an excessively aggressive attempt to undermine provincial autonomy. Other areas examined included the Supreme Court and Senate, both of which were seen as unfair, if not hostile, to provincial interests.

The new PQ government was, however, in a conflicted situation. On the one hand, it wanted more evidence that federalism did not and could not work to address Quebec's problems, a goal that required fighting with Ottawa. On the other, it had to provide good government and deliver services, a goal that required co-operation with Ottawa. The result was four years of co-operation on issues such as immigration and economic development, coupled with conflict on the constitution. Evidence of co-operation included seven new projects that were announced in 1978 and provided over half a billion dollars for roads, infrastructure, and cultural sites, 60 per cent of it paid by Ottawa. Quebec also accepted changes to the financing of shared-cost programs, although it was not happy with the details.

Trudeau's response to the PQ victory was to forge straight ahead with his existing plans, rather than seriously address any of the issues that had led a majority of the Québécois to vote for a separatist party. In 1977, he put his toughest and most trusted ally, Marc Lalonde, in charge of federal-provincial relations. In Parliament, Lalonde introduced the *Constitutional Amendment Bill*, which contained much of the agreement reached at the Victoria Conference and proposed that Ottawa unilaterally patriate the constitution. By now, however, Ottawa's attempt to control resources in the western provinces had changed their views on the constitution, and they wanted a stronger constitutional guarantee of provincial control of resources. The *Bill* was referred to the Supreme Court, and in 1979, the Court declared that the federal government could not change matters affecting the provinces. On January 19, 1977, Trudeau repeated the earlier proposal of patriation first, to be followed by the discussion of responsibilities. This led to a series of meetings in 1978 and 1979. At the conference in October 1978, Trudeau presented a list of seven matters Ottawa might give to the provinces, but the gap between him and the premiers was much too wide and his mandate was running out. The provinces could wait him out because Liberal popularity was at a low point, and the Conservatives of Joe Clark were much more flexible on matters of federal-provincial relations.

One of Trudeau's responses to the new situation was the appointment of a commission to study all the issues. It was called the Task Force on Canadian Unity and was headed by former Ontario Premier John Robarts and respected Quebec federal cabinet minister Jean-Luc Pépin. The choice of chairmen was curious; indeed, it was a mistake. Normally, prime ministers select chairmen who agree with what the government wants and produce reports recommending that course of action with supporting documentation and argument. But Robarts had fought Ottawa's centralization throughout his premiership, and Pépin sympathized with many of Quebec's concerns. The Commission's conclusions were more in line with Quebec's traditional views, namely that the provinces were not equal, that

Canadian federalism was asymmetrical, and that there should be some decentralization of power. That was the opposite of Trudeau's view, and he allegedly threw the report in a waste basket. It was another blow to his plans, as was the replacement of Bourassa by the much more nationalistic Claude Ryan as head of the Quebec Liberal party.

During this period Trudeau grew increasingly concerned with the idea that Canadian citizens had stronger loyalties to, and identification with, their provinces and provincial governments than with the country and the federal government. It is not clear that there was such a problem, as most Canadians identified with their communities, provinces, regions, country, and the global community. The relative strength of those overlapping identities shifted over time, were different between individuals and provinces, and were not necessarily in conflict or a source of problems. It was clear, however, that many Québécois felt a stronger sense of identity with each other and with Quebec than with other Canadians and Canada. That had been true for centuries, but it particularly bothered Trudeau.

Ottawa therefore launched a series of measures to increase the federal presence in Quebec. There was more emphasis on "national" interests and institutions, and the word Dominion went out of fashion. The Royal Mail became Canada Post. Ottawa created pro-federal constituencies by funding special groups—youth, women, environmentalists, and municipalities—and by ensuring that the provinces told their citizens that half the money for shared-cost programs came from Ottawa. Between 1970 and 1976, the cost of federal advertising increased 400 per cent. This competition between Ottawa and Quebec for the hearts and minds of the Québécois had to be copied to some degree across the country, which magnified the steep increase in the costs of government. The competition accelerated rapidly after the PQ came to power. Far more federal money was spent in Quebec per capita than anywhere else, an implicit recognition of Quebec's political "special status."

Natural Resources: Ottawa vs. the West

In the 1970s, the constitutional issue was about to be severely complicated by developments in the relationship between Ottawa and the three westernmost provinces. Indeed, relations between Ottawa and those three provinces were about to deteriorate to a level approaching those between

Ottawa and Quebec. The cause was a doubling of the international price of oil that produced a massive increase in revenue, especially for Alberta. It was perfect timing for the new regime of Progressive Conservatives under the young, smart, dynamic, and tough Peter Lougheed. At the same time as Ottawa was trying to increase its political and economic power across Canada, Lougheed emerged as a key proponent of greater co-operation among provinces in defending their constitutional responsibilities and rights from an assertive federal government. The Trudeau-versus-Lougheed battles would soon be as dramatic and important as those between prime ministers and Quebec premiers. Ottawa was about to enter a very bitter, two-front battle with the West and Quebec, something unprecedented in the history of federal-provincial relations.

Although Ottawa had given the three Prairie provinces control of natural resources in 1930, there were still those in central Canada and in the federal government who apparently believed that the resources of the Prairie provinces belonged to all Canadians, unlike the resources of other provinces. Federal politicians argued that all Canadians had the right to a share of "windfall" profits that resulted from the jump in oil prices, and they decided to tax oil and gas revenue. The problem with this argument was that numerous resources and industries in various provinces had experienced "windfall" profits, but Ottawa had never before suggested that such profits be shared across the land. Profits from the sale of hydro-electricity increased in tandem with oil prices, and Ontario and Quebec earned "windfall" profits on those natural resources, but there was no attempt to tax them and redistribute that wealth. What was particularly galling for the West was that their economy had always been used to support industrialization in central Canada, and now that fate had given them a chance to grow and diversify, it was being denied by a federal government based overwhelmingly on voters in central Canada.

In late 1973, the federal government imposed an export tax on oil and gas shipped to the United States, used that revenue to subsidize imports into eastern Canada, and froze the domestic price of oil to the benefit of consumers, voters, and Liberals from coast to coast. Both measures transferred Albertan tax dollars to Ottawa and the rest of Canada. Lougheed described it as "the most discriminatory act by a federal government against a provincial government in the entire history of Confederation . . ." He pointed out that Alberta had always paid world prices for minerals from central Canada and asked why there were two prices for oil and one for other resources. He also questioned why there was no similar tax on the exports of products from other provinces.

After very difficult negotiations, on March 27, 1974, Ottawa and Alberta agreed to increase the domestic price of oil, partly because Ottawa was facing a huge deficit and needed to collect more taxes. One day later, Lougheed announced a new royalty rate that would raise an additional $900 million in revenue. Two months after that, the federal budget stated that the royalties oil companies paid to the province could no longer be deducted from their federal income tax, a measure that significantly raised the amount of taxes those companies paid to Ottawa, and one that was not applied to royalties on other resources. Lougheed said that measure interfered with provincial ownership of resources and violated the agreement they had reached in March. He saw the federal actions as a naked money grab, a power play, an attempt by the federal Liberal government to buy votes in central Canada with revenue taken from a provincial Conservative administration, and a means to interfere in provincial jurisdiction. Those with memories of the twenty-five-year battle to gain control of natural resources saw it as an attempt by Ottawa to return Alberta to the status of second-class province. Lougheed had no choice but to enter a bitter and lengthy dispute. Ottawa's position was basically untenable, and further agreements with Alberta in 1975 and 1977 produced a step-by-step plan to move Canadian prices to the level of world ones. By 1978, this problem seemed well on its way to solution.

Ottawa's taxation of oil and gas in the three western provinces and the maintenance of below-world prices across Canada represented, in effect, another equalization program. But unlike the formal one, redistributing revenue from this single economic sector was not based on any identifiable economic or financial criteria, other than the fact that the three western provinces were experiencing rapidly increasing revenues. Paradoxically, the policy transferred money from Saskatchewan, which was still technically a have-not province, to Ontario, which was still a have province. It was thus becoming increasingly difficult to know exactly how much money Ottawa was transferring from rich to poor provinces, one more example of how federalism was becoming so complex that neither politicians, bureaucrats, nor experts fully understood it.

Next door in Saskatchewan, the taxing and control of natural resources was also a dominant issue for the NDP government of Allan Blakeney, first elected in 1970. Though the two Prairie governments represented opposite ends of the political spectrum, they soon became close allies in the battles with Ottawa over the control and taxation of their resources. Their goals, tactics, and policies were different, however. Blakeney was determined that the people of Saskatchewan would receive almost all the benefits from the rise in oil prices. To achieve this objective, he established Saskatchewan Oil and Gas Corporation, SaskOil, in March 1973. Ottawa could not tax provincial Crown corporations, and SaskOil could help the government obtain a clear understanding of how the industry operated while also giving it a direct share in production, retailing, and profits. New legislation imposed special taxation on windfall profits and led to a series of battles with Ottawa. One company went to court to challenge the province's tax on windfall profits. In an unprecedented move, Ottawa intervened in the case to support the private company against another order of government.

Saskatchewan won in the first court case and the first appeal, but on November 27, 1977, it lost 7–2 in the Supreme Court. The ruling stated that Saskatchewan's surcharge on the royalties of oil and gas companies was beyond its powers because it was an indirect tax, which companies did not pay since they passed it on to their customers. Also, since almost all the oil and gas was sold outside the province, provincial taxes interfered with trade, which was federal. These arguments were seen by the provinces as a serious distortion of tax law and of federal jurisdiction. All companies collect the money they pay in taxes from their customers. Almost all of Canada's exports come from within provinces, and provinces had always taxed resource exports such as minerals and timber. The Supreme Court decision strengthened the view in the West that the federally appointed Court was an instrument of the central Canadian–dominated federal government. In a tough speech to the Canadian Club in Toronto, Blakeney said, "I have become convinced that (Ottawa's) unrelenting attack on our resource policy is prompted . . . by a desire to extend the . . . powers of the federal government at the expense of provincial powers." Blakeney's government then devised different forms of taxation, in search of one the courts would accept as being within provincial power.

Unlike Alberta, Saskatchewan was also a major producer of potash and was in a position to influence global supply to prevent overproduction and disastrous fluctuations in price. It had been doing this by pro-rationing production among companies, but in December 1972, one of them took the government to court for restricting production, and Ottawa supported the company as a co-plaintiff. The Saskatchewan government was shocked—it was the companies that had asked for regulation; it was the former provincial Liberal government of Ross Thatcher that had introduced it; and Ottawa had previously shown no interest in the issue. Now, if the company won the case, not only would a stable industry become subject to boom and bust, but Blakeney's government would have to pay back millions of dollars the companies had allegedly lost because of the previous pro-rationing of their output. Blakeney was infuriated and vowed to "use all weapons open to us to defend the people of Saskatchewan and their resources."

In 1975, the Supreme Court found against Saskatchewan, arguing that the issue was more a matter of trade than of resources. Blakeney responded by establishing the Saskatchewan Potash Corporation, which soon bought up 40 per cent of the province's potash industry. The issue of pro-rationing continued to percolate and on October 3, 1978, the Supreme Court ruled 9 -0 that the pro-rationing system for potash was beyond provincial power. The decision came during a provincial election, and Blakeney argued that Ottawa was using the Court to take control of provincial resources. Lougheed supported him, and the two premiers argued for provincial input into the appointment of Supreme Court judges and for clarification of wording of the constitution to reduce the Court's capacity to interpret federal and provincial jurisdiction. Their attitude towards the Supreme Court also made them hostile to Trudeau's goal of adding a charter of rights to the constitution, since that would give the Court even more power at the expense of elected governments. Blakeney won the election and became one of the major actors in the continuing battle over the constitution.

Another indication of increasing nationalism in Ottawa was the establishment of Petro-Canada. The oil and gas sector was largely foreign-owned, second only to the automobile sector, so nationalizing had much left-wing support. It would be a fully integrated company involved in exploration, development, refining, and marketing oil and gas products, and it would have a network of highly visible service stations across the land. They would probably charge the same prices as the privately owned companies, but at least Canadians would know that its profits were added to federal revenues and not the dividends of American shareholders. And, as a federal Crown corporation, Petro-Canada would be difficult for Alberta to regulate.

The pay-off for Trudeau's battles with the West occurred in Ontario. Premier Bill Davis seemed to believe that the energy-producing provinces should subsidize Ontario's consumers and industry, something Ontario had never done in terms of its own sales to other provinces. Conservative Ontario became a firm ally of Liberal Ottawa on both energy and constitutional issues. Ontario had evolved from being the strongest defender of provincial rights to being Ottawa's strongest provincial partner. The alliance was highly successful for both parties and would prove crucial in the constitutional negotiations in the following decade.

Inflation, Immigration, UI, and the Balance of Power

Another of the major problems Canadians faced in the mid-1970s was a very high rate of inflation. After the 1975 election, Trudeau introduced price and wage controls to bring down the rate. The premiers saw that legislation as yet another attempt by Ottawa to centralize power and invade provincial jurisdiction. The issue went to the Supreme Court, which sided with Ottawa in a 7–2 decision. Failure to stop Ottawa on that matter further hardened provincial opposition to other federal initiatives and narrowed the gap between Quebec and the English-speaking provinces, which were now moving closer to positions similar to those Quebec had championed on federal-provincial issues for decades.

A rare bright spot on the Ottawa-Quebec relationship concerned immigration, which was constitutionally a shared jurisdiction with Ottawa paramount. As Quebec's birth rate plummeted and its share of Canada's population declined, its governments became more interested in using immigration to maintain a significant Francophone population. A Department of Immigration was created in 1968, and in 1971, Quebec began stationing immigration officers in Canadian missions abroad, where they had a role in the selection of immigrants. Other provinces could have become involved in the selection of immigrants, but none did. These arrangements made Quebec more "special," but Ottawa was willing to recognize Quebec's need, and the program worked quite well, a good example of asymmetrical federalism and of flexibility.

In 1976–77, Trudeau introduced one of the most important and radical changes to several shared-cost programs, a change that transferred back to the provinces a considerable amount of the power Ottawa had taken from them when it created the programs. The provinces had been complaining about the shared-cost programs since they began in 1927, but more importantly, Ottawa's financial situation was becoming precarious. Federal spending surged due to high interest rates on the debt, the 1972 expansion of unemployment coverage and benefits, subsidies for oil and gas imports into eastern Canada, new programs for regional economic development and urban renewal, and the rapidly increasing federal payments for the shared-cost programs.

In December 1976, Trudeau proposed to replace Ottawa's direct funding of half the costs of shared-cost programs for Medicare, hospital insurance, and post-secondary education with a combination of 50 per cent grants and 50 per cent tax abatements. The amount was tied to GDP and was therefore fixed, stable, and predictable. Provinces could no longer spend money knowing that Ottawa had to match their expenditure. The money still had to be spent on the three shared-cost programs, but in effect the provinces could spend the half that came from tax abatements almost any way they chose. Ottawa could still use the half it provided as cash to ensure the provinces followed the general conditions of the three programs. Ottawa thus gave up a considerable amount of control over the programs, but that was not, in fact, a serious problem, as provinces were always under pressure to spend much more on health and education. The new system gave all the provinces greater flexibility and met many of their concerns. Since the amount was based on Canada's GDP rather than on the amount each province spent, the amounts were equal per capita rather than being a subsidy to the richest provinces. And since it applied to all provinces, opting out ceased to be an option and Quebec was no longer "special" in this regard. As part of this process, Ottawa abandoned any attempt to control its contributions for post-secondary education.

Other skirmishes developed as the two orders of government sought to deal with the problems created by the ad hoc approach both had taken to introducing the welfare state. One such area of friction was unemployment insurance. Relaxing the criteria in the early 1970s had produced a drain on federal coffers, so Ottawa reversed direction and tried to save money by increasing the time one had to work in order to qualify. That impacted provincial welfare programs, and Ottawa made compromises. In 1978, Ottawa proposed making eligibility more difficult for seasonal workers, another reversal of the changes of the early 1970s, and the provinces protested because that shifted costs to their welfare programs. Faced with the same deteriorating financial situations, the provinces proposed making it more difficult for one member of a family to draw unemployment insurance if another was working, but Ottawa rejected that proposal. A few reforms were made, but the fundamental problem was not addressed, namely the fact that the federal UI program was still not fully integrated with the provincial welfare ones.

The arrival of new technologies often raised questions as to which order of government had responsibility, and one of the latest was cable television. In the 1920s, the courts had ruled that radio was federal because broadcasts crossed provincial and international borders. That interpretation applied to TV when it appeared on the scene in the 1950s. But, in 1974, Quebec argued that cable TV should be a provincial responsibility because it was a local system, did not cross provincial or international borders, and was becoming an important element in education. Although Ontario, BC, Alberta, and Saskatchewan supported Quebec, the Supreme Court ruled that cable TV was a federal responsibility, because it was part of the TV system. The decision was 6–3, the three dissenting judges being from Quebec. English-speaking provinces saw this case as one more example of the Supreme Court supporting the centralizing tendencies of the federal government; Quebec saw it as proof the Supreme Court could not deal fairly with its interests.

In the late 1970s, the question of minority language rights continued to bedevil relations between provinces and between Ottawa and the provinces. Trudeau's position was that Canadians should have the right to go to schools in English or French anywhere in Canada. That would have weakened provincial control over education, and was, in effect, an attempt to reverse the outcomes of the battles over education in New Brunswick, Manitoba, Ontario, and the North-West Territories. Even John A. Macdonald had avoided those battles. At their annual meeting in February 1978, the premiers rejected Trudeau's proposal. They agreed that English and French minorities should have access to education in their own language where numbers warranted, but that it was up to each province to implement that policy.

As Trudeau failed to achieve his objectives, he became increasingly convinced that the problem was not the objectives themselves, but rather the inability of the federal government to force the provinces to accept them. He and many others began arguing that Canada was becoming highly decentralized with an increasingly weak federal government whose capacity to govern the entire country was in danger. It was argued that Canada was the most decentralized federation in the world, but one of the world's federations had to be the most decentralized; Canada was the largest and, unlike Australia, Germany, or the United States, was the only one with a minority group of 25 per cent of the population concentrated in a single province. Comparisons to the US ignored the fact that Washington achieved dominance over the states as a result of a civil war that had cost six hundred thousand lives. Whether Canada was over- or under-centralized was a subjective opinion, and the assertion that it was overly decentralized was essentially an argument for a stronger central government.

The theory that the provinces had become too strong was supported by comparisons of federal and provincial spending, with the assumption that spending equalled power. The shrinking federal proportion was exaggerated by using Second World War figures as a base, a period when federal spending had been maximized. The financial power of provincial governments was exaggerated by including municipal spending. In the 1970s, a growing population spilled into the suburbs, requiring schools, roads, sewers, and parks. The municipalities had to collect more taxes, and the provinces had to assist the municipalities. Building suburbs for a growing population did not make provincial governments "stronger" than Ottawa, and it actually made the Atlantic provinces even more dependent on Ottawa. There was no evidence that Ottawa was too weak to govern the country and, in fact, federal involvement in regional development and urban affairs was still expanding.

Trudeau's concern with the alleged growing power of the provinces was summed up in several phrases: that if the trend to decentralization continued, Canada would not be able to act "in unison"; that it would become a "Confederation of semi-independent states"; and in the question, "Who speaks for Canada?" These phrases strongly suggest that Trudeau no longer believed in a federation, because federalism exists precisely so the provinces do not have to act "in unison." Second, Canada had always been a "Confederation of independent states," in terms of the matters that were provincial. Third, there had never been any question about who spoke for Canada. If the issue was federal or national, then the prime minister spoke for all Canadians; if the matter was provincial or local, then the premiers spoke for the Canadians in their province and the ten premiers spoke for all Canadians. No premier was asking to speak for Canada on national or international matters; it was Trudeau who was upset because he could not speak for all Canadians on provincial matters.

Another conference in February 1979 failed, and Trudeau called an election for March 26. He had come to Ottawa to counter Quebec nationalism and arrest what he saw as the erosion of federal power. Fourteen years later, the nationalists had evolved into outright separatists, had won an election, and were preparing to launch a referendum campaign, seeking a mandate to negotiate the breakup of the country. Ottawa's attempts to gain control of the revenue from natural resources had alienated the three westernmost provinces and moved them from indifference about the constitution to being allies of Quebec. As an academic, Trudeau had been regarded as an expert on federalism; as a politician, he pursued contradictory policies, some increasing Ottawa's power, some transferring power to the provinces. First Ministers' meetings had become commonplace, one following on the heels of the previous one in a dreary pattern of failure and public recrimination. In 1979, Ottawa's relations with the provinces were at their lowest ebb in history, and the man who had been prime minister for eleven years was widely regarded as a failure. That was but one of many factors that suggested Canadians were headed for a new government and perhaps a new chapter in relations between the two orders of government.

CHAPTER 13
The Second Trudeau Regime, 1980-1984

The election of 1979 brought Joe Clark and the Progressive Conservatives to power in a minority government. Trudeau announced his resignation, and an era in Canadian history seemed to have come to a close. The new government did not share Trudeau's belief that the country had become overly decentralized and the provinces too powerful, and it was therefore in a position to have much better relations with the provinces. That possibility disappeared as it almost immediately faced confrontation with two strong Conservative provincial regimes.

Another sharp jump in the international price of oil had created a new gap between that price and the one Lougheed and Trudeau had agreed upon. Lougheed was again demanding that Canadian prices rise to international levels. Although Alberta had voted solidly Conservative and the West had strong representation in the federal government for the first time since 1963, that government was managing a country whose population had enjoyed the benefits of buying oil products at less than international prices. Clark was caught between the interests of his western base of support and the majority population of central Canada, and especially between the Alberta and Ontario Conservative governments.

Energy prices were to be addressed in Clark's first budget, which was presented on December 11. Clark assumed that with the Liberals leaderless and the election only a few months in the past, his minority government faced no danger of defeat and could govern as though it had a majority. Both assumptions proved wrong. The wily Liberal politician Allan MacEachen calculated that Clark might not have a majority for his first budget and it was he, not Clark, who had done the arithmetic correctly. The Clark government fell on December 13, and whatever beneficial effect it might have had on federal-provincial relations was lost. The next election was set for February 18, 1980.

Trudeau did not require much persuasion to withdraw his resignation. There had been no renewal of the federal Liberals in terms of leadership, personnel, or policy, but the party and Trudeau were rejuvenated by the surprising turn of events. They won a convincing victory, their seat total rising from 114 to 147. Equally important was the distribution of seats: 126 of 170 in central Canada, nineteen of twenty-five in Atlantic Canada, and only two in the West, both in Winnipeg. Canada had an eastern Canadian government, not a national one, and that would be very clearly reflected in Ottawa's policies towards the provinces.

The reborn Liberals had a very different attitude than the one they had carried into the previous election. Given the polls in 1979, they were not surprised to have lost that election. But they had been shocked by the political obituaries that appeared after Trudeau announced his resignation. They focused on the failures, the economic mismanagement, the dismal state of relations with the provinces and with the United States, the contradictions, and the aimlessness in both policy and action. Trudeau had been rated as one of the worst prime ministers in Canadian history. Changing that reputation would drive the second Trudeau regime as much as any policy goals.

Surprised to be back in power, Trudeau and his colleagues were suddenly energized, focused, disciplined, united, and determined. They narrowed their agenda to four specific issues: Quebec, the constitution, energy, and the economy. They were not going to let any obstacles stop them or even slow them unnecessarily, including the provinces, the constitution, the public, or the British government. The word "compromise" was not in their vocabulary, and they were determined, for example, to patriate the constitution with or without the support of the provinces, and to expand Ottawa's control of energy resources regardless of what the constitution said about provincial ownership. Observers would later describe the government's newfound determination and its unilateralism as unprecedented in a federal state and, indeed, as a contradiction of federalism as a form of government.

The Liberals were determined to promote Canadian nationalism, to ensure that Canadians identified more with their national government than with their province, and to promote the view that all Canadians should have the same rights and access to government services. However laudable these goals, they implied a major shift in power from the provinces to Ottawa and, indeed, a denial of some fundamental principles of federalism. In particular, Trudeau was determined to ensure that Quebec be treated the same as other provinces. This was a denial of the very purpose of Confederation and of the fact that Canadian federalism had always been asymmetrical, that Quebec had always had "special status," and that all provinces were different in some ways and had all been treated differently by Ottawa since 1867. Oddly, his actions did not conform to his stated intentions as he treated Quebec as special in many ways.

Trudeau's concept of a charter of rights reflected his desire to have one set of values for the whole country, rather than ten slightly different ones as the *BNA Act* allowed. Some provinces already had bills or charters of rights, and if they differed from those of other provinces, it was because the respective populations had different circumstances and views of human rights, not that they did not respect rights. Since the main differences were between English-speaking and French-speaking Canadians, Trudeau's proposed national charter represented, in effect, a new attempt to assimilate the Québécois and was seen by many in Quebec as a threat to *la survivance*, the preservation of their unique situations, society, values, language, and culture.

Canadians began to realize that there had been a significant shift in Liberal thinking when Trudeau spoke to the House of Commons on April 15, 1980. It would take some time, however, for people to understand that his new strategy was to use Canadian nationalism to counter Québécois nationalism; after all, he had condemned all nationalism for decades. One problem with nationalism, as he had written, is that in a highly nationalist people there is room for only one political identity. He saw Canadians having a choice between identifying with the country or with their province, and he seemed to reject the idea that people could see themselves as Montrealers, Québécois, and Canadian at the same time. For Trudeau, identification with Canada had to outweigh identification with a province because he was, above all, a Canadian nationalist.

The Quebec Referendum

One of the first items on the new federal government's agenda was the Quebec referendum on separation. In the 1976 provincial election, Premier Lévesque had promised a referendum seeking authority to negotiate sovereignty-association with Ottawa. On November 1, 1979, the PQ released its arguments for separation in the form of a white paper entitled *Quebec-Canada: A New Deal*. The date was set for May 20, 1980. Claude Ryan and the provincial Liberals had undertaken a massive study of the province's place in the federation and advocated remaining a province provided there was a large degree of decentralization. Their position was presented in detail in a document called the Beige Paper. It was the sort of nationalist program that had troubled Trudeau for decades: more power and special status for Quebec, the very things he had gone to Ottawa in 1965 to fight.

The first debate on the referendum took place in the Quebec Assembly on March 4, 1980, and the PQ won it convincingly. It continued to do well in the early stages of the campaign. Trudeau convinced Ryan to stop referring to the Beige Paper, to the consternation of provincial Liberals who had put so much work into it and saw it as the vision that was needed to counter separatism. But while it was no longer emphasized, the voters knew that it was the vision and the policy the provincial Liberals had put forth as an alternative to separation. It was and remained the platform of the *No* side.

The two official sides were the PQ and the Quebec Liberals, but that left unanswered the question of what role would be played by the seventy-four federal Liberal MPs, thirteen of whom were ministers and, of course, by Trudeau himself. A prominent role for Trudeau would make Ryan look weak, so it was decided that Trudeau would make only three speeches. Jean Chrétien was put in charge of the federal forces and became co-chair of the *No* side. He and the Quebec federal MPs were massively engaged in the campaign in their own ridings, those who were ministers used their departments to promote federalism, and federal funds poured into the province. Ottawa had a huge advertising budget, allegedly informing the public of federal programs but effectively providing masses of pro-federal propaganda.

The debate was in theory about seeking a mandate to negotiate, but it quickly centered on the question of separation itself. That gave the advantage to the *No* side, and it edged ahead in the polls. It was aided by PQ blunders and by leaders from English-speaking Canada who said there would be no association if Quebec separated. Trudeau asked the key question that Lévesque could not answer: if the other provinces would not accept an association with Quebec, how could the PQ promise that it could deliver sovereignty with association? Trudeau's role in the campaign was and remains highly controversial. In a speech on May 14, he promised that he would ensure that the constitution was renewed if the *No* side won. He did not provide details on what he meant by renewal, but constitutional renewal had been demanded since the mid-1960s by five successive premiers from three different parties. The renewal they demanded was a re-examination, rewriting, and re-allocating of the division of responsibilities between the two orders of government, the renewal outlined in the Beige Paper. If Trudeau meant something different, then it was his responsibility to say so.

The outcome was a resounding victory for the *No* side, 60 per cent to 40 per cent. It was a disaster for the PQ: if it could not even win a mandate to negotiate, then a mandate to separate was out of the question. The outcome was a disaster for the soft nationalists as well, regardless of whether they were Liberal, PQ, or Union National. The rest of Canada had shown some sympathy for a number of Quebec's demands, but that was partly out of fear for the future of a Canada without Quebec. Now 60 per cent of Quebeckers had rejected the PQ's strategy, and the threat of separation was gone, at least for the immediate future. But constitutional talks were now high on Ottawa's agenda, and Lévesque would be going to those talks in the weakest position of any Quebec premier.

With the victory in Quebec, Trudeau claimed that he represented 60 per cent of Quebec's population to Lévesque's 40 per cent. But it was Ryan's Quebec Liberals who had won the referendum, and they could argue that their vision of a Quebec within a decentralized Canada had received 60 per cent of the vote. Ryan probably expected that he would win the next Quebec election and pursue the object of decentralization at the upcoming constitutional talks. Trudeau could avoid that situation by forcing the pace of the talks, which is exactly what he did. As a result, Ryan and the Quebec Liberals' vision of a decentralized Canada was not part of the official constitutional talks, and the side that had actually won 60 per cent on the referendum question was marginalized.

On the day of the referendum, no one knew just how high on Ottawa's agenda the constitutional talks ranked. They found out within twenty-four hours, when Trudeau sent Chrétien to discuss the issues with the nine English-speaking premiers. They were quite surprised with what Ottawa was proposing—agreement on a charter of rights and an amending formula followed by patriation from London. A charter of rights and an amending formula would be additions to the constitution, not the renewal of anything in it, and patriation was a change of residence for the constitution. There was, in fact, no "renewal" in Chrétien's brief to the premiers.

Trudeau had misled the public. There was outrage in Quebec when his definition of "renewal" became public knowledge. That was especially the case within the Quebec Liberal Party, which had won the referendum debate after offering a large degree of decentralization. Even his speech writer for the campaign—André Burelle—interpreted Trudeau's "renewal" to be a promise of radical change and was extremely disillusioned when he found out otherwise. Trudeau said that it was very clear where he stood on constitutional issues, so people had no right to be surprised. But he had hardly been consistent in his negotiating positions on the constitution. He had agreed at different times to a number of the demands and proposals coming from the provinces. He had gradually become a strong centralist, but in 1978, he had agreed to meet a number of the premiers' specific demands.

On his tour of provincial capitals, Chrétien discovered some support for a new round of talks, but the premiers' mood grew steadily more negative as the summer wore on. At the first post-referendum conference on June 7, 1980, the premiers heard Trudeau's own version of what he wanted, and most of them were strongly opposed. Premiers Lougheed and Blakeney wanted to start discussions where they had ended before the 1979 election, that is, after Trudeau had offered a number of concessions. But Trudeau now dropped that list. Indeed, he announced that he wanted to strengthen the common market by removing interprovincial barriers to the movement of goods, services, and labour. That idea had much merit and support, but it also represented a new assertion of federal control over the economy and a decline in the provinces' ability to manage their own economies in matters that were constitutionally theirs. Trudeau also had a new plan for breaking any continuing deadlock over the constitution, namely adding a referendum option: if there was no agreement on a proposed amendment in two years, Ottawa could hold a national referendum on it. This was a brand new amending formula that would be controlled by Ottawa and denied the veto to any and all of the provinces.

Trudeau needed to give the impression that he was still flexible so he agreed to re-establishing the Continuing Committee of Ministers on the Constitution, the CCMC. It held a series of meetings over the summer and drafted some possible language for the new constitution. In the meantime, Trudeau told the Liberal caucus that all his efforts had failed, that the only means of solving Canada's constitutional problems was unilateral patriation and that they did not need the agreement of the provinces to proceed. Cabinet and caucus agreed.

Chrétien continued his talks with the relevant ministers and reported to Trudeau that there was some progress, but that their premiers were not enthusiastic about constitutional issues. It was decided to hold another First Ministers' meeting in Ottawa on September 8, 1980. After Trudeau's re-election, a memorandum had been prepared under the direction of Michael Kirby, outlining the strategy to be pursued. Its authors assumed that they could not obtain provincial agreement and concluded that Ottawa should go ahead with a unilateral request for patriation. To make that credible with the British government, however, there had to be a First Ministers' meeting on the constitution, which the authors assumed and probably hoped would fail. That was the strategy Ottawa was following in the months before the September meeting, and the Kirby memorandum made clear that Chrétien's discussions with the provincial governments were not being held in good faith.

It was traditional for the governor general to host a dinner for the first ministers on the eve of their meetings, and Governor General Edward Schreyer had such an event arranged for that Sunday evening. The discussion quickly degenerated into nasty barbs. Trudeau had to ask Schreyer to speed up dessert so they could all escape from the poisonous atmosphere. Jean Chrétien, who was there as minister in charge of relations with the provinces, described it as "the most unpleasant reception I have ever . . . [attended]," a view confirmed by others who were present.

Unfortunately for Ottawa, the Kirby memorandum had been leaked to the Quebec government and it eagerly distributed copies to the premiers that evening. That made a poisonous atmosphere even worse, and it deteriorated further when Trudeau began the conference with the threat of unilateral patriation. Manitoba Premier Sterling Lyon said that would tear the country apart. Trudeau replied that if the constitution could not be patriated "then the country deserves to be torn up." This was another example of Trudeau's arguing style. The fact that the *BNA Act* had resided in London had caused no problem before the 1930s, and only upset some English-Canadian nationalists and Trudeau after that. The idea that the country could be "torn up" over a matter of consequence to so few was an extreme exaggeration. The provinces were not opposed to patriation or an amending formula, and the crisis, if there was one, was over Trudeau's desire to add his *Charter of Rights* before patriating it.

Lyon said that a charter would be an invasion of provincial jurisdiction and a violation of parliamentary democracy. The inclusion of a charter in the constitution itself meant that some power would be transferred from elected legislatures to appointed courts and ultimately the Supreme Court. Trudeau had already made clear what direction he wanted that Court to lean when he appointed the strong federalist and nationalist Bora Laskin in 1970. Just three years later, Trudeau made him Chief Justice ahead of others with far more experience and arguably more balanced views on federalism. This was the very type of politicization and bias in the Supreme Court that the premiers feared.

Trudeau argued that including the *Charter* did not affect the balance of power between Ottawa and the provinces, because Parliament was also losing power. The provinces were hardly fooled since it was Trudeau who appointed the Supreme Court judges. He was saying, in effect, that his team could pick the referees, but that was fair since they then applied the rules to both teams. The premiers knew that most of the rights listed in the *Charter* were provincial rather than federal, and their power would be reduced more than Ottawa's. The premiers were also very aware of how politicized the American Supreme Court was and how it had been making law rather than just interpreting it for decades. And they could hardly have forgotten that, in the 1970s, the Supreme Court had repeatedly sided with Ottawa on federal-provincial disputes.

Constitutional Paralysis

To no one's surprise, the conference was a disaster. On September 27, Trudeau met the Liberal caucus to say that the premiers were demanding more and more, and he could not wait for agreement. The urgency was in the minds of the caucus and did not reflect any Canadian problem, especially as the government was just beginning a five-year mandate. The next day, cabinet confirmed the decision to proceed with unilateral patriation. That proposal was introduced into Parliament on October 2. The new constitution would be drafted and controlled by Ottawa alone and would include Ottawa's version of an amending formula and a charter of rights, plus reform of the Senate and Supreme Court. There would be no changes to the division of responsibilities between the two orders of government. There would also be a referendum to obtain final approval, which would make clear that the people were sovereign and not the governments of Canada or the UK. Trudeau told the public that Canada had to end fifty years of constitutional paralysis. That was odd, as the constitution had been amended fourteen times, more than those of the United States and Australia over the same period. Paradoxically, it was after the Constitution of 1982 was adopted that it became almost impossible to amend it. The premiers met on October 14 to discuss a response to Trudeau's proposed initiative, but there was no agreement.

A deadline was set for going to London by Christmas. That timetable was upset when the federal Progressive Conservatives began a very successful filibuster in the House of Commons, a tactic that was reinforced by a strong demand for public hearings. The hearings produced many submissions, and the proceedings were televised. The government's deadline had to be moved to July 1, 1981, the 114th anniversary of Confederation. With Ontario and New Brunswick supporting Ottawa, the other English-speaking premiers began co-operating to fight Trudeau's strategy. In London, provincial politicians and officials began a campaign to inform and lobby British MPs. It was only then that the British seemed to understand that Trudeau planned to change the constitution in ways the provinces did not accept before having Britain patriate it. British Prime Minister Margaret Thatcher asked why Canada did not patriate the *Act* and then change it; her question went unanswered. Lévesque decided that the advantages of co-operation with the other premiers outweighed the disadvantages, and they became known as the Gang of Eight.

They made a historic compromise, one as potentially significant as those that had led to Confederation itself. Lévesque accepted the amending formula that the others wanted, the so-called Vancouver formula, which stated that general amendments required the agreement of Ottawa and two-thirds of the provinces with 50 per cent of the population. By this formula, neither Quebec nor Ontario had a veto. In return, the seven premiers accepted the demand Quebec had been making since Lesage's day: when Ottawa launched a program in provincial areas of jurisdiction, the provinces could opt out of it with full financial compensation, which they could spend as they chose and not necessarily on a similar program. Ottawa and the English-speaking provinces could have shared-cost programs with Ottawa setting the standards, but Quebec would no longer be coerced into participating through Ottawa's use of the spending power. The Gang of Eight would insist on both these elements in any renewed constitution, and they did not think Britain would patriate the constitution against the will of eight out of ten provinces.

It has been argued that Lévesque made a major tactical error in giving up Quebec's veto and that no previous premier would have done so. But Lévesque did not "give up" the veto. He traded it for the support of seven other provinces for a matter far more important to Quebec, namely regaining control over education, health, welfare, and culture, the areas of "exclusive provincial" control that had been steadily encroached upon by the federal government. Amendments were very rare so Quebec's veto had hardly ever mattered. But by 1980, there were eighty-seven shared-cost programs and Quebec had been forced to accept them, along with Ottawa's conditions. Opting out with full compensation now seemed within grasp and it was well worth surrendering the veto. Also, no previous premier had ever faced a federal government determined to patriate the constitution unilaterally with a charter of rights that would permanently weaken Quebec.

The English-speaking premiers had made a major concession: they had effectively abandoned the policy of assimilating Quebec that was being gradually achieved by Ottawa's use of the spending power. This agreement was the twentieth-century equivalent of the one between George Brown and George-Étienne Cartier in 1864, the basis of the compromise that made Confederation possible. Trudeau was, of course, horrified. He had no intention of abandoning the long list of federal encroachments on provincial jurisdiction dating back to 1927 and was, in fact, heading in the opposite direction, of increasing federal power vis-á-vis the provinces. The compromise between Lévesque and the premiers was a major challenge to this trend. It would ensure *la survivance* of Québécois culture, the goal pursued doggedly since 1763, the goal achieved at Confederation but since undermined. If adopted, this formula would almost certainly have avoided the following decades of constitutional turmoil and the referendum of 1995.

It was also said that by abandoning the veto, Lévesque accepted that all provinces were equal. That was theoretically correct, in that under the agreement no province would have a veto and all of them would have the right to opt out of federal programs. But it had been clear since the mid-1960s that Quebec was the only province that would take advantage of opting out. When it alone did, it ceased to be equal to the others. More precisely, the other provinces chose not to be equal to Quebec, since they would not be exercising the right all of them would gain. That is precisely why Trudeau was so strongly opposed to opting out—it would result in Quebec being more special and distinct. Six days after Lévesque joined the Gang of Eight, they announced an accord that constituted their reply to Trudeau's proposal to make a unilateral request to Britain for patriation. The accord called for the Vancouver amending formula, opting out of federal programs that infringed provincial responsibilities with full compensation, no charter of rights, and then patriation. Now the main issues were that Trudeau wanted the charter, which the provinces opposed, while the provinces wanted a new formula for the spending power, which Trudeau opposed.

Throughout this period, the attitudes of other provinces towards Ottawa had been hardening. That was particularly the case of Alberta Premier Peter Lougheed. In his view, Ottawa was launching an all-out assault on the provinces with its proposed changes to the constitution. It was also assaulting the oil-producing provinces with the National Energy Program of October 1980. He saw the constitutional and energy issues as being related. His concern was that Ottawa was attempting to take control of oil and natural gas resources, which were found mainly in western Canada. His view was clearly expressed: under Trudeau's proposed constitutional changes, there would be "a very different kind of Canada. . . . It will be a much different federal state—if a federal state at all . . . it will primarily be a unitary state . . . with provinces other than Ontario and Quebec being in a second-class position . . . [Ottawa's plans] change the rules of Confederation . . . in a very significant way . . . in terms of resource ownership of the provinces."

An important part of the Gang of Eight's strategy was court challenges to the idea that the federal government could unilaterally patriate the constitution. They decided to launch three challenges, for Quebec, Manitoba, and Newfoundland. In Manitoba, the provincial court found for Ottawa 3–2, a legal victory but not a very convincing one politically. In Quebec, the provincial court found for Ottawa 4–1, another legal victory but not a perfect one. Then, on March 31, the Newfoundland court unanimously rejected Ottawa's plan: in its view, the *Charter* did indeed infringe on provincial jurisdiction, and by convention provincial support was required for such an amendment. The federal government could not unilaterally alter the constitution without the agreement of some provinces. Trudeau had no choice but to appeal that ruling to the Supreme Court, accept yet another delay, and hope for the best.

The precedents were quite clear: the constitution had never been amended in areas that affected the provinces except with the unanimous agreement of the provinces. Eighteen months earlier, in the *Senate Reference* case, the Supreme Court unanimously said that provincial agreement was necessary to change the Senate. In reaching that decision, it noted that all previous amendments affecting the provinces had been made with unanimous provincial consent. On September 28, 1981, the Supreme Court decided by a vote of 7–2, that although it had never done so in the past (that is, in spite of all precedents), Ottawa did have the legal right to make the amendments on its own. But by a vote of 6–3, it also said that doing so would violate convention and that Ottawa needed the support of a "substantial" number of provinces to make the amendments. The word "substantial" changed the amending process from unanimous provincial consent to less than unanimous provincial support, a major but undefined shift in Ottawa's favour. The Supreme Court was continuing with its recent tradition of centralizing power and, predictably, Chief Justice Laskin had sided with Ottawa. The decision did not specify a minimum number of provinces or how much of Canada's population they had to represent, as those were political decisions. Key questions were thus left unanswered: how many provinces, with what proportion of the population, and was Quebec one of them? If Quebec was not, then it was neither "distinct" nor "significant," and it could not count on the courts to protect the rights and responsibilities given it in the *BNA Act*.

The court decision forced Trudeau to make one more attempt to reach agreement with at least some of the Gang of Eight and a First Ministers' Conference was scheduled for November 2. For two days, there was stalemate at the table but some indications of flexibility in the private conversations that always accompanied formal meetings. That, of course, made Lévesque very nervous. He did not trust the other premiers, and vice versa —not a good situation for a group that had to remain united if they were to succeed. There was also some flexibility on the federal side in terms of Chrétien's views, but not those of Trudeau. Trudeau did not think a deal could be made; Chrétien thought there was a possibility, but he knew that to achieve a deal they had to break the unity of the Gang of Eight.

The *Constitution of 1982*

On the morning of the third day, Trudeau reiterated a proposal he had made previously and that had received little attention and no endorsement. He suggested they patriate the constitution with the amending formula adopted at Victoria and then spend two years discussing the other issues. If there was no agreement at the end of that period, then Ottawa would submit its proposed changes to the people in a referendum. The proposal was a direct challenge to Lévesque, who had put his province's future to a referendum only two years earlier. It would be very difficult for him to say that a national referendum was not acceptable. Perhaps more importantly, he probably thought that in a referendum Quebeckers would reject a constitutional proposal that would increase federal power over matters of importance to the Québécois.

Lévesque immediately agreed to Trudeau's proposed referendum. The other seven members of the Gang of Eight were stunned, as were others who heard him, including journalists from Quebec. None of the other seven premiers wanted a referendum because they knew the *Charter* was popular. More importantly, Lévesque had inadvertently broken the Gang of Eight's rule that none of them would make a deal with Ottawa without first discussing it with the others. Lévesque had risen to Trudeau's bait and seriously undermined, if not destroyed his own position. He had betrayed and broken the Gang of Eight and confirmed their worst suspicions about dealing with a separatist premier. This was somewhat of a repeat of Lesage's repudiation of the Fulton-Favreau amending formula in 1964 and of Bourassa's reversal on the *Victoria Charter* in 1971, and the English-speaking premiers had had enough of dealing with Quebec premiers. After lunch, Trudeau cleverly presented the idea of a referendum to the other premiers as an Ottawa-Quebec deal. For years, English-speaking premiers had been upset with bilateral deals between Ottawa and Quebec City, such as the CPP/QPP of 1964, which they had had to accept. There had been other such deals going back to the 1950s that affected them, and they were in no mood for another one. What little trust existed on Monday morning had disappeared by noon on Wednesday. Lévesque tried to argue that he had not properly understood the proposal, but they had all heard him accept it.

Since none of the English-speaking premiers wanted a referendum, Trudeau thought the Conference had failed. That was what he expected and probably still hoped for. Failure would prove the impossibility of obtaining provincial agreement and presumably a reluctant Britain would then agree to the unilateral patriation of a constitution containing only his changes. Chrétien still thought a deal was possible. He convinced Trudeau to keep the Conference going and continued his talks, mainly with his colleagues from Ontario and Saskatchewan, Roy McMurtry and Roy Romanow. That choice of partners was interesting—Ontario was not in the Gang of Eight, Saskatchewan favoured centralization unlike most of its partners, and they were definitely not representative of the opposition to Trudeau's plan.

That evening, Chrétien brought a rough outline of an agreement to 24 Sussex Drive, where Trudeau was huddled with his key ministers and advisers. Trudeau did not like it and remained adamant until 10 PM, when he received a call from his main ally, Ontario's Premier Davis. Davis said the compromise was acceptable to himself and New Brunswick Premier Richard Hatfield. Trudeau could not go to London against the wishes of all the provinces, and he gave in. There would be patriation but the *Charter* would not contain everything he wanted, and there would be compromises on other federal positions.

The talks went on throughout the night of November 4–5. Various players met in hotel rooms, various proposals were made and debated, and numerous phone calls kept the participants informed as the issues evolved. The essential compromises became clear, and Chrétien, McMurtry, and Romanow are generally regarded as the prime drafters, although a number of premiers played key roles, including Newfoundland's Brian Peckford and Saskatchewan's Allan Blakeney. By breakfast time on Thursday, the federal government and the nine English-speaking premiers had arrived at an agreement. Peckford gave a copy of it to Lévesque, the first he knew that a deal was afoot. He immediately realized that he had been outmanoeuvred by Trudeau, Chrétien, and his recent allies in the Gang of Eight. The Quebec delegation had also very seriously mishandled the tactics of the negotiations. Lévesque thought the Conference had failed by Wednesday afternoon, and his officials did not attempt to find out if other delegations were still negotiating. None of the participants in those talks bothered to inform them because, as far as they were concerned, Lévesque had deserted the Gang of Eight when he accepted the proposal for a referendum.

That morning Trudeau and nine premiers signed the agreement. Lévesque returned to Quebec City a depressed, angry, frustrated, and defeated man. He could not acknowledge that he had misplayed his cards, so he claimed that he had been betrayed by his partners in the Gang of Eight. That argument would be received in Quebec with much sympathy, where the events of November 4 became known as the "night of the long knives," the night Canada's English-speaking premiers conspired to stab Quebec in the back. The theory entered the mythology of Quebec, but not that of Ottawa or the rest of Canada. Outside Quebec, there was little or no sympathy for Lévesque and perhaps a little too much satisfaction over the way things had unfolded.

The question then was what exactly had Trudeau and the English-Canadian premiers agreed upon. This was a very good question given all the changes of position, compromises, and horse-trading on the last night of the Conference, not to mention the previous three days and, indeed, the fifteen years of negotiations. The most important fact was that the premiers had accepted Trudeau's beloved *Charter of Rights*. It was not, however, a total victory, as Trudeau had to accept a caveat stating that provinces could overrule the courts on certain rights, the famous "notwithstanding clause." Alberta had developed that concept in 1971, and Lougheed introduced it into the discussion partly to test Trudeau's interest in compromising. The clause made it possible for the legislatures to pass laws "notwithstanding" the fact they might violate some *Charter* rights. This was a victory, especially for Lyon and Blakeney. The notwithstanding clause did not apply to language or democratic rights, but it did preserve provincial power over other rights such as labour mobility or free speech.

Most amendments would require the agreement of Parliament plus two-thirds of the provinces with 50 per cent of the population so no province had a veto. Extremely important matters required the approval of Parliament plus all the provinces. The condition that Trudeau found so objectionable was dropped, namely the proposal that any province could opt out of federal programs with full compensation. That was what Lévesque had traded Quebec's veto for when he joined the Gang of Seven. The premiers had thus kept Lévesque's surrender of the veto but not honoured their half of the bargain. Quebec emerged from the conference with no veto, no opting out clause, none of the changes it wanted to the division of responsibilities, and no progress on any of the issues it had been raising since 1960.

Trudeau also dropped his proposal for a referendum mechanism, so his deal with Lévesque on Wednesday morning did not last until dinnertime. This was significant in constitutional terms. Trudeau had argued that sovereignty rested with the people, and one of his main reasons for wanting to patriate the constitution was so that it would be an act of the Canadian people and not that of a foreign government. But the *Constitution of 1982* was, in fact, another British Act of Parliament, which, when ratified by the Canadian House of Commons, became a Canadian document. Unlike the *BNA Act*, it was not approved by a single provincial legislature. In the new constitution, sovereignty still flowed from the Crown downwards to the people. That was not much of a change, although the Crown was now Queen Elizabeth of Canada rather than Queen Elizabeth of Great Britain. Ottawa also accepted a strengthening of provincial control of natural resources and the right to tax them, the only change made to the 1867 division of responsibilities. That met Lougheed's and Blakeney's main goal for the talks, but it did not solve the conflict of jurisdiction between provincial control of resources and federal control of trade.

In a symbolic bow to Quebec, any province could opt out of an amendment that transferred provincial power in the fields of education or culture to Ottawa. This was hardly of significance because Ottawa had used its spending power, rather than constitutional amendments to launch programs in those areas. In response to demand from Atlantic Canada, the new constitution enshrined the equalization system—a future federal government could change it but not abolish it without provincial consent. There was also agreement on holding a First Ministers' meeting including Aboriginal leaders to address the large number of issues that had been ignored. This was highly significant because until then First Ministers' meetings had never included Aboriginal leaders, but the new constitution now elevated them in principle to a status bordering on that of premiers. From then on, they would be involved in federal-provincial talks, attempting to parley their new status and treaty rights into effective bargaining chips. That changed the nature of First Ministers' meetings, but there is little evidence that the presence of Aboriginal leaders led to improvement in the situation of the people they represented. The premiers of Yukon and the Northwest Territories were also working to gain admittance to First Ministers' meetings, so federal-provincial relations would represent more interests but be more complicated in the future. Within decades, the phrase "Ottawa and the Provinces" had been replaced by "Ottawa and the Provinces and Territories," and Territorial premiers eventually took their turns being chairmen and spokesmen for the association of premiers.

The *Charter* identified a number of rights that all Canadian citizens enjoy and gave the courts the power to interpret those rights. These rights were not new, but now they were legally enshrined in the constitution, a change from British convention to American-style practice. That power had belonged to Parliament and the provincial legislatures now belonged to the courts and ultimately the Supreme Court. This represented a significant transfer of power from the legislative to the judicial branch of government, and was seen as a major step in the Americanization of Canadian politics. The *Charter* gave the right to education in English or French to all people born in Canada where numbers warranted it. That overruled the provision in Quebec's *Bill 101* that only English Canadians born in Quebec had that right.

There was some updating, as a few obsolete Sections of the *BNA Act* were repealed but others were retained, such as Ottawa's right to disallow provincial legislation, which had not been used since 1943. One of the most significant conventional changes to the constitution since 1867, the idea that the federal government could spend money on programs in areas of provincial jurisdiction, was not written into the constitution, and nearly one hundred shared-cost programs remained in constitutional limbo. Thus the federal encroachments into health, welfare, education, local matters, municipal affairs, culture, and language remained legal by convention, not by enshrinement in the written constitution.

Canada was fully independent at last, with a revised but not renewed constitution, one that could be amended in Canada itself, but only with considerable difficulty. The monarch was still Queen Elizabeth but that was by Canadian choice, not a vestige of colonialism. Failure to address the division of responsibilities left all those issues unsolved, except provincial control of natural resources. The constitution did not indicate that foreign affairs was assigned to Ottawa, and trade remained in theory an exclusive federal responsibility, although in reality it was now shared. New issues such as the environment were not dealt with. In effect, the main change in 1982 was the addition of the *Charter of Rights and Freedoms*. Apart from that, the *Constitution of 1982* was profoundly unimpressive, the language that of the mid-nineteenth century. It left Quebec with the special status it had under the 1867 *BNA Act*, and it left Canada with an asymmetrical federalism in which none of the provinces were exactly the same. Trudeau had argued for years that all provinces were the same, but he made little or no effort to make the *Constitution of 1982* reflect that view. That was probably because the idea that they were the same had no basis in history or current reality or even in the way he treated them. The *BNA Act* was renamed the *Constitution Act, 1867*, which eliminated the word *British* with its connotations of colonialism, and the new *Act* with its additions was called the *Constitution Act, 1982*. The deal was approved by the House of Commons by a vote of 246–24; the British Parliament passed the necessary legislation; and Elizabeth II, Queen of Canada, signed it in Ottawa on a rainy April 17.

The subsequent history of court cases under the *Charter* did not indicate that Supreme Court decisions would strengthen the federal government as so many expected, hoped, or feared. In the first decade of the *Charter*, eighteen provincial laws were rejected, as were twenty-three federal ones. In a number of cases, the Court's decisions reinforced the right of provinces to do things differently. On these matters, Canadians do not have equal rights in every province, and provinces can interpret and administer federal laws differently according to local circumstances. In the case of *Haig v. Canada* (1993), the Court specifically said that differences between federal and provincial law did not violate equality, and the guarantee of equality did not change the division of powers. The constitution did not solve the basic problems between English and French. It did not resolve the two fundamental competing visions of Canada: of a country including a Québécois nation in control of its own destiny, or of Canada as a single nation with one set of values including bilingualism. It did not resolve the question of what kind of federalism should prevail—Trudeau's vision of one in which the federal government had primacy, or the premiers' view that both orders of government had control over the responsibilities that were not shared. And Quebec, which had championed constitutional change, was weaker and more discontented in 1982 than when it first raised the issues back in 1966!

Prime Minister Pearson's goal in calling the first conference in 1968—to make changes that would halt Quebec's drift towards independence—had been thwarted. There were elements of both decentralization and centralization in the new constitution, but overall, it moved Canada towards centralization. The *Charter* strengthened identification with the nation at the expense of provincial identities but the latter did not disappear. In short, none of problems that gave rise to the debate were resolved. The period of 1968–1982 could be viewed as a series of missed opportunities, and the consequences of that failure would linger for decades and almost lead to the destruction of the country in 1995.

Quebec refused to sign, but was bound by the constitution anyway. It rejected both bilingualism and multiculturalism, and the Quebec government continued to fight Ottawa on *Charter* rights. The PQ refused to attend federal-provincial meetings, and federalism became more dysfunctional. In an act of defiance, the PQ passed legislation applying the notwithstanding clause to all relevant bills that were on the books and applied it to future bills as long as it was in power. Each such use made Quebec more different from the rest of Canada, more distinct, more special, and each was more annoying to the rest of Canada, the reverse of the national unity that Trudeau had sought. His vision of a charter that would bring Canadians together failed in the short term: the *Charter* carried English-speaking Canadians to a new level of national identity, it had the reverse effect amongst the Québécois, and the two groups were more divided in 1983 than in 1980.

Trudeau's failure to shift the primary allegiance of the Québécois from Quebec to Canada was confirmed by public opinion polls. In 1970, 34 per cent of Francophones in Quebec identified themselves primarily as Canadians; twenty years later the number had fallen to 9 per cent. In 1970, 44 per cent of them identified themselves primarily as French Canadians; twenty years later that had declined to 28 per cent. In 1970, 21 per cent of them identified themselves primarily as Québécois; twenty years later that had more than doubled to 59 per cent. The idea that Trudeau spoke for the Québécois was shattered in the 1984 election when Liberal strength in Quebec fell from seventy-three MPs to seventeen, with those elected mostly in non-Francophone constituencies.

Natural Resources: Ottawa and the West Again

Equally high on the agenda of the newly elected government was energy policy. After the 1980 election campaign began, Marc Lalonde convinced Trudeau that a new energy policy should be a key plank in the platform. Trudeau then announced the comprehensive policy in a speech in Halifax on June 25, 1980, almost as far from Alberta as it was possible to be. There was no agreement on it in cabinet, and the committee process established in 1968 made it very difficult for the government to adopt any legislation unless broad agreement had been achieved in the relevant committees. To avoid discussion with the ministers who questioned or opposed it, the National Energy Program, or NEP, was inserted in the budget so only the prime minister and the ministers of finance and energy were involved.

The NEP of October 28 implemented a number of the new government's major goals. They included centralizing political and economic power in Ottawa, asserting federal power over the economy, substantially increasing federal revenues, increasing the political visibility of the federal government, solidifying Liberal support in central and Atlantic Canada, increasing Canadian ownership of the oil and gas industry, and maintaining a price below international levels. It was a regional oil and gas policy, not a national energy one, and it was as much political as economic.

A major feature of the NEP was maintaining prices below international levels. Ottawa increased some old taxes and brought in a number of new ones, especially the Natural Gas Tax and the Petroleum and Gas Revenue Tax. The revenue was needed to subsidize the cost of oil being imported into eastern Canada at world prices. Ottawa allegedly needed more money in order to manage the economy and ensure that the equalization program gave all Canadians a minimum level of governmental services, but Ottawa had the tools to manage the economy, and there were many ways to ensure that the equalization program was functioning adequately.

The 1970s goal of self-sufficiency in energy production was maintained. In order to increase the proportion of oil and gas being produced in areas controlled by Ottawa, expensive incentives were offered to companies exploring in the North and offshore. A number of other measures were designed to increase Ottawa's influence over the entire sector. The architects of the NEP had apparently not read Adam Smith's 1776 classic, *Wealth of Nations*, which explained why trade makes countries richer while protection and the quest for self-sufficiency makes them poorer. The NEP's goals were at odds with increasing globalization and international trade, an attempt to turn the clock back to an era of mercantilism and economic autarchy.

Saskatchewan and BC were predictably angry; Alberta's Premier Lougheed was enraged. In October 1980, he addressed Albertans on TV: "Without negotiation, without agreement, [Ottawa] simply walked into our house and occupied the living room." Lougheed began referring to the federal government as "the Ottawa government," suggesting that it was the government of central Canada. Alberta's energy minister, Merv Leitch, asked why it was not possible for Canadians to pay world prices for energy when they had always paid more than world prices for manufactured goods. And he pointed out that Ottawa was not taxing the windfall profits on hydro exports from Ontario and Quebec.

Albertans were so upset that a separatist movement began to emerge, and Lougheed had to prove that the provincial government could stand up to Ottawa to head off the threat. He told Albertans, "You will determine whether or not you want to see more and more of your lives directed and controlled from Ottawa or . . . a fair portion of decision-making determined by Albertans . . ." Premier Blakeney regarded the NEP as a new assault on the provinces. The disallowance of the oil industry's royalties as a provincial tax deduction was, he said in his *Memoirs*, unprecedented and aggressive, did not apply to royalties on other natural resources, and "there could not be any reason in accounting, taxation, or government principles for this."

Lougheed was determined to force the federal government to compromise. Alberta announced that it would reduce its oil shipments to central Canada by 180,000 barrels a day, and it would do so in three stages of sixty thousand barrels each on April 1, June 1, and August 1, 1981. That would force Ottawa to increase imports by the same volume, but at world prices. In order to pay for the additional costs, Ottawa responded to the first cut by adding a tax of half a cent per litre on gasoline, plus another tax of 1.6 cents per litre after the second cut. While Lougheed and Trudeau fought in public, their officials met privately and agreement was reached on September 1, 1981. Alberta won on the main issue, as Ottawa recognized provincial control of energy resources and agreed that the Canadian price would continue to rise towards international levels. Ottawa abandoned its gas and export taxes, and the Petroleum and Gas Revenue Tax was modified. Alberta reduced its royalty rates on companies and took over the Petroleum Incentive Program.

Similar agreements were negotiated with BC on September 24 and with Saskatchewan on October 26. On March 2, 1982, Ottawa negotiated an agreement with Nova Scotia. Ottawa would manage the offshore resources, but the province would reap all of the economic benefits until it ceased to be a have-not province. This was another qualification to the equalization program making Nova Scotia "a province not like the others." There was no similar agreement with Newfoundland since it insisted that offshore resources were completely provincial, as they had belonged to Newfoundland before Confederation and had not been transferred to Ottawa. That also made it "a province not like the others."

Shortly after Ottawa and the provinces reached their agreements, the foundation of the NEP crumbled. The key assumption underlying it was that international prices would rise to $100 per barrel. Instead, in March 1983, OPEC reduced the price to $29—it only approached the $100-mark two decades later, only to fall back toward $50 again. The windfall that Ottawa, the producing provinces, and industry were squabbling over disappeared. Ottawa and the producing provinces found themselves giving new subsidies to the oil companies to encourage exploration. The NEP was in ruins, leaving Canadians with the world price, no self-sufficiency, a recession in Alberta, inefficient industry in central Canada, and a bitter legacy of distrust between western Canadians and their national government. Politically, the NEP virtually destroyed the Liberal party in the West at both the federal and provincial levels.

New Federal Programs, New Battles

By that time, Canada was heading for a financial crisis as the federal deficit rose at a rate that was unsustainable. One of the main causes was the series of policies Trudeau had adopted to dominate the provinces and "put Quebec in its place." They included competition with Quebec City for the hearts and minds of the Québécois, support for declining industries and regions, spending on local infrastructure, generous increases to the unemployment and welfare programs, and subsidized oil prices and incentives for the oil industry. Even with the oil and gas revenue grab, Ottawa financed its programs in the provinces by borrowing, and the annual deficit had risen to $40 billion by 1984.

In 1982, Ottawa's drive to become more involved in local economic development led to yet another reorganization of several of the main departments involved and the way they spent their money. The Department of Regional Economic Expansion (DREE) and the Department of Industry, Trade, and Commerce (ITC) were combined into the Department of Regional and Industrial Expansion (DRIE). It planned to contribute its funds through agreements with the provinces, which were to be called Economic Regional Development Agreements (ERDAs). Seven provinces were willing to enter such agreements, but Quebec was very wary of them. Its position was summed up in the claim that "the provinces were being reduced to simple federal agencies." It stated: "This short-circuiting of Quebec . . . will never be tolerated . . . If . . . Ottawa has lost sight of . . . viable federalism . . . then Quebec has only one option: to demand the amounts that it is entitled to . . . [as] unconditional financial transfers." This, in 1984, was what Lesage had demanded in 1960, and once more Ottawa rejected Quebec's demand.

The constitution and energy policy were not the only issues where Ottawa decided it could act unilaterally. In 1981, it made a radical decrease in transfer payments with little consultation so it could spend that money directly, providing assistance to institutions and the public that had previously been funnelled through the provinces. In June 1982, Ottawa announced radical changes to regional development programs, taking direct control rather than co-operating with the ones administered by the provinces. In June 1983, it established an exclusive job creation program to replace shared-cost ones. These attempts to make Canadians look to Ottawa for support reflected the government's increasingly nationalistic agenda.

Another assault on provincial power occurred in 1982 when the 1977 taxation agreement, the Established Programs Financing, the EPF, arrangement was due for renewal. Ottawa's plan was to reduce transfer payments by tying them to increases to the rate of growth of the GDP. That would cut payments by 15 per cent, yielding savings of $6 billion over the term of the new arrangement. Ottawa presented its proposals only five months before the expiry of the current agreement, leaving the provinces with insufficient time to develop proper responses. In spite of unanimous provincial opposition, Ottawa imposed its new conditions in April 1982. Significantly, federal transfers to the provinces, which had been increasing for decades, peaked in 1982 and the trend line from then on was steadily downwards.

The money saved by these cutbacks was spent in part on investments to support regional economic development. Many of these programs were aimed specifically at Quebec in the competition for the hearts and minds of Quebeckers. In 1983, Ottawa began a huge program for the development of the Lower St. Lawrence-Gaspé region, the first time such a program was launched without consultations with the relevant province. This was followed a year later with another large program, the two costing $500 million. Other provinces were not treated the same, a paradoxical example of the "special status" Trudeau claimed to reject. These programs were called regional economic development. This was an Orwellian use of the word *regional*, because in Canadian politics, that word refers to one of the five major regions such as Quebec or Atlantic Canada, not a small local area such as southeastern Quebec.

Ottawa's relations with municipal governments also changed. The provinces, especially Quebec, had objected when Ottawa attempted to deal directly with municipal governments. In an agreement of 1978, Ottawa accepted that it had to deal with the municipalities through the provincial governments, which would control programs, with the caveat that any federal contributions would be publicly acknowledged. In 1981, that form of co-operation was cancelled, to Quebec's dismay. The new policy was denounced by all the provinces, and new unilateral federal programs naturally led to problems and conflict with the provinces. Quebec threatened to penalize any municipality that accepted federal funds directly, and Ottawa was forced to sign an agreement covering its programs.

Medicare was another area of disagreement. By 1984, Ottawa's share of Medicare had declined considerably from the initial 50 per cent of the costs covered. The increased burden on the provinces and the loosening of federal controls over the program had led hospitals and doctors to begin extra-billing and charging user fees for services they thought were not covered by Medicare. Defenders of Medicare argued that this was creating a two-tier system, which benefited the rich who could pay those extra fees. In fact, Medicare had never covered all aspects of health and was a two-tier system from the beginning. A visit to the doctor was covered, for example, but not the drugs or eyeglasses the doctor prescribed, and a broken jaw bone was covered, but not a broken tooth.

The extra-billing and user fees provoked public protest, and Ottawa responded with the *Canada Health Act* of April 1, 1984. It imposed dollar-for-dollar penalties on provinces that allowed user fees and extra-billing. That was an additional condition to the original four. Provincial governments were enraged over yet another invasion of provincial jurisdiction, done without consultation. BC, Alberta, and Quebec took Ottawa to court over the issue. They lost, and proponents of Medicare bragged incorrectly that Canada had avoided a two-tier system. The *Act* did reduce extra-billing and user fees, but Medicare's monopoly could not be fully enforced. People resented the violation of the principle of freedom of choice; some went abroad and paid for quicker or better service; some provinces began allowing medical clinics to charge for services such as MRIs; people crossed provincial borders to obtain faster service at their own expense; and uniform standards between provinces simply could not be completely enforced.

Throughout Trudeau's second term, Ottawa's relations with the four Atlantic provinces were quite harmonious. Their governments were receiving around half their revenue from federal grants of one kind or another, and federal spending on things like regional economic development provided another major boost to their economies, hence the population's level of satisfaction with their provincial governments. Maintaining the flow of federal funds was thus a top priority for all these provincial governments and rocking the boat on mere constitutional issues was furthest from their minds. For a while, the NEP brought them cheap oil and gas, which was particularly important given their lack of hydro-electricity. Equalization grants and other spending had effectively turned the four provinces into clients of the federal government, and they played only a small role in the great federal-provincial debates of the period. The exception was Richard Hatfield's government, which was a staunch ally of Trudeau on the constitutional debate because of the large Acadian population in the province. The degree to which such dependence undermined the work ethic and the ability of Atlantic Canadians to manage their own affairs was noted, but it was of minor concern within and outside of the region.

CHAPTER 14
Mulroney, Meech, and Charlottetown, 1984-1993

Trudeau retired for a second time on February 29, 1984, and this time there would be no resurrection as prime minister. He did not, however, abandon politics, and came out of retirement two more times to play a major role in defeating Prime Minister Brian Mulroney's attempts to correct or, in Trudeau's view, destroy his constitutional package of 1982. Trudeau was replaced by his old rival, John Turner. Turner had a much more positive view of the role of the provinces, but any attempts he might have made to improve Ottawa's relations with them or restore a more balanced federalism were cut short when he called an election for September 4. Unfortunately for him, Brian Mulroney led the Progressive Conservatives to an overwhelming majority of 211 out of 282 seats.

Mulroney was a sharp contrast to Trudeau. Mulroney strongly believed that provinces should have a large degree of independence and that the way to defeat separatism was to meet the legitimate goals of the "soft" or moderate nationalists. Trudeau treated provincial governments almost as enemies; Mulroney treated them as partners. Mulroney believed that the provinces should have some input into trade policy and that in foreign affairs they could have a major role in matters within provincial jurisdiction. As he stated in his *Memoirs*, "To me, the Canadian federation is not a test of strength between different governments," and "If Quebec is strong, then Canada is strong. There is room in Canada for all identities to be affirmed, for all aspirations to be respected, and for all ideals to be pursued . . ."

In the election campaign, Mulroney made his position towards the provinces very clear: in Calgary, he said that Ottawa would address Western grievances such as the NEP, and in his home riding of Sept-Isles, he said he would find a way to have Quebec accept the *Constitution of 1982* with "dignity and enthusiasm."

The federalism that Mulroney inherited was different from the one Prime Minister Pearson left to Trudeau in 1968. By 1985, there were one hundred agreements covering federal payments to the provinces, ninety-three agreements for joint federal-provincial activities, fifty for the purchase of goods and services, sixteen for intergovernmental liaison, twelve covering economic development, eleven for the purchase of land, five more between Ottawa and the municipalities, and thirty-four for other matters. It was difficult to identify provincial responsibilities that Ottawa was not involved in, and it had become impossible to separate the roles of the two governments. Both were involved in municipal issues, making those areas subject to co-operation by three governments. The nation's capital was perhaps the worst example of overlap as building a bridge over the Ottawa River required the agreement of five governments and was debated for decades without any decision being made. Genuine or classical federalism with its "watertight compartments" of exclusive areas of responsibility had long since ceased to exist and could not be recreated.

Mulroney's government was probably the first to genuinely accept that Ottawa could not afford all its programs, the first to reflect growing public awareness that government could not solve all social problems by throwing money at them. He ended universality in family allowances and old age benefits, ended direct subsidies to UI, and capped the CAP, the Canada Assistance Program. These trends were continued and expanded by the Chrétien government as the Canadian welfare state continued to weaken, and federalism became more co-operative and less confrontational as a result.

Mulroney came to office with a fairly clear idea of what he wanted to accomplish in terms of federal-provincial relations and a strategy for how to go about it. The first element was to set a new tone of conciliation and to promise that the provinces would be treated differently than under the Trudeau regime, a process he began with his first meeting with the premiers. The next element in the strategy was to address some major economic issues, in the hope that progress on that front would take some of the bitterness out of political discourse.

Half the provinces had experienced particularly abrasive relations with Trudeau, namely Newfoundland, Quebec, Saskatchewan, Alberta, and BC. In Mulroney's view, Quebec was the most important and the most difficult. Lévesque and the PQ were still in power and still dedicated to separation, but their position was weak due to the accumulated problems of years in office, their defeats at the hands of Trudeau, and their success in addressing grievances such as the threat to the French language. The West, however, believed that, for decades, Quebec had driven the nation's political agenda and had received far too many "concessions." Given these contradictory beliefs and challenges, Mulroney's strategy called for dealing with a minor Quebec problem first to put that relationship on an upwards trend. Then he would address Ottawa's major problems with Newfoundland and the West, partly because of the merits of the complaints and partly to put those four provinces in a better mood so he could tackle Quebec's major grievances.

Mulroney established decent working relations with Lévesque, and the PQ began attending federal-provincial meetings and submitted a list of twenty-two matters that it wanted resolved. Lévesque was replaced on September 29, 1985, by Pierre-Marc Johnson, the son of Daniel Johnson, one of the last Union National premiers. Mulroney worked with him to solve the problem of provincial representation at La Francophonie, the French equivalent of the British Commonwealth of Nations Quebec had insisted on its right to belong to the organiza- tion as an equal partner, and the squabble between it and Ottawa had stalemated its development, because France was unwilling to become involved in Canada's domestic affairs.

The compromise was that the federal government would lead Canadian delegations, but Quebec, Ontario, and New Brunswick could be part of those delegations and could engage in discussions that affected provincial matters. That allowed France to proceed with a Summit of La Francophonie in October 1985. Mulroney represented Canada, Richard Hatfield represented New Brunswick, and the re-elected Robert Bourassa represented Quebec. Quebec then hosted the next such Summit, and an important but largely symbolic example of poor relations between

Ottawa and *la belle province* disappeared. Mulroney and Bourassa also played important roles in establishing the international French-language channel TV5.

Better Relations with Atlantic Canada and the West

The second item on the agenda was the question of control of the mineral resources off the coast of Newfoundland. It believed it had the same ownership of offshore resources as all provinces had for those on land. This issue had helped make Premier Brian Peckford one of Trudeau's strongest critics on constitutional issues, and that was the sort of animosity Mulroney was determined to eliminate. He understood that offshore resources were different because of international complications and foreign claims but, unlike Trudeau, he did not believe that those differences gave Ottawa the right to manage and tax those resources.

On February 11, 1985, Mulroney signed the Atlantic Accord with Premier Brian Peckford. The resources would be managed by a commission of three, one nominated by Ottawa, one by St. John's, and a third by the Newfoundland Chief Justice, a Newfoundlander appointed by the federal government. This composition would ensure a role for Ottawa on any matter affecting relations with foreign countries. The benefits from development would flow to Newfoundland, just as the benefits from other resources flowed to the provinces in which they were located. The revenue from offshore oil would not affect Ottawa's equalization payments for a decade. This further confused the equalization program, tilting it even more to the advantage of Atlantic Canada. The Accord was hailed in Newfoundland as a historic breakthrough.

Next was the Western Accord of March 1985 and a series of measures to deal with discontent in the West. The most important was the dismantling of some remaining features in the NEP and the deregulation of the industry. Prices would reflect international levels and several federal taxes were eliminated, such as the hated Petroleum and Gas Revenue Tax. Ottawa terminated the taxes on natural gas that had been BC's main complaint. Ottawa also ended its favourable treatment of Petro-Canada and its attempts to lure Canadian-owned companies from the provinces to the areas it controlled.

In a major policy reversal, Mulroney eliminated the *Foreign Investment Review Act, FIRA*. That legislation made it more difficult for foreign companies to invest in Canada. *FIRA* was a response to left-wing, nationalist, and central Canadian concerns over the amount and power of foreign investment. The views of Albertans were the opposite—energy development there stemmed almost entirely from foreign investment. *FIRA* infuriated them, and Mulroney made it an agency that promoted rather than restricted foreign investment.

The Meech Lake Accord

Now Mulroney could turn to the main problem: Quebec. The timing was fortuitous because his old friend Robert Bourassa had led the provincial Liberals back to power in December 1985. He was in a strong position with a mandate based on a 56 per cent popular vote and ninety-eight seats, friendship with Mulroney, and a reputation as a staunch federalist. He could argue that concessions to him would undermine separatism rather than encourage it and save Canada from another referendum and possible breakup. An older and wiser Bourassa had given up on the demand for provincial paramountcy on welfare issues that had wrecked the Victoria Conference of 1971, and he came to power promising reconciliation.

During the election, Bourassa had expressed the desire for Quebec to sign the *1982 Constitution* and had spelled out some of the conditions that would have to be met. These were identified in a policy document called "Mastering Our Future," which was adopted by the party on March 3, 1985. In May 1986, a large group of Canada's top academics, officials, journalists, and businessmen met at Mont Gabriel, Quebec, for a conference on constitutional affairs. The audience was pleasantly shocked by the speech of Quebec's Minister of Intergovernmental Affairs Gil Rémillard, a leading constitutional expert. He spelled out the five conditions Quebec now demanded, and they were the least onerous the audience had ever heard. In particular, the demand for opting out with full compensation was missing. The new approach was welcome news across Canada, because many people still understood that there was something fundamentally wrong with a constitution that resulted from an agreement between Ottawa and the nine English-speaking provinces.

Bourassa's five demands were not new, and all of them had been accepted in at least one of the dozens of conferences and draft agreements over the previous two decades. Quebec wanted its agreement with Ottawa on immigration, the Cullen-Couture understanding of 1978, enshrined in the constitution. That agreement had been negotiated by the Trudeau government and caused Ottawa no problems. Bourassa wanted Quebec's veto restored—it had that veto de facto from 1867 to 1982, and a number of the formulas for constitutional change that Trudeau had approved maintained its veto. He wanted the constitution to state that three of the Supreme Court justices must come from Quebec, which would enshrine traditional practice and had been agreed at the 1971 Victoria Conference. Quebec also wanted a say in the selection of justices by the prime minister, another issue that had been debated for years and approved in some of the draft agreements. A fourth demand was that the constitution include wording on opting out, but without compensation, that is, the legalization of the process that was in place. Again, there was no apparent problem with this issue. The difficult demand was for the constitution to state that Quebec was a "distinct society." Everyone knew that Quebec had always been distinct: the issue was recognizing that reality in a specific clause in the constitution, identifying exactly what it meant, and ensuring that it did not give Quebec more power than other provinces had.

Mulroney was well aware of the pitfalls involved in constitutional negotiations, and he proceeded very slowly and carefully. The more issues that were on the table, the more difficult it would be to reach agreement. The more compromises that were made, the less clear and meaningful the result would be. His plan, then, was to have a conference to address Quebec's concerns, followed by further conferences to address other issues. This strategy was similar to that of Trudeau, who concentrated on the *Charter*, the amendment process, and patriation with everything else postponed to the future. Mulroney informed the premiers of Bourassa's five points and asked if they were prepared to deal with just those in a Quebec round of talks. He appointed Senator Lowell Murray as his Minister for Federal-Provincial Relations and sent him on a round of talks with the provinces. Quebec Minister Rémillard also visited the other capitals, and Mulroney was in contact with them directly and on the phone on numerous occasions.

These contacts and confidence-building exercises proceeded throughout the spring and summer of 1986.

The nine English-speaking premiers accepted the process Mulroney had proposed. A First Ministers' meeting in Vancouver on December 1 maintained the momentum and was followed by six more months of meetings between Murray and the provinces, plus meetings of deputy ministers and officials. A First Ministers' Conference was scheduled at the government retreat at Meech Lake on April 30, 1987. There, the first ministers met for eleven hours of intense negotiations and the nine English-speaking premiers accepted all of Quebec's demands. The months of effort, consultation, co-operation, and homework had paid off. At 10 PM, Mulroney proclaimed success and stood up to go and meet the press. He received a standing ovation, something not seen at a First Ministers' meeting in decades, if ever. On June 2, the Meech Lake Accord was signed by Mulroney and the ten premiers.

The distinct society clause stated that the constitution should be interpreted to reflect the fact that Quebec was distinct. That was not an addition of powers, but rather the acknowledgement that in interpreting the constitution, the courts should recognize that fact. Thus the courts would simply be doing the same as Ottawa and the provinces were doing—accepting the obvious fact of Quebec's distinctiveness within a federal system. It also acknowledged that the Quebec government had a role to preserve and promote its distinct society, something Quebec governments had been doing since 1867 under the provisions of the *BNA Act*. Now, with the Québécois feeling that their survival as a unique society was still threatened, the constitution would make that role explicit. That added no power to the Quebec government, took nothing away from Ottawa, and was balanced by the statement that French Canadians outside Quebec and English Canadians inside Quebec were "a fundamental characteristic of Canada and Parliament and the provinces have a role in preserving their fundamental characteristics." In return for these "concessions," Quebec would accept the *1982 Constitution* even though it met almost none of Quebec's traditional demands.

In addition, Mulroney met an old provincial demand that prime ministers select senators and Supreme Court justices from lists submitted by the provinces. If a prime minister did not like any of the suggested names, he could request more nominees until the provinces produced ones acceptable to the federal government. The power of appointment thus remained with the prime minister, but Canada would now have senators and justices that both orders of government agreed on. For the first time ever that would make the Senate and the Supreme Court "federal" in the true sense of the word, that is, institutions of both orders of government and not just parts of the central government. The Senate would have no more power, and Mulroney had sacrificed the patronage prime ministers had always enjoyed with these sought-after appointments. Given his fondness for patronage, this was a huge personal sacrifice.

The Meech Lake Accord was initially well received. The governments of the eleven first ministers were all pleased. The media was favourably impressed, experts and editorials hailed the decisions, and public opinion polls were favourable. Both Mulroney and Bourassa sent envoys to give Trudeau detailed briefings and to point out that, in the past, he had supported the elements in the new Accord. Several days later, on May 27, he came out of political retirement to attack the Accord in an article published in the *Toronto Star* and *L'Actualité*. Unfortunately, he wrote it before the legal text had been released, and that text demonstrated that a number of his concerns did not reflect the facts. Basically, he accused it of giving powers to Quebec, which it did not do. He also launched a personal attack on Mulroney, calling him a weakling and an unworthy successor of all previous prime ministers. Former prime ministers had criticized the policies of other prime ministers, but it was unprecedented for one to launch a personal attack on a successor.

The vehemence of that attack took many by surprise, especially those with expertise in the constitution and in the debates of the previous two decades. His article was criticized by others who pointed out the errors in his analysis. The facts, however, did not seem to matter, because what his article did was make the Meech Lake Accord an emotional issue, one that appealed especially to English-Canadian nationalists. In yet another paradox of his career, Trudeau, who believed passionately in the unity of a single Canadian nation, was pitting English- and French-speaking Canadians against each other. Trudeau also addressed the Senate for six hours, knowing that a majority of them had been appointed by himself and Pearson. He urged them to reject the Accord, not simply to suggest amendments, that is, to overrule the elected House of Commons. That would violate the most basic principle of democracy. He ignored the fact that the federal Liberals under his successor, John Turner, were supporting it, dismissing them as just an opposition party.

Trudeau's condemnation was odd for other reasons. On immigration, the Accord merely put into the constitution an agreement he had made with Quebec. He had agreed previously to amending formula that included a veto for Quebec. The new language on opting out denied Quebec the right to spend any compensation as it chose, something he had always insisted on. It was in many ways a victory, in fact, for his version of federalism, certainly for his earlier views on federalism and for constitutional conventions he had created or endorsed. Provincial input into the appointment of senators and justices did not force Ottawa to accept their nominees, and all provinces wanted qualified people in those positions. And the best constitutional experts said that the distinct society clause did not transfer power to Quebec, an opinion later confirmed by Chief Justice Brian Dickson after retirement allowed him to speak on political issues.

Three days after Trudeau's article appeared, the *Globe and Mail* published an article by Mulroney identifying a number of factual errors in the article and pointing out that Trudeau had offered most of the points previously. Gordon Robertson, Canada's top civil servant throughout the negotiations from 1968 to 1979, also wrote in the *Globe and Mail* that Trudeau's article contained serious factual errors. Trudeau replied that while he had offered most of these concessions in the past, he had never offered them at the same time and had linked them to concessions by the provinces. That argument ignored the fact that he had obtained the concessions he had demanded in the previous negotiations—it was the things that Quebec wanted that had been excluded.

The Meech Lake Accord of April 30, 1987, was a general statement, and the meeting to approve the wording of the legal text began on the morning of June 2. It was a marathon session, and at dawn the next day, Mulroney emerged to tell the impatient and exhausted press that an agreement had been reached. It would be submitted to the eleven legislatures for ratification as a package because all the issues were related, the compromises were balanced, and no agreement could be reached if every legislature could suggest changes that it alone wanted and send the entire package back into the negotiating process. That was the same process Trudeau had followed for the 1971 *Victoria Charter*, but not for the *Constitution of 1982*. The 1982 amending process called for approval no later than three years after the first legislature had approved it.

The Failure of Meech

The time-frame was a very serious potential problem, because it allowed provincial governments to delay ratification or change their positions or for new elections to produce different governments. Mulroney and Bourassa were well aware of the danger, and the Quebec Assembly passed the legislation on June 23 creating a final deadline of June 23, 1990. In Ottawa, the federal Liberals and the NDP both supported the agreement, and it easily passed in Parliament.

Trudeau's attack galvanized all those who agreed with his vision of a highly centralized Canada. Other critics soon emerged, including all the groups who had their own demands for constitutional change—women, Aboriginal peoples, labour unions, the Territories, other special interests. Members of these groups did not accept the argument that Quebec's needs should be addressed in a single round, followed by more rounds to deal with additional issues. Their position was essentially that if they could not get what they wanted in the current round, then neither could Quebec. The political left was generally opposed, as they had always wanted a stronger federal government and saw the Accord as weakening federalism. They were also angry with Mulroney over the free-trade agreement with the United States.

Other concerns related to the process: that the agreement had been negotiated behind closed doors; that the first ministers were all male; that the public had not been consulted; and that the legislatures could not suggest changes. These factors differed little from previous negotiations, including the ones that led to the *Constitution of 1982*, but the situation had changed. People had been following the debate for years and had views on the issues. The *Charter* had changed people's concepts about how democracy functioned and had given them the impression that they had more power, that legislatures had less, and that if laws were passed that they objected to, they could take their concerns to the courts and the courts could overrule governments. Many were now concerned as much or more with individual rights as with provincial ones, and Meech was all about the rights of just one province, the one many English Canadians viewed as an obstacle to the nation's progress.

Another problem was that in selling the Meech Lake Accord, politicians did what politicians do—while addressing their respective constituencies, they exaggerated the positive effects and minimized the problems. Thus Bourassa argued that the distinct society clause gave Quebec more power to protect its unique culture, and in the rest of Canada the premiers argued that the clause gave Quebec no additional powers. This was an almost per- fect replay of the Confederation debates, when Macdonald argued that the *BNA Act* created a strong federal government while his French-Canadian ally, Cartier, told Quebeckers that it created strong provinces.

The first serious setback for the process resulted from the fact that New Brunswick Premier Richard Hatfield failed to have his legislature approve it. In October 1987, Frank McKenna won an overwhelming victory, and the new legislature rejected the Accord. In Manitoba, the NDP government of Howard Pawley did not obtain the approval of the legislature before it was defeated by the Progressive Conservatives under Gary Filmon. Filmon withdrew the Accord from consideration by the legislature, leaving it in limbo. Nevertheless, by mid-1988, Parliament and eight provinces with over 90 per cent of the population had ratified the Accord. That was far more support than the "substantial" amount that the Supreme Court's rul- ing of 1980 demanded and far more than obtained for the *Constitution of 1982*. But it did not yet meet the bar of unanimous support that Trudeau and the nine provinces had put back in the amending process after using a much lower threshold to approve it.

Quebec's language law then dealt another blow to the Accord. In spite of the success of a series of increasingly tough language laws, many Québécois still felt their language was threatened by English. Bourassa's government passed a law saying that the signs outside stores had to be in French only, but on December 15, 1988, the Supreme Court unanimously struck down the law as a violation of *Charter* rights for freedom of expression. Many Québécois saw the issue as a matter of principle, as justifying their worst fears regarding the *Charter* and the power of a majority English-speaking federal court to dictate language policy to their province.

Bourassa was under enormous pressure to use the *Charter*'s notwithstanding clause to overrule the verdict. Such a situation was, in fact, what the clause was designed for, namely, to allow an elected government to overrule appointed judges if the government believed the issue to be sufficiently important, and if it was one of the issues subject to the notwithstanding clause, as this one was. Mulroney and others told Bourassa that utilizing the notwithstanding clause would touch off a furor in the rest of Canada and place the ratification of the Accord in doubt. But the sign issue was urgent, and he vetoed it.

Meanwhile, in Newfoundland Premier Peckford had been defeated by the Liberals under Clyde Wells. Wells was strongly opposed to the Accord, partly because he believed all provinces should be treated the same. This was odd since they never had been. Newfoundland was a case in point—the way it joined Confederation was unique and a violation of the *BNA Act*, and the subsidies and other favours extended to the province substantially exceeded those given to any other province. Wells was, however, a staunch ally of Trudeau on constitutional matters, and Newfoundland had poor relations with Quebec over disagreement on the price of electricity from Newfoundland's Churchill Falls. His arguments against the Accord were refuted by experts and federal and provincial politicians, but Newfoundland rescinded its approval on April 6, 1990.

As opposition mounted, federal cabinet minister Jean Charest consulted widely on possible solutions to the issues being raised across the land. His committee's report was tabled on May 17, 1990. Lucien Bouchard, Mulroney's friend and Quebec lieutenant, did not agree with the proposed changes or with the new process. In his view, the possibility of changes violated the agreement that only Quebec's concerns would be addressed in the current round of talks. Including other issues was, he said, yet another humiliation for Quebec. He resigned from the government and formed the separatist Bloc Québécois with several defectors from the Progressive Conservative and Liberal caucuses. Another First Ministers' Conference was called for June 3, a marathon, last-ditch effort that lasted an entire week. It resulted in an agreement that the additional issues would be dealt with after the June 23 deadline for ratifying Meech.

McKenna was satisfied with that, and New Brunswick approved the Accord on June 15, 1990. That left Manitoba, which had not voted, and Newfoundland, which had voted yes and then no, but which might vote yes again now that more negotiations had been approved. Wells had promised to allow another vote in the Assembly, and there was a suspicion that a number of Liberal MLAs might approve it. Wells had to be seen as being open to discussion and debate, so he invited proponents of the Accord to speak to the Assembly.

In Manitoba, time was running out, and an extension on the debate required unanimous support of the MLAs. When it was requested, a back-bench NDP MLA, Elijah Harper, refused. He was Aboriginal, a member of one of the groups most upset that their issues had not been dealt with. The real question, however, was not why and how a single opposition MLA vetoed the Accord, but why the government had waited three years until it needed a procedural vote to gain another two days for debate. Elijah Harper was credited or blamed for the failure of Meech, but it was the Pawley and Filmon governments that had dithered for three years. Then the spotlight shifted back to Newfoundland, because there was still one day left until the deadline. Mulroney and others had just addressed the Assembly, but with a few hours left for a vote, Wells adjourned the legislature. The Meech Lake Accord did not have the approval of either Manitoba or Newfoundland, and the three-year ratification process lapsed. Meech was dead.

Wells's action was a violation of his own promise to allow another vote in the Assembly and a violation of the process for constitutional reform established by Trudeau's *1982 Constitution*. In the past, dozens of attempts to reform the constitution had failed, none by an arbitrary act of a premier or the procedural vote of one MLA. Wells's action was one of the most undemocratic steps ever taken by a Canadian premier. The opponents of Meech were overjoyed; the supporters dismayed. The inevitable comparison to 1982 was instructive. Trudeau's constitution was approved in spite of overwhelming opposition in Quebec; Mulroney's Meech Lake deal died at the hands of two men, Elijah Harper and Clyde Wells. Paradoxically, one of the complaints against Meech was that it had been negotiated by eleven men, but critics were pleased when it was defeated by just two.

The Charlottetown Accord

In Quebec, support for separatism jumped to between 30 and 40 per cent, with support for sovereignty-association rising to the 50 to 60 per cent range. Had the PQ been in power and launched a referendum, separation would almost certainly have been approved. And the PQ was now under the leadership of Jacques Parizeau, one of the politicians who had wanted a clear question on separation on the 1980 referendum ballot. He and the hardliners were finally in control of the party, promising a referendum and separation almost immediately after winning an election. Bourassa remained a federalist, but his view of federalism changed dramatically, as did the views of the provincial Liberal party, which became far more nationalist.

Two commissions were established to examine the province's options. One was headed by two businessmen, Michael Bélanger and Jean Campeau, the other by two MLAs, Jean Allaire and Mario Dumont. The National Assembly received the Bélanger-Campeau Report in September 1990. A majority of the six hundred submissions favoured independence. The report documented two decades of failure and said that the stalemate had to be broken. The Allaire Report of January 1991 was intended to shock the rest of Canada. The list of matters that were to be made provincial jumped from Bourassa's five back to Lévesque's twenty-two. It called for a far more decentralized Canada and came very close to demanding sovereignty-association. It clearly indicated how the failure of Meech Lake had driven moderate Quebec nationalists in the Liberal party towards more extreme nationalism. These reports reverted to the type of demands Quebec had been making before Bourassa's re-election in 1985. They also rekindled a tactic Quebec had been using, now described as the "knife at the throat" strategy, the idea that the only way English-speaking Canada would agree to any of Quebec's demands was if it was threatened with the breakup of the country.

There was little difference now between the Quebec Liberals and the moderate PQ, and both now favoured the strategy of the "knife at the throat" of Canada. The policy was endorsed by the provincial Liberals on March 10, 1991, and the ultimatum was issued on March 27. The rest of Canada would be asked to make Quebec an offer, and Quebec would hold a referendum to determine if the new offer was satisfactory. If the rest of Canada did not make an offer, the referendum would be on separation. The Quebec Assembly passed a bill in June 1991, providing for a referendum in October 1992.

Though the federal government, the nine English-speaking provincial governments, the public, the media, and even the experts who staffed the large cottage industry of constitutional consultations were exhausted, Quebec's position and its deadline left them no alternative but to go back to the drawing boards. On April 21, 1991, Mulroney gave ex-prime minister Joe Clark the task of making the next round a success. Clark criss-crossed the country for five months and ensured that every group's demands for change were heard. This extensive effort at consultation was a direct response to the criticisms of the secret, male-dominated Meech Lake process. Ottawa also commissioned several studies, which involved consultations with interested members of the public.

Mulroney's strategy for addressing Quebec's demands alone followed by further conferences had failed, so the new strategy was to address all of the issues in a single document. One issue was the strong demand in western Canada for major reform to the Senate. They wanted a Senate that would be equal, elected, and effective and would therefore balance the enormous power that central Canada wielded in Parliament. A number of studies had been done, and Senate reform had been discussed as early as the first Premiers' Conference back in 1878. There was support for an elected and effective Senate, but in an equal one, Ontario or Quebec would have no more senators than PEI, and both Atlantic Canada and the West would outnumber central Canada two to one. The system of 1867 that had put central Canada in control of the federal government and both houses of Parliament was under attack. Ontario and Quebec had no intention of allowing their influence over the central government to be watered down by a Triple-E Senate.

Throughout the rest of 1991, consultations proceeded with various groups that had demanded input and a series of papers were released, including *Shaping Canada's Future Together.* On February 28, 1992, the *Report of the Special Joint Committee on a Renewed Canada* was released. After a number of preliminary conferences, a major one was scheduled for Charlottetown. This time it included the prime minister, the ten provincial premiers, the two leaders of the governments of the northern territories, and four Aboriginal leaders. In more marathon sessions, this group hammered out an agreement that seemed to satisfy all of the interests they represented to a degree they could all accept. That meant, of course, that many of them had not obtained all they wanted, although getting all they wanted was never possible in a negotiation such as this.

Quebec obtained less than it had in Meech, far less than it had demanded in the 1960s and 1970s, a clear reflection of the reluctance of the rest of Canada to meet its demands and of the failures and mistakes of its governments since 1960. Quebec agreed to an equal Senate in return for a guarantee of a minimum of 25 per cent of the seats in the Commons. There was a new Canada clause to balance the distinct society clause and confirm the equality of provinces and protection for Quebec's Anglophone minority. The Accord increased federal power by putting the spending power in the constitution, that is, the concept that Ottawa could spend money on provincial matters without provincial approval. It strengthened the Senate by having provincial input into appointments so that senators did represent their provinces for the first time. It also delegated some federal power to the provinces, so it was relatively balanced in terms of centralization versus decentralization of power. Bourassa was accused of caving in and failing to gain as much as at Meech. Interestingly, Premiers Wells and Filmon accepted an agreement that contained the essence of the Meech Lake Accord, even if watered down, the agreement they had allowed to die or killed only two years earlier.

The Charlottetown Accord was approved by the premiers in August 28, 1992, by the House of Commons by a vote of 233–12, by the provincial governments and opposition parties, and by Aboriginal leaders. That compared very favourably to Confederation, which was approved by only one of three assemblies, and to the *Constitution of 1982*, which was not approved by Quebec. By now, however, it was accepted that approval by the eleven legislatures was not sufficient. The *Charter* had empowered the people, or so they thought, and they were not interested in government by executive federalism, by deals made in secret that legislatures could not change. The first ministers agreed that it had to be ratified by referendum, the date being set for October 26, 1992.

When the public saw the Charlottetown Accord, they noted, as they might have done with any previous constitutional agreement, that compromises had been made. In some cases, they did not get all they wanted; in others cases, someone else got more than what they thought they should. The fact that their leaders had been negotiating these issues for decades, had made the best deals they thought they could, and had signed the agreement as the best outcome possible did not resonate with a lot of Canadians. Most importantly, many inside Quebec thought it did not give their province enough, and many outside Quebec thought it gave that province too much. Had the *BNA Act* been submitted to the public, it would almost certainly have been criticized for the same reasons, as would almost any trade treaty. In matters such as these, individuals do not have to compromise but political leaders do. That is why referenda are used so rarely to make major national decisions, and why the results of referenda are often criticized.

Once more Trudeau came out of retirement to challenge the latest attempt to alter his *1982 Constitution*. His views were presented in an article in *McLean's* and *L'Actualité* on September 28 and in speech at a Montreal restaurant with the wonderful bilingual and multicultural name of Maison du Egg Roll. That speech was broadcast. Trudeau argued that the Charlottetown Accord would render the federal government "impotent," as it was "an unprecedented abdication of sovereign powers." This was a highly emotional attack, as few people would want to live in a country with an impotent central government that lacked sovereign powers.

The comment helped galvanize opposition to the Accord, but it caused puzzlement amongst those who actually read the details of the agreement. All the provincial governments were Canadian governments, and he was suggesting that if they had any more power, then the Canadian government was "impotent." This suggested that only the central government should have power, and the slightest hint of a reduction in its power would render it completely powerless. Experts on the constitutional talks such as Gordon Robertson were amazed by the use of the phrase, and a number of Trudeau's supporters deserted him. Trudeau helped create the strong view that the Accord gave Quebec too much power, although it gave no more power than the *Victoria Charter*, which he and the nine other premiers had accepted. The Accord reflected the recommendations of Ottawa's Pépin-Robarts Commission, which he had appointed; the Beige Paper, which was the platform of the *No* side in the 1980 referendum; other proposals that had been discussed during his years in office; and other items that simply reflected current practice, such as the federal spending power, which he had used.

Many factors conspired to destroy the Charlottetown Accord. A crucial one was that Mulroney had become one of the most unpopular prime ministers in Canadian history. It followed that if he was strongly in favour of the Accord, then it must be a very bad deal for Canada. The constitutional talks also coincided with the negotiations for a free-trade deal with the United States. Many Canadians favoured that deal, especially in the West and in Quebec. Many did not, especially those on the left of the political spectrum and those in Ontario. The opponents linked the constitution with free trade—if they opposed the latter, that led them to oppose the former.

In the referendum that followed, Canadians rejected the Charlottetown Accord by a vote of 54.4 per cent to 45.6 per cent. That included Quebec, where the vote was 55.4 per cent to 42.4 per cent. This was the first and only time Canadian citizens ever voted on a constitutional amendment. Those delighted with the result celebrated, but their victory was premature: over the next two decades, a number of the elements of Meech and Charlottetown were implemented by federal legislation or agreement between Ottawa and the provinces, and by both Conservative and Liberal regimes. While Trudeau played a major role in defeating the Meech and Charlottetown initiatives, he thus failed to prevent the implementation of many of their provisions, including the ones he had most strongly opposed.

As with the Meech Lake Accord, the immediate aftermath of Charlottetown's failure was a dramatic increase in nationalism in Quebec. The day after the Charlottetown Accord was rejected, Bourassa spoke in the Assembly. He said, "English Canada must clearly understand that whatever is said, whatever is done, Quebec is today and forever a distinct and free society, capable of ensuring its own destiny and its own development." There was a huge ovation, and PQ leader Parizeau congratulated him. The more nationalist wing of the Quebec Liberal Party left to form the Action Démocratique du Québec, the ADQ, under Mario Dumont. In the 1993 federal election, the soft-nationalist Quebec wing of the Conservative party was decimated as Lucien Bouchard's Bloc won 49 per cent of the popular vote and fifty-four of seventy-five seats in Quebec. In the provincial election of September 12, 1994, the PQ returned to power under the hardline separatist Parizeau, with a promise of a referendum on separation. That was a very serious threat, as support for separatism rose from 40 per cent in 1980 to over 50 per cent after the rejection of the Charlottetown Accord.

Free Trade, Immigration, and Deficits

While constitutional talks dominated Canadian politics, one of the most important thrusts of the Mulroney government was towards a free trade deal with the United States. In terms of federal-provincial relations, the question was what role the provinces would play in the negotiations. Ottawa's answer was to consult the provinces while developing the Canadian position, after which Ottawa alone would negotiate while keeping the provinces informed and considering their feedback. Mulroney met the premiers on June 2, 1986, and let them know that while Ottawa alone would be engaged in the negotiations, the federal government would keep them informed. The minister responsible, Joe Clark, and officials updated the provinces regularly, and an elaborate mechanism was established to ensure that they were briefed as the talks progressed.

The provinces were briefed on other trade negotiations such as the Uruguay Round on the General Agreement on Tariffs and Trade (GATT), which lasted from 1986 to 1989, and they were sent reports on international meetings such as the G7. The Free Trade Agreement, or FTA, reduced regional tensions, as the West and Maritimes had always complained about tariffs that favoured central Canada. One negative result of the agreement in terms of federal-provincial relations was that many English-speaking Canadians wanted a stronger federal government to protect the economy and culture from American influence.

Immigration was another sphere of activity that experienced considerable evolution under Mulroney. The Cullen-Couture agreement of 1978 allowed Quebec a role in the selection of immigrants, and other provinces gradually became more involved in the selection of economic migrants and in settlement programs. Under the 1991 Ottawa-Quebec agreements, the federal government withdrew completely from settlement programs and provided Quebec with compensation so it could finance Ottawa's former role. Mulroney wanted to prove that federalism still worked for Quebec in the aftermath of the Meech Lake disaster, and there were no conditions on the funds, which were quite generous. Other provinces followed Quebec, and Canada experienced one more example of successful, flexible, collaborative federalism.

One of the most difficult challenges Mulroney faced was the federal deficit, which was roughly $40 billion a year when he came to power. Finance Minister Michael Wilson had no choice but to make significant cuts to the rate of spending increases. Transfers to the provinces accounted for 20 per cent of the federal budget. The reductions affected the EPF, which covered health care and higher education, and the CAP, which covered welfare and social services. The 1990 budget limited the growth of the CAP to 5 per cent for the three richest provinces, and became known as the "cap on the CAP." BC took the issue to the provincial court, arguing that the CAP could only be changed with provincial agreement. That court backed BC, but the Supreme Court reversed the verdict. That decision confirmed Ottawa's use of the spending power by stating that Ottawa could change the amounts if it chose. The "cap on the CAP" was, in effect, yet another equalization program as it affected the three richest provinces but not the seven poorest.

These changes meant that the fifty-fifty ratio of tax points to cash in the original 1977 policy would change fairly quickly as the cash portion declined, while the value of the tax points grew with the economy. And as the cash portion declined, so too did Ottawa's ability to use it to ensure that the provinces met the conditions for the programs. This was particularly the case for the portion of the CAP designated to support higher education, where Ottawa's ability to influence provincial spending practically disappeared.

Naturally, the provinces that could escape or modify federal conditions changed their policies in different ways, depending on local conditions, and uniform federal standards became more and more of a patchwork. Relatively speaking, the provinces grew stronger, the federal government weaker, and the federal encroachment on provincial jurisdiction became less and less important. And with no money to spend, the Mulroney government did not launch new shared-cost programs, eliminating that long-standing source of provincial annoyance.

From the quasi-unitary state that Trudeau envisioned and almost created, the country evolved back towards the genuine or classical model of the *BNA Act*. Ottawa was still able to enforce many standards, especially on Medicare, but the Canada of Brian Mulroney was neither a genuine federation nor a unitary state. The paradox for Trudeau's legacy was that the overspending during his regime partly destroyed his goal of uniform standards from coast to coast in provincial areas of responsibility. The paradox of Mulroney's legacy was that in spite of the failure of Meech and Charlottetown, he presided over the restoration of a balanced federalism due to the financial crisis inherited from Trudeau.

CHAPTER 15
The Chrétien Regime, 1993-2003

On October 25, 1993, Jean Chrétien led the federal Liberals to a convincing victory, winning 177 seats out of 295 based on 41 per cent of the popular vote. Of the other two national parties, the NDP elected only nine MPs and the Progressive Conservatives only two. The separatist, Quebec-based Bloc became the Official Opposition with fifty-four seats, and the western-based Reform Party came third with fifty-two seats. Canada had never been as divided.

The new government soon faced two crises that had been brewing for decades—a financial crisis that almost cost the country its economic sovereignty, and another Quebec referendum that almost cost the country its unity. For ten years, the Chrétien government lurched from centralist to decentralist policies, from unbalanced to balanced budgets, from sharp cuts to expenditure to sharp increases, from being tough with Quebec to being soft. Some of these conflicting trends were pursued simultaneously, and it was sometimes difficult to tell what was happening to federalism under Prime Minister Chrétien.

Given the failure of the Charlottetown Accord, Mulroney's strategy of attempting to make massive, all-inclusive changes to the constitution was abandoned for the traditional approach of dealing with one issue at a time by legislation or federal-provincial agreement. One of the first examples was the July 1994 Agreement on Internal Trade, the AIT. The proposal had been in the Charlottetown Accord and was designed to reduce barriers to trade involving government procurement and the movement of goods, labour, and professional employees across provincial borders. Another agreement facilitated better co-operation on the environment. Both showed that progress could be made and that elements of the Meech and Charlottetown Accords could and should be implemented.

The Financial Crisis

One of the biggest problems the Chrétien government faced was a very serious financial situation. The national debt had ballooned to $500 billion and the deficit for 1993–94 was an all-time record of $42 billion. Interest on the debt was consuming 36 per cent of revenue, and that proportion was growing. The first budget of Finance Minister Paul Martin made fairly modest cuts to spending, and Chrétien said that there would be no more cuts after the first two rounds. Then, in December 1994, Mexico plunged into a financial crisis, and in January, the influential *Wall Street Journal* published a front-page article saying that Canada was heading for a similar crisis. There was a good possibility that international bankers would downgrade Canada's credit rating, which would lead to a sharp rise in interest charges. Ottawa could not afford higher interest payments, and the IMF might have had to save Canada from bankruptcy. If it did, it would impose conditions on the Canadian government's financial and economic policies, and while those were in effect, Canada would not be completely independent.

This threat produced a complete reversal in thinking by Chrétien and Martin. They now decided that the entire deficit had to be eliminated, and that it should be done quickly. Their goal jumped from cutting a few billion dollars to chopping over $40 billion, an unheard of change to government financing. That required massive cuts to almost every program, including the ones providing financial transfers to the provinces. The financial situation thus put federal-provincial relations near the top of the new government's priorities, because it had to figure out what programs to cut and how to manage the negative reaction from the provinces.

There was strong opposition within cabinet and caucus to this plan. It undermined a main Liberal policy dating back to the Second World War, namely the centralization of power based on conditional shared-cost programs in provincial areas of responsibility. If Ottawa substantially reduced its share of funding, its leverage would also be reduced. The threat of losing the levers of power touched off bitter fights within cabinet and the party. Ministers who tried to fight Martin lost almost every battle. Those who appealed to Chrétien over Martin's head also lost, and the cuts could not have been made without Chrétien's full support. Martin's second budget, delivered in February 1995, is justly famous in the annals of Canadian constitutional history, as well as financial, economic, and political history.

During that first year in office, Marcel Massé, one of the most powerful and knowledgeable ministers, headed a bureaucratic initiative known as program review. The object was to study every program to determine whether it was needed, whether it was meeting its objectives, and whether it was efficient, the main goal being to reduce costs. Such exercises are fairly routine when new governments take over, but this one took on enormous significance when it became clear that departments had to make massive cuts to their spending. In effect, Chrétien, Martin, and Massé forced an unprecedented level of slashing on almost every department and program.

The budget cuts and program review led to one of the most significant changes ever in Ottawa's relations with the provinces. Ottawa had been transferring money to the provinces through the EPF, which covered health care and post-secondary education, and the CAP, which covered welfare and social services. The 1995 budget combined both into the Canada Health and Social Transfer, the CHST, to be financed by a combination of federal tax points and cash transfers tied to growth in the GDP. Ottawa then reduced the cash portion of the CHST by $4.2 billion for April 1, 1996, and a further $2.8 billion the following year, a total reduction of $6 billion, from $18 billion to $12 billion, in its transfers to the provinces. In future, the cash component was not to fall below $12 billion in order to leave Ottawa with some leverage over the provinces. The conditions for Medicare were maintained, along with the rule that provinces could not make residence a requirement to receive welfare. The CHST now covered Ottawa's transfers for welfare, child welfare, social services, post-secondary education, hospitals, and Medicare. The CHST cuts reduced Ottawa's share of provincial health spending by 25 per cent, leaving it somewhere between 15 per cent, the figure the provinces calculated, and 30 per cent, the figure the federal government calculated.

The cost-cutting exercise was remarkably successful in financial terms.

Within two years, the deficit was reduced from $40 billion to $20 billion, the next budget was the first to be balanced in twenty years, and there was a surplus of $12 billion in 1999–2000. But while Ottawa could maintain its conditions for Medicare, it lost the ability to impose conditions on the other programs. There, the increased flexibility allowed the provinces to adjust their systems to local circumstances, and Canada clearly had ten different systems with some important common elements. There were safety nets for the poor in every province, but they varied and no longer reflected the "national standards" that had been a primary objective of the federal programs introduced after the Second World War. By 2000, Canada had moved part-way back towards a more even balance of power between the two orders of government. When a CBC reporter asked Chrétien if the cuts would change the nature of federalism, he replied, "Yes, for years the provinces said, 'Let us run these programs . . .' I said, 'Fine. Run them . . .' This is changing . . . yeah. It's changing to respond to the request of the provinces that say, 'We need more flexibility.'"

The provinces had no choice but to make major cuts to programs. They also had to reduce assistance to municipalities, so the federal, provincial, and municipal governments all reduced the level of their services to the public. In just two years, Canadians saw spending by all three orders of government decline sharply, while levels of taxation remained the same or rose slightly. In effect, the citizens of 1995 were suddenly paying for three decades of government extravagance. The provincial governments were enraged with the cuts to their revenues; the fact that they were imposed without any consultation; the fact that it was Ottawa that had launched most of these programs and imposed them on the provinces; the fact that the provinces had argued since the 1960s that the programs were unaffordable; and finally, the fact that they would face most of the political backlash from the cuts. There was, needless to say, a sharp deterioration in Ottawa's relations with the provinces, and the howls were as loud in the wealthy provinces as in the poorer ones, and in English-speaking Canada as much as in Quebec.

The Second Quebec Referendum

At the same time, the new government faced an even more challenging problem in Quebec. Canada was heading for the most serious crisis of national unity in its history, more serious than the problems that had forced the colonies to embrace federalism in 1867, more serious than the referendum of 1980. On September 12, 1994, the PQ romped back to power in Quebec and Jacques Parizeau became premier with seventy-seven seats based on 44.8 per cent of the vote. Their election was virtually inevitable given the failure of Bourassa's Liberals and Mulroney's soft Quebec nationalists to meet Quebec's demands in the Meech and Charlottetown Accords.

Parizeau was a hard nationalist and an out-and-out separatist who believed that Quebec should become fully independent. After achieving that status, it would attempt to negotiate some sort of arrangement with the rest of Canada. To him, independence was the important and immediate goal, and any subsequent arrangement with Canada might be desirable but was not essential. His party had promised another referendum on separatism, and he was determined to carry it out early in his mandate. Bouchard, leader of the Bloc of MPs in Ottawa, was a soft nationalist who wanted sovereignty-association, but not outright independence. Mario Dumont and the ADQ were soft nationalists who definitely wanted change and could have been appeased by minor concessions. Chrétien refused to make any gesture, and Dumont joined the PQ and the Bloc for the referendum campaign. On June 12, the three leaders reached a compromise. The referendum would ask: "Do you agree that Quebec should become sovereign, after having made a formal offer to Canada for a new economic and political partnership . . . ?"

It was a clever compromise, and the Quebec Liberals and the federal government naturally condemned it for being vague. But whatever the wording, everyone knew what it meant—if 50 per cent of the electorate voted *Yes*, Quebec would be headed for independence, and Canada would be sundered into two parts minus its biggest province. The referendum was scheduled for Monday, October 30. Canada was launched on perhaps the most gut-wrenching exercise in its history. Since Ottawa had no plans for dealing with a victory by the *Yes* side, the short-term effects of such an outcome would be chaos.

Chrétien's policy towards Quebec was roughly the same as Trudeau's and the opposite of Mulroney's, namely, that no concessions should be made because concession would demonstrate weakness and whet the appetite for more. According to this argument, if enough concessions were made, Quebec would eventually become practically independent. This was the opposite of Mulroney's view that many of the demands of the soft nationalists and Quebec governments were justified and should be met in order to undermine support for separatism. Mulroney and three successive leaders of the Quebec Liberals—Bourassa, Ryan, and Johnson—had tried that approach, but it had failed. Now it was back to the Trudeau-Chrétien tough-love approach. Trudeau's and Chrétien's policy defied all the rules of negotiating, which by definition is based on a willingness to compromise. Their goal was the all-out defeat of Quebec nationalism. It was all or nothing, and nothing was now a possible outcome.

At the onset, Chrétien said, "I have a good and clear strategy: it's faith in Canada. If we provide a good, honest, solid working government, everybody will want to remain in Canada." The "everybody" obviously did not include the 25 to 45 per cent of Quebeckers who had been telling the pollsters for over two decades that they did not want to remain in Canada. And the idea that Canada enjoyed a "good . . . solid working government" was not necessarily the view of a majority of the Québécois.

The *Yes* side was headed by Parizeau, with help from Bouchard and Dumont; the *No* side was headed by Daniel Johnson, leader of the provincial Liberal Opposition, aided by the federal Liberals. It was not clear how Bouchard and Dumont would help Parizeau, and there were animosities and differences amongst them, but few major problems were envisioned in the *Yes* camp. The *No* side faced a very different situation. Chrétien and Johnson and their supporters did not like each other, had different if not opposite views of federalism, and there was definitely no trust between the two groups of politicians.

The provincial Liberals believed strongly that a significant amount of power should be transferred back to the provinces from Ottawa, while the federal Liberals believed in maintaining the status quo or making Ottawa even stronger relative to the provinces. This was the same situation that had prevailed during the first referendum campaign, only at that time Prime Minister Trudeau had created the impression that he agreed with the provincial Liberals. The official document issued by the Quebec Liberal Party for the 1995 referendum campaign said that Quebec was a distinct society and should have full autonomy in areas of provincial jurisdiction. That, then, was the official position of the *No* side, so when the federal Liberals supported the *No* side, they were endorsing a policy they strongly opposed. Few Quebeckers would be fooled. On constitutional issues, Johnson's Liberals were closer to their PQ opponents than to their federal allies. Taking advantage of this ambiguity, Parizeau asked Chrétien if Ottawa would withdraw from provincial areas of responsibility as the Quebec Liberals wanted; Chrétien would not and could not give a clear answer.

As the campaign began, polls put the *No* side ahead by roughly 55 per cent to 45 per cent. Those polls reinforced the view of both the provincial and federal parts of the *No* side that Quebeckers would never vote to separate from Canada. The softer question had been defeated by a 60–40 margin in 1980; now the harder question would certainly be defeated by at least 55–45. In Ottawa, this complacency reinforced the view that the federal Liberals did not have to do much to support Johnson. That fit well with Johnson's intentions and strategy, because he did not believe he needed any assistance and probably suspected that help from the federal Liberals could be counter-productive. Chrétien was very unpopular in Quebec, and it was understood that his involvement would be limited to three speeches, while Trudeau was not asked to participate at all. Federal MPs would campaign in their own constituencies, and various departments in Ottawa would continue to pour federal money into the province, especially on advertising the benefits of federal programs and spending with the unsubtle message that all that would be lost in an independent Quebec.

Little changed during the first three weeks of the campaign. Neither Parizeau nor Johnson were inspiring leaders or speakers, the positions were all well known, the polls showed little movement, and the outcome seemed predictable. The responsible federal minister, Lucienne Robillard, was a member of the *No* committee, but no one there was interested in her views. Federal ministers such as Deputy Prime Minister Sheila Copps were not welcome. When they did contact the *No* side, they were surprised at how poorly it was organized and how badly its campaign was going, but the polls still pointed to a decisive victory. Chrétien and his Quebec ministers repeatedly assured cabinet that all was well.

In his first speech, Chrétien bragged about French power in Ottawa. This may not have had the desired effect because, over the past three decades, federal ministers from Quebec had not produced the changes the nationalists wanted. Indeed, Quebec's position within the federation had grown weaker due to the policies and actions of Trudeau and Chrétien, two of the best examples of "French power." And the drastic budget cuts had been carried out by the three Quebec ministers, Chrétien, Martin, and Massé. Under Mulroney, a weaker team of Quebec ministers had obtained much of what Quebec wanted in Meech and Charlottetown, but that government had failed to implement those agreements. Apart from encouraging bilingualism, having more Francophones in senior positions, and spending billions in Quebec, it was difficult to identify many achievements stemming from the presence of more cabinet ministers and senior officials from Quebec in Ottawa. With the federal debt at $500 billion and Martin's cuts to transfers to the provinces, it was no longer possible to argue convincingly that separation would make Quebec a lot poorer. In addition, the FTA had shifted part of Quebec's trade from the rest of Canada to the United States. That was an argument for independence and closer relations with the United States, not for staying in a pan-Canadian economic union. Fortunately for the *No* side, Chrétien's Quebec City speech received little coverage.

The *Yes* side was, of course, fully aware that it was heading for defeat if things did not change. So they made a change. On Saturday, October 7, it was announced that Bloc leader Lucien Bouchard would be the chief negotiator for whatever arrangement might be made with Canada after a *Yes* vote on independence. Parizeau remained premier, but Bouchard was now de facto head of the *Yes* campaign. Chrétien thought that changing horses in mid-stream was a sign of weakness and confusion. That was another miscalculation, because Bouchard was the most popular politician in Quebec, a brilliant speaker, a man of intelligence, passion, charisma, and integrity. There was no comparison between him and Parizeau, Johnson, or Chrétien, and he changed the debate from one based on reason to one based on passion, an advantage for the *Yes* side.

Polls taken between October 15 and 17 showed the *No* side's lead narrowing to forty-seven to forty-five. As the *Yes* side gained momentum, federal ministers grew more alarmed. On October 17, Martin gave a speech in Quebec City in which he argued that there was no guarantee that an independent Quebec would be admitted to NAFTA. That was seen as odd since the United States wanted to expand NAFTA, not shrink it. He also said that 90 per cent of Quebec's exports could be affected by independence and that a million jobs could be lost. Parizeau immediately pointed out the absurdity of these claims and accused Ottawa of scare-mongering, a view shared and publicized by most of the Quebec media.

The day after Martin's speech, Chrétien gave his second speech of the campaign, this one to the Quebec City Chamber of Commerce. In it, he raised doubt that there could be a partnership between Quebec and Canada. This was a questionable strategy when decade after decade, between 45 and 55 per cent of the population supported sovereignty-association, proving that they did believe a partnership was possible if not inevitable. Chrétien failed to correct Martin's musings about Quebec losing a million jobs should it separate.

Although the polls still showed a victory for the *No* side, Johnson realized he had to promise something to turn the momentum around. On October 21, he reiterated a key statement in the *Yes* side's position, saying that the Canadian constitution should recognize Quebec as a distinct society. That, of course, had been Bourassa's key demand in 1985 and was the main element of both the Meech Lake and Charlottetown Accords. Chrétien was caught off-guard, and when asked to comment, he said that the real issue was separation rather than the constitution. That statement was half right and half wrong. The referendum was indeed about separation, but it was the constitution that had created the referendum, and the solution to Quebec's grievances lay in constitutional reform, not in simply winning the referendum campaign. His comment was therefore seen as a direct contradiction of Johnson.

The polls changed the following weekend. One on Monday, October 23, showed the *Yes* side ahead; another on the following day showed it seven points ahead. The complacency of the *No* side then became a major problem, because they had made no plans for how to campaign if the momentum shifted to the *Yes* side, as it clearly had done. What they did have was ineffective leadership at both levels, a sharp difference of views about Quebec's place in Canada, and, in Ottawa, an inability to comprehend the reasons for the strength of separatist sentiment. Suddenly,

Chrétien, his cabinet ministers, his backbenchers, and much of the rest of Canada realized that Bouchard and Parizeau could very well win. The question was how to turn the vote around, a question for which Chrétien had no answers. Anglophone ministers from outside Quebec, such as David Collonette, Sheila Copps, and Brian Tobin, urged him to make the two concessions that might win the vote: promising to recognize Quebec as a distinct society and restoring the veto it had lost in 1982.

Chrétien's position on both issues was ambivalent, a tribute to the political deftness he had demonstrated in his in three decades in politics, but not an advantage in the dying days of the campaign. He would probably have no political problem endorsing both the veto and the distinct society, but doing so on the eve of the vote would look like death-bed conversion. It would also raise a number of questions. If he believed in them, why had he not spoken earlier or reacted positively to Johnson's request? How could he deliver the two concessions when every previous effort to do so had failed? And what, exactly, would recognizing Quebec as a distinct society mean this time? Though Trudeau was not active in the campaign, no one could forget that he strongly opposed both these key elements in the Meech and Charlottetown Accords and that Chrétien was his key minister for federal-provincial affairs before 1984.

These questions could not be answered, but something had to be done. On Tuesday, October 24, Chrétien told cabinet that he would offer Quebec hope for change in his third and final speech, to be delivered that evening in the Verdun Arena near Montreal. Was this a repeat of Trudeau's 1982 promise to "renew" the constitution? He gave no details and allowed no discussion. In the speech that evening, he promised to restore Quebec's veto and recognize the province as a distinct society. Thus two of the most important policy promises in modern Canadian history were decided by Chrétien alone, without the approval of either cabinet or caucus. The following day, he met the Liberal caucus in Ottawa, a group who knew that the country was in danger of disintegrating and that one of the main reasons was the prime minister's mismanagement of the relationship with Quebec. Chrétien wept; the party remained united; and the federal Liberals seemed to agree at last that Quebec should have a veto and be recognized as a distinct society. Chrétien repeated those promises that evening in a TV address to the nation.

It was not clear at all that the two last-minute promises would turn the tide. Quebeckers were well aware that Chrétien needed support from the nine English-speaking provinces and that Mulroney had failed to implement them in two major attempts over a period of ten years. Unsurprisingly, the PQ scoffed at the promises. Johnson and the provincial Liberals were not impressed either, and Johnson criticized Ottawa for not promising change until defeat was staring them in the face. Nevertheless, the speech appeared to have had a positive effect with the next poll showed the *No* side in front again by a scant 3.5 per cent margin.

The feeling in Ottawa was that something else had to be done, but no one seemed to know what. Then Fisheries Minister Brian Tobin heard that the Montreal Chamber of Commerce was organizing a rally in Place du Canada for Friday, October 27, three days before the vote. The thought emerged: what if thousands of people from across Canada joined that rally as an expression of their love for Quebec? The idea was immediately and enthusiastically endorsed and plans launched for its execution. Air Canada, Canadian Airlines, and bus companies offered discounts as high as 90 per cent for travel to Montreal. Federal civil servants and employees in many companies were given time off to attend the rally. Tens of thousands of Canadians converged on Montreal, where they were conveniently supplied with a giant maple leaf flag. The rally may have been counter-productive, as some had predicted, because the *No* side's lead dropped from 3.5 to 2.5 per cent. As the weekend began, the race was too close to call, and as polling ceased, an anxious nation wondered whether they would have one or two countries come Tuesday.

On Monday, October 30, the referendum was defeated by a vote of 50.6 to 49.4 per cent. The turnout was 93.5 per cent, the largest in Quebec history. Of the electors, 2,362,648 voted to stay in Canada, and 2,308,360 voted to leave, a difference of just 54,288. Quebec would have been independent if 55,000 *No* sympathizers had stayed at home, if 55,000 more *Yes* sympathizers had come out to vote, or if 28,000 people had voted differently. Bouchard had almost led them to victory, but his role ended with the campaign. Parizeau was in charge of the Quebec government, and he had a clear plan should the *Yes* side win. He would immediately declare Quebec independent, take the necessary steps to implement that decision, and see how Ottawa reacted. That would take time, since Ottawa had no plan for dealing with a *Yes* victory or an immediate declaration of independence. It was not clear what role, if any, Quebec MPs and ministers, including Chrétien, could play after their provincial government declared Quebec independent, and many people in the rest of Canada believed that Quebec MPs and ministers could not represent Ottawa in negotiations with a Quebec that had declared independence.

One of the first results of a Quebec declaration of independence would therefore have been a political crisis in Ottawa over whether Quebec politicians could still be MPs and ministers, including Chrétien himself. The declaration would have violated the Supreme Court's ruling, but it was not clear whether that ruling would have any meaning—how could a court with six English-speaking justices overrule the democratic decision of several million Quebeckers? As far as Parizeau was concerned, the Court would no longer have any influence over Quebec's destiny, as its sovereignty lay in the hands of the people who had just voted for independence.

But the *Yes* side lost, and an infuriated Jacques Parizeau said that the outcome reflected money and the ethnic vote. This was probably true, as non-French Quebeckers voted overwhelmingly against independence and Ottawa had been pouring billions of dollars into Quebec for decades with the goal of buying support. That included the enormous advertising budget launched after the election of the PQ in 1994. The travel subsidies for the Montreal rally probably also violated the referendum rules. But Parizeau's statement was a political blunder because it suggested that independence was designed for the Québécois and not the rest of the population. He resigned immediately and was replaced by Bloc leader Bouchard.

Quebec: A Veto and Status as a Distinct Society

Back in Ottawa, Chrétien faced some enormous problems. Many in the cabinet, caucus, and party remained opposed to his two promises. He wanted to put an end to the Quebec problem as quickly as possible, but few others agreed. The rest of Canada had not been consulted, and in the past, it had repeatedly made clear its opposition to recognizing Quebec as a distinct society. Two days after the referendum, Chrétien met with new Ontario Premier Mike Harris, but he was strongly opposed to the changes. Harris and the premiers also opposed a hasty approach to the Quebec problem. Clearly, Chrétien would not be able to obtain an amendment to the constitution to implement his two promises.

The next best option was unilateral federal action, and Chrétien decided to use that means to "lend" its own veto to Quebec. If Quebec made clear that it objected to some proposed amendment, Ottawa would veto that proposal on Quebec's behalf, even if Ottawa favoured the proposal. That would be unfair to the other provinces, a case of "special status" that went far beyond anything envisioned in either the Meech or Charlottetown Accords, so Chrétien had to devise a suitable formula covering all the provinces. The one he proposed was familiar to anyone who remembered the aborted *Victoria Charter* of 1971. By it, four regions had vetoes: Ontario and Quebec, and any two Atlantic provinces and any two western provinces with 50 per cent of their respective populations. Ottawa would thus pass legislation saying it would refuse its own approval to any amendment that any of these regions opposed, and Quebec would have its veto back.

British Columbia had never seen itself as merely part of a western Canadian region—that was a view from east of the Rockies. In 1971, it had reluctantly gone along with the *Victoria Charter*, but since then its growth had substantially outstripped that of the Prairies and its sense of identity as a separate region had grown as fast or faster. Now, BC demanded that it be treated as a region and have its own veto, just like Ontario and Quebec, and Chrétien agreed. Alberta did not see itself as inferior to BC, but oddly, if BC was no longer part of the western region, then Alberta had over half the remaining population of the Prairies and would therefore have its own veto too.

Instead of requiring the support of any seven provinces with 50 per cent of the population as the constitution dictated for most amendments, change would now require the support of Ottawa, Ontario, Quebec, BC, and two more provinces from Atlantic Canada and the Prairies. So the number of provinces required had changed to seven or eight, but the population they represented had jumped from 50 per cent to 90 per cent, which actually made constitutional change almost impossible. Parliament passed the legislation on February 2, 1996, leaving political scientists mystified and Canadians confused. What, exactly, had the five decades of debate about the amending formula been about? Was the outcome worth the effort? And what was the outcome—the amending formula in the *Constitution of 1982*, or the one in the new federal legislation? And how could a federal law over-rule the constitution? Apparently, Chrétien had contacted Trudeau over the issue, but what they discussed was not revealed, possibly because a crucial part of Trudeau's 1982 constitutional package was now being trashed.

Alberta was not the only province to object to BC being recognized as a separate region. Chrétien's new legislation was designed to give Quebec back its veto, but now BC also had one and it was smaller than Quebec! The Québécois noted that in six days of discussion, BC gained something Quebec had been fighting for ever since 1982, and had gained it only because of Quebec's referendum. And Alberta, with a fraction Quebec's population and much less "distinctiveness," had not even demanded a veto but got one anyway. Once more, Bouchard, the Bloc, the PQ, and the soft and hard nationalists could complain that Quebec was being "slighted." They were also well aware that the Chrétien government itself and any future government could take away the veto by simply repealing the federal legislation. That only required a vote in the Commons of 50 per cent of the MPs, and Parliamentary majorities often represented only 40 per cent of the population, certainly not the 90 per cent required in the new formula.

Fifty years of debate had produced this mess of an amending formula and guaranteed that most future constitutional changes would be made by legislation and federal-provincial agreement, not by the process agreed in the constitution. The *Constitution of 1982* would thus grow more and more irrelevant. It was no wonder that Canadians increasingly honoured the *Charter of Rights and Freedoms*, because it was one of the few parts of the constitution that still made sense. In a bizarre twist to constitutionalism, Chrétien's compromise reversed the concept that a constitution overrode legislatures because his new formula overrode the one in the constitution! This process only operated in one direction though—Quebec could now have a change it did not want vetoed by Ottawa, but it would be almost impossible to obtain any change it wanted. Some might have wondered if patriating the constitution had been worth it.

Honouring the second major promise—recognizing Quebec as a distinct society—was much easier as it could be done through federal legislation that did not involve any province other than Quebec. The objection of

Trudeau, English-speaking Canada, and the other nine provincial governments to inserting a distinct society clause in the constitution was that it supposedly gave Quebec powers the other provinces did not have. Recognizing Quebec as a distinct society through federal legislation clearly did not bestow any addition power on the Quebec government and could be ignored or repealed by any federal government. On December 11, 1995, Parliament recognized Quebec as a distinct society.

Whether Quebec had obtained half a loaf, a slice of bread, or some crumbs depended on one's point of view. What observers could clearly see, however, was that the two most important and controversial elements of the defunct Meech and Charlottetown Accords had now been implemented. And since the Charlottetown Accord had been rejected by the Canadian people in a referendum, Parliament was now overriding the will of the people. Thirteen years after the adoption of the *Charter of Rights and Freedoms*, Canadians once more discovered that sovereignty still lay with the government, not the people, and with the legislative branch, not the judiciary. This time, Trudeau was strangely quiet as Chrétien implemented Mulroney's main Meech and Charlottetown proposals.

Carrots and Sticks

Chrétien then decided to bury whatever remained of the threat of separatism. For decades, Quebec provincial Liberals and some federal Liberals had been calling for concessions, for a positive federal approach to Quebec's demands. More recently, the Reform Party had been calling for a tough approach to Quebec. Chrétien decided to embrace both approaches more or less simultaneously and they became known as Plan A, the soft approach, and Plan B, the tough one, a classic example of carrots and sticks.

A key element in that strategy was recruiting the Quebec academic and constitutional expert Stéphane Dion. As the new Minister of Intergovernmental Affairs, Dion mapped out a clear strategy to replace the fuzzy thinking that had almost led to disaster. To implement Plan A, the government would use legislation to provide a number of the concessions that had been demanded by Quebec Liberals for decades. The list was outlined in the Speech from the Throne in February 1996. Ottawa would devolve to all provinces control of mining, forestry, social housing, recreation, tourism, and manpower training. Ottawa's spending power was also to be clarified and perhaps limited. The list was hardly surprising—all these elements had been in the defeated Charlottetown Accord.

All Ottawa had to do to satisfy the provinces on social housing, recreation, and tourism was reduce or suspend its programs. In the case of mining and forestry, the responsibilities were really being transferred back to the provinces, because the *BNA Act* listed them as exclusively provincial. Ottawa also signed another agreement with the provinces on harmonizing environmental policies, which reduced that area of friction. Plan A also included a continuation of massive federal spending on advertising in Quebec, a program that would play a crucial role in the defeat of the federal Liberal government in January 2006.

Abandoning manpower training was more complicated. Ottawa had managed the UI plan since 1940, but in some cases the unemployed needed more than half a dozen monthly payments to tide them over until they found another job. Sometimes they needed training for a different type of work. Federal bureaucrats and politicians had long concluded that federal government responsibility for "unemployment insurance" could be expanded to mean responsibility for "unemployment," and that could include retraining the unemployed. Ottawa began using part of its unemployment fund for the retraining of unemployed workers. These programs were often shared-cost with the provinces administering them.

As usual, the nine English-speaking provinces welcomed the federal program because it freed up provincial funds for other purposes. As usual, Quebec objected because manpower training was education and education was a provincial responsibility. Manpower training thus joined the long list of conflicts between Quebec and Ottawa. Now, in 1995, Ottawa was retreating from shared-cost programs. There did not appear to be any compelling reasons for the federal government to be involved in programs, which all provinces were operating and where needs differed widely. The downside included duplication, waste, and, with Quebec, a fight in which political dimensions were vastly out of proportion to any economic benefits of federal involvement.

Chrétien was still opposed to transferring manpower training to the provinces, but two of his most powerful cabinet ministers—Paul Martin and Treasury Board Secretary Marcel Massé—wanted to downsize and rationalize the federal bureaucracy, and both, as MPs from Quebec, wanted to decentralize power to Quebec to undermine support for separatism. That, of course, was Mulroney's policy. Neither saw how federal involvement in training unemployed people was essential for the preservation of national unity or the power of the federal government. Chrétien finally agreed, and Ottawa withdrew from manpower training, or, as the Québécois would say, from one part of the exclusive provincial field of education. There were separate agreements with each province, and Ottawa provided the provinces with the amounts it had previously been spending on the program with relatively minor conditions. The manpower agreement was signed in November 1997, and it did not undermine national unity.

Going hand in hand with the carrots in Plan A were the sticks in Plan B. At the top of the list was ensuring that the next referendum question, if there was one, would be worded clearly, something the Reform Party had been demanding. Only the government of Quebec could draft the question, which meant some mechanism had to be established so that the rest of Canada could decide whether they accepted that the wording was clear. A second matter was whether a vote of 50 per cent plus 1 was sufficient for Quebec to achieve independence. By participating in both the 1982 and 1995 referendums, and by making it clear how important those referenda were, Ottawa had de facto recognized that Quebec's 50 plus 1 formula was the benchmark for those votes. What it wanted to do now was move the goalposts by requiring a higher percentage vote to separate.

The PQ, for its part, could point out that 50 per cent plus 1 was the normal rule for democratic decisions, and had been the accepted number for the referendum on the Charlottetown Accord and for Newfoundland's referendum on joining Confederation. The counter-argument regarding the Newfoundland vote was that breaking up a country should require a higher threshold than joining one. That, however, implied that for joining a country, *Yes* votes counted the same as *No* votes, but for separating, *No* votes carried more weight than *Yes* votes. For Quebec, that meant that the *No* vote of an English-speaking Quebecker was worth more than the *Yes* vote of a Québécois voter, a rather blatant discrimination against a majority and a clear distortion of democracy. The matter was tricky indeed.

In September 1996, Ottawa made a reference case to the Supreme Court for an opinion on Quebec's right to independence. Premier Bouchard was furious. He believed that only the people of Quebec had the right to decide how their future would be determined and that the issue was political, not constitutional. For him and others, the matter certainly should not be decided by a court that was appointed by the federal government, with six of its nine judges being Anglophones from outside Quebec. Almost 70 per cent of Quebeckers opposed the reference to the Supreme Court, including Johnson, Ryan, and federal Progressive Conservative leader Jean Charest.

On August 20, 1998, the Court handed down its unanimous decisions. It said that Quebec did not have the automatic right to secede and that secession must meet four criteria: constitutionalism, federalism, democracy, and respect for minorities. Thus the will of the majority had to be given weight, but so must the will of affected minorities. Quebec could secede only through the legal process, the rule of law. That meant that Quebec's separation required an amendment to the Canadian constitution, and an amendment of this importance fell under the unanimous rule by which all provinces would have to agree. This was a major victory for the federal government and for Quebec's minorities.

But the Court also said that in the event of a clear decision on a clear question, the rest of Canada had an obligation to negotiate. That was a firm rejection of the position of Ottawa and the other provinces. The Court also said that the size of the majority and the wording of the question were political, not constitutional, issues. The verdict was generally seen as a balanced, important, and judicious decision, with both sides having won partial victories and the issues tossed back into the political and federal-provincial arenas.

The Court's rejection of Quebec's right to secede unilaterally may not have been as valuable as some people thought. Premier Bouchard said that Quebec was not bound by the decision, just as it had not been bound by the *1982 Constitution*. On the day of the 1995 referendum, Parizeau was prepared to declare unilateral independence if the *Yes* side won, and the Supreme Court had no power to prevent a future Quebec government doing the same after another referendum. However satisfying the decision, it left the rest of Canada with the problem of what to do if a future Quebec government defied the Supreme Court and sending in the army was not an option. The importance of the Court's decision lay, rather, in its effects on the voting in a future referendum as it would certainly strengthen the *No* side.

The Supreme Court decision left unanswered the question of what was a clear majority and a clear question. The federal Liberals were sharply divided on whether the government should introduce legislation setting out its views on the two issues. The danger was that such legislation could inflame opinion in Quebec and create the very "winning conditions" the PQ said it wanted to see before launching another referendum. A large majority of ministers and MPs were opposed, but Chrétien's gut instinct told him it was the right thing to do. The Department of Justice had great problems trying to draft the legislation, and its minister, Allan Rock, tried several times to talk Chrétien out of it.

Eventually, the *Clarity Act* was presented to Parliament in 1998 and passed in January 2000. It did not say what a clear question or majority was, but it stated that soon after Quebec tabled its referendum question, Parliament would determine whether it accepted that the wording was clear. If it decided the wording was not clear, and Quebec did not change it to meet Parliament's demands, then Ottawa would not have to negotiate. If it was clear, then Parliament would determine whether the majority was adequate. Again, if it found the majority too small, then Canada did not have to negotiate any new arrangement with Quebec.

The *Clarity Act* thus put a future Quebec referendum under the control of a Parliament with over three-quarters of its members drawn from outside Quebec. In 1949, the British writer George Orwell published *Nineteen Eighty-Four*, the book which famously predicted that, in the future, government statements would reach a level of distortion in which words would be used to mean the opposite of what they said. The *Clarity Act* was a wonderful Canadian contribution to the Orwellian lexicon, because it was anything but clear. With no fixed time limit to decide if the majority was adequate, Canadians might not know for days, weeks, or months whether the majority was acceptable to Ottawa. What if the House of Commons said it was, and the Senate said it wasn't? What if MPs from Quebec said it was, and those from the rest of Canada said it wasn't? Or vice versa?

The Bloc and the Reform Party had said that 50 per cent plus 1 was adequate; the Liberals had said it was not, at least not any longer, since they had campaigned in 1980 and 1995 on the basis that a 50 per cent margin would lead to separation. A Commons decision on the acceptability of a Quebec referendum would therefore depend on the strength of various parties in the House at the time of the next referendum, something that was totally unpredictable. An important question that had already arisen was whether MPs from Quebec would have any legitimate status in the Commons after their province had voted to separate. Another question was how the Commons would interpret the vote if most Quebeckers wanted to leave but the west end of Montreal, the Quebec side of the Ottawa valley, and the north voted substantially or overwhelmingly to remain in Canada, as most people expected.

For Quebec, this was another example of Ottawa both making the rules governing the hockey game and being one of the teams playing the game. In this case, it would decide if the game was being played fairly, and after the game, it would decide how many goals were required to win, whether controversial shots counted, and when the winner would be announced. One thing the *Clarity Act* did make clear was that Ottawa and the rest of Canada would decide whether Quebeckers had voted for separation. If its purpose was to tell the Québécois that separating was going to be far more difficult than they previously imagined, then that purpose was well served. The *Act* was, of course, rejected by all of Quebec's provincial political parties and was opposed by federal Progressive Conservatives, the NDP, and the Bloc. It was opposed by parties representing a majority of Canadians and the overwhelming majority of Quebeckers. Then to avoid appearing to give recognition to Quebec's special status, it was applied to all provinces, none of which had any interest in separation, a move that theoretically weakened federalism.

As a reaction to the *Clarity Act*, the Quebec Assembly unanimously passed the *Fundamental Rights Act* on December 7, 2000. It stated that the required majority was 50 per cent plus 1, that Quebec's territorial integrity could not be compromised, that Quebec was sovereign in provincial areas of responsibility, and that it had the right to self-determination. It also stated that the legitimacy of the Assembly flowed from the sovereignty of the people; that treaties affecting provincial matters could apply to Quebec only if approved by its Assembly; that French was the language of the province; and that minority rights, including the rights of eleven named Aboriginal nations, had to be respected. Unlike the federal *Clarity Act* or the *Constitution of 1982*, it was a model of clarity.

Another part of Ottawa's hardball strategy was to raise a number of questions that would cause unease amongst many Québécois who might be leaning towards separation. Accordingly, Stéphane Dion stated that if Canada were divisible, then so was Quebec. This referred to the possibility of west-end Montreal, the eastern half of the Ottawa Valley, and the Inuit-dominated north remaining in Canada. Quebec, however, was a province with a government, recognized borders, geographical unity, and the presence of a number of foreign consulates, which implied that foreign countries understood it to be a political state. The three regions in question had none of those characteristics. The statement was inflammatory and divisive, even within the federal and Quebec Liberal parties and among Quebec's minorities. It raised serious questions such as where any borders would be, how they would be decided, and whether force would have to be used to separate the three areas from Quebec. The questions helped serve the purpose of sowing unease over separation. Bouchard said Quebec's territory was indivisible and denounced the statement, and both Bourassa and Johnson supported him.

In the years following the near-death experience of the referendum, support for separatism declined significantly. Chrétien claimed credit, but a number of factors were responsible. Losing the second referendum took the steam out of the separatist campaign. Parizeau's post-referendum comments and resignation were serious blows. The restored veto, recognition of distinct society status, and Ottawa's withdrawal from mining, forestry, recreation, tourism, and manpower training addressed some of the grievances that had led so many Québécois to see separatism as the only way to be masters in their own house. And Plan B probably made a number of those who voted *Yes* in the referendum think twice about voting that way again.

Perhaps more importantly, the loosening of federal control over shared-cost programs that accompanied the cuts in Ottawa's contribution to those programs removed part of the grievance that had first led Lesage to challenge federalism as it existed in 1960. Many of the grievances that had produced separatism had been solved by Quebec governments themselves, especially the threat to the survival of the French language, the domination of the economy by non-Francophones, and the disparity in income between Francophone and Anglophone Quebeckers. Though the referendum had been very close, it revealed an important and growing demographic gap: younger Québécois did not share their parents' dislike and distrust of the federal government and of English-speaking Canada. They were likely to be comfortable speaking French in Montreal and English in Florida, and as the separatist generation died off, support for separatism declined.

More Changes to the Functioning of Federalism

While the nine English-speaking provinces were not interested in constitutional change, they were still very interested in changes to the functioning of federalism. They wanted a clarification of the responsibilities of the two orders of government, the elimination of duplication and overlap of federal and provincial programs, stability and predictability in federal financing, co-operation in implementing programs, a provincial role in the development of new ones, and a legitimization of the whole shared-cost system. Some of these issues would have been solved by the Meech or Charlottetown Accords, which they had negotiated and signed, and they now intended to see such resolutions implemented through federal-provincial agreements. This would provide a considerable degree of the renewal of federalism that had been promised repeatedly and would demonstrate to Quebec that federalism was flexible. The nine English-speaking premiers reached agreement on this package of demands at a conference in 1996. This was the sort of thing Bouchard wanted, and he joined the process.

The most important element was the section on the federal spending power. Gradually all of the provinces had come to share Quebec's concerns, but none to the same degree. After the experience of the 1995 referendum, the nine English-speaking provinces decided to address it, and they agreed on the formula Quebec had been advocating since the 1960s. Ottawa could launch programs on provincial matters, but if any province decided not to participate, it was to receive its share of the money to spend as it chose. That, of course, was what the Gang of Eight had agreed on in 1982. Ottawa remained inflexible: a province could opt out of the federal financial arrangements for a program only if it had a similar program. The federal government would continue to dictate priorities to the provinces and articulate the broad outlines of the policies they had to implement in those programs. Ottawa did respond to the provinces' demand for prior consultation and input, saying that any new programs would require the agreement of any six provinces.

The nine English-speaking provinces accepted this position, but Quebec was furious. Ottawa had now obtained provincial agreement to its ability to use the spending power. Not only that, the formula—approval by any six provinces—meant that the six smallest could legitimize a new federal encroachment on provincial responsibilities, and they accounted for less than 15 per cent of the population! Politically, the new arrangement provided an even lower bar because the six smallest provinces were also the six poorest, the ones that benefited most from shared cost programs, the ones that had supported Ottawa's encroachment on provincial jurisdiction for half a century. That made Ottawa's "loan" of a constitutional veto to Quebec meaningless, because the federal initiatives that mattered to Quebec came under the weak spending power rules rather than the tougher constitutional amendment rules.

This was one of the most centralizing policies ever enacted in Canada, the reversal of whatever trend towards decentralization Chrétien had been forced to implement in the wake of the 1995 referendum. Once more, Ottawa and the nine English-speaking provinces had shifted the balance in federalism significantly towards English-speaking Canada and Ottawa. Once more, Quebec was helpless to prevent the new concentration of power in the nation's capital. Once more, Ottawa was managing the federation through the policies of divide and conquer, this time playing the poor provinces against the rich and the English-speaking ones against Quebec. In this constitutional repeat of the Battle of the Plains of Abraham, Quebec had suffered another conquest.

The new arrangements were documented in the Social Union Framework Agreement, or SUFA, which was signed by Ottawa and the nine English-speaking provinces in February 1999. There was agreement that both orders of government would advise the other of any major change to social policy that might affect the others' programs, and both would consult on implementing them. Ottawa had to inform and consult the provinces three months before implementing new agreements. Any new federal program negotiated with one province had to be available to all. Quebec was more isolated than ever, but it was also more "distinct" and "special" because it alone refused to sign the new agreement. SUFA marked the further implementation of elements of the Charlottetown Accord, but in this case they were ones Quebec did not want.

Meanwhile, Martin's cuts to federal spending were so severe that the budget was balanced by 1997, and the surplus mounted rapidly due also to a burgeoning economy and the success of the GST in raising revenue. Ottawa spent part of the surplus on large tax reductions—good economics and good politics. Part went to pay down the debt of $500 billion, which was the cause of the financial crisis. The government had three options for the large remaining surplus: increase spending in federal areas of responsibility, such First Nations, that were drastically underfunded; restore part of the reductions it had made to transfers to the provinces, which had left them in such dire circumstances; or launch new initiatives in provincial areas of responsibility.

Old habits die hard, and Ottawa began launching new programs with all the dangers and problems they implied for the state of federal-provincial relations. The centre of the new initiatives was Paul Martin and the Department of Finance, fresh from their victories over the deficit and greatly enjoying the power within government that those successful battles had yielded. Martin was concerned with the state of higher education and issues such as Canadian weaknesses in the fields of innovation and research. The logical focus for any federal programs in these fields would be the Department of Industry, which had just faced a budget cut of 60 per cent, but Martin was planning to establish the Canadian Foundation for Innovation, CFI, as an arms'-length organization to support research in universities and research foundations. He not only ignored the relevant department but also the fact that previous federal grants to universities had created so many problems that Ottawa had gradually withdrawn from shared-cost programs in that field.

Another new program was the National Child Benefit. It was announced in July 1998 and was the first new social program in three decades. This plan was aimed at lower-income families and addressed the fact that, under provincial social assistance, a family could be worse off if the parents obtained a low-paying job and lost the benefits of welfare, a policy that encouraged them to remain on welfare. Under the NCB, the family did not lose those benefits. Quebec had its own program in this area and did not participate, but the program did not create problems between Quebec and Ottawa. Another example of successful federal-provincial co-operation from this era was the Canada-Wide Accord on Environment Harmonization of January 28, 1998.

The 1998 Millennium Scholarship program was another new and controversial federal incursion into the field of education. An endowment of $2.5 billion was given to a foundation in order to provide $325 million annually in university scholarships, mainly for poorer students. Canadian universities were facing serious financial problems, partly because of the cutbacks in provincial funding as a result of Martin's budgets. They and the provinces were wrestling with all the problems that created, and raising tuition fees was only one part of the solution. The Millennium Scholarships helped tens of thousands of students pay higher tuition, but did nothing for the students who did not receive them and nothing for all other areas where universities were facing difficulties. That was not the way provinces and universities would have used the money, especially as circumstances varied between universities and provinces. This was another "one-size-fits-all" program launched by a government with little or no expertise on the situation in the dozens of institutions of higher education across the country, but with a sharp eye to the political appeal of such a program.

Quebec predictably condemned the program as a violation of the constitution. In his memoirs, Martin says that he consulted the Ontario and Alberta finance ministers and a number of Quebec universities, but he does not mention contacting any ministers of education or anyone in the Quebec government. The provinces were furious and they demanded that, instead of scholarships, Ottawa should restore the previous level of funding. The initiative was a contradiction of other thrusts towards better co-operation, especially the spirit of SUFA, which carried the promise to consult.

Ottawa was also expanding its role in other areas, one being using the UI fund to cover maternity leave. That duplicated a Quebec program, and Quebec regarded maternity leave as a matter of welfare. UI was designed to help unemployed people who were able to work until they found another job; pregnant women were unemployable and needed paid maternity leave. Both governments proceeded to develop their own programs, and the fact that there were provincial ones called into question the need for a federal one. The dispute went to court where the Quebec Court of Appeal upheld Quebec's position. Ottawa appealed that to the Supreme Court and won, leaving both governments with overlapping programs and a new issue of constitutional conflict and confusion. Canada was becoming even more asymmetrical as Quebec refused to join these new federal programs while the other nine provinces welcomed them.

The Chrétien government knew that the cuts in transfers to the provinces had weakened Ottawa's ability to impose conditions on the provinces. One of Chrétien's top priorities was therefore to restore some of the federal funding for health care to get back more leverage over the provinces. Transfers to the provinces were thus increased substantially in the budgets of 1999 and 2000. These increases did not bring Ottawa's contribution close to the 40 per cent of the original health schemes, and the provinces desperately wanted Ottawa to raise funding towards that level. Ottawa saw this provincial desperation as an opportunity to assert more control. At the federal-provincial meeting on health in September 2000, Chrétien announced that the amount of the new federal offer was non-negotiable, but in return for that money the provinces had to commit more expenditure to four specific areas: primary care, home care, drug costs, and hospital equipment. It also demanded new accounting practices for the monies. These were additional conditions to the original four of the 1967 Medicare scheme, which had grown to five in 1984.

Any province that did not agree would receive no money. Six provinces, including Quebec, objected but eventually had to accept. This incident indicates that after cutting its share of health to around 25 per cent and promising co-operation, Ottawa was still acting unilaterally and was restoring part of that money in return for new and additional conditions. It had returned to the policy of using the federal spending power to encroach on provincial responsibility, the policy that had produced three decades of political crisis and the rise of separatism, as well as contributing heavily to the financial crisis of the 1990s. It was also cherry-picking provincial priorities for spending, because the four areas it identified were among dozens that needed more money, each having different priorities in the ten different provincial health budgets.

The Chrétien era had been a roller-coaster of conflict between Ottawa and Quebec, the decline and resurgence of Ottawa's ability to use its spending power to impose its views on provincial programs, the near-death experience of the 1995 referendum, the soft Plan A attempt to meet Quebec's legitimate concerns combined with the tough Plan B effort to make separatism unpalatable and more difficult, and the federal government's reassertion of its right to impose its programs on the provinces in their areas of responsibility with the money freed up by the cancellation of its previous commitments. On November 13, 2003, a reluctant Chrétien passed the federation to the overly eager Paul Martin, whose long list of proposals and priorities included many that affected the provinces. Martin's optimism was welcomed, because polls taken at the end of the previous century had revealed deep pessimism about the future of Confederation.

CHAPTER 16

Federalism in the Twenty-First Century, 2003-2017

On December 12, 2003, Paul Martin was sworn in as prime minister. Seeking a mandate, he called an election for June 28, 2004, and the three main issues he campaigned on were aid to municipalities, child care, and health, all matters of provincial jurisdiction. Federal-provincial relations would thus be a major theme of his government, and once more Ottawa was in the driver's seat because the provinces and the municipalities were desperate for federal funds. The provinces had no intention, however, of reverting to the situation of the 1980s and 1990s, when Ottawa sharply reduced its contribution to shared-cost programs but tried to ensure that its influence and conditions were maintained.

Health, Municipalities, Energy, and Daycare

After winning a minority victory, Martin tackled one of his top priorities, health care. The provinces had long complained about the lack of predictability, and he was determined to make his mark as a champion of health care. He was also determined to use the partial restoration of funding to impose more conditions. One problem that had developed was the lengthening wait times for some medical services, and Martin planned to trade increased funding for a new mechanism of provincial accounting for progress in reducing wait times. Long wait times were just one of many problems, and once more Ottawa was cherry-picking an issue that was receiving more attention than others and therefore had political appeal. It was not necessarily the top priority of the provinces and was certainly not the same in every hospital and province. If it had been their main priority, they would have devoted more resources to it and another issue would have been getting more media attention.

Martin called a First Ministers' meeting for September 13, a meeting that lasted for five days and was partly televised. The provinces did not see increased federal funding as "new," but rather as a partial restoration of some of the funds Martin had cut in 1995. The idea of accepting new conditions for partial restoration of funding was unacceptable, as was the amount offered. Martin desperately wanted to succeed, and he caved to the premiers. Funding was more than doubled, from the original offer of $11 billion over six years to $41 billion over ten years. The provincial commitments extracted in return were symbolic—they were to account to their citizens for the spending, something all governments had to do anyway. In his memoirs, Martin says it was a mistake to televise the meeting as the premiers then berated Ottawa over real and imagined grievances. That, of course, had been the pattern of federal-provincial meetings since the 1920s.

Quebec refused to sign, and Martin made a separate deal allowing it to establish its own method of measuring results. This was a recognition of its distinctiveness and of the fact that it was not "a province like the others," and demonstrated that on the matter of Quebec's place in Confederation, Martin was distancing himself from Chrétien and moving closer to the positions of Mulroney and the Quebec provincial Liberal party. The agreements ended the bickering over health funding for a decade, but was not the "fix of a generation" he had promised.

High on Martin's agenda was aid to the municipalities. He believed that in the twenty-first century, cities were the engines of growth and that their development should be a major focus of any central government's programs. He noted that, in order to fulfill their roles, they had to have adequate infrastructure. Martin promoted these ideas as if they were a new revelation, though cities had always been centres of civilization, learning, and economic activity, and Canadian cities had never had as much infrastructure as they needed. His discovery that the municipalities were suffering was interesting too, in that their current problems resulted in part from his cuts to transfers to the provinces.

Martin arranged meetings with the mayors of the largest cities, who were, of course, delighted with the prospect of federal funds. The initiative, the first federal one in urban affairs in twenty-five years, was called the New Deal for Cities and Communities. Of all the challenges the municipalities faced, Martin chose to help with infrastructure. That was more cherry-picking, because municipalities needed more funds for all their activities, but infrastructure was more visible. Ottawa negotiated agreements with the provinces to facilitate funding for municipal projects, with BC as the first province to sign on. The revenue was to come from a refund of the GST paid by municipalities, plus five cents of the federal tax on gasoline.

Once more Ottawa imposed conditions. One of them was that the municipalities had to spend part of the funds on projects that would enhance the environment. That was no problem, because the municipalities and their citizens cared as much about the environment as did the federal government. It was another example of Ottawa acting as the nanny state for reasons of public relations. The two orders of government represented the same citizens and voters, and cities had been dealing with environmental issues for centuries. They did not have to be told to take the environment into consideration, but they now had to report to Ottawa on how the projects improved the environment.

In his memoirs, Martin says that the deal "offered" the municipalities more autonomy in planning their projects. Since the municipalities were provincial creations, Ottawa was not in a position to "offer" them greater autonomy on anything, and in fact, the federal conditions and the fact that the deal only covered infrastructure restricted their ability to plan according to their own priorities. That represented a loss of autonomy. Martin also said that the deal made municipalities "full partners," but local infrastructure was their responsibility anyway, and in reality, what he was trying to do was make the federal government a full partner.

The energy accords signed by the Trudeau and Mulroney governments with Nova Scotia and Newfoundland maintained their level of equalization payments in spite of increasing revenue from energy. Those agreements had expired, and during the election campaign, Martin called Newfoundland's Premier Danny Williams to offer to continue the energy accord, a deal that would have to be extended to Nova Scotia. These offers did not sit well with the other have-not provinces, which were being discriminated against by being left out of this additional equalization system. Since Martin's offer came when the polls indicated he might not win a majority, Newfoundland and Nova Scotia were in good bargaining positions. Martin therefore had to provide more than he had planned to fix a problem that might not have existed, and then make a similar deal with Saskatchewan and respond to complaints from Ontario and Quebec. The new deals included the condition that the provinces had to spend most of the additional funds paying down their debt, a condition that, in effect, ordered them to balance their budgets.

High on Martin's very long list of priorities was daycare. There had been no new federally initiated shared-cost programs in health and welfare since Medicare in 1968, because Ottawa could not afford additional ones. Now, however, Ottawa was flush with cash, and daycare was one of the few remaining building blocks for a complete welfare state. Martin put one of his best ministers, Ken Dryden, in charge. The idea was to establish a national program in co-operation with the provinces in order to create a large number of daycare spots. By now, the government had realized that one-size-fits-all policies were not always appropriate for a nation as diverse as Canada, so Dryden negotiated separate deals with the ten provinces. The conditions were designed to ensure that the provincial programs were better regulated and emphasized learning, with stated provincial objectives and accounting of progress on achieving those goals.

This approach led to a major ideological clash between the Liberals and the Conservative Opposition, now led by Stephen Harper. Martin's program provided very good daycare spots to a large number of families, nothing for others, and the benefit would vary from province to province. Harper regarded the program as the worst form of policy, the "nanny state" in which governments made decisions for families, plus needless meddling in provincial affairs, duplication, bureaucracy, and standards that might not be appropriate everywhere. The federal money only existed because of cuts to federal transfers to the provinces—if they were restored, the provinces could have launched their own programs if that was their priority and that of the families in their jurisdictions.

Harper's alternative plan was to provide every family with $1,200 annually, a significantly larger expenditure than Martin's plan, which could be used to purchase daycare or whatever individual parents regarded as the priority needs of their children. In Harper's view, parents made better decisions regarding their children than did governments. The "nanny state" accusation against the government was given much credibility when Martin's communications director, Scott Reid, said that under Harper's scheme parents could spend the money on beer and popcorn. That, of course, was true of every government payment, but there was no evidence that families spent government cheques recklessly. Dryden had completed his negotiations before the election, but Martin lost it. Harper cancelled the program and implemented his own.

One of Martin's last forays into federal-provincial relations related to the situation facing Canada's Aboriginal population. The conditions in which they lived both on and off reserves were appalling and produced high rates of crime, disease, mortality, suicide, welfare, and high school drop outs. Since problems existed both on the reserves, which were federal, and off reserves, which was partly within provincial jurisdiction, Martin decided to hold a federal-provincial conference to develop a comprehensive and well-funded plan. The question the initiative raised was why Martin spent time on a federal-provincial agreement when many of the problems were on reserves, which were exclusively under federal authority and had been underfunded since they were established. Provinces and cities were well aware of the situation of Aboriginals under their jurisdiction, where they were more likely to be receiving government services at the same level as other Canadians. The Kelowna Accord was signed just before the election, and Harper cancelled it.

Relations with the provinces often played a role in federal elections, but that of 2006 was one of the rare examples when federal policies became one of the main causes of a government's defeat. From the earliest stirrings of separatism in Quebec in the 1960s, a key element in Ottawa's strategy was advertising. The goal was to make the Québécois fully aware of the advantages of being Canadian, to make the federal government a more important part of their lives, to make them look to Ottawa rather than Quebec City for government services. One reason Ottawa contributed to local infrastructure such as sports arenas was to create opportunities for federal MPs to attend the opening and unveil the plaque identifying Ottawa's contribution. Maple leaf flags were distributed by the millions. After the 1995 election, advertising was an important part of the Chrétien governments' Plan A, the effort to permanently undermine support for separatism.

Advertising contracts were not covered by normal procurement rules, and the party in power gave them to friendly companies who naturally contributed to party funds to keep the contracts coming. Rumours began to circulate, suggesting that no advertising at all had been done for some of the contracts. Martin claimed that he was not aware of any wrongdoing, but as finance minister and a prominent MP from Quebec, it was difficult to accept that he knew nothing about the way one of the government's key strategies for dealing with Quebec was being handled. As the scandal dominated the media day after day, Opposition leader Stephen Harper took full advantage. Martin's government went down to defeat, and the Sponsorship Scandal played a key role in that outcome.

Harper's Federalism

On January 23, 2006, Stephen Harper led the Conservative Party to a minority victory. He was somewhat unique amongst prime ministers in a number of ways and that would have a significant influence on relations with the provinces. He was one the most profoundly "small c" conservatives ever to be prime minister. He believed very strongly in the concept that people make wiser decisions about spending, family, and other matters than governments do. He believed that provinces make decisions at least as well as Ottawa does. He believed in small government, in minimal government regulation, in the fewest possible number of federal organizations, and in the minimal degree of overlap and duplication between the two orders of government.

As a young policy adviser with the Reform Party, Harper strongly opposed the use of the spending power to encroach on provincial jurisdiction. He called for a genuinely federal state, with a strong national government and strong provinces with the power to protect the things that made them distinct. He believed the provinces should be equal and was an advocate of the Triple-E Senate—elected, equal, effective. One of his first statements on federalism was that "Canada is a country of regions with widely differing geography, culture, and economic interests. These differences are best secured and reconciled by allowing differences to exist among the provinces in a wide array of policy areas."

Harper's views on federalism were summarized in the famous "Firewall Letter" that he and five other Albertans sent to Premier Ralph Klein on January 24, 2001. It stated, "We believe the time has come for Albertans to take greater charge of our own future. This means resuming control of the power that we possess under the constitution of Canada but which we have allowed the federal government to exercise." This was the western Canadian version of Quebec's slogan from the Quiet Revolution, the demand to be "masters in our own house." Harper's views, policies, and actions also reflected conclusions he had drawn from watching several Liberal regimes in Ottawa doing things that he thought were not only unnecessary but simply wrong. One of Harper's main goals was to reverse as many of those policies as possible and to make it very difficult for future governments to revert to such policies or initiate new ones.

Harper was possibly the first prime minister since Laurier to believe in classical or genuine federalism. His job was to handle the things Ottawa was responsible for; it was the job of the provinces to handle matters such as education, health, and welfare. When they asked for federal involvement, which usually meant more money, he ignored the requests. This was made explicit in a speech in the Commons in 2007 when Harper said the provinces were autonomous in their areas of responsibility and that there should be limits on Ottawa's ability to use the spending power. But while he avoided federal-provincial meetings where he would be outnumbered ten to one, he was quite willing to discuss specific problems and work out solutions with any premier. Harper largely stayed out of provincial politics except for some sniping back and forth, especially with the Liberal regime in Ontario.

Like Mulroney, Harper regarded the relationship between Ottawa and Quebec City as one of the most serious problems facing his new government, and like Mulroney, he was determined to tackle it quickly. His views had been outlined in a speech given in Quebec City during the 2004 election. He spoke about respect for federalism and provincial jurisdiction and promised to deal with a number of Quebec's grievances. It was a message of conciliation and understanding and was seen in Quebec as significant coming from a western Canadian founder of the Reform Party.

After the 2006 election, he established a good working relationship with Quebec Premier Jean Charest. On April 20, he outlined several goals in a major speech to the Montreal Board of Trade. One problem he promised to solve was the "fiscal imbalance" that Quebec and the other provinces had complained about for decades. Harper promised predictable, transparent, and long-term transfers to the provinces based on principles and policies, and he honoured that with a ten-year commitment in the 2007 budget. Those statements sent a positive message to the provinces as the Chrétien and Martin governments had refused to acknowledge that there was such a thing as a fiscal imbalance and had continuously surprised the provinces with changes to federal transfers and policies. Another promise concerned Quebec's desire to participate in UNESCO as a full partner. UNESCO's rules did not allow that so Harper gave Quebec a place in Canadian delegations. That was the best he could do, and it set the stage for better relations.

The Québécois as a Nation

Harper unexpectedly met another long-standing demand for recognition of the Québécois as a nation. Chrétien had Parliament recognize the province of Quebec as a distinct society, but recognizing French Canadians within Quebec as a nation was quite different, something Trudeau and much of English-Canada, including Harper, had strongly opposed. On November 21, 2006, Bloc leader Gilles Duceppe tabled a motion calling for the House of Commons to recognize Quebeckers, that is, all the people in Quebec, as a nation. The Bloc probably thought it would fail, but that it would embarrass the government and provide some fuel for the separatist cause, which had been in decline since the 1995 referendum.

Though he had previously opposed it, Harper had recently been considering this issue as part of his strategy to improve relations between Quebec and Ottawa and widen the Conservatives' base. He had kept these thoughts to himself, however. Suddenly he had to deal with Duceppe's manoeuvre, so he had a motion drafted saying, "That this House recognize that the Québécois form a nation within a united Canada." Unlike Duceppe's motion, Harper's applied only to French-Canadian Quebeckers and did not refer to the province of Quebec. This was a 180 degree change for Harper and the former Reform politicians. The morning after Duceppe tabled his motion, Harper announced his draft to a surprised Conservative caucus, none being more shocked than the minister responsible for relations with the provinces, Michael Chong. He immediately challenged it on the grounds that it violated party policy and allegedly gave an advantage to the separatists for the next referendum.

Harper refused to drop the initiative or to make any changes, and the caucus remained united. He introduced the motion that afternoon, and it passed in the House of Commons by a vote of 265–16. It was a political coup going beyond anything the Liberals had done and beyond both the Meech and Charlottetown Accords in terms of symbolism. The Quebec Assembly approved it 107–0. Now Parliament had recognized Quebec as a distinct society and the Québécois as a nation, and to the degree politically possible, two of Quebec's oldest demands had been met. Chong resigned on principle, but time proved him wrong. The motion helped pacify opinion in Quebec, and it caused no problems for Ottawa, federalism, or the other provinces. Once more, thrusts in the failed Meech and Charlottetown Accords were being implemented by Parliament without recourse to amendment to the constitution. And federalism was working to the satisfaction of more and more Quebeckers.

The Fiscal Surplus, Equalization, and UI

In terms of relations with the provinces, what Harper did not do was as important as what he did. He thought that First Ministers' Conferences were counter-productive to good government with important decisions being hastily made under the influence of TV coverage and instant public pressure. He only met the premiers three times, once to get acquainted soon after his election, twice more to discuss the economy in general. More important, he did not use the federal spending power to invade areas of provincial responsibility. That ended, for a time at least, the federal policy that began in earnest in 1927, accelerated rapidly after the Second World War, and eventually produced separatism in Quebec.

For the first time in decades, Canada was spared the fighting between Ottawa and the provinces that accompanied St. Laurent's policies on education, Diefenbaker's adoption of a series of shared-cost programs, Pearson's fights over pensions and Medicare, and continued confrontation over these programs under Trudeau, Chrétien, and Martin. Harper also made little effort to enforce the conditions in existing programs such as health care. While this was decried by those who believed in "national standards," the loosening of control followed the trend that began in the 1980s when Ottawa could no longer afford its programs. The looser controls also allowed provinces to experiment and to copy each other as new and better ways of implementing health services were developed.

For Harper, the way to ensure that Canada never went back to the system of shared-cost programs was to address permanently the source of the problem. In his view, since 1945, Ottawa had collected billions of dollars more than it needed for its responsibilities and used that unnecessary surplus to impose poorly planned and executed shared-cost programs on the provinces. The combination of federal surpluses and provincial deficits was known as the "fiscal imbalance." Harper decided to eliminate the imbalance and make it very difficult for future federal governments to accumulate large surpluses and face the irresistible desire to spend them on provincial matters.

His plan was to squeeze the surplus from two sides—reduce the amount Ottawa was collecting and allocate part of the surplus in ways that could not easily be reversed. These initiatives were carried out by Finance Minister Jim Flaherty, who introduced the changes in his budgets of 2006 and 2007. On the revenue side, the main policy was the reduction of the federal sales tax from 7 to 5 per cent. That reduced the size of the surplus by an estimated $10 billion annually and created the same amount of "tax room" for the provinces to increase their sales tax by 2 per cent without paying any political penalty, since the effects on the taxpayer would be neutral. It was up to the provinces to take advantage of the situation, and they were expected to as they had been demanding more "tax room" since 1945. If they did, they would have a lot more revenue for their needs and the freedom to spend it according to their priorities; if they did not, they could no longer credibly complain that they needed federal transfers to meet their needs. In addition, Harper cut a number of taxes so that citizens and organizations would have more money to spend. His government also proceeded to harmonize the collection of the GST with the sales tax in a number of provinces in order to simplify their administration, a good example of co-operation and flexibility. By 2015, federal revenue as a percentage of GDP had fallen from over 19 per cent under Trudeau to around 14 per cent, the lowest in over half a century, a staggering 25 per cent decline in Ottawa's tax take.

On the expenditure side, Harper maintained the Health Care Accord that Martin had signed with the provinces in 2004. That provided $41 billion over ten years and meant that there should be no wrangling over financing health until near the end of that period. A second major expenditure was contained in a substantial increase to the unconditional equalization payments to the provinces, something future governments would not likely reverse. The increase was announced in the 2007 budget and provided for growth in equalization payments at the rate of 3.5 per cent for ten years— stable, predictable, transparent, and above the projected rate of inflation. Close to half those funds went to Quebec, reflecting a key political priority of addressing that province's grievances. This was somewhat unexpected of a western-based Conservative party containing Harper's old Reform Party. Over the years, Quebec had been one of the most outspoken critics of the fiscal imbalance, and it had been an important element in separatist propaganda. Now the "fiscal imbalance" dragon had been slain.

Harper believed he had addressed one of Quebec's major grievances, but Premier Jean Charest was facing an election and decided to offer the citizens a tax break made possible by the increased transfers. Harper was furious, because he had gone out of his way to befriend Charest and thought they had an understanding. Charest's tax break also proved that Quebec's complaints about the fiscal imbalance had been exaggerated. Harper was not one to forgive or forget an alleged betrayal, and his relationship with Charest never recovered. It did not, however, become acrimonious as had previous relationships between prime ministers and Quebec premiers.

Harper also wanted to address the fact that equalization had gradually been built into a number of federal programs, which gave the have-not provinces larger shares of those funds than their population warranted. Many of these programs were between Ottawa and just one or several of the have-not provinces, four of which were in Atlantic Canada. These distortions had always annoyed the richer provinces because, while they had accepted the official equalization program where the transfers were transparent, the other deals represented additions to the equalization formula and were anything but transparent. They also annoyed federal and provincial Conservatives, because the traditional pay off for those programs was substantial support for federal and provincial Liberals and the extra money tended to come from provinces with Conservative governments.

By 2005, it had become difficult, if not impossible, for anyone to figure out how much money was being transferred to the poorer provinces, and they were receiving different amounts with no necessary connection to their relative income levels. The equalization program carried no conditions but most of the others did, so it was impossible to know how much influence Ottawa had over spending and the degree to which it varied from province to province. Two good examples were the offshore energy agreements with Nova Scotia and Newfoundland, which allowed them to retain the revenue from energy for ten years before equalization payments would start declining to reflect that additional revenue. By those agreements they could, in theory, become the richest provinces in Canada and still receive equalization grants from Ottawa.

That also disadvantaged the have-not provinces that did not produce energy, and eventually meant that rich provinces were receiving equalization payments while some formerly rich ones were not, although they should have been. It had become difficult, for example, to know whether Saskatchewan and Ontario were have or have-not provinces. Harper decided to include part of energy revenue of the have-not provinces in the calculations for their equalization payments. That provoked a harsh reaction from Newfoundland's Conservative Premier Danny Williams, who organized an "Anything But Conservatives" campaign in the next federal election. This may have cost Harper a seat, but it may also have been counter-productive in terms of Williams's ongoing relations with the federal government.

Unemployment Insurance had long since ceased to be a self-supporting insurance program for unemployed workers. Instead, it was more and more a form of taxation of the employed plus welfare programs for people who could not work and people who seemed not to want to if it meant travelling some distance to an available job. It had also become a method of transferring money from prosperous industries to struggling ones, and another form of equalization in which premiums collected in richer provinces subsidized workers in poorer ones. Harper attacked all these alleged problems by making it more difficult to qualify. That was bitterly resented in Atlantic Canada, but Harper would not trim his sails for political advantage.

Health and Infrastructure

Martin's ten-year accord on health care was due to expire in 2014. Based on the history of such matters, it was anticipated that the lead-up to the renegotiation would involve numerous televised conferences, squabbles, demands from the provinces for more money, attempts by Ottawa to introduce new conditions, and pressure from the general public for Ottawa to yield to the demands of the provinces. Harper had watched in dismay as the provinces forced Martin to double the money he planned for the 2004–2014 deal, and he had no intention of repeating that process or that result.

Instead, at a meeting of provincial finance ministers in Vancouver on December 19, 2011, Finance Minister Flaherty announced the amount of increase in transfers for the period 2014–2024. It was a unilateral announcement, and there had been no consultation or warning. There would be no First Ministers' Conference, no televised sessions with the premiers complaining about shortages of funds, no public squabbling. That also meant there would be no sensational stories for the media, a let-down that may have influenced their opinions of the deal and of Harper's tactics. The program provided for Ottawa's contribution to continue increasing at the same rate as in the existing one, 6 per cent per year, for two more years, and then drop to the level of inflation or 3 per cent, whichever was greater for the next eight years. That was a reasonably generous amount, and the provinces would have to live with it or raise their own taxes. Like the Martin program, this one met the provincial demands for transparency, stability, and predictability. It forced the provinces to look for efficiencies in their health care systems without Ottawa telling them how to do it. It also took health off the federal-provincial agenda for another ten years, or at least as long as the Conservatives were in power.

One exception to Harper's laissez-faire attitude towards the provinces concerned the initiative to adopt a common securities market for the whole of Canada. Under the constitution, the regulation of securities was provincial, which resulted in ten different sets of rules and forced companies operating in more than one province to duplicate their administration, even if some provinces had the same rules. With the increasing globalization of international financial markets, the fact that Canada had ten systems was seen as a growing problem. Pressure mounted for Ottawa to bring the provinces into a single system, but they jealously guarded their autonomy on this matter and the Harper government failed to produce a single system.

In 2008, Canada and the world slipped into the most serious recession in decades. The Harper government was slow to respond, but reality could not be denied and the government decided to go heavily into deficit spending to create jobs and stimulate the economy. The fastest and best way to do that was through building infrastructure. Many projects could be launched quickly, the spending would produce a multiplier effect as unemployed workers got jobs and paycheques to spend on goods and services, and the projects would constitute a permanent investment in things such as roads and sewers. Provinces and municipalities normally have a list of such projects just waiting for financing, and Ottawa's program was to provide money so the provinces and municipalities could launch those projects.

This was a difficult decision for the Harper government, because the old Reform Party was adamantly opposed to the very concept of governments not living within their means. That internal opposition had to be overruled and other means found to keep them happy. Then, over the next seven years, Ottawa provided billions of dollars to the provinces and municipalities. Canada enjoyed one of the best records in the industrialized world in dealing with the recession. In the history of federalism, this effort was a model of co-operation between Ottawa, the provinces, and the municipalities. Given the haste with which the projects were launched, there was a surprising absence of problems and no scandals. All regions benefited, so there was little provincial criticism or jealousy.

One of Harper's priorities was the negotiation of more free trade agreements, especially with Europe and Asia. He expanded the degree of provincial involvement in these talks. This was essential, given the number of issues that were in provincial jurisdiction such as procurement, labour, the environment, state enterprises, and investment. In the negotiations with Europe, for example, over fifty provincial officials were involved, and the provinces had seats at the table when matters of provincial jurisdiction were being discussed. Such negotiations produce winners and losers, but they were handled in such a way as to avoid federal-provincial problems.

Harper's approach to federalism and relations with the provinces was quite successful overall, especially in the first years. For ten years, there were no major federal-provincial fights, no new federal initiatives leading to outrage, push-back, acrimony, and criticism. Spats like the one with Premier Williams made the headlines, but were insignificant compared to previous battles. Premiers got on with their jobs, Harper got on with his. There were numerous meetings and contacts between Harper and various premiers in which specific issues and problems were discussed and resolved. The number of meetings between ministers and officials continued to grow, with numerous agreements being achieved outside the glow of the media, probably known only to those directly affected and experts who followed the arcane issues. One notable proof of the better atmosphere was the steady decline in support for separatism and the Bloc. Oddly, one big loser was probably the media as federal-provincial bickering had been a mainstay of reporting and analysis for decades, and Harper probably paid a price for taking away one of their favourite issues.

Growing Tensions: Culture, the CPP, and the Environment

Harper's policy on federalism and relations with the provinces was, of course, a reversal of the thrust of federal politics since 1945. That thrust had always reflected a strong desire by English-speaking Canadians for a more active federal role in social services and economic development. Interestingly, by the time Harper became prime minister, Quebec had not only accepted the federal role but was also demanding more. Over the years, criticism mounted of Ottawa's alleged indifference to the issues many Canadians wanted to see the federal government involved in and, especially, helping to pay for.

In his eagerness to restore a more genuine or classical federal system, Harper misread the degree to which Canadians had moved in their views of the roles of the two orders of government and their acceptance of overlapping responsibilities and co-operation. Few things demonstrated that better than the issue of federal support for culture in the 2008 election. As part of his policy of cost-cutting and reducing federal involvement in society and in provincial matters, Harper announced a reduction in federal spending on culture. Quebec had fought for decades to stop Ottawa from involving itself in culture, but the announced cuts were denounced in Quebec and may have been a factor in the loss of several Conservative seats. Harper had not noticed that the Québécois had gone from being strongly opposed to federal involvement in culture to being strongly supportive, the sort of change in attitude that was also undermining support for separatism. The Québécois remained very nationalistic, but identification with Canada was strengthening, especially among younger voters. The differences between them and Canadians were now narrowing, and while Harper's attitudes would have avoided much of the Ottawa-Quebec squabbling of past decades, it was somewhat out of date by 2008.

One of the negative features of federalism is that it inevitably leads to one order of government criticizing another for the policies it is or is not pursuing. Sometimes that criticism is justified, sometimes it is simply politically driven, and opinions as to its justification are often subjective. The fact that Canadians often elect different political parties at the provincial and federal level contributes to the "blame game." The Harper government sincerely believed that high levels of taxation were seriously harming Canada's economic prospects. That problem would not be solved if Ottawa alone cut taxes while large provinces continued to run huge deficits. Since Ontario's Liberal government was running deficits, Finance Minister Flaherty criticized it and made the unhelpful and controversial statement that Ontario was not a good place to invest because of its high rate of corporate taxes. There are few examples of such a criticism of a provincial government coming from a federal cabinet minister.

Another problem with Ontario arose over the latter's desire to expand the coverage of the CPP, a demand driven in part by the fact that the population was aging and many employees were not covered. Harper was well aware of the problems and introduced a number of changes to address it, but he was not interested in expanding the CPP. Any change would require collecting contributions from employees and employers, and he felt that a recession was the wrong time to impose such costs because the higher contributions would reduce consumer spending. The original CPP/QPP deal had given provinces billions of dollars to invest before payouts began, and there was a suspicion that one of the Ontario government's goals was, in fact, to use the fund instead of taxes to pay for infrastructure.

Harper believed that pensions were within provincial jurisdiction, different provinces had different needs and desires, and Ontario's Premier Kathleen Wynne was free to introduce any plan she chose as an addition or supplement to the CPP. Changing the CPP itself was a completely different matter, which would require similar changes to Quebec's QPP and approval by seven provinces. Accordingly, Harper refused to support Wynne's initiative, and the two first ministers criticized each other publicly. Wynne requested a meeting; Harper refused. To him it was a lose-lose proposition—if they agreed on anything, she would claim credit; if they didn't, she would blame Ottawa. The fact that a federal election was approaching enhanced the importance of these issues.

Another issue that caused increasing strain with the provinces was environmental policy. Harper regarded the previous government's commitment to the Kyoto Accord as fraudulent and hypocritical, because Canada could not possibly meet the targets for greenhouse emissions that it had endorsed. Nor was he convinced that action by Ottawa was the best solution. Much of the environmentalists' criticism within Canada was directed at the energy industry in Alberta, and the last thing Harper wanted was another NEP-style federal policy in which central Canadians used the federal government to tell the western provinces how to manage their energy industry. The provinces all had their own programs, and he was not interested in sharing those endeavours or attempting to impose national standards and targets on them.

Those who saw global warming as a serious threat wanted Ottawa to be much more active and to partner with the provinces. One genuine concern was that problems would develop if each province adopted different programs, which would affect their economies, tax rates, cost-of-living, and attractiveness for investment. That could cause the more determined provinces to lower their targets to the level of less-capable provinces, to the disadvantage of Canada's overall contribution. Many provinces wanted Ottawa to become engaged, to take a leadership role, and to ensure a level playing field between the provinces and a far more active Canadian response to climate change. Implicit in the demand, of course, was that Ottawa would pay a large share of costs, something immediately apparent to Harper. The criticism also came from Canadian nationalists who believed that Canada should take a leadership role globally, that it had long "punched above its weight" on various issues, and that Harper was not carrying on that tradition. Premier Wynne in particular repeatedly criticized Ottawa for not showing leadership, which meant not supporting her position, but Harper ignored those demands.

By the time of the 2015 election, Canadians' views of Harper's handling of federal-provincial relations were changing, and not in Harper's favour. Many of the positive things he had done were fading into history, such as the recognition of the Québécois as a nation, the solution of the fiscal imbalance problem, and enhanced equalization. While fights with the provinces paid dividends to previous federal governments, peace with them did not make the headlines while small differences did. As the battles at First Ministers' meetings faded into memory, Harper's refusal to meet the premiers as a group looked increasingly like simple stubbornness—why not sit down with the other ten or thirteen heads of government who were responsible for so many issues and have a good, frank discussion of them?

A New Era Dawns

Once more, relations with the provinces played a role in a federal election, though not a major one. The practice of citizens to vote for one party federally and another provincially so that one order of government becomes a balance or check on the other caught up to Harper in 2015. Thus, as Conservative rule in Ottawa stretched to ten years, provincial Conservative regimes fell one by one. By 2015, there were no Conservative provincial governments at all, and Liberals ruled in seven provinces, the NDP in Manitoba and Alberta, and the Saskatchewan Party in between. On October 19, 2015, Justin Trudeau led the federal Liberals to a majority government. They won 184 of 238 seats, showing strength in every region. That included all thirty-two seats in Atlantic Canada, forty of seventy-eight in Quebec, eighty of 121 in Ontario, and forty of seventy-eight in the West.

Almost immediately after the federal election, the pendulum began swinging against the new Liberal regime with the re-election of the Saskatchewan Party, which had had excellent relations with the federal Conservatives, and the emergence of the first new Conservative provincial regime with the defeat of the NDP in Manitoba on April 19. Six months later, those were the only provinces to reject the new federal government's climate change deal. If history is our guide, Trudeau can expect that as time goes by, fewer provinces will be ruled by fellow Liberals and the provinces will become more and more of a check on federal power, as has always happened in the past.

The new harmonious relationship with the provinces reflected Liberal promises to do a number of things differently and to rule through "Sunny Ways," a slogan copied from the Laurier regime more than a century earlier. One promise was to hold more First Ministers' meetings and that was honoured within a month of the election, although it was more about building relationships than solving problems. Within a year, Prime Minister Trudeau met the provincial premiers two more times, as many meetings as Harper had held in ten years, and more meetings were expected in 2017. Behind the scenes, federal ministers and bureaucrats continued to hold numerous meetings with their provincial counterparts—that was not new, but it was better publicized and may have constituted a higher level of consultation.

Changing Directions: The CPP, Deficits, and Pipelines

One of the Harper government's failures in the eyes of the provinces was its reluctance to become involved in any expansion of the CPP. The Trudeau government quickly worked out an agreement in principle with the provinces to increase the coverage of the CPP. The speed and ease with which agreement was reached suggested that a very different atmosphere had been established in considerable measure because of the positive federal response to provincial concerns. Skeptics could point out, however, that they had reached agreement in principle and the drafting of the details might identify some disagreements. Another example of a new and more positive relationship was the quick and relatively problem-free settlement of 25,000 Syrian refugees, which required good co-operation with the provinces and cities.

During the election, the Liberals capitalized on the fact that an incumbent government can be blamed for slow economic growth such as Canada was experiencing in the last years of Harper's mandate. One of the new government's major promises was to "jump start" the economy by doubling the budget for Harper's infrastructure program. Harper allowed the provinces and municipalities to decide on specific projects for which Ottawa would pay half the costs if the projects met Ottawa's criteria. Trudeau required the cities and provinces to agree on lists of projects that would form the basis for negotiation with Ottawa. This proved to be difficult, and by late August 2016, only five provinces had signed infrastructure agreements. The program is long-term, the economy had definitely not been "jump started" in its first year, and the mounting deficit is of concern to some observers. The program does, however, demonstrate that on this issue, both the Harper and Trudeau regimes were working with the provinces and cities and not imposing federal decisions on them, the old practice that had produced so much conflict in the second half of the twentieth century, especially between Ottawa and Quebec.

One of the more difficult problems facing governments is the approval of pipelines that pass through other provinces on the way from Alberta to ocean ports. During the Harper regime, three such projects were under consideration: the Northern Gateway line to Kitimat on the BC coast, the Kinder Morgan Trans Mountain line to Vancouver, and Energy East to the Atlantic. They all faced stiff provincial opposition as different governments tried to maximize the benefits to their constituents and deal with environmental concerns.

Harper approved Northern Gateway, but that did not lead to construction due to numerous challenges. Trudeau promised to make progress on pipelines and prove that protecting the environment could go hand-in-hand with energy development. On November 29, 2016, the government announced that Harper's approval for the Northern Gateway line was cancelled, and Kinder Morgan was approved. In a sense, that did combine protection of the environment (the Northern Gateway cancellation) with promotion of energy development (Kinder Morgan), but the latter still faces challenges from the BC government, First Nations, and environmental groups. The Energy East pipeline is strongly supported by New Brunswick and equally strongly opposed by Quebec, and one of those two Liberal regimes will likely be displeased by whatever decision the federal government makes. While there is optimism on pipeline construction, there is no guarantee that the Trudeau government has solved Canada's pipeline problems to the satisfaction of the provinces, and it remains to be seen whether or when these interprovincial pipelines will be built. Another line from Alberta to North Dakota presented no problems with other provinces.

The Environment

Trudeau's policy on relations with the provinces on environmental issues was presented as a sharp break with his predecessor's policy or lack thereof. Harper left it to the provinces to achieve Canada's fairly modest goals by whatever means they chose, which meant that there was neither meetings, confrontation, nor co-operation between the two orders of government. Trudeau's plan was to work with the provinces to establish a national framework that would incorporate all the provincial plans acceptable to Ottawa, but also impose a minimum target that each province would have to meet. That meant that there would be federal-provincial meetings, and both co-operation and confrontation, the opposite of the situation under Harper.

Trudeau met the premiers to discuss overall issues, and they were invited to be part of the large Canadian delegation to the United Nations Climate Change Conference in December 2015, which set new global goals. Talks continued between environment ministers and civil servants, and co-operation was the order of the day in the early months of the Trudeau regime. A First Ministers' meeting was scheduled for March 2016 to draft a plan and co-ordinate the work of the two orders of government. It failed primarily because the programs of Saskatchewan and Nova Scotia did not meet Ottawa's criteria. Instead, the meeting produced a plan to draft a plan, plus agreement to establish working groups to examine the various issues to be covered by the plan.

Although Ottawa implied that it was going to be far more active and take a "leadership role" in establishing a pan-Canadian plan as opposed to ten provincial ones, several of its decisions made co-operation with the provinces fairly easy. One was the maintenance of Harper's climate change goals, because raising them as many people expected would almost certainly have led to conflict with the provinces. Ottawa also declared acceptable the plans already adopted by the four largest provinces: Quebec, Ontario, Alberta, and BC. For them, there was no change from Harper's policy in terms of goals or the effects on 80 per cent of the population, but the plans of those four provinces were now part of the "national framework."

The main problem with Saskatchewan and Nova Scotia was Trudeau's criteria for accepting provincial plans. Ottawa determined that the provinces had to place a "price on carbon," and that there were only two ways to do so, namely through a straight carbon tax or a cap-and-trade system. Nova Scotia, however, was reducing its gas emissions through a system of regulations, and although it was one of the most successful provinces in meeting Canadian goals, Ottawa rejected that option. Saskatchewan had adopted a system of "capture and store" by which gas emissions from one of its coal-fired power plants were stored rather than released into the atmosphere, but Ottawa did not approve that program. Premier Brad Wall was adamantly opposed to any tax on carbon, arguing that it would raise the cost of energy-intensive activities such as agriculture and mining, as well as deal another blow to an economy already suffering from the recent dramatic fall in prices for oil and gas.

As talks continued during the summer, a First Ministers' meeting was scheduled for December. In November, however, Trudeau announced in the House of Commons that putting a price on carbon was the only acceptable plan. The announcement was made at the same time as environment ministers were meeting to discuss that very issue, an act that reminded observers of past federal unilateralism and clearly violated Trudeau's promise of meaningful consultation with the provinces. Ottawa also issued a warning—if any province failed to adopt a tax on carbon, Ottawa would impose one and return the money to its government. Premier Wall pointed out that the unilateral announcement violated Ottawa's promise to negotiate and called into question the purpose of the First Ministers' meeting scheduled for December after Ottawa had announced its decisions.

On December 9, first ministers, including those from the Territories, assembled in Ottawa to hammer out the pan-Canadian position. Ottawa had by then announced a specific target for achieving the overall goal—all provinces had to implement a $50-per-ton tax on carbon by 2022 beginning with $10 in 2018 and rising annually by $10, until reaching the $50 target. Apart from Saskatchewan, no province seemed to have problems with these targets partly, cynics said, because they were so low. BC, for example, has a tax of $30 per ton so it has already met the target for 2020. Premier Christy Clark insisted that some mechanism be adopted to measure the results of all the provincial programs in order to ensure fairness. This was agreed, though the details have yet to be worked out, and it is difficult to compare the results of the cap-and-trade and the carbon tax systems. It remains to be seen what Ottawa will do if any provinces miss their targets between 2018 and 2022.

As expected, there were no changes in Saskatchewan's strong opposition to any carbon tax. Premier Wall's objections were outlined again, both before the meeting and at the news conference, and Saskatchewan may challenge any federal action in the courts. The length and outcome of any such challenge cannot be predicted. Oil prices are also impossible to predict, and Saskatchewan could be experiencing boom times or a desperate situation before any deadline for imposing a carbon tax arrives. Premier Wall also pointed out that there are no good public studies of how the carbon tax will affect the economy, and Ottawa refused to share an uncensored report of the study it had made. Federal and provincial positions may change when Canadians see more clearly the answers to the three main questions: what is the cost, what is the benefit, and what is the ratio between them? Manitoba's new government does not have problems with the federal plan, but withheld its approval as a bargaining lever for larger federal transfers for health care. It remains to be seen how that confrontation will be resolved.

Agreement on climate change was greatly facilitated by the fact that Alberta has an NDP government, which has excellent credentials on environmental issues and needs federal support for pipelines to get its energy to market. If no progress is actually made building the necessary pipelines, Alberta will likely grow increasingly cool towards co-operating with Ottawa on climate change. Given the glacial speed at which pipelines are approved and built, and the uncertainties of politics, the Albertan election of 2019 could result in a dramatic shift in that province's positions on climate change. Many other provincial and federal elections are scheduled before new deadlines have to be met, with many unpredictable results on environmental policy and federal-provincial relations.

Coal-fired power plants are a major source of gas emissions, and on November 21 Ottawa dramatically announced that the deadline for Canada to phase out these plants was being advanced by twelve years, from 2042 to 2030. Since four provinces use coal to generate electricity the announcement appeared to raise serious potential problems for Ottawa's relations with them. That, however, did not materialize. Alberta, the biggest user of coal, was already on course to phase out its plants by 2030. Saskatchewan and Nova Scotia negotiated "equivalency agreements" with Ottawa which allow them to continue using coal after 2030 providing they achieve an equivalent reduction by other means. Thus at the time of writing, the new deadline only applies to one plant in rural New Brunswick, a plant that already uses advanced technology to reduce emissions, and an equivalency agreement similar to Nova Scotia's could exempt it too.

Confrontation over Health Care

Health care is perhaps the most difficult file for Trudeau and the provinces. The Harper program of 2014 was imposed unilaterally, and the provinces were highly critical of the process and the proposed decline in the rate of increase of federal transfers from 6 to 3 per cent for the period from 2017 to 2024. Negotiations for a new program did not have to begin until 2022, and Trudeau did not specifically promise to raise the rate of growth of the transfers. But the Liberals had criticized it, and Trudeau did promise better relations with the provinces. Since their main demand was an increase to that 3 per cent rate of growth, it was understandable if they believed that the promise of better relations meant an increase to that rate.

To the provinces' surprise, a year after the election, Ottawa unilaterally announced that the rate of growth in Harper's program would be maintained. The provinces tried to use Trudeau's need for co-operation on climate change as a lever to force federal movement on the health transfers, and demanded that there be a First Ministers' meeting on health care before any meeting on climate change. Ottawa prevailed on that issue, and the First Ministers' Conference of December 9 was dedicated to climate change, but was followed by an informal dinner with health care as the main topic for discussion. That dinner conversation produced no movement towards resolving the dispute.

Instead of an expected First Ministers' meeting, health and finance ministers met in Ottawa on December 19. Ottawa offered to increase the rate of increase in transfers from 3 to 3.5 per cent and provide $11.5 billion over ten years for home care and mental health. Most of the $11.5 billion would come in the last half of the ten-year period after the agreement on the annual transfers has expired, so it is impossible to know what the actual federal transfer would be over the next ten years. Harper's program provided growth of 3 per cent, or the rate of growth of GDP if it was larger. The Trudeau offer is for 3.5 per cent and no provision for a higher rate if GDP growth is greater. Since GDP growth is projected to be above 3.5 per cent, the new offer could well be less than Harper's, which is one reason the provinces rejected it and the Harper formula still covers the period to 2024.

The provinces argued that their health budgets will increase by more than 3.5 per cent in the future, resulting in Ottawa's share of health spending falling from around 23 per cent to around 20 per cent. Ottawa's proposal reverted to the practices of the past, namely, cherry-picking which of the dozens of areas of health spending are most in need of money. There were familiar echoes of the nanny state attitude when Health Minister Jane Philpott suggested that the provinces were not sufficiently aware that home care and mental health were underfunded. And in another familiar pattern, Ottawa's interference in provincial health budgets comes at a time when federal spending on its own responsibilities for the health of Indigenous peoples and veterans remains woefully inadequate. The allocation of additional funds to home care and mental health implies yet another federal condition on health transfers at a time when Ottawa's overall share is falling, for the first time since 2004. This is, in fact, the third time in twenty years that Ottawa earmarked additional funds for specific purposes with new conditions added to the original four, while Ottawa's overall share of health care spending continues to decline.

The provinces were united in rejecting the proposal, but within days Ottawa had negotiated separate deals with New Brunswick, Newfoundland and Labrador, and Nova Scotia, the old politics of divide and conquer and Ottawa's reliance on Canada's poorest provinces to accept new federal programs with the conditions Ottawa applies. As of the time of writing, four provinces were still united in demanding that Ottawa provide greater transfers if the existing levels of health care are to be maintained, and the two sides were waiting to see which one would blink first. One advantage for the provinces was the fact that Trudeau promised both better relations and more First Ministers' meetings, and the provinces are demanding a First Ministers' meeting on health. If that occurs, Trudeau will face the choice of maintaining the tough positions of his ministers or improving relations with the provinces by increasing the transfers. In the meantime, the debate became a dialogue of the deaf with Ottawa talking about the conditions of health care for all Canadians while the provinces talked about the cost of providing them. Quebec Premier Philippe Couillard also pointed out that the proposed federal funding for home care and mental health would lapse in ten years, leaving the provinces to pay the full amounts of those enhanced programs.

A new issue seemed to arise when Health Minister Philpott claimed that she did not know how Ottawa's contribution to provincial health budgets was being spent. The provinces reacted angrily, saying that Ottawa had all the information it needed. Philpott's assertion was odd indeed, since provincial health budgets are published every year, and this was not a problem in the previous five decades of Medicare. Ottawa's contribution covers around 20 per cent of provincial spending on health, so presumably Ottawa pays for one-fifth of every medical bill and has done so ever since 1968.

A variation on this theme was Ottawa's assertion that the provinces had not spent all of the recent 6 per cent growth in transfers for health, and instead had used some of those funds for other programs. The problem, if there was one, stemmed from the success of Harper's program. He made clear that there would be no more increases, that the provinces had to use their money more efficiently, and that Ottawa would not tell them how to do so since Ottawa did not have detailed knowledge of provincial health programs. Although this non-interventionist approach was heavily criticized at the time, it appeared to have worked, as the provinces reduced the growth in their health expenditures to less than 3 per cent. That seems to be the basis for the Trudeau government's assertion that some of the 6 per cent had been shifted to other departments. In fact, the annual 6 per cent increases from 2004 to 2016 did not move Ottawa's overall share of provincial spending back towards the original 40 per cent, and health was still the largest element in provincial budgets and was still growing faster than inflation.

As part of the propaganda battle, federal Health Minister Philpott also asserted that Ottawa has always led the way on health. In fact, it was hardly involved in the health of most Canadians before 1967, and it was Tommy Douglas and Saskatchewan's CCF who led the way on both hospital insurance and Medicare. Ottawa's only exclusive responsibility for health care is with the Indigenous peoples and veterans, and those programs have been woefully underfunded compared to provincial ones and still are. No province would accept the idea that Ottawa was the "leader" on health care issues, but many Canadians might. That, of course, is part of the age-old battle for power, the competition to convince Canadians that Ottawa is in a better position than the provinces for calling the shots on health care decisions.

Perhaps the most important challenge the Trudeau government will have in dealing with the provinces is financial. Promises to act meaningfully on urban infrastructure, the environment, Indigenous peoples, pension reform, health transfers, military procurement, and the international scene, along with the need to meet the expectations of Atlantic Canada and support the oil and gas industry, will require substantial increases in federal spending. Harper's major tax cuts were deliberately designed to force future governments to finance new spending with either tax increases or borrowing. Major tax hikes have been ruled out, so the financing will have to come from massive borrowing. If that is not sufficient to meet provincial expectations, as seems likely, then relations with the provinces will deteriorate.

Meanwhile, two ancient problems in federal-provincial relations have seemingly been laid to rest. By giving the prime minister the right to appoint senators, the BNA Act made the Senate a part of the central government and not a true "federal" institution representing the interests of both Ottawa and the provinces. When the Supreme Court was established in 1870, it too was appointed solely by the prime minister and was therefore a part of the central government. The provinces have always viewed both institutions as instruments of central government authority and have advocated provincial input into appointments since 1878. During the decades of constitutional debate, this issue was discussed and agreements reached for provincial input, but none were ever implemented. Trudeau addressed the question of appointments to both Senate and Supreme Court by appointing committees to recommend names for his consideration, a process still completely controlled by the prime minister. Their consultations are secret, so it is not clear what input provinces might have, but the proposals for the prime minister to select names from lists submitted by the provinces has been abandoned, and the two institutions remain parts of the central government and not joint institutions of Ottawa and the provinces.

Like many of its predecessors, the Liberal government of 2016 seems to be learning that dealing with the provinces is relatively easy immediately after an election that replaces an old government with fresh faces and new promises and is of the same political stripe as most provincial governments. Managing the relationship then starts to become difficult as questions of financing new initiatives arise, the different interests and priorities of Ottawa and the provinces begin to assert themselves, the differences between Canada's regions pit provinces against province, and friendly provincial governments lose office. Not everyone can be satisfied in a federation, and Ottawa and the provinces have to work out who will be satisfied and who will not. Those decisions will set the pattern for federal-provincial relations into the future, and history suggests that harmony will not prevail for long. Problems between the two orders of government are both inevitable and unpredictable, and the management of them is one of the severest challenges for both the central and the provincial governments. The coming years will reveal how Ottawa and the provinces manage the relationship, and how their stewardship compares to that of their predecessors.

Conclusion

Canada is one of the oldest and most successful federations in the world. One can make a case that it is *the* most successful federation. Unlike those of similar size and varied geography, such as the United States and Australia, Canada contains an ethnic minority of 25 per cent concentrated in one province. Unlike those such as Switzerland with large minorities, Canada has an enormous geographic mass with a wide variety of regional economies and interests. The unique combination of factors that make federalism essential for Canada also make it the most decentralized federation in the world, and that is one of the reasons it has been so successful. Unlike the United States, Canada was not held together by a war, and unlike the former Yugoslavia, it was not held together by a one-party dictatorship. The *BNA Act* has never been changed significantly because it reflects Canadian realities, and it is so flexible that Canada became a unitary state for the duration of two world wars by a simple Act of Parliament.

On July 1, 1867, few people had any right to expect such success, though some dreamers spoke and wrote about an unlimited future. In the late 1850s, there was no reason to think that the seven British North American colonies would adopt a federal system of government or unite into a single colony. At the time hardly any politician or interest group endorsed such revolutionary changes, including the government of Great Britain. A few years later, many had changed their minds, mainly as a result of political stalemate, Britain's desire to see the colonies united, economic factors, and the real or imagined threat posed by the United States.

Of the two elements that made up Confederation—adopting a federal system of government and uniting the colonies—the first was the easiest. By August 1864, a strong majority of French-Catholic and English-speaking politicians in the Province of Canada had agreed to adopt federalism and had agreed on the broad outlines of that scheme. Subsequent conferences in Charlottetown, Quebec City, and London worked out the details, but the broad outline of what those Canadian politicians agreed upon was not altered in any significant way. What was meant by the clauses they drafted remained a matter of dispute and still does—that is the nature of federal constitutions.

The more difficult part of the Confederation scheme was uniting the seven colonies—Newfoundland, Prince Edward Island, Nova Scotia, New Brunswick, Canada, British Columbia, and Vancouver Island. The Canadian Assembly was the only one to endorse the Confederation proposal. New Brunswick was manipulated into joining, and Nova Scotia was forced to become a province. PEI rejected the scheme but had to join to avoid bankruptcy, and Newfoundland said no in 1869. Later, BC was bribed with the promise of a railway, and Newfoundland approved joining in a 1949 referendum that many saw as being manipulated. Manitoba, Saskatchewan, and Alberta were created by the central government, but with inferior status to the other provinces, a matter that created difficulties until 1930 and arguably up to the present day.

It took eighty-two years to complete the process of uniting the colonies, and the twists and turns on that long road suggested that there was nothing inevitable about the process at all. It was a triumph of people over obstacles, of politics over geography, and it might have turned out quite differently. Along the way, the super-colony created in 1867 gradually became more and more independent, the best date for achieving sovereignty being 1931. But there were so many stages in that evolution that there is little agreement on any date, the lack of clarity and agreement apparently being another characteristic of Canadian federalism. That lack of clarity facilitated the myth that Confederation brought independence, along with the companion myth that it created an instant nation.

Federalism was adopted in 1867 because English-speaking Canadians had failed to assimilate French Catholics, and the cultural differences between the two groups were so great that they could not agree on policies to govern matters that had cultural elements. The solution to that problem was to create separate provinces for Lower and Upper Canada and give them responsibility for most of the things on which the two groups had different views. Each was then *maîtres chez nous*, masters in our own house, and neither could dominate the other. Ottawa was given general matters, the things the two groups could agree on. These were more important for English Canadians, who later created the argument that the federal government should be stronger or dominant on the grounds that it had the important responsibilities.

But the things the provinces controlled were the ones important to French Canadians, and indeed almost all of a citizen's dealings with governments or institutions after Confederation were with the provinces, not Ottawa. Many English-speaking Upper Canadians also wanted local matters to be handled by their provincial government and not by a central government in which French Catholics might wield considerable power, and many Maritimers did not want a central government dominated by central Canadians managing their local issues. While they haggled over details, there was very broad agreement on the division of responsibilities between the two orders of government.

The Fathers of Confederation did not treat the provinces the same for the very simple reason that they were all different. English-speaking Canadians were a minority in Lower Canada within a French-Catholic minority in the Province of Canada, and those two minorities required special treatment, namely provincial status for French Catholics and full protection for the English-speaking minorities in Quebec. To the Fathers, it did not make sense that small provinces should have the same number of senators as large ones, and a great deal of effort went into allocating Senate seats. The structure of the Senate was copied from the United States, its more limited powers were modelled on the British House of Lords, and it has never represented the provinces or been a fully satisfactory partner to the House of Commons. Other examples of asymmetrical federalism included different subsidies, powers, and law codes. Ever since 1867 central governments have treated the provinces differently, and one of the puzzles of recent history is the fact that many people seemed to believe that all provinces were the same. One of the defining characteristics of Canadian federalism is the fact that it is asymmetrical, that no provinces are "like the others," especially Quebec.

With three colonies united into one and a federal constitution in place, the new Dominion of Canada set out to establish a working federal system. It went through many stages and crises, and the journey is still underway because a federal constitution can never be fixed in time. Whether a federation survives depends on the flexibility of the citizens in adjusting the framework to new circumstances and dealing with inevitable tensions and conflicts between groups, regions, and the two orders of government. The first 150 years saw Canadian federalism meet those many challenges, but not without a number of major battles along the way. Indeed, in 1995, federalism came within a whisker of failing.

The new central government of 1867 was entrusted to Sir John A. Macdonald, who executed the responsibilities with enormous success. He implemented the new scheme at the federal level and, to a degree, in the new provinces of Quebec and Ontario; pacified disgruntled provinces; added the North-West Territories and the provinces of Manitoba, BC, and PEI; and knitted the whole together with the CPR and his economic policies. He helped establish viable two-party systems at the federal level and in some provinces. He established the precedent that the central government would not interfere in education—it was up to the local Protestants and Catholics to work out the education systems within their provinces.

Macdonald was also a rather strange choice to implement federalism since he clearly preferred a unitary system of government. He never did accept federalism and set out to make the central government superior to the provinces. The result was a long series of battles with various provinces, especially Ontario. Macdonald lost most of those battles and, in the process, discredited legitimate federal powers such as disallowance. The question as to what kind of federalism Canada enjoyed had been answered by 1896—a political entity as diverse as Canada required a genuine federal system with both orders of government autonomous in their areas of responsibility. That was the outcome of political and court battles and the will of the people.

The first decade of the twentieth century was the Golden Age of Federalism. Not only had Macdonald's attempts at centralization failed, but Prime Minister Wilfrid Laurier and his cabinet and party believed in classical or genuine federalism. Aided by a wave of prosperity and the arrival of millions of immigrants, Ottawa got on with the tasks the constitution assigned to it and the provinces got on with theirs. Alberta and Saskatchewan became the eighth and ninth provinces in 1905, and the inevitable problems of creating new provinces and adjusting the Dominion to accommodate them were handled reasonably well. Laurier also made a major effort to correct one of the most significant faults in the original agreement, the fact that none of the provinces except Ontario received adequate subsidies from Ottawa to allow them to execute their responsibilities properly.

After 1911, Ottawa's budgetary surplus led the new Conservative regime of Robert Borden into a new phase of federalism. The exercise of power is central to politics in any regime, and money is central to power. Competition between the orders of government is inevitable in federal systems, and no written constitution can prevent governments and political parties competing with each other. If governments have money, they will use it, and Borden did. Amongst his first acts was the launching of new programs in provincial areas of responsibility in spite of the fact that the constitution said they were "exclusively provincial." The constitutionality of those programs was challenged unsuccessfully, revealing one of the most significant problems with constitutions. That is, if a government can get away with doing something unconstitutional according to the written document, then it becomes constitutional by convention or the passage of time. Borden had begun seriously blurring the lines between federal and provincial responsibilities in one direction only—federal encroachments on provincial jurisdiction. Since it has usually been the federal government that had more money than needed, the pattern ever since has been federal encroachments on provincial jurisdiction, with very little movement in the opposite direction.

After the Great War, things would never go back to "normal," and among those things affected were federal-provincial relations. Four years of exercising enormous power affected politicians, bureaucrats, and their supporters.

New conditions such as the health and welfare of veterans and the challenge of dealing with post-war economic problems gave Ottawa legitimate interests in areas of responsibility that were provincial under the constitution but could hardly be ignored because of that fifty-year-old document. So it was the constitution that was ignored, not the pressing demand for federal action on these new problems.

The war gave Ottawa a new tool to carry on with its encroachments into provincial jurisdiction, a tool that became the centre of bitter conflict that has never ended. The *BNA Act* gave Ottawa the right to collect taxes by any means and limited the provinces to the unimportant and unpopular fields of direct taxes. Ottawa left that field alone, and by 1914, it was "convention" that only the provinces collected income taxes on corporations or individuals. In 1917, Ottawa entered the field and has collected income taxes ever since. The rise of the welfare state then produced a new and challenging era in federal-provincial relations that has endured to the present. Welfare is very clearly a provincial matter under the constitution, and the reasons for that never have changed, namely the fact that different regions have different views on welfare as well as different needs and capacities. In 1927, however, Ottawa decided to establish the Old Age Pension program.

The argument advanced to justify this encroachment on provincial jurisdiction was called the "spending power," the idea that since Ottawa could collect money by any means, it could spend it on anything, and that would not violate the constitution if the provinces accepted it. Five did, three could not afford to, and Quebec refused because the program violated the constitution and, in effect, imposed English-Canadian values. That was precisely what federalism and the *BNA Act* were designed to avoid, but the program was gradually adopted by all provinces because they could not afford to remain aloof. The fiction developed that their acceptance was "voluntary," and de facto the constitution had been changed to allow Ottawa to initiate programs in almost any area of provincial responsibility. In fact, however, the provinces could not reject such federal programs so their acceptance was not really voluntary. "Exclusive" provincial responsibility for welfare ceased to exist and the most significant precedent for changing the constitution had been established, but the spending power was never legitimized by a formal amendment to the *BNA Act*.

The Depression marked the low point of federalism. The municipalities could not meet the welfare needs of their populations, and the poorer provinces could not provide adequate help to them. The federal government alone had the financial means to enable those on welfare to survive with a minimum of suffering. It provided huge amounts of financial support, but it was never enough and never nearly as much as it could have been. Ottawa had all the constitutional powers it needed to mount massive spending programs and increase the amount of money in circulation. Instead, the Conservative regime wound up proposing a series of measures that were clearly in provincial jurisdiction, and the successor Liberal regime proposed a study of the problem. Desperate provinces proposed real solutions that were also beyond their powers. It was the politicians that failed the people, not federalism and the constitution.

The Second World War turned Canada into a unitary state once more, with the full support of the provinces. To help finance the war, the provinces allowed Ottawa to collect their taxes and return a fixed amount to cover their expenses, which were basically frozen. During the war Ottawa's revenue and spending vastly increased, creating an enormous shift in the balance between the budgets and power of the provinces and Ottawa. A number of civil servants and politicians decided that Ottawa should retain much of the enormous power it had exercised politically and financially in wartime, and that the means to do so was for Ottawa to implement the welfare state with programs in welfare, health, and perhaps education. The federal government was determined to maintain control of taxation and a high level of spending with the provinces limited to the role they had been reduced to by the Depression and the war. Most of the poorer provinces agreed, the richer ones and several others did not, and Canada was set for a half-century struggle over which order of government would provide the welfare state. The fact that the constitution clearly said it was the provinces cut little ice in Ottawa or the poorer provinces, but was crucial to the thinking of Ontario and Quebec.

Ottawa's wartime efforts to encroach on provincial affairs were rebuffed in conferences at the end of the war. Ottawa's fallback position was to implement programs one by one as circumstances permitted, a strategy that made the process ad hoc and highly political. The baby bonus, for example, was introduced just before the 1945 election. Federal aid to universities resulted from a tax windfall and provoked a bitter battle with Quebec. A crucial development in federal-provincial relations in the post-war period centered on the attempts by Ottawa to retain control of taxes, collecting them for the provinces and returning a proportionate amount plus a bit more. Quebec's Premier Maurice Duplessis refused to participate on the grounds that doing so would make his province subordinate to Ottawa. That began to drive huge wedges between Quebec and Ottawa and between Quebec and the other provinces. Eventually, every other province followed Quebec's lead and accepted its principle—provinces cannot be independent if Ottawa collects taxes for them.

The federal encroachment into provincial matters continued under the regimes of Louis St. Laurent and John Diefenbaker, with new or enhanced programs in pensions, hospital insurance, higher education, infrastructure such as local roads, winter works to ease unemployment, and housing. Federalism changed when a western Canadian, John Diefenbaker, formed a cabinet in which central Canadian ministers were in a minority for the first time in history. That government was the first to place a high priority on federal support to the West and Atlantic Canada. It also institutionalized equalization payments so that poorer provinces could offer their citizens services comparable to those of richer provinces without excessive taxation. From then on, one of Ottawa's major roles in federalism was the transfer of wealth from the regions that benefited the most to the ones that benefited the least.

The adoption of the equalization system in the late 1950s changed forever the functioning of federalism in Canada. Essentially, central Canadians accepted that federalism worked to their advantage more than to that of the other regions, and that it was only fair for Ottawa to provide money to the have-not provinces so they could provide services similar to those of the richer, have provinces. The formula was changed several times, and the system was entrenched in the *1982 Constitution*. The program did not, however, stop the have-not provinces asking for special deals on shared-cost programs and other federal initiatives, and politics being what it is, Ottawa often responded positively. The result was that, by 2005, a degree of equalization had been built into so many federal programs that it was virtually impossible to know how much money was being transferred from richer to poorer provinces. These programs did, however, reflect the modern reality of federalism, which is the involvement of all three orders of government in many of the programs that assist the nation's citizens. It was easy, however, to overemphasize the importance of the equalization program because, to a certain extent, it merely balanced the shared-cost programs that always provided more federal money to the richer provinces.

In the early 1960s, two developments converged to produce decades of conflict within Canadian federalism. The first was the Quiet Revolution in Quebec, which saw the government replace the Church as the provider of health, welfare, and education. That made Quebec more like the other provinces where governments handled such matters. Paradoxically, it also made Quebec less like the other provinces because its government was far more determined to ensure that those matters would be handled by Quebec City and not Ottawa. Then, in 1963, the federal Liberals returned to power, determined to complete the federal welfare state through a number of new programs, especially the two most expensive ones: a national contribu tory pension fund and Medicare. The stage was set for a major showdown between Quebec and Ottawa over power and money. It was also ethnic and religious: who would determine social policy in Quebec, the provincial government dominated by French Catholics or the federal government in which French Catholics wielded little power? Confederation had been designed and adopted to avoid problems like this, and the battles that escalated in the 1960s demonstrated the degree to which Ottawa had successfully invaded "exclusive" provincial jurisdiction, as well as the degree to which English-speaking Canadians agreed with that policy.

The clashes dominated Canadian politics, and while Quebec lost most of the battles, many in English-speaking Canada mistakenly thought it had won most of them. The failure to protect Quebec's autonomy in its own areas led more and more Québécois to embrace more nationalistic parties and even separatism. English-speaking Canada was moving in the opposite direction, becoming more nationalist and more determined to have Ottawa impose "national standards" on health and welfare and become more involved in "local" matters that were, of course, provincial. One prominent French Canadian, Pierre Elliott Trudeau, saw Quebec nationalism as a force for evil, and when he became a champion of federalism and the darling of the English-Canadian nationalists, he quickly rose to the leadership of the federal Liberal party and then became prime minister.

Trudeau's first regime witnessed some of the worst battles between Ottawa and the provinces, with Ottawa's relations with the West deteriorating to the level of its relations with Quebec, where the people elected their first separatist government. In 1980, Trudeau found himself back in power with roughly the same agenda he had started with twelve years earlier. He was determined to add a charter of rights and an amending formula to the constitution, patriate it from Britain, share western Canada's energy wealth with the rest of Canada, defeat Quebec nationalism, tip the balance of power strongly towards Ottawa, assert Canadian nationalism over any other identities, and reform various aspects of the relationship with the provinces to Ottawa's advantage. Canada was in for the worst period ever of federal-provincial relations, issues that would dominate politics across the land and produce an entire cottage industry of experts and participants.

The first challenge the country faced was a Quebec referendum on separating from Canada, which was defeated by the wide margin of 60–40. That was followed by two years of fighting, which produced a compromise between Ottawa and the nine English-speaking provinces: the constitution was patriated with a charter and an amending formula, but none of Quebec's goals were achieved and it refused to sign. At the same time, the attempt to control western energy resources was a failure financially, constitutionally, and politically.

In 1984, Brian Mulroney's Conservatives swept to power, determined to reverse the federal policies that had placed such strains on the federation. He succeeded with negotiations with the Atlantic provinces and the West but the attempt to deal with Quebec's major objections to the state of federalism—the Meech Lake Accord—foundered, as did the successor arrangement, the Charlottetown Accord. Fortunately, federalism is infinitely flexible, and many of the main elements in those Accords were later implemented by Acts of Parliament or by agreements between Ottawa and one or more provinces. That was the way most changes had been made before 1982, and the main advantage of the new amending formula was to facilitate patriation of the constitution.

During this period another factor dramatically changed the functioning of federalism. In the 1970s, Ottawa began to run huge deficits to finance all its programs and to buy the hearts and minds of the Québécois. The deteriorating financial situation ended the search for new initiatives in provincial areas of jurisdiction and also led to cutbacks in transfers to the provinces. Though Ottawa attempted to maintain control of the programs and the conditions the provinces had been forced to accept, the provinces knew that a shrinking federal share of the burden meant a shrinking federal ability to call the shots. Over the next two decades, more and more federal conditions were loosened, Canada became more asymmetrical, and relations between Ottawa and the English-speaking provinces improved. By 2000, Medicare was almost the only shared-cost program in which Ottawa could impose conditions on the provinces, and the other programs have run relatively smoothly ever since.

In the mid-1990s, Canada approached its worst crisis ever. The Parti Québécois was back in power with a Quebec government determined to secede as soon as a referendum could be held. The *No* side was now weaker politically at both the provincial and federal levels, and arguments that had helped to defeat the separatist referendum of 1980 were no longer of value. Panic on the eve of the vote forced Prime Minister Jean Chrétien to reluctantly promise two of the main features from the defeated Meech and Charlottetown Accords—restoring Quebec's veto and recognizing it as a distinct society. The *No* side won a narrow victory, and Chrétien restored the veto and recognized Quebec as a distinct society through legislation, since constitutional amendment had become virtually impossible.

Chrétien had the federal government withdraw from a number of areas of provincial jurisdiction and took a number of steps to make separation much more difficult. These measures, coupled with the loss of the two referenda and their best leaders and the emergence of a new generation of Québécois, produced a steady decline in support for separatism. Canada finally lapsed back into a peace on the constitutional front not seen since 1960. After 2006, Prime Minister Stephen Harper took a number of steps to improve the state of the relationship, including addressing the "fiscal imbalance" and recognizing the Québécois as a nation. The federal election of 2015 then produced a new Liberal regime promising to make even more improvements to the functioning of federalism. If implemented, the 150th year of Confederation could be one of the most harmonious ever.

As Canada celebrates the 150th anniversary of Confederation, federalism is functioning very well compared to its historical record, possibly better than at any time since 1911. One only has to look back on the problems that bedevilled Canada in the past to note that there are no such problems on the agenda today. Sir John A. Macdonald's attempt to turn the provinces into municipalities was a complete failure, and they are much stronger now than they were in his day. Federal powers that could be used against provinces, such as that of disallowing provincial legislation, have long since been abandoned. There are no international wars on the horizon to turn the country back into a unitary state, but the constitution is sufficiently flexible to allow that to happen if necessary. Co-operation between Ottawa, the provinces, and the municipalities to deal with the 2008 recession was a model for federalism, especially compared to the decade of squabbling, buck-passing, ideological intransigence, and failure that passed for governance in the Depression.

The fiscal imbalance that the Fathers bequeathed the provinces, the problem that led to so much conflict for over a century, was resolved by the Harper government, and the current government's promises of support for provinces and municipalities are based on a plan to borrow rather than the disposal of excess revenue. The main cause of federal-provincial friction was power as federal politicians and bureaucrats sought to dominate the provinces. By 2015, however, it appeared that the politicians and bureaucrats in both orders of government had come to the conclusion that co-operation was more desirable than confrontation and that they all had sufficient challenges to absorb all their time and money. Time will tell how long the current balance and relationship between Ottawa and the provinces will last, and what changes lie in the future. History provides good grounds for optimism; it also provides much evidence that the future cannot be predicted.

Bibliography

Glossary
An excellent glossary defining 124 terms and issues relevant to federalism can be found in Bakvis, Herman, and Grace Skogstad. *Canadian Federalism*. 3rd ed. Don Mills: Oxford University Press, 2012.

Biographies
One of the best sources of information on Canadian politicians is the individual entries in the *Dictionary of Canadian Biography*, available online at http://www.biographi.ca/en/. There are too many to list separately.

Primary Sources, listed chronologically

The *Proclamation Act*, October 7, 1763

The *Quebec Act*, June 22, 1774

The *Constitutional Act*, June 10, 1791

The Durham Report, February 11, 1839

The *Act of Union*, July 23, 1840

The *Quebec Resolutions*, August 27, 1864

The *London Resolutions*, December 4, 1866

The *British North America Act*, March 29,1867

The *Manitoba Act*, May 12, 1870

The *British Columbia Terms of Union*, May 16, 1871

The *Prince Edward Island Terms of Union*, June 26, 1873

The *Alberta Act*, July 20, 1905

The *Saskatchewan Act*, July 20, 1905

The *Constitution Act*, August 9, 1907 (covering federal transfers to the provinces)

The *War Measures Act*, August 22, 1914

The *Constitution Act*, July 10, 1930 (covering the transfer of natural resources to Manitoba, Saskatchewan, Alberta, and BC)

The *Statute of Westminster*, December 11, 1931

The *War Measures Act*, 1939

The *Report of the Royal Commission on Dominion-Provincial Relations*, May 3, 1940 (the Rowell-Sirois Report)

The *Constitution Act*, July 10, 1940 (giving Ottawa control of unemployment insurance)

The *Report on Social Security for Canada*, January 17, 1943 (the Marsh Report)

The *Newfoundland Act*, March 23, 1949

The *British North Act*, May 31,1951 (giving Ottawa some responsibility for pensions)

The *British North America Act (NO. 2)*, 1949 (giving Ottawa the power to amend the BNA Act on federal issues)

The *Report of the Royal Commission on National Development in the Arts, Letters, and Sciences*, June 1, 1951 (the Massey Report)

The *Report of the Royal Commission of Inquiry on Constitutional Problems*, 1956 (the Tremblay Report)

The *Preliminary Report of the Royal Commission on Bilingualism and Biculturalism*, February, 1965

The *War Measures Act*, October 17, 1969

The *Victoria Charter*, June 16, 1971

The *Task Force Report on Canadian Unity*, January 25, 1979 (*A Future Together*, the Pépin-Robarts Report)

The *Constitution Act*, April 17, 1982 (patriating the *BNA Act* to Canada)

An Act Respecting the Constitutional Act, June 1982 (Quebec's response to the *Constitution Act*)

The Atlantic Accord, February 11, 1985

The Western Accord, June 1, 1985

The Constitutional Accord, April 30, 1987 (the Meech Lake Accord)

The *Report of the Commission on the Political and Constitutional Future of Quebec*, 1991 (the Bélanger-Campeau Report)

Consensus Report on the Constitution, August 28, 1992 (the Charlottetown Accord)

Bill C-110, December 13, 1995 (provincial agreement required for Ottawa to approve an amendment to the constitution)

The Social Union Framework Agreement (SUFA), February 4, 1999

The *Clarity Act*, June 29, 2000

The *Fundamental Rights Act*, December 7, 2000 (Quebec's reply to the *Clarity Act*)

Books and Articles

Ajzenstat, Janet. *Canadian Constitutionalism: 1791–1991*. Ottawa: Canadian Study of Parliament Group, 1991.

———. *The Canadian Founding: John Locke and Parliament*. Montreal: McGill-Queen's University Press, 2007.

———. *Discovering Confederation: A Canadian's Story*. Montreal: McGill-Queen's University Press, 2014.

Ajzenstat, Janet, Paul Romney, Ian Gentles, and William D. Gardner. *Canada's Founding Debates*. Toronto: University of Toronto Press, 1999.

Ajzenstat, Janet, and Peter J. Smith. *Canada's Origins: Liberal, Tory, or Republican*. Montreal: McGill-Queen's University Press, 1995.

Anderson, George. *Federalism: An Introduction*. Don Mills: Oxford University Press, 2008.

———. *Fiscal Federalism: An Introduction*. Don Mills: Oxford University Press, 2010.

Archer, John. *Saskatchewan: A History*. Saskatoon: Prairie Books, 1980.

Armstrong, Christopher. *The Politics of Federalism: Ontario's Relations with the Federal Government, 1867–1942*. Toronto: University of Toronto Press, 1981.

Atkinson, Michael. *Governing Canada: Institutions and Structures*. Toronto: Harcourt Brace, 1993.

Aunger, Edmund. *In Search of Political Stability: A Comparative Study of New Brunswick and Northern Ireland*. Montreal: McGill-Queen's University Press, 1981.

Axworthy, Lloyd. "Regional Development: Innovations in the West." In *Towards a Just Society: The Trudeau Years*, edited by Thomas Axworthy and Pierre Elliott Trudeau. Toronto: Viking, 1990.

Axworthy, Thomas, and Pierre Elliott Trudeau, eds. *Towards a Just Society: The Trudeau Years*. Toronto: Viking, 1990.

Baier, Gerald. "The Courts, the Constitution, and Dispute Resolution." In *Canadian Federalism*. 3rd ed., edited by Herman Bakvis and Grace Skogstad. Don Mills: Oxford University Press, 2012.

Baier, Thomas. "The Law of Federalism: Judicial Review and the Division of Powers." In *New Trends in Canadian Federalism*. 2nd ed., edited by François Rocher and Miriam Smith. Peterborough: Broadview Press, 2003.

Bailey, Alfred. "The Basis and Persistence of Opposition to Confederation in New Brunswick." In *Canadian Historical Readings*, Vol. III, *Confederation*, edited by Ramsay Cook, Craig Brown, and Carl Berger. Toronto: University of Toronto Press, 1967.

Bakvis, Herman, and Grace Skogstad. *Canadian Federalism*. 3rd ed. Don Mills: Oxford University Press, 2012.

Bakvis, Herman, Gerald Baier, and Douglas Brown. *Contested Federalism: Certainty and Ambiguity in the Canadian Federation*. Don Mills: Oxford University Press, 2009.

Bakvis, Herman. *Federalism and the Organization of Political Life: Canada in Comparative Perspective*. Montreal: McGill-Queen's University Press, 1981.

Banting, Keith. "Remaking Immigration: Asymmetrical Decentralization and Canadian Federalism." In *Canadian Federalism*. 3rd ed., edited by Herman Bakvis and Grace Skogstad. Don Mills: Oxford University Press, 2012.

———. "The Three Federalisms Revisited: Social Politics and Decision-Making." In *The Welfare State and Canadian Federalism*. 2nd ed., edited by

Keith Banting. Montreal: McGill-Queen's University Press, 1987.

Banting, Keith, Douglas M. Brown, and Thomas Courchene, eds. *The Future of Fiscal Federalism*. Montreal: McGill-Queen's University Press, 1994.

Banting, Keith, and Richard Simeon, eds. *And No One Cheered: Federalism, Democracy, and the Constitution Act*. Toronto: Methuen,1983.

Banting, Keith G., and Richard Simeon. *Redesigning the State: The Politics of Constitutional Change in Industrial Nations*. Toronto: Palgrave,1985.

Barnhart, Gordon L., ed. *Saskatchewan Premiers of the Twentieth Century*. Regina: University of Regina Press, 2004.

Barman, Jean. *The West Beyond the West: A History of British Columbia*. Toronto: University of Toronto Press, 1991.

Bastien, Frederic. *The Battle for London: Trudeau, Thatcher, and the Fight for Canada's Constitution*, translated by Jacob Homel. Toronto: Dundurn Press, 2014.

Beck, J. Murray. *Joseph Howe*. 2 vols. Montreal: McGill-Queen's University Press, 1984.

———. *The Government of Nova Scotia*. Toronto: University of Toronto Press, 1957.

———. *The Politics of Nova Scotia*. 2 vols. Toronto: Four East Publications, 1985.

Behiels, Michael D. "Mulroney and a Nationalist Quebec: Key to Political Realignment in Canada?" In *Transforming the Nation: Canada and Brian Mulroney*, edited by Raymond Blake. Montreal: McGill-Queen's University Press, 2007.

Bélanger, Claude. "The Power of Disallowance and Reservation in Canadian Federalism." Westmount, QC: Marianopolis College, 2001.

Bélanger, Gerard. "The Division of Powers in a Federal System." In *Division of Powers and Public Policy*, edited by Richard Simeon. Toronto: University of Toronto Press, 1985.

Bell, David V.J. *The Roots of Disunity: A Study of Canadian Political Cultures*. Rev. ed. Toronto: Oxford University Press, 1992.

Bercuson, David, and Barry Cooper. *Deconfederation: Canada Without Quebec.* Toronto: Key Porter Books, 1991.

Berger, Carl. *The Sense of Power.* Toronto: University of Toronto Press, 1970.

Bergeron, Gérard. "Quebec in Isolation." In *And No One Cheered: Federalism, Democracy, and the Constitution Act,* edited by Keith Banting and Richard Simeon. Toronto: Methuen, 1983.

Bernard, André. *What Does Quebec Want?* Toronto: James Lorimer & Company, 1978.

Bickerton, James. *Nova Scotia and the Politics of Regional Development.* Toronto: University of Toronto Press, 1990.

Bickerton, James, and Alain-G. Gagnon. *Canadian Politics.* 5th ed. Toronto: University of Toronto Press, 2009.

Bird, Richard M. *The Growth of Government Spending in Canada.* Toronto: Canadian Tax Foundation, 1970.

Black, Conrad. *Duplessis.* Toronto: McClelland and Sewart, 1977.

———. *Rise to Greatness: The History of Canada, from the Vikings to the Present.* Toronto: McClelland and Stewart, 2014.

Black, Edwin. *Divided Loyalties: Canadian Concepts of Federalism.* Montreal: McGill-Queen's University Press, 1975.

Blair, R.S., and J.T. McLeod, eds. *The Canadian Political Tradition: Basic Readings.* 2nd ed. Toronto: Metheun, 1995.

Blake, Raymond. *From Fishermen to Fish: The Evolution of Canadian Fishery Policy.* Toronto: SAGE, 2000.

Blake, Raymond B., Penny E. Bryden, and J. Frank Strain, eds. *The Welfare State in Canada: Past, Present and Future.* Concord, ON: Irwin Publishers, 1997.

Blake, Raymond, Jeffrey Keshen, Norman Knowles, and Barbara Messamore. *Narrating A Nation: Canadian History Pre-Confederation.* Toronto: McGraw-Hill Ryerson, 2011.

Blake, Raymond, ed. *Transforming the Nation: Canada and Brian Mulroney.*

Montreal: McGill-Queen's University Press, 2007.

Blakeney, Allan. *An Honourable Calling; Political Memoirs*. Toronto: University of Toronto Press, 2008.

Bliss, Michael. *Right Honourable Men: The Descent of Canadian Politics from Macdonald to Mulroney*. Toronto: HarperCollins, 1995.

Boase, Joan Price. "Trends in Social Policy: Towards the Millennium." In *Provinces: Canadian Provincial Politics*, edited by Christopher Dunn. Peterborough: Broadview Press, 1996.

Bolger, Francis. *Canada's Smallest Province: A History of Prince Edward Island*. Charlottetown: Prince Edward Island Centennial Commission, 1973.

Bothwell, Robert. *A Short History of Ontario*. Edmonton: Hurtig, 1986.

———. *Canada and Quebec: One Country, Two Histories*. Vancouver: UBC Press, 1995.

———. *The Penguin History of Canada*. Toronto: Penguin Canada, 2006.

Bothwell, Robert, Ian Drummond, and John English. *Canada since 1945: Power, Politics and Provincialism*. Rev. ed. Toronto: University of Toronto Press, 1989.

Bothwell, Robert, and Jack Granatstein. *Our Century: The Canadian Journey in the Twentieth Century*. Toronto: McArthur and Company, 2000.

Bothwell, Robert, and William Kilbourn. *C. D. Howe: A Biography*. Toronto: McClelland and Stewart, 1979.

Boucher, Edith, and Arndt Vermaeten. "Changes to Federal Transfers to Provinces and Territories in 1999." In *Canada: The State of the Federation, 1999/2000: Toward A New Mission*, edited by Harvey Lazar. Kingston: Queen's University, 1999.

Bowker, Alan. *A Time Such as There Never Was Before: Canada After the Great War*. Toronto: Dundurn Press, 2014.

Boychuk, Gerard W. "Social Assistance and Canadian Federalism." In *New Trends in Canadian Federalism*. 2nd ed., edited by François Rocher and Miriam Smith. Peterborough: Broadview Press, 2003.

Bray, Matt, and Ernie Epp, eds. *A Vast and Magnificent Land: An Illustrated History of Northern Ontario.* Thunder Bay: Lakehead University, 1984.

Brock, Kathy. "Executive Federalism: Beggar Thy Neighbour." In *New Trends in Canadian Federalism.* 2nd ed., edited by François Rocher and Miriam Smith. Peterborough: Broadview Press, 2003.

Brodie, Janine. *The Political Economy of Canadian Regionalism.* Toronto: Harcourt Brace Jovanovich, 1990.

Brown, Douglas M. "Fiscal Federalism: Maintaining a Balance." In *Canadian Federalism.* 3rd ed., edited by Herman Bakvis and Grace Skogstad. Don Mills: Oxford University Press, 2012.

Brown, Douglas M., and Janet Hiebert. *Canada: The State of the Federation, 1994.* Kingston: Queen's University, 1994.

Brown, Keith, and Michael Howlett, eds. *The Provincial State in Canada.* Peterborough: Broadview Press, 2001.

Brown, R.C., and Ramsay Cook. *Canada, 1896–1921: A Nation Transformed.* Toronto: McClelland and Stewart, 1964.

Bruce, Harry. *An Illustrated History of Nova Scotia.* Halifax: Nimbus Publishing, 1997.

Brunet, Michel. "Canadians and Canadiens." In *French-Canadian Nationalism,* edited by Ramsay Cook. Toronto: Macmillan, 1969.

———. "The French Canadians' Search for a Fatherland." In *Nationalism in Canada,* edited by Peter Russell. Toronto: McGraw-Hill Ryerson, 1966.

Bryden, Kenneth. *Old Age Pensions and Policy Making in Canada.* Montreal: McGill-Queen's University Press, 1974.

Bryden, Penny E. "Brian Mulroney and Intergovernmental Relations: The Limits of Collaborative Federalism." In *Transforming the Nation: Canada and Brian Mulroney,* edited by Raymond Blake. Montreal: McGill-Queen's University Press, 2007.

Burgeis, Michael. "Canadian Federalism and Federation in Comparative Perspective." In *New Trends in Canadian Federalism.* 2nd ed., edited by François Rocher and Miriam Smith. Peterborough: Broadview Press, 2003.

Burns, R.M., and John J. Deutsch, eds. *One Country or Two?* Montreal: McGill-Queen's University Press, 1971.

Cadigan, Sean. *Newfoundland and Labrador, A History.* Toronto: University of Toronto Press, 2009.

Cairns, Alan C. *Charter versus Federalism: The Dilemmas of Constitutional Reform.* Montreal: McGill-Queen's University Press, 1992.

———. *Constitution, Government and Society in Canada: Selected Essays,* edited by Douglas E. Williams. Toronto: McClelland and Stewart, 1988.

———. "The Politics of Constitutional Conservatism." In *And No One Cheered: Federalism, Democracy, and the Constitution Act,* edited by Keith Banting and Richard Simeon. Toronto: Methuen, 1983.

———. "The Politics of Constitutional Renewal in Canada." In *Redesigning the State: The Politics of Constitutional Change in Industrial Nations,* edited by Keith G. Banting and Richard Simeon. Toronto, 1985.

———. *Reconfigurations: Canadian Citizenship and Constitutional Change: Selected Essays,* edited by Douglas E. Williams. Toronto: McClelland and Stewart, 1995.

Cameron, David. "Quebec and Canadian Federalism." In *Canadian Federalism.* 3rd ed., edited by Herman Bakvis and Grace Skogstad. Don Mills: Oxford University Press, 2012.

Campbell, Terry, and George Rawlyk. "The Historical Framework of Newfoundland and Confederation." In *The Atlantic Provinces and the Problems of Confederation,* edited by George Rawlyk. St. John's: Breakwater, 1979.

Canadian Tax Foundation. *The National Finances 1970–71.* Toronto: Canadian Tax Foundation, 1970.

Careless, J.M.S. *Brown of the Globe,* Vol. I, *The Voice of Upper Canada, 1818-1859.* Toronto: Dundurn Press, 1989.

———. *Brown of the Globe,* Vol. II, *Statesman of Confederation, 1859-1880.* Toronto: Dundurn Press, 1996.

———. *Canada: A Story of Challenge.* Toronto: Macmillan, 1970.

———, ed. *The Pre-Confederation Premiers.* Toronto: University of Toronto Press, 1980.

Carter, George E. *Canadian Conditional Grants since World War II*. Toronto: Canadian Tax Foundation, 1971.

Chandler, Marsha A., and William M. Chandler. *Public Policy and Provincial Politics*. Toronto: McGraw-Hill Ryerson, 1979.

Cheffins, R.I., and R.N. Tucker. *The Constitutional Process in Canada*. 2nd ed. Toronto: McGraw-Hill Ryerson, 1976.

Chodos, Robert, Rae Murphy, and Eric Homovich. *The Unmaking of Canada: The Hidden Themes in Canadian History since 1945*. Toronto: James Lorimer & Company, 1991.

Chrétien, Jean. "Bringing the Constitution Home." In *Towards a Just Society: The Trudeau Years*, edited by Thomas Axworthy and Pierre Elliott Trudeau. Toronto: Viking, 1990.

———. *My Years as Prime Minister*. Toronto: A.A. Knopf Canada, 2007.

Clark, Andrew Hill. *Three Centuries and the Island*. Toronto: University of Toronto Press, 1959.

Clarkson, Stephen, and Christina McCall. *The Magnificent Obsession*, Vol. I, *Trudeau and Our Times*. Toronto: McClelland and Stewart, 1990.

Clift, Dominique. *Quebec Nationalism in Crisis*. Montreal: McGill-Queen's University Press, 1982.

Cohen, Andrew. *Lester B. Pearson*. Toronto: Penguin Canada, 2008.

Coleman, William. *The Independence Movement in Quebec 1945–1980*. Toronto: University of Toronto Press, 1984.

Conrad, Margaret, and J. Hiller. *Atlantic Canada: A Region in the Making*. Don Mills: Oxford University Press, 2001.

Conrad, Margaret, and J. Hiller. *A Concise History of Atlantic Canada*. Toronto: Oxford University Press, 2006.

Conrad, Margaret, Kadriye Ercikan, Gerald Friesen, Jocelyn Létourneau, Delphin Muise, David Northrup, and Peter Seixas. *Canadians and Their Pasts*. Toronto: University of Toronto Press, 2013.

Conway, John F. *Debts to Pay; English Canada and Quebec from Conquest to Referendum*. Toronto: James Lorimer & Company, 1992.

———. *The West: The History of a Region in Confederation.* 2nd ed. Toronto: James Lorimer & Company, 1994.

Cook, Ramsay. *Canada and the French Canadian Question.* Toronto: Macmillan, 1966.

———. *Canada, Quebec, and the Uses of Nationalism.* 2nd ed. Toronto: McClelland and Stewart, 1986.

———. *Confederation.* Toronto: University of Toronto Press, 1967.

———. *Provincial Autonomy, Minority Rights, and the Compact Theory, 1867–1921.* Ottawa: Queen's Printer, 1963.

Cormier, Michel, and Achille Michaud. *Richard Hatfield: Power and Disobedience.* Fredericton: Goose Lane Editions, 1991.

Corry, J.A. "Constitutional Trends and Federalism." In *Evolving Canadian Federalism*, edited by A.R.M. Lower and F.R. Scott. Durham, NC: Duke University Press, 1958.

Courchene, Thomas J. *Redistributing Money and Power: A Guide to Canadian Health and Social Transfer.* Toronto: C.D. Howe Institute, 1995.

Coutts, Jim. "Expansion, Retrenchment and Protecting the Future: Social Policy in the Trudeau Years." In *Towards a Just Society: The Trudeau Years*, edited by Thomas Axworthy and Pierre Elliott Trudeau. Toronto: Viking, 1990.

Craig, Gerald. *Upper Canada: The Formative Years.* Toronto: McClelland and Stewart, 1963.

Creighton, Donald. *Canada's First Century, 1867–1967.* Toronto: Macmillan, 1970.

———. *Dominion of the North.* Toronto: Macmillan, 1962.

———. *The Forked Road: Canada 1939–1957.* Toronto: McClelland and Stewart, 1976.

———. *The Road to Confederation.* Toronto: Macmillan, 1964.

Crepeau, P.A., and C.B. Macpherson, eds. *The Future of Canadian Federalism.* Toronto: University of Toronto Press, 1965.

Crawley, Brian Lee. *Fearful Symmetry: The Fall and Rise of Canada's Founding Values.* Toronto: Key Porter Books, 2009.

Eager, Evelyn. *Saskatchewan Government and Politics*. Saskatoon: Western Producer Prairie Books, 1980.

Crosbie, John C. "Governing from the Centre: Reflections on the Mulroney Cabinet." In *Transforming the Nation: Canada and Brian Mulroney*, edited by Raymond Blake. Montreal: McGill-Queen's Press, 2007.

Decter, Michael B. "Harper on Health Care: A Curious Mix of Continuity, Unilateralism and Opportunities Lost." In *The Harper Factor: Assessing a Prime Minister's Policy Legacy*, edited by Jennifer Ditchburn and Graham Fox. Montreal: McGill-Queen's University Press, 2016.

Dicey, A.V. *Introduction to the Study of the Law of the Constitution*. 10th ed. London: Macmillan, 1961.

Dickinson, John, and Brian Young. *A Short History of Quebec*. 4th ed. Montreal: McGill-Queen's University Press, 2008.

Ditchburn, Jennifer, and Graham Fox, eds. *The Harper Factor: Assessing a Prime Minister's Policy Legacy*. Montreal: McGill-Queen's University Press, 2016.

Doern, Bruce, and Glen Toner. *The Politics of Energy: The Development and Implementation of the NEP*. Agincourt, ON: Methuen, 1985.

Doyle, Arthur T. *The Premiers of New Brunswick*. Fredericton: Brunswick Press, 1983.

Drummond, Ian. *Progress Without Planning: The Economic History of Ontario from Confederation to the Second World War*. Toronto: University of Toronto Press, 1987.

Dubec, Alfred. "The Decline of Confederation and the New Nationalism." In *Nationalism in Canada*, edited by Peter Russell. Toronto: McGraw-Hill Ryerson, 1966.

Dufour, Christian. *A Canadian Challenge; Le Défi Québécois*. Montreal: McGill-Queen's University Press, 1990.

Dunn, Christopher, ed. *Provinces: Canadian Provincial Politics*. Peterborough: Broadview Press, 1996.

Dupré, J. Stefan. "Taming the Monster: Debt, Budgets, and Federal-Provincial Fiscal Relations at the Fin de Siècle." In *Provinces: Canadian Provincial*

Politics, edited by Christopher Dunn. Peterborough: Broadview Press, 1996.

Dyck, Rand. *Provincial Politics in Canada*. Scarborough: Nelson, 1996.

English, John. *Just Watch Me: The Life of Pierre Elliott Trudeau, 1968–2000*. Toronto: A.A. Knopf Canada, 2009.

———. *Years of Growth, 1948–1967*. Toronto: Grolier, 1986.

Evans, Margaret. *Sir Oliver Mowat*. Toronto: University of Toronto Press, 1992.

Fingard, Judith, Janet Guilford, and David Sutherland. *Halifax, The First 250 Years*. Halifax: Formac Publishing, 1999.

Finkel, Alvin. *Our Lives: Canada after 1945*. Toronto: James Lorimer & Company, 1997.

Finkel, Alvin, and Margaret Conrad. *History of the Canadian Peoples*, Vol. II, *1867 to the Present*. 2nd ed. Toronto: Copp Clark Pitman, 1998.

Finlay, John, and Keith Sprague. *The Structure of Canadian History*. Scarborough: Pearson, 1979.

Fitzmaurice, John. *Quebec and Canada*. London: C. Hurst & Company, 1985.

Fletcher, Frederick J., and Donald C. Wallace. "Federal-Provincial Relations and the Making of Public Policy in Canada." In *Division of Powers and Public Policy*, edited by Richard Simeon. Toronto: University of Toronto Press, 1985.

Forbes, Ernest. *Challenging the Regional Stereotype*. Fredericton: Acadiensis Press, 1989.

———. *The Maritime Rights Movement*. Montreal: McGill-Queen's University Press, 1979.

Forbes, Ernest, and D.A. Muise, eds. *The Atlantic Provinces in Confederation*. Toronto: University of Toronto Press, 1993.

Fortin, Sarah, Alain Noël, and France St.-Hilaire. *Forging the Canadian Social Union: SUFA and Beyond*. Ottawa: Institute for Research on Public Policy, 2003.

Fournier, Pierre. "The Future of Quebec Nationalism." In *And No One*

Cheered: Federalism, Democracy, and the Constitution Act, edited by Keith Banting and Richard Simeon. Toronto: Methuen, 1983.

Fox, Graham. "Unfinished Business: The Legacy of Stephen Harper's Open Federalism." In *The Harper Factor: Assessing a Prime Minister's Policy Legacy,* edited by Jennifer Ditchburn and Graham Fox. Montreal: McGill-Queen's University Press, 2016.

Francis, Douglas, Richard Jones, and Donald B. Smith. *Destinies: Canadian History since Confederation.* Toronto: Holt, Rinehart & Winston, 1988.

———. *Origins: Canadian History to Confederation.* 6th ed. Toronto: Nelson, 2009.

Gagnon, Alain-G., ed. *Quebec State and Society.* 3rd ed. Toronto: University of Toronto Press, 2008.

Gagnon, Alain-G., and Raffaele Iacovino. *Federalism, Citizenship, and Quebec: Debating Multinationalism.* Toronto: University of Toronto Press, 2007.

Gagnon, Alain-G., and Mary Beth Montcalm. *Quebec: Beyond The Quiet Revolution.* Scarborough: Nelson Canada, 1990.

Gibbins, Roger. *Conflict and Unity: An Introduction to Canadian Political Life.* 3rd ed. Scarborough: Nelson Canada, 1995.

———. "Constitutional Politics." In *Canadian Politics.* 5th ed., edited by James Bickerton and Alain-G. Gagnon. Toronto: University of Toronto Press, 2009.

———. "Constitutional Politics and the West." In *And No One Cheered: Federalism, Democracy, and the Constitution Act,* edited by Keith Banting and Richard Simeon. Toronto: Methuen, 1983.

Gillespie, W. Irwin. *Tax, Borrow and Spend: Financing Canadian Federalism in Canada, 1867–1990.* Ottawa: Carleton University Press, 1991.

Gillmor, Don, Achille Michaud, and Pierre Turgeon. *Canada: A People's History,* Vol. II. Toronto: McClelland and Stewart, 2001.

Glazebrook, G.P. De T. *A History of Transportation in Canada.* New York: Greenwood Press, 1969.

Godin, Sylvain, and Maurice Basque. *Histoire des Acadiens et des Acadiennes.* Tracadie: La Grande marée, 2007.

Gossage, Peter, and J.I. Little. *An Illustrated History of Quebec*. Don Mills: Oxford University Press, 2012.

Gourgeon, Gilles. *A History of Quebec Nationalism*. Toronto: James Lorimer & Company, 1994.

Gow, James Iain. *Histoire de l'Administration publique québécoise 1867–1970*. Montreal: Presses de l'Université de Montréal, 1986.

Graham, Fraser. *René Lévesque and the Parti Québécois in Power*. Toronto: Macmillan, 1984.

Graham, Roger. *Old Man Ontario: Leslie Frost*. Toronto: University of Toronto Press, 1990.

Graham, Ron. *All the King's Horses: Politics among the Ruins*. Toronto: Mcfarlane, Walter and Ross, 1995.

———. *One-Eyed Kings: Promise and Illusion in Canadian Politics*. Toronto: HarperCollins, 1986.

Granatstein, J.L. *Canada 1957–1967: The Years of Uncertainty and Innovation*. Toronto: McClelland and Stewart, 1986.

———. *Canada's War: The Politics of the Mackenzie King Government, 1939–1945*. Toronto: University of Toronto Press, 1990.

———. *The Ottawa Men: The Civil Service Mandarins, 1935–1957*. Toronto: Oxford University Press, 1982.

———. *W.L. Mackenzie King*. Markham: Fitzhenry & Whiteside, 2002.

Granatstein, J.L., Irving M. Arbella, T.W. Acheson, David J. Bercuson, R. Craig Brown, and H. Blair Neatby. *Nation. Canada since Confederation*. 3rd ed. Toronto, 1990.

Granatstein, J.L., and Kenneth McNaught, eds. *English Canada Speaks Out*. Toronto: Doubleday Canada, 1991.

Gray, John. *Paul Martin in the Balance*. Rev. ed. Toronto: Key Porter Books, 2004.

Greenspon, Edward, and Anthony Wilson-Smith. *Double Vision: The Inside Story of the Liberals in Power*. Toronto: Doubleday Canada, 1996.

Groulx, Canon Lionel. "Why We Are Divided." In *French-Canadian*

Nationalism, edited by Ramsay Cook. Toronto: Macmillan, 1969.

Guest, Dennis. *The Emergence of Social Security in Canada.* 3rd ed. Vancouver: UBC Press, 1997.

Guindon, Hubert. *Quebec Society: Tradition, Modernity, and Nationhood.* Toronto: University of Toronto Press, 1988.

Gwyn, Richard. *Nation Maker: Sir John A. Macdonald: His Life, Our Times,* Vol. II, *1867–1891.* Toronto: Random House Canada, 2011.

———. *The Northern Magus: Pierre Trudeau and Canada.* Toronto: McClelland and Stewart, 1980.

Hale, Geoffrey. "The Tax on Income and the Growing Decentralization of Canada's Personal Income Tax System." In *Canada: The State of the Federation, 1999/2000: Toward A New Mission,* edited by Harvey Lazar. Kingston: Queen's University, 1999.

Hamelin, Jean, and Jean Provencher. *Brève Histoire du Québéc.* Quebec: Éditions du Boréal, 1997.

Harper, Stephen, Tom Flannagan, Ted Morton, Rainer Knopf, Andres Crooks, and Ken Boessenkool. "Letter to Alberta Premier Ralph Klein." January 24, 2001. [The Firewall Letter].

Heard, Andrew. *Canadian Constitutional Conventions: The Marriage of Law and Politics.* Toronto: Oxford University Press, 1991.

Harris, Michael. *Party of One: Stephen Harper and Canada's Radical Makeover.* Toronto: Viking, 2014.

Hébert, Chantal, and Jean Lapierre. *The Morning After.* Toronto: Penguin Random House, 2014.

Hébert, Chantal. *French Kiss: Stephen Harper's Blind Date with Quebec.* Toronto: A.A. Knopf Canada, 2007.

Heick, W.H. "Alexander Mackenzie and Canadian Federalism." In *Federalism in Canada and Australia: The Early Years,* edited by Bruce Hodgins, Don Wright, and W.H. Heick. Canberra, NSW: Australian National University Press, 1978.

Hiebert, Janet. "The Charter and Federalism: Revisiting the Nation-Building Thesis." In *Canada: The State of the Federation, 1994,* edited by Douglas M.

Brown and Janet Hiebert. Kingston: Queen's University, 1994.

Hiller, James K. *Confederation: Deciding Newfoundland's Future, 1934–1949.* St. John's: Newfoundland Historical Society, 1998.

Hiller, James, and Peter Neary. *Newfoundland in the Nineteenth and Twentieth Centuries.* Toronto: University of Toronto Press, 1980.

Hoberg, George. "Unsustainable Development: Energy and Environment in the Harper Decade." In *The Harper Factor: Assessing a Prime Minister's Policy Legacy*, edited by Jennifer Ditchburn and Graham Fox. Montreal: McGill-Queen's University Press, 2016.

Hobson, Paul A.R., and France St-Hilaire. "The Evolution of Federal-Provincial Fiscal Arrangements: Putting Humpty Together Again." In *Canada: The State of the Federation, 1999/2000: Toward A New Mission*, edited by Harvey Lazar. Kingston: Queen's University, 1999.

Hockin, Thomas A. *Government in Canada.* Toronto: McGraw-Hill Ryerson, 1976.

Hodgins, Bruce W., Richard P. Bowles, James L. Hanley, William Mackenzie, and George A. Rawlyk. *Canadiens, Canadians, and Québécois.* Scarborough: Prentice-Hall, 1974.

Hodgins, Bruce W., and Robert C. Edwards. "Federalism and the Politics of Ontario 1867–1880." In *Federalism in Canada and Australia: The Early Years*, edited by Bruce Hodgins, Don Wright, and W.H. Heick. Canberra, NSW: Australian National University Press, 1978.

Hodgins, Bruce W., Don Wright, and W.H. Heick. Federalism in Canada and Australia: The Early Years. Canberra, NSW: Australian National University Press, 1978. Horn, Michiel. "Federalism and Social Legislation: Past and Present." In Canada Speaks Out, edited by J.L. Granatstein and Kenneth McNaught. Toronto: Doubleday Canada, 1991.

Hoy, Clair. *Bill Davis.* Toronto: Metheun, 1985.

Hudon, Raymond. "Quebec, the Economy and the Constitution." In *And No One Cheered: Federalism, Democracy, and the Constitution Act*, edited by Keith Banting and Richard Simeon. Toronto: Methuen, 1983.

Hueglin, Thomas O., and Alan Fenna. *Comparative Federalism.*

Peterborough: Broadview Press, 2006.

Humphries, Charles W. *The Life and Times of James Pliny Whitney*. Toronto: University of Toronto Press, 1985.

Ibbitson, John. *Loyal No More: Ontario's Struggle for a Separate Destiny.* Toronto: HarperCollins, 2001.

———. *Stephen Harper*. Toronto: Signal, 2015.

Ismael, Jacqueline S., ed. *Canadian Social and Welfare Policy: Federal and Provincial Dimensions*. Kingston: McGill-Queen's University Press, 1985.

Jackson, James A. *A Centennial History of Manitoba*. Toronto: McClelland and Stewart, 1970.

Janigan, Mary. *Let the Eastern Bastards Freeze in the Dark: The West vs. the East Since Confederation*. Toronto: A.A. Knopf Canada, 2012.

Johnson, A.W. *Dream No Little Dreams: A Biography of the Douglas Government, 1944–1966*. Toronto: University of Toronto Press, 2004.

Johnson, Charles M. *E.C. Drury: Agrarian Idealist*. Toronto: University of Toronto Press, 1986.

Johnson, Hugh, ed. *The Pacific Province*. Vancouver: Douglas and McIntyre, 1966.

Johnson, William. *Stephen Harper and the Future of Canada*. Toronto: McClelland and Stewart, 2005.

Laforest, Gerald V. *The Allocation of Taxing Power Under the Canadian Constitution*. 2nd ed. Toronto: Canadian Tax Foundation, 1981.

Laforest, Guy. *Trudeau and the End of the Canadian Dream*. Montreal: McGill-Queen's University Press, 1995.

Lalonde, Marc. "Riding the Storm: Energy Policy 1968–1984." In *Towards a Just Society: The Trudeau Years,* edited by Thomas Axworthy and Pierre Elliott Trudeau. Toronto: Viking, 1990.

LaSelva, Samuel. *The Moral Foundations of Canadian Federation*. Montreal: McGill-Queen's University Press, 1996.

———. "Understanding Canada's Origins: Federalism, Multiculturalism, and the Will to Live Together." In *Canadian Politics*. 5th ed., edited by

James Bickerton and Alain-G. Gagnon. Toronto: University of Toronto Press, 2009.

Latouche, Daniel. "The Constitutional Misfire of 1982." In *And No One Cheered: Federalism, Democracy, and the Constitution Act*, edited by Keith Banting and Richard Simeon. Toronto: Methuen, 1983.

Laurendeau, André. "Is There a Crisis of Nationalism?" In *French-Canadian Nationalism*, edited by Ramsay Cook. Toronto: Macmillan, 1969.

Laxer, James. *The Acadians: In Search of a Homeland*. Toronto: Anchor Canada, 2006.

Lazar, Harvey, ed. *Canada: The State of the Federation, 1999/2000: Toward A New Mission*. Kingston: Queen's University, 1999.

Lazar, Harvey. "The Social Union Framework Agreement." In *Canada: The State of the Federation, 1999/2000: Toward A New Mission*, edited by Harvey Lazar. Kingston: Queen's University, 1999.

Lazar, Harvey, and France St. Hilaire, eds. *Money, Politics and Health Care: Reconstructing the Federal-Provincial Partnership*. Kingston: Institute for Research on Public Policy and Queen's University, 2004.

Lederman, W.R., ed. *The Courts and the Canadian Constitution*. Toronto: McClelland and Stewart, 1965.

Lederman, W.R. "The Supreme Court of Canada and Basic Constitutional Amendments." In *And No One Cheered: Federalism, Democracy, and the Constitution Act*, edited by Keith Banting and Richard Simeon. Toronto: Methuen, 1983.

Léger, Jean-Marc. "Where Does Neo-Nationalism Lead?" In *French-Canadian Nationalism*, edited by Ramsay Cook. Toronto: Macmillan, 1969.

Lemco, Jonathan. "Speculations on Canada With (or Without) a Committed Quebec." In *Provinces: Canadian Provincial Politics*, edited by Christopher Dunn. Peterborough: Broadview Press, 1996.

Leslie, Peter M. *Federal State, National Economy*. Toronto: University of Toronto Press, 1987.

Linteau, Paul André, René Durocher, Jean-Claude Robert, and François Ricard. *Quebec since 1930*. Toronto: James Lorimer & Company, 1991.

Lower, A.R.M. *Colony to Nation*. 4th ed. Don Mills: Longmans Green, 1964.

Lower, A.R.M., and F.R. Scott. *Evolving Canadian Federalism*. Durham, NC: Duke University Press, 1958.

Lower, A.R.M. "Theories of Canadian Federalism—Yesterday and Today." In *Evolving Canadian Federalism*, edited by A.R.M. Lower and F.R. Scott. Durham, NC: Duke University Press, 1958.

MacDonald, Edward. *If You're Stronghearted: Prince Edward Island in the Twentieth Century*. Charlottetown: Prince Edward Island Museum and Heritage Foundation, 2000.

MacDonald, L. Ian. *From Bourassa to Bourassa: Wilderness to Restoration*. 2nd ed. Montreal: McGill-Queen's University Press, 2002.

MacGregor, James G. *A History of Alberta*. Edmonton: Hurtig, 1972.

MacKinnon, Frank. *The Government of Prince Edward Island*. Toronto: University of Toronto Press, 1951.

MacKinnon, Wayne. *The Life of the Party: A History of the Liberal Party of Prince Edward Island*. Summerside: Prince Edward Island Liberal Party, 1973.

Mackintosh, W.A. *The Economic Background of Dominion-Provincial Relations*. Toronto: McClelland and Stewart, 1964.

Maioni, Antonia. "Health Care." In *Canadian Federalism*. 3rd ed., edited by Herman Bakvis and Grace Skogstad. Don Mills: Oxford University Press, 2012.

Maioni, Antonia, and Miriam Smith. "Health Care and Canadian Federalism." In *New Trends in Canadian Federalism*. 2nd ed., edited by François Rocher and Miriam Smith. Peterborough: Broadview Press, 2003.

Mallory, J.R. *The Structure of Canadian Government*. Rev ed. Toronto: Gage, 1984.

Malone, Greg. *Don't Tell the Newfoundlanders*. Toronto: A.A. Knopf Canada, 2012.

Martin, Ged. *Britain and the Origins of Canadian Confederation, 1837–67*. Vancouver: UBC Press, 1995.

———. *The Causes of Canadian Confederation*. Fredericton: Acadiensis Press, 1990.

———. *John A. Macdonald: Canada's First Prime Minister*. Toronto: Dundurn Press, 2013.

Martin, Lawrence. *Chrétien: The Will to Win*. Toronto: Lester Publishing, 1995.

———. *Harperland: The Politics of Control*. Toronto: Viking, 2010.

———. *Iron Man: The Defiant Reign of Jean Chrétien*. Toronto: Viking, 2003.

Martin, Paul. *Hell or High Water: My Life in and out of Politics*. Toronto: McClelland and Stewart, 2008.

McCall-Newman, Christina. *Grits: An Intimate Portrait of the Liberal Party*. Toronto: Macmillan, 1982.

McCall, Christina, and Stephan Clarkson. *The Heroic Delusion*, Vol. II, *Trudeau and Our Times*. Toronto: McClelland and Stewart, 1994.

McConnell, W.H. "The Judicial Review of Prime Minister Bennett's New Deal." *Osgoode Hall Law Journal* 6, no. 1 (October, 1968): 39–86.

McDougall, A.K. *John P. Robarts: His Life and Government*. Toronto: University of Toronto Press, 1986.

McInnis, Edgar. *Canada: A Political and Social History*. Toronto: Holt, Rinehart and Winston, 1958.

McLeod, Thomas H., and Ian McLeod. *Tommy Douglas: The Road to Jerusalem*. Edmonton: Hurtig Publishers, 1987.

McNaught, Kenneth. "The National Outlook of English-Speaking Canadians." In *Nationalism in Canada*, edited by Peter Russell. Toronto: McGraw-Hill Ryerson, 1966.

———. *The Penguin History of Canada*. Rev. ed. Markham: Penguin Books, 1988.

McNutt, W.S. *The Atlantic Provinces*. Toronto: McClelland and Stewart, 1965.

———. *New Brunswick, A History, 1784–1867*. Toronto: Macmillan, 1963.

McWhinney, Edward. *Quebec and the Constitution 1960–1978*. Toronto: University of Toronto Press, 1979.

McRoberts, Kenneth. "Conceiving Diversity: Dualism, Multiculturalism, and Multinationalism." In *New Trends in Canadian Federalism*. 2nd ed., edited by François Rocher and Miriam Smith. Peterborough: Broadview Press, 2003.

McRoberts, Kenneth. "Federal Structures and the Political Process." In *Governing Canada: Institutions and Structures*, edited by Michael Atkinson. Toronto: Harcourt Brace, 1993.

———. *Misconceiving Canada: The Struggle for National Unity*. Toronto: Oxford University Press, 1997.

———. *Quebec: Social Change and Political Crisis*. 3rd ed. Toronto: McClelland and Stewart, 1988.

McRoberts, Kenneth, and Dale Pasgate. *Quebec: Social Development and Political Crisis*. Toronto, 1976.

Meekison, J. Peter. *Canadian Federalism: Myth or Reality*. 3rd ed. Agincourt: Metheun, 1977.

Meekison, J. Peter, Hamish Telford, and Harvey Lazar, eds. *Canada: The State of the Federation 2002*. Kingston: Queen's University, 2004.

Messamore, Barbara. *Canada's Governors General, 1847–1878*. Toronto: University of Toronto Press, 2006.

Michaud, Nelson, and Kim Nossal. "Out of the Blue: The Mulroney Legacy in Foreign Policy." In *Transforming the Nation: Canada and Brian Mulroney*, edited by Raymond Blake. Montreal: McGill-Queen's University Press, 2007.

Milne, David. *The New Canadian Constitution*. Toronto: James Lorimer & Company, 1982.

———. *Tug of War: Ottawa and the Provinces Under Trudeau and Mulroney*. Toronto: James Lorimer & Company, 1986.

Milner, Henry. *Politics in the New Quebec*. Toronto: McClelland and Stewart, 1978.

Milner, Henry, and Sheilagh Milner. *The Decolonization of Quebec: An Analysis of Left-Wing Nationalism*. Toronto: McClelland and Stewart, 1973.

Moore, A. Milton, J. Harvey Perry, and Donald J. Beach. *The Financing of Canadian Federalism: The First 100 Years*. Toronto: Canadian Tax Foundation, 1966.

Monahan, Patrick. *Politics and the Constitution: The Charter, Federalism and the Supreme Court of Canada*. Toronto: Carswell, 1987.

Moore, Christopher. *1867: How the Fathers Made a Deal*. Toronto: McClelland and Stewart, 1997.

Morin, Claude. *Quebec vs. Ottawa: The Struggle for Self-Government 1960–1972*. Toronto: University of Toronto Press, 1976.

Morton, Desmond. *Confederation: A Short History of Canada's Constitution*. Toronto: Umbrella Press, 1992.

———. *A Short History of Canada*. 5th ed. Toronto: McClelland and Stewart, 2001.

Morton, William L. *The Critical Years: The Union of British North America, 1857–1873*. Toronto: McClelland and Stewart, 1964.

———. *The Kingdom of Canada*. Toronto: McClelland and Stewart, 1963.

———. *Manitoba: A History*. Toronto: University of Toronto Press, 1957.

Mulroney, Brian. *Memoirs*. Toronto: Emblem Editions, 2007.

Neary, Peter. *Newfoundland in the North Atlantic World*. Montreal: McGill-Queens's University Press, 1988.

Neatby, H. Blair. *The Politics of Chaos: Canada in the Thirties*. Kemptville, ON: Golden Dog Press, 1972.

Nelles, H.V. *A Little History of Canada*. Don Mills: Oxford University Press, 2004.

Neufeld, E.P. *The Financial System of Canada: Growth and Development*. Toronto: Macmillan, 1972.

Newfoundland Historical Society. *A Short History of Newfoundland and Labrador*. St John's: Newfoundland Historical Society, 2008.

Newman, Peter C. *The Distemper of Our Times*. Toronto: McClelland and Stewart, 1968.

———. *Renegade in Power: The Diefenbaker Years.* Toronto: McClelland and Stewart, 1963.

Nish, Cameron. *Quebec in the Duplessis Era, 1935–1959: Dictatorship or Democracy.* Toronto: Copp Clark, 1970.

Noel, S.J.R. *Patrons, Clients, Brokers: Ontario Society and Politics, 1791–1896.* Toronto: University of Toronto Press, 1990.

———. *Politics in Newfoundland.* Toronto: University of Toronto Press, 1971.

Norrie, Kenneth, Douglas Owram, and J. C. Herbert Emery. *A History of the Canadian Economy.* 4th ed. Toronto: Nelson, 2008.

Nossal, Kim Richard. "Anything but Provincial: The Provinces and Foreign Policy." In *Provinces: Canadian Provincial Politics*, edited by Christopher Dunn. Peterborough: Broadview Press, 1996.

Oliver, Peter. *G. Ferguson: Ontario Premier.* Toronto: University of Toronto Press, 1977.

Ormsby, Margaret. *British Columbia: A History.* Vancouver: Macmillan, 1958.

Ouellett, Fernand. "The Historical Background of Separatism in Canada." In *French-Canadian Nationalism*, edited by Ramsay Cook. Toronto: Macmillan, 1963.

Owram, Douglas. *The Government Generation: Canadian Intellectuals and the State 1900–1945.* Toronto: University of Toronto Press, 1986.

Palmer, Howard. *Alberta: A New History.* Edmonton: Hurtig, 1990.

Panitch, Leo, ed. *The Canadian State: Political Economy and Political Power.* Toronto: University of Toronto Press, 1977.

Peach, Ian. "Building or Severing the Bonds of Nationhood? The Uncertain Legacy of Constitution Making in the Mulroney Years." In *Transforming the Nation: Canada and Brian Mulroney*, edited by Raymond Blake. Montreal: McGill-Queen's University Press, 2007.

Pelletier, Gérard. "Language Policy and the Mood in Quebec." In *Towards a Just Society: The Trudeau Years*, edited by Thomas Axworthy and Pierre Elliott Trudeau. Toronto: Viking, 1990.

Perry, David P. *Financing the Canadian Federation, 1867 to 1995: Setting the Stage for Change*. Toronto: Canadian Tax Foundation, 1997.

Perry, J. Harvey. *A Fiscal History of Canada—the Postwar Years*. Toronto: Canadian Tax Foundation, 1989.

———. *Taxes, Tariffs, and Subsidies: A History of Canadian Fiscal Development*. 2 vols. Toronto: University of Toronto Press, 1955.

Plamondon Bob. *Blue Thunder: The Truth about Conservatives from Macdonald to Harper*. Toronto: Key Porter Books, 2009.

———. *The Truth about Trudeau*. Ottawa: Great River Media, 2003.

Poliquin, Daniel. *René Lévesque*. Toronto: Penguin, 2009.

Pratte, André. *Wilfrid Laurier*. Toronto: Éditions du Boréal, 2011.

Prince, Michael. "SUFA: Sea Change or Mere Ripple for Canadian Social Policy." In *Forging the Canadian Social Union: SUFA and Beyond*, edited by Sarah Fortin, Alain Noël, and France St.-Hilaire. Ottawa, 2003.

Prince, Michael, and James J. Rice. "Governing Through Shifting Social-Policy Regimes: Brian Mulroney and Canada's Welfare State." In *Transforming the Nation: Canada and Brian Mulroney*, edited by Raymond Blake. Montreal: McGill-Queen's University Press, 2007.

Pryke, Kenneth G. *Nova Scotia and Confederation*. Toronto: University of Toronto Press, 1979.

Quinn, Herbert. *The Union Nationale: Quebec Nationalism from Duplessis to Lévesque*. 2nd ed. Toronto: University of Toronto Press, 1979.

Radwanski, George. *Trudeau*. Toronto: Macmillan, 1978.

Rawlyk, George, ed. *The Atlantic Provinces and the Problems of Confederation*. St. John's: Breakwater, 1979.

Rawlyk, George. "The Historical Framework of the Maritimes and Confederation." In *The Atlantic Provinces and the Problems of Confederation*, edited by George Rawlyk. St. John's: Breakwater, 1979.

Rea, K.T. *The Prosperous Years: The Economic History of Ontario 1939–1975*. Toronto: University of Toronto Press, 1985.

Rennie, J. Bradford, ed. *Alberta's Premiers of the Twentieth Century*. Regina:

Canadian Plains Research Centre, University of Regina, 2004.

Resnick, Philip. *The Masks of Proteus: Canadian Reflections on the State.* Montreal: McGill-Queen's University Press, 1990.

———. *Thinking English Canada.* Toronto: Stoddard Publishing, 1994.

Ricci, Nino. *Pierre Elliott Trudeau.* Toronto: Penguin Canada, 2009.

Riendeau, Roger. *A Brief History of Canada.* Markham: Fitzhenry & Whiteside, 2000.

Riker, William H. *Federalism: Origin, Operation, Significance.* Boston: Little, Brown and Company, 1964.

Rioux, Marcel. *Quebec in Question.* Toronto: James Lorimer & Company, 1978.

Robertson, Gordon. *Memoirs of a Very Civil Servant.* Toronto: University of Toronto Press, 2000.

Robin, Martin, ed. *Canadian Provincial Politics.* 2nd ed. Scarborough: Prentice-Hall, 1978.

———. *The Rush for Spoils: The Company Province.* Toronto: McClelland and Stewart, 1972.

———. *Pillars of Profit: The Company Province.* Toronto: McClelland and Stewart, 1973.

Robinson, Ian. "Neo-Liberal Trade Policy and Canadian Federalism Revisited." In *New Trends in Canadian Federalism.* 2nd ed., edited by François Rocher and Miriam Smith. Peterborough: Broadview Press, 2003.

Rocher, François, and Miriam Smith, eds. *New Trends in Canadian Federalism.* 2nd ed. Peterborough: Broadview Press, 2003.

Romney, Paul. *Getting It Wrong: How Canadians Forgot Their Past and Imperilled Confederation.* Toronto: University of Toronto Press, 1999.

———. "Why Lord Watson Was Right." In *Canadian Constitutionalism: 1791–1991,* edited by Janet Ajzenstat. Ottawa: Canadian Study of Parliament Group, 1991.

Roy, Patricia, and John Herd Thompson. *British Columbia: Land of Promise.* Don Mills: Oxford University Press, 2005.

Russell, Peter. *Constitutional Odyssey: Can Canadians Become a Sovereign People?* 3rd ed. Toronto: University of Toronto Press, 2004.

Russell, Peter, ed. *Nationalism in Canada.* Toronto: McGraw-Hill Ryerson, 1966.

Ryerson, Stanley. *Unequal Union: Roots of Crisis in the Canadas, 1815–1873.* Toronto: Progress Books, 1973.

Savoie, Donald. *Breaking the Bargain: Public Servants, Ministers, and Parliament.* Toronto: University of Toronto Press, 2003.

———. *Federal-Provincial Collaboration: The Canada-New Brunswick General Development Agreement.* Montreal: McGill-Queen's University Press, 1981.

———. *Governing from the Centre.* Toronto: University of Toronto Press, 1999.

———. *Power: Where Is It?* Montreal: McGill-Queen's University Press, 2010.

———. *Pulling Against Gravity.* Montreal: Institute for Research on Public Policy, 2001.

———. *What Is Government Good At?* Montreal: McGill-Queen's University Press, 2015.

Saywell, John. *Canada Past and Present.* Toronto: Clarke Irwin, 1981.

———. *Just Call Me Mitch: The Life of Mitchell F. Hepburn.* Toronto: University of Toronto Press, 1991.

———. *The Lawmakers: Judicial Power and the Shaping of Canadian Federalism.* Toronto: University of Toronto Press, 2002.

———. *The Office of Lieutenant Governor: A Study in Canadian Government and Politics.* Toronto: University of Toronto Press, 1957.

———. *The Rise of the Parti Québécois, 1967–1976.* Toronto: University of Toronto Press, 1977.

Schull, Joseph. *Ontario since 1867.* Toronto: McClelland and Stewart, 1978.

Scott, F.R. "French Canada and Canadian Federalism." In *Evolving Canadian Federalism,* edited by A.R.M. Lower and F.R. Scott. Durham, NC: Duke University Press, 1958.

Scott, Frank, and Michael Oliver. *Quebec States Her Case*. Toronto: Macmillan, 1964.

Séguin, Maurice. *Histoire de deux Nationalisms au Canada*. Montreal: Guérin, 1997.

———. *L'Idée d'indépendance au Quebec, Genèse et Historique*. Montreal: Boréal Express, 1977.

Shelton, George. *British Columbia and Confederation*. Victoria: Morriss Printing Co., 1967.

Shoyama, Thomas. "Fiscal Federalism in Evolution." In *Towards a Just Society: The Trudeau Years*, edited by Thomas Axworthy and Pierre Elliott Trudeau. Toronto: Viking, 1990.

Silver, A.I. *The French Canadian Idea of Confederation, 1864–1900*. 2nd ed. Toronto: University of Toronto Press, 1997.

Simeon, Richard, ed. *Division of Powers and Public Policy*. Toronto: University of Toronto Press, 1985.

Simeon, Richard. *Federal-Provincial Diplomacy; The Making of Recent Policy in Canada*. Toronto: University of Toronto Press, 2006.

———, ed. *Intergovernmental Relations*. Toronto: University of Toronto Press, 1985.

———, ed. *Must Canada Fail?* Montreal: McGill-Queen's University Press, 1977.

Simeon, Richard, and Amy Nugent. "Parliamentary Canada and Intergovernmental Canada: Exploring the Tensions." In *Canadian Federalism*. 3rd ed., edited by Herman Bakvis and Grace Skogstad. Don Mills: Oxford University Press, 2012.

Simeon, Richard, and Ian Robinson. "The Dynamics of Canadian Federalism." In *Canadian Politics*. 5th ed., edited by James Bickerton and Alain-G. Gagnon. Toronto: University of Toronto Press, 2009.

Simeon, Richard, and Ian Robinson. *State, Society and the Development of Canadian Federalism*. Toronto: University of Toronto Press, 1990.

Simpson, Jeffrey. *Discipline of Power: The Conservative Interlude and the Liberal Restoration*. Toronto: University of Toronto Press, 1996.

———. *The Friendly Dictatorship*. Toronto: McClelland and Stewart, 2001.

———. *The Anxious Years: Politics in the Age of Mulroney and Chrétien*. Toronto: Lester Publishing, 1996.

———. *Spoils of Power: the Politics of Patronage*. Toronto: HarperCollins, 1988.

Skogstad, Grace. "International Trade Policy and the Evolution of Canadian Federalism." In *Canadian Federalism*. 3rd ed., edited by Herman Bakvis and Grace Skogstad. Don Mills: Oxford University Press, 2012.

Smallwood, Joey. *I Choose Canada: The Memoirs of the Honourable Joseph R. "Joey" Smallwood*. Toronto: Macmillan, 1973.

Smiley, Donald. *Canada in Question: Federalism in the Eighties*. 3rd ed. Toronto: McGraw-Hill Ryerson, 1980.

———. *The Canadian Political Nationality*. Toronto: Methuen, 1967.

———. *Conditional Grants and Canadian Federalism*. Toronto: Canadian Tax Foundation, 1963.

———. "A Dangerous Deed: The Constitutional Act, 1982." In *And No One Cheered: Federalism, Democracy, and the Constitution Act*, edited by Keith Banting and Richard Simeon. Toronto: Methuen, 1983.

———. *The Federal Condition in Canada*. Toronto: McGraw-Hill Ryerson, 1987.

———. "Federalism, Nationalism and the Scope of Public Activity in Canada." In *Nationalism in Canada*, edited by Peter Russell. Toronto: McGraw-Hill Ryerson, 1966.

———. "The Two Themes of Canadian Federalism." In *The Canadian Political Tradition: Basic Readings*. 2nd ed., edited by R.S. Blair and J.T. McLeod, Toronto: Nelson Canada, 1995.

Smiley, Donald, and Ronald Watts. *Intrastate Federalism in Canada*. Toronto: University of Toronto Press, 1985.

Smith, Jennifer. "The Constitutional Debate and Beyond." In *New Trends in Canadian Federalism*. 2nd ed., edited by François Rocher and Miriam Smith. Peterborough: Broadview Press, 2003.

———. *Federalism*. Vancouver: UBC Press, 2004.

Smitheram, Verner, David Milne, and Satadal Dasgupta, eds. *The Garden Transformed*. Charlottetown: Ragweed Press, 1982.

Stanley, Della. *Louis Robichaud: A Decade of Power*. Halifax: Nimbus Publishing, 1984.

Stanley, G.F.G. "Act or Pact? Another Look at Confederation." In *Confederation*, edited by Ramsay Cook. Toronto: Macmillan, 1967.

———. *A Short History of the Canadian Constitution*. Toronto: Ryerson Press, 1969.

Starr, Richard. *Equal as Citizens: The Tumultuous and Troubled History of a Great Canadian idea*. Halifax: Formac Publishing, 2014.

———. *Richard Hatfield: The Seventeen Year Saga*. Halifax: Goodread Biography, 1987.

Stevens, Geoffrey. *Stanfield*. Toronto: McClelland and Stewart, 1973.

Stevenson, Garth. "The Division of Powers." In *Division of Powers and Public Policy*, edited by Richard Simeon. Toronto: University of Toronto Press, 1985.

———. *Ex Uno Plures: Federal Provincial Relations in Canada, 1867–1896*. Montreal: McGill-Queen's University Press, 1993.

———. *Unfulfilled Union: Canadian Federalism and National Unity*. 5th ed. Montreal: McGill-Queen's University Press, 2009.

———. "The Political Economy of Regionalism and Federation." In *Canadian Federalism*. 3rd ed., edited by Herman Bakvis and Grace Skogstad Don Mills: Oxford University Press, 2012.

Strain, J. Frank. "Debts Paid and Debts Owed: The Legacy of Mulroney's Economic Policies." In *Transforming the Nation: Canada and Brian Mulroney*, edited by Raymond Blake. Montreal: McGill-Queen's University Press, 2007.

Struthers, James. *No Fault of Their Own: Unemployment and the Canadian Welfare State*. Toronto: University of Toronto Press, 1983.

Stursberg, Peter. *Diefenbaker: Leadership Gained, 1956–62*. Toronto: University of Toronto Press, 1975.

———. *Lester Pearson and the Dream of Unity*. Toronto: Doubleday, 1978.

Swainson, Donald. "Canada Annexes the West: Colonial Status Confirmed." In *Federalism in Canada and Australia: The Early Years*, edited by Bruce Hodgins, Don Wright, and W.H. Heick. Canberra, NSW: Australian National University Press, 1978.

———, ed. *Oliver Mowat's Ontario*. Toronto: Macmillan, 1972.

Sweeney, Alastair. *George-Étienne Cartier: A Biography*. Toronto: McClelland and Stewart, 1976.

Taylor, Charles. *Reconciling the Solitudes: Essays on Canadian Federalism and Nationalism*. Montreal: McGill-Queen's University Press, 1993.

Thompson, John Herd, and Allan Seager. *Canada 1922–1939: Decades of Discontent*. Toronto: McClelland and Stewart, 1985.

Thomson, Dale. *Alexander Mackenzie: Clear Grit*. Toronto: Macmillan, 1960.

———. *Jean Lesage and the Quiet Revolution*. Toronto: Macmillan, 1984.

———. *Louis St. Laurent: Canadian*. Toronto: Macmillan, 1967.

———, ed. *Quebec Society and Politics: Views from the Inside*. Toronto: McClelland and Stewart, 1973.

Thorburn, Hugh G. *Politics in New Brunswick*. Toronto: University of Toronto Press, 1961.

Toner, Peter. "New Brunswick Schools and the Rise of Provincial Rights." In *Federalism in Canada and Australia: The Early Years*, edited by Bruce Hodgins, Don Wright, and W.H. Heick. Canberra, NSW: Australian National University Press, 1978.

Trudeau, Pierre Elliott. *Memoirs*. Toronto: McClelland and Stewart, 1993.

———. "The Values of a Just Society." In *Towards a Just Society: The Trudeau Years*, edited by Thomas Axworthy and Pierre Elliott Trudeau. Toronto: Viking, 1990.

Vaillancourt, François. "Federal-Provincial Small Transfer Programs in Canada, 1957–1998." In *Canada: The State of the Federation, 1999/2000: Toward A New Mission*, edited by Harvey Lazar. Kingston: Queen's University, 1990.

Veilleux, Gérard. *Les Relations Intergouvernementales au Canada 1867–1967*. Montreal: Les Presses de l'Universitié du Québec, 1971.

Verney, Douglas V. *Three Civilizations, Two Cultures, One State: Canada's Political Traditions*. Durham, NC: Duke University Press, 1986.

Vigod, Bernard. *Taschereau*. Sillery, QC: Septentrion, 1996.

Vipond, Robert. "The Federal Principle and Canadian Confederation Reconsidered." *Canadian Journal of Political Science* 22, no. 1 (March, 1989): 3–25.

Vipond, Robert C. *Liberty and Community: Canadian Federalism and the Failure of the Constitution*. Albany: State University of New York Press, 1991.

Wade, Mason. *The French Canadians*, Vol. I, *1760–1911*. Toronto: Macmillan, 1968.

Waiser, Bill. *Saskatchewan: A New History*. Calgary: Fifth House Publishers, 2005.

Waite, P.B. "Edward Cardwell and Confederation." In *Confederation*, edited by Ramsay Cook. Toronto: Macmillan, 1967.

———. *In Search of R. B. Bennett*. Montreal: McGill-Queen's University Press, 2012.

———. *The Life and Times of Confederation*. Toronto: University of Toronto Press, 1962.

———. *Canada 1874–1896: Arduous Destiny*. Toronto: McClelland and Stewart, 1971.

Walker, Michael, ed. *Canadian Confederation at the Crossroads: The Search for a Federal-Provincial Balance*. Vancouver: The Fraser Institute, 1978.

Wardhaugh, Robert. "Brian Mulroney and the West." In *Transforming the Nation: Canada and Brian Mulroney*, edited by Raymond Blake. Montreal: McGill-Queen's University Press, 2007.

Warkentin, John. *A Regional Geography of Canada*. Scarborough: Prentice-Hall Canada, 2000.

Watts, Ronald. *Comparing Federal Systems in the 1990s*. Kingston: Queen's University, 1996.

———. *Executive Federalism: A Comparative Analysis*. Kingston: Queen's University, 1989.

Wells, Paul. *Right Side Up: The Fall of Paul Martin and the Rise of Stephen Harper*. Toronto: Douglas Gibson Books, 2006.

———. *The Longer I'm Prime Minister: Stephen Harper and Canada, 2006–*. Toronto: Random House Canada, 2013.

Westell, Anthony. *Paradox: Trudeau as Prime Minister*. Scarborough: Prentice-Hall, 1972.

Wheare, K.C. *Federal Government*. 3rd ed. London: Oxford University Press, 1953.

Whitcomb, Ed. *A Short History of Alberta*. Ottawa: From Sea to Sea Enterprises, 2005.

———. *A Short History of British Columbia*. Ottawa: From Sea to Sea Enterprises, 2006.

———. *A Short History of Manitoba*. Ottawa: Canada's Wings, 1982.

———. *A Short History of New Brunswick*. Ottawa: From Sea to Sea Enterprises, 2010.

———. *A Short History of Newfoundland and Labrador*. Ottawa: From Sea to Sea Enterprises, 2011.

———. *A Short History of Nova Scotia*. Ottawa: From Sea to Sea Enterprises, 2009.

———. *A Short History of Ontario*. Ottawa: From Sea to Sea Enterprises, 2007.

———. *A Short History of Prince Edward Island*. Ottawa: From Sea to Sea Enterprises, 2010.

———. *A Short History of Quebec*. Ottawa: From Sea to Sea Enterprises, 2012.

———. *A Short History of Saskatchewan*. Ottawa: From Sea to Sea Enterprises, 2005.

White, Randall. *Ontario, 1610–1985*. Toronto: Dundurn Press, 1985.

Whyte, John D. "Constitutional Aspects of Economic Development Policy." In *Division of Powers and Public Policy*, edited by Richard Simeon. Toronto: University of Toronto Press, 1985.

Wiseman, Nelson. "Provincial Political Cultures." In *Provinces: Canadian Provincial Politics*, edited by Christopher Dunn. Peterborough: Broadview Press, 1996.

———. *In Search of Canadian Political Culture*. Vancouver: UBC Press, 2007.

Woodcock, George. *British Columbia*. Vancouver: Douglas and McIntyre, 1990.

Young, Brian. "Federalism in Quebec: The First Years After Confederation." In *Federalism in Canada and Australia: The Early Years*, edited by Bruce Hodgins, Don Wright, and W.H. Heick. Canberra, NSW: Australian National University Press, 1978.

———. *George Étienne Cartier: Bourgeois Montréalais*. Montreal: McGill-Queen's University Press, 2004.

———. *The Struggle for Quebec: From Referendum to Referendum*. Montreal: McGill-Queen's University Press, 1999.

Books by Ed Whitcomb

Napoleon's Diplomatic Service (1979)

A Short History of Manitoba (1982)

Canadian Fiddle Music, Volume I (1990)

Canadian Fiddle Music, Volume II (2001)

A Short History of Alberta (2005)

A Short History of Saskatchewan (2005)

Λ Short History of British Columbia (2006)

The Great Canadian Songbook (2006)

A Short History of Ontario (2007)

A Short History of Nova Scotia (2009)

A Short History of New Brunswick (2010)

A Short History of Prince Edward Island (2010)

A Short History of Newfoundland (2011)

A Short History of the Canadian North (2011)

A Short History of Quebec (2012)

Index